RELIG

SPIRITUALITY AND CIVILIZATION SUSTAINABILITY IN THE 21ST CENTURY

Religion and Spirituality

Additional books in this series can be found on Nova's website under the Series tab.

Additional e-books in this series can be found on Nova's website under the e-book tab.

Focus on Civilizations and Cultures

Additional books in this series can be found on Nova's website under the Series tab.

Additional e-books in this series can be found on Nova's website under the e-book tab.

RELIGION AND SPIRITUALITY

SPIRITUALITY AND CIVILIZATION SUSTAINABILITY IN THE 21ST CENTURY

ANDREW TARGOWSKI
AND
MAREK J. CELINSKI
EDITORS

nova publishers
New York

For permission to use material from this book please contact us:
Telephone 631-231-7269; Fax 631-231-8175
Web Site: http://www.novapublishers.com

NOTICE TO THE READER

Additional color graphics may be available in the e-book version of this book.

Library of Congress Cataloging-in-Publication Data

Spirituality and civilization sustainability in the 21st century / editors: Andrew Targowski (Western Michigan University, MI, USA) and Marek J. Celinski. pages cm Includes index.
ISBN 978-1-53610-729-6 (softcover)
1. Religion and civilization. 2. Spirituality. 3. Civilization--21st century. 4. Civilization--Forecasting. I. Targowski, Andrzej. II. Celinski, Marek J.
BL55.S65 2013 204--dc23
2013011828

Published by Nova Science Publishers, Inc. † New York

Contents

PREFACE

This book sets out to investigate the following challenges:

1. To what extent human spirituality can affect civilization,
2. Whether human spirituality can cause a rebirth of civilization, particularly the western and global variety as well as save those from the ongoing crisis and perhaps their decline and fall in the 3rd millennium. What is spirituality supposed to be about so that man will not destroy civilization?

The immediate reason for taking up these issues is the crisis of 2008, which is commonly thought to have been caused by ethical shortcomings – a shortage of *spirituality* in business, particularly big (global) business.

One can understand spirituality as a belief in the ultimate or an alleged immaterial reality[1] an inner path enabling a person to discover the essence of their being; or the deepest values and meanings by which people live[2.] The term "spiritual" is often used in contexts in which the term "religious" was formerly employed[3.] However, this is a limited understanding of spirituality, which can be of a secular nature, too, since secular spirituality emphasizes humanistic ideas about qualities such as love, compassion, patience, tolerance, forgiveness, contentment, responsibility, harmony, and a concern for others4. Therefore secular spirituality includes aspects of life and human experience which go beyond a purely materialist view of the world, without necessarily accepting a belief in a supernatural reality or divine being. A modern definition of spirituality is as follows:

> "Spirituality exists wherever we struggle with the issues of how our lives fit into the greater scheme of things. This is true when our questions never give way to specific answers or give rise to specific practices such as prayer or meditation. We encounter spiritual issues every time we wonder where the universe comes from, why we are here, or what happens when we die. We also become spiritual when we become moved by values such as beauty, love, or creativity that seem to reveal a meaning or power beyond our visible world. An idea or practice is "spiritual" when it reveals our personal desire to

---

[1] Ewert Cousins (1992) in a preface to Antoine Faivre and Jacob Needleman, Modern Esoteric Spirituality, Crossroad Publishing.

[2] Philip Sheldrake (2007). A Brief History of Spirituality. Hoboken, NJ: Wiley-Blackwell. pp. 1-2.

[3] James, W. (1985). The varieties of religious experience. Cambridge, MA: Harvard University Press. (Original work published 1902)

[4] Dalai Lama (1999). Ethics for the New Millennium. New York:Riverhead Books. p. 22.

establish a felt-relationship with the deepest meanings or powers governing life (Fuller 2011)[5]."

Eighteen scholars, members of the International Society for the Comparative Study of Civilization have been called up to investigate religious and secular spirituality in the way civilization operates, as the society have been looking into the issue for half a century.

Issues related to spirituality are usually investigated within theology and comparative study or religion, whereas in life, particularly social and business life, man makes these decisions on the basis of the following basic processes: a secular process of genetic (biological) evolution as well as a process of religious and secular spirituality. But when the two clash or require deliberations of a higher kind, man uses a decision-making process oriented towards right judgment and choice – seeks a wise decision. Whereas the processes of biological evolution and optimal decision-making are subjects of numerous scholarly studies, the process of secular and religious spirituality and their influence on the level and quality of civilizational (also cultural and economic) progress and operation has been researched to a lesser extent.

Max Weber's classic *The Protestant Ethics and the Spirituality of Capitalism*[6], published at the beginning of the 20th century (1904-1905), should be the constant reminder of the importance of the connection between spirituality and politics.

This present book seeks to fill the current gap in the business studies, while research in human spirituality and their influence on the social life leads, in the large-scale dimension, to the comprehension of the premises of civilization. This scale affects the way smaller entities such as a business or the state operate. The authors of this book believe that the way these lower entities work should be reflected in a higher being such as civilization which, as a holistic system, sets the tone for the lives of its component parts.

The book is made up of 24 chapters, divided into three parts, investigating the condition, cause and the part spirituality – both secular and religious – plays in the social life of man.

Part A posits a diagnosis of the plight of civilization in the 21st century. It follows that not only civilization but also the planet are in a plight that endangers their existence. The reason is the nascent Civilization Death Triangle, caused by the explosion of population, ecological and resources exhaustion bombs. The initial small explosions may start cropping up around 2050. The reasons include the rate of population expansion and the aggression of modern technology which used to support human culture but now seeks to eliminate man from an active life in civilization by our excessive reliance on automatons, robots and computers. Mankind has a potential for a wise resolution of their problems but – as we learn from history – man is wise in misery and stupid in prosperity. This kind of life can best be seen in the Western Civilization.

Part B investigates the role of the most popular sacral religions that determine the spirituality of man, particularly that of a believer. It turns out that none of these can become a universal religion even though each of these affirms ideas that can be considered universal and worthy of dissemination. The sum total of these individual ideas/values ought to constitute Spirituality 2.0 ("Pseudo-religion" 2.0), which might inspire a further progress of

[5] Fuller, R. C. Spiritual, But Not Religious. beliefnet.com. Retrieved on: 2011-12-03.

[6] Archive fur Socialwissenschaft und Socialpolityk, vol. XX and XXI (2004, 2005), in English New York: Charles Scribner's Sons, 1958.

humanity even upon an assumption that the majority would continue to profess traditional religions, discussed in Part C.

Part C proposes solutions that go beyond the sphere of sacral spirituality – on the one hand, that sphere has generated a reason for the crisis of civilization and, on the other, provides possible assistance in its overcoming. The transformation of the Western Civilization into Global Civilization is controlled by global business that has become a „global religion." This kind of business leads to exorbitant profit and is a major source of corruption in the 21st century, irrespective of civilizational level and kind. Today, a noticeable solution is a requirement of making ethical decisions in business, promoting automatization with a human face, postulating a more consistent application of selflessness in social processes or the development of Spirituality 2.0, which – rather than replacing the existing religions 1.0 – is supposed to establish a shared framework for the universal and accepted values practiced by organized religions. Spirituality 2.0 is to proclaim tolerance among people, taught at home as well as in schools, universities, at work and in all social activity.

Part D synthesizes deliberations on the role of spirituality in the way the society functions. Considering bad morality we now see in global business, a proposition was posited that since the beginning of the Great Crisis we have witnessed II Great Crisis of Civilization, similar to the I Great Crisis following the fall of the Roman Empire in 476. The reason for both these crises is the downfall of morality in the ruling elites of the two Romes (the second being the USA). Just as the invention of print and the spread of printed material caused a revival of civilization in the Renaissance, so did the 20th century invention of the Internet create conditions and arouse expectations for full expression on the part of its users which, in effect, makes it possible to promote immoral ideas and behavior – factors that contribute to the downfall of the civilization we know.

The book contains a rather pessimistic picture of our civilization. However, it sees its revival mainly in a more intensive growth of a universal and complementary spirituality of man by way of recognizing and developing a universal Spirituality 2.0 and the application of the strategy of Wise Civilization. Man has a potential to enforce this solution as long as they are guided by wisdom in the service of survival and further development rather than placing instantaneous material profit first.

Our authors speak of spirituality inside and outside of religion; the proponents call themselves *"spiritual but not religious"* and believe in the existence of different "spiritual paths," emphasizing the importance of finding one's own individual path to spirituality. They argue that in order to save civilization, both kinds of spirituality should be applied in agreement. The main ideas of that agreement have been defined in this book.

Part A

Individuals, World, Planet and Civilizations

In: Spirituality and Civilization Sustainability ... ISBN: 978-1-53610-729-6
Editors: Andrew Targowski and Marek J. Celinski

Chapter 1

SPIRITUALITY: ITS POTENTIAL FOR INSPIRATION AND DYSFUNCTIONALITY IN CIVILIZATION

Marek J. Celinski*
Private practice in psychology, Toronto, Canada

"How our life would be changed if we could see that Greek geometry and the Christian faith have sprung from the same source!"
(Simone Weil, *Letter to a priest*, p.85)

ABSTRACT

In this chapter, spirituality is described from a psychological perspective as one of the components of the human regulatory system that has functional significance to modify instinctual reactivity. As both spirituality and instincts influence our behavior in a compulsive and absolute manner, psychosocial evolution requires a mental construct that would provide a bridge between the two, taking into consideration reality constraints. This construct is represented in wisdom that acknowledges the need for both instincts and spirituality, but enables us to act with prudence and courage, based on reason and convictions, while facing novel and challenging situations. Modern spiritual values and approaches created cultures based on human rights, freedom and democracy, and developed technologies and civilizations that offer a possibility for almost everybody to live with dignity and opportunities for fulfillment of the best of human potential.

THE THEORY OF EVOLUTION AND SPIRITUALITY

One of the objectives of this chapter is to document the importance of spirituality for the human awareness of being- in- the world (Heidegger, 1962). To this end, it is necessary to acknowledge two assumptions that underlie the organization of material, as presented in this chapter. One concerns a distinction between spirituality and religion. Religion is considered

* Ph.D, C. Psych; Email: marekcelinski1@rogers.com

divisive in that, more so in the past than now, it led to numerous wars, prejudices, intolerance and persecutions of non-believers; on the other hand, spirituality offers a possibility of finding the common core for all religions that will make it possible to unite people in the spirit of solidarity (Tischner, 1981). That would enable them to face the challenges of life, either because of their shared belief in our creation by a divine and benevolent Being or because we share the ubiquitous human conditions and dilemmas that require our mutual support.

The second assumption stems from psychology and its accumulated knowledge of human nature (Fromm, E. and Xirau, R., 1968; Schwartz, B.,1986; Stevenson, L.,1987; Mandler, G.,1997). As an empirical science, psychology has developed various theoretical understandings of how people feel, think and act in the world. Whereas each individual's activity is usually a manifestation of some goal-oriented behavior, one can ask if this is primarily for the purpose of satisfying our instinctual needs. If we consider that instincts are not the main or only force that guides us, the further question is: What is the origin of spirituality and its function within human nature? In this respect, the difference between religion and spirituality is particularly important, as typically religions emphasize a necessity to accept a particular perspective on reality and on the appropriateness of people's behavior in order to qualify for happiness in eternity, which is a reward only available to the members of a particular religious denomination. By contrast, spirituality refers to the way that people make decisions and live their lives based on attitudes and beliefs that are not primarily an expression of instinctual pleasures and self-interests, but which are not necessarily a manifestation of any denominational rules of conduct.

The present chapter will attempt to describe what role spirituality plays in helping people become aware of their developmental potential, and how it enables them to better cope with adversity (Gow et al, 2011). Once again, a distinction between religion and spirituality needs to be considered; while belonging to a particular religious denomination manifests as observance of dogmatic morality and the following of certain rituals, spirituality emphasizes a greater awareness and desire for betterment of the self and the expectation of progress inspired by "irrational" faith in the transformative power of goodness and a need for self-actualization.

It is the primary tenet of this chapter that the origin of spirituality can be regarded as a reflection of the two primary functions of the human brain: one is sense-making (Miller, 1981) and the other one is the ability to transcend visible or material reality. The first function manifests in establishing connectivity between separate objects, phenomena and events so that our vision of reality would make subjective sense and enable for purposeful behavior. In psychological theories and conceptualizations, this capacity of the human mind was an object of exploration by the 19th century school of Gestalt psychology. It postulated that the mind organizes perceptions in a holistic way, so that in our mental representation of reality objects and events do not exist separately, but appear integrated by common principles. Miller (1981) explained the concept of Gestalt in the following way:

> "In the Gestalt the whole is more than the sum of the parts simply because the parts can be related in many ways other than by summation" (p. 50)… "Just as there is no theoretical limit to the possible associations *between* Gestalts there is no limit to the association *within* Gestalts, which consciousness may be called upon to make (p. 51)."

In such a way, various meanings for a particular concept or construct are created.

With respect to understanding what philosophical inquiry is about, Watson (2006) stated the following:

> "The writers of the *Encyclopédie* in France in the eighteenth century, thought this approach would advance knowledge: 'Since "everything in nature is linked together," since "beings are connected with one another by a chain of which we perceive some parts as continuous, though in the greater number of points the continuity escapes us, the art of the philosopher consists in adding new links to the separated parts, in order to reduce the distance between them as much as possible" (p. 11-12).

More recently, Frankl (1966, 2000) postulated that the primary human orientation to life is manifesting as search for meaning. One can imagine that at the dawn of humanity's awareness of its own existence, the mind of the hominid experienced a sense of chaos and unpredictability. To this, the ancient hunters responded through physical strength forcing weaker beings into submission, and giving a stronger individual a sense of power and control along with confidence that the desired objects will be obtained when the opportunity appears. Use of primitive tools (such as stones or sticks) was an extension and enhancement of oneself. The further step in the development of hominids' minds was made with a change of the focus from primarily on external control, to awareness of the self and one's own associative processes that would allow them to see objects and events as somehow mutually connected. While reviewing the stages of human developments, Watson (2006) identifies the period of 60,000-40,000 years ago as "creative explosion." The characteristic feature of this period is appearance of "very beautiful, very accomplished, and very modern–looking *art* that captures the imagination of all who encounter it" (p. 44). This art is expressed in three forms: "cave paintings, Venus figurines and multicolored beads" (p. 44)"

In this manner, externalizing and storing images manifested two important developmental achievements for humanity: first, a shift of attention to one's internal processes, as before the image was externalized, it must have been internally visualized; the second point is possiblity to manipulate the representation of reality embedded in the externalized image. In such a way the artist became aware of one's impact on reality through activity of his /her mind and of a possibility to communicate through images something meaningful (coherent and important) to others. This initial expression of transcendence which extended the presence of a singular event beyond its concrete, momentary, here and now existence must have triggered further wishes, perhaps initially on the unconscious level, and then attempts to search for something which is more fundamental and unifying behind diverse phenomena separated by space and time; likewise, seeing how things change over time may have triggered, again perhaps subconsciously, search for timeless and stable existence which continues as the perpetual and ubiquitous "search for meaning" that is expressed in tales and myths. Campbell (1990) described commonalities of themes across diverse cultures and recognized their metaphysical nature, and their being an expression of human destiny by saying: "They are not invented but occur, and are recognized by seers, and poets, then cultivated and employed as catalyst of spiritual (i.e.,psychological) well-being"(p. 6).

Whereas the specific answers to the eternal questions change through history, vary across cultures and with the advancement of knowledge, the most important task for humanity is to never stop asking who we are and what are our relations to Being, to visible reality and to another person. These questions will likely remain as constant inspirations for people efforts as providing answers gives meaning to people's lives.

With reference to dialectic philosophy (which postulates that phenomena have their opposite representation in physical and psychological reality), spiritualty may be hypothesized to originate as a mind construct that unites the opposite states of mind and that continues to play this role in our psychological functioning. While being guided by this philosophical insight, it is possible to imagine that as an ancestral mind associated pain and suffering with unpredictability of events and one's own helplessness, these experiences activated "hunger" for the opposite qualities which Steiner (1974, p. 5) described as "certitude" and "total explanation" that express "deep- seated nostalgia for absolute." The natural need for absolute manifests in the phenomenon that "Those great movements (Steiner specifically refers to Marxist social class theory, Freud's psychoanalysis and Lévi-Strauss's anthropology)...which have tried to replace religion in the West and Christianity in particular, are very much like the churches, like a theology, they want to replace."

Could biological evolution (Dawkins 1995) by itself raise hominids' awareness to the level that the experience of chaos (Gleick 1987) and unpredictability could be contrasted with a concept of timelessness and yearning for absolutes which offer a prospect of continuity and stability on a highly cognitive level? It is difficult to understand why biological evolution would develop spirituality to provide a sense of stability and predictability considering that, previously, reliance on instincts alone offered the best assurance in this respect by strongly motivating and structuring animal's behaviour.

Any departure from the instinctual regulation of behavior would create chaos and unpredictability that negate the primary advantage that evolution gives to those individuals who have the greatest ability to act on their instinctual drives and become best adjusted. In case of humans, increasing utilization of the self as an agency that is capable of modifying its own perception of reality and, even more importantly, of making decisions about what is important, valuable (and thus desirable) to individuals, violates the rigorous consistency and stability of behavior governed by instinct.

The regulatory processes alternative to instincts originate from the primary intuitive insights about our relation to the world, to ourselves and to others, and are open to modifications, as no interpretation of reality can be regarded as final. One cannot deny that for a biologist the origin of this specifically human quality of mind must be a mystery, which may be summarized in these questions: Why did evolution release its grip on life, which ensured that life would continue through the best adapted individuals, by leaving this task to the fancy of a species endowed with a potentially free will, but feeble mind that is not fully capable of grasping the fundamental truths about physical reality and one's own existence? Should we assume that the evolution inevitably leads to development of beings endowed with higher levels of awareness, and to discovery of objective principles of morality that become an alternative regulatory system based on free will? Considering that in human beings impact of spirituality causes that meaning and values motivate us more than instinctual drives, biologically weak individuals get a greater opportunity to survive and contribute to the genetic pool. This changes the way in which future generation will develop (and it remains an open questions which values will guide future evolution of civilizations).

Another possibility is that human beings "outsmarted " the guardians of the evolutionary flow and set for themselves the path of development. Were they predestined to to so from the very begining ?. In any case, compared to the evolutionary past, humanity manifests an entirely novel perspective on life development; at this stage, evolution allowed that the very existence of life on earth be no longer securely grounded in the survival instinct, but that it be dependent on values and moral judgments of individuals and nations. The 20th century confrontation of values manifesting during the "the Cold War" period should forever remind us of a possibility of the self-annihilation if we cannot agree on what is more important.

The major insights which change the instinctual ways we act in the world refer to the concepts and ideas which are reflected in the laws, religious beliefs and conscience of every person regardless of cultures, civilization or tradition. Jacob Bronowski and Bruce Mazlish (1960) in their book *The Western Intellectual Tradition* specify that the people's cognitive activities focus on the three domains: seeking truth in approaching reality, expressing a sense of beauty (a good taste) and searching for what is right.(p. 495). With respect to the latter, in psychosocial sense, this means showing love, compassion, and kindness in relations to people, which is an extension of the ethical principle that we should treat others in the manner we wish to be treated ourselves. This spiritual principle is reflected in various religions, even predating Judeo- Christian and is known as a "golden rule" (Wikipedia, the free encyclopedia; en.wikipedia.org/wiki/Golden_Rule); its violation, according to Kant's categorical imperative, represents the ultimate evil. James Rachels (1986) in his book, *The Elements of Moral Philosophy,* stated the following (public.callutheran.edu/~chenxi/phil345_022.pdf - United States):

> "Like many other philosophers, Kant believed that morality can be summed up in one ultimate principle from which all our duties and obligations are derived. He called this principle The Categorical Imperative. In the Groundwork of the Metaphysics of Morals (1785) he expressed it like this: Act only according to that maxim by which you can at the same time will that it should become a universal law. However, Kant also gave another formulation of The Categorical Imperative. Later in the same book, he said that the ultimate moral principle may be understood as saying: Act so that you treat humanity, whether in your own person or in that of another, always as an end and never as a means only (p. 1)"

Before any laws were developed to formally guard and enhance these specifically human insights, there must have been some tacit acknowledgement on an intuitive subconscious level, that these are the desirable ways to lay foundations for societal organization and for promoting individual growth through social interactions, whereas violation of these principles will be the cause of suffering and pain. These insights established guidelines for the future course of human development in recorded history, and it is not that important whether it was actually Moses or somebody else who presented the Ten Commandments (Book of Exodus; 20:1-17) to the people.

What is, however, important is that the commandments were given in their legalistic form at the time when people's awareness had already advanced to the level that the commandments could be widely accepted. Their broad acceptance expressed people's common understanding what are the important life questions and how they "should" be answered with reference to who we are as human beings, what should be our mutual relations, and what should be our future course of development. It is therefore not surprising that as "natural laws", these commandments are reflected in various religions and in the beliefs and behaviors of people in many cultures.

The importance of spirituality is recognized by those who intend to influence people's thinking and acting. Through recorded human history a primary effort was directed at shaping people to be part of a certain social order by referring to its devine origin, laws of history, high morality or people's best interests.

Formal education, religious teaching along with political and cultural ideas change human behavior through presenting certain programs as ultimately good for humanity and individuals. Political manipulation and propaganda is about giving different meaning to the well-known values; this may result in redefining expropriation of property as a way of implementing social justice, annihilation of the opposition on the pretense that they create obstacles to progress, concealment of facts because such knowledge would cause mind corruption, etc.

Inspirational Value of Spirituality

The greatest inspirational value of spirituality is that it is poorly defined. This is a cause of innumerable disputes, confusions, misunderstandings and wars which created a lot of human misery. On the other hand, spirituality also offers a possibility of progress which typically emerges from the confrontation of the opposite or conflicting views (Celinski, 2011). Following on the primary obligation to be committed to truth results in countless battlefields where opposite sides have at their disposal accumulated knowledge, creative insights and the skills that enable sophisticated expressions. Similarly, possibilities for showing love and kindness are not only numerous, but potentially unlimited because there is no other restriction, other than personal capabilities and boundaries. However, misunderstanding and confusion about the meaning of various values and concepts create the primary reason for difficulties in interpersonal, political, legal and familial relationships.

To achieve balance in people's involvement with others, awareness of personal boundaries was needed that is reflected in morality, culture and the laws of the land. Only from such a perspective would it make sense to follow on the postulate to reach to others (which obviously requires crossing personal boundaries) or, as in Buddhist's tradition, to achieve a sense of unity with all creation (His Holiness the Dalai Lama, 2005). Personal boundaries are also a source of conflicts pertaining to privacy, intimacy and the nature of assault; they create a sense of entitlement and the right to defend oneself and one's own possessions (to list the most important). One cannot deny that historically there have been divers and still evolving viewpoints about "boundaries" and "rights" that result in modifications of the penal systems, but also in riots and wars.

Thus, to summarize, introduction of spirituality to self-regulation enabled people to partially free their attention away from instinctual drives as the primary source of individual's motivation for any activity. The alternative regulatory principle is based on individuals' beliefs and values, and on judgment that needs to take into consideration objectively recognized opportunities and constraints, individual and collective capabilities along with consequences of one's behavior on personal relations and physical reality. There are profound consequences that result from such an understanding of people's being-in –the -world. As we have inadequate cognitive capabilities to comprehend reality in the complete and truthful manner, this leaves room for various errors in judgment which makes us vulnerable to unforeseen negative consequences and to suffering (Celinski and Gow, 2008).

Individuals' awareness of vulnerability and mortality, shared with the rest of humanity, should prompt everybody to approach social reality with love, compassion and kindness expressed especially towards those who are disadvantaged or weak. This attitude could be further extended to all the living, sensing creatures, as postulated by the spiritual orientation embedded in Buddhist's beliefs. The degree to which we are to extend ourselves to meet needs of others is expressed in the spiritual obligation to measure love for others proportionately to the love which we feel for ourselves; this also means that in our practical decisions, we have to consider guarding our own personal boundaries and not to "stretch" ourselves beyond our personal capabilities, as these would be harmful or disadvatagous to our own survival. However, love for others may sometimes override such concerns. These are great insights and expressions of wisdom, and it is not surprising that there have been continuous attempts to formalize and to quantify in a dogmatic way the intrinsic goodness of spirituality so that it will be accepted and practiced in daily life in accordance with local laws and various religious, moral as well as cultural rules and traditions. Such efforts are well intended as they promote uniform ethical standards that may uphold social order; nonetheless, continuous reference to freedom is essential to allow spirituality to maintain its inspiration and to use wisdom (Targowski, 2011 a,b) to choose and to combine various values in a creative way that would manifest cohesive vision while disregarding more superficial diversity. Tension created by awareness of both unity and diversity represents the kind of dialectic challenge that humanity will have to continuously struggle with, in attempts to provide solutions so that some stability and continuity be preserved (Celinski and Gow, 2011); this gives meaning to our lives and satisfaction if we even partially succeed in such an effort. Dogmatic and formalized approaches to spirituality would contradict its very inspirational nature.

According to Jewish tradition, God gave Moses the Ten Commandments (Book of Exodus; 20:1-17), thus endorsing their objective validity as a representation of humanity interests. The belief in their divine origin gives hope in their power to inspire ideas that would transform people's relationships, attitudes and behaviors when people acknowledge the intrinsic and eternal goodness of these Commandments. Psychologically, both in individual lives and historically people experience a sense of righteousness and satisfaction from doing what they recognize as being in accordance with the fundamental laws of life, and they would develop a sense of guilt if they transgress them. Awareness of these mental states creates an obsessive-compulsive need to pay attention and to be vigilant to whether particular values are observed or violated. Freud (1961) focused on the negative aspects of civilization as suppressing the free expression of our instincts and stated that "the price we pay for our advance in civilization is loss of happiness through the heightening of the sense of guilt." (p. 81)...this primal guilt ... was also the beginning of civilization..." (p. 83)..."the two urges, the one towards personal happiness and the other towards union with other human beings must struggle with each other in every individual" (p. 88).

While recognizing this eternal struggle, we need to acknowledge that it is also a motivating force as, in the end, people are naturally compelled to reconcile instinctual needs and behaviors with spirituality in order to achieve "peace of mind."

From this review, the path to progress may be described as follows: people have the freedom to pursue spiritual values which allow them to interpret them in accordance with their level of self-awareness and objective circumstances. Acting from such an inspiration gives people confidence in doing right things, and enables them to gain satisfaction from their achievements. Departure from spiritual values results in personal dissatisfaction, a sense of unfulfilled life, and guilt feeling. This is the reason why it is so difficult for a normal human being to live with the knowledge of wrongdoing, even if committed under pressure or in a moment of weakness, without feeling guilty. Dostoyevsky (1917) presented this state of mind in "*Crime and Punishment*" where the poor student Raskolnikov, after killing a greedy pawnbroker for money, tried to find various justifications for his action, but finally admitted to his guilt and decided to bear punishment for his crime. In Raskolnikov's case the power of the self-punishing guilty conscience was exemplified; in psychoanalytic theory (Freud, 1961) a punishing super-ego serves the purpose of taming instinctual drives, especially the sexual drive. Development of super-ego is explained as stemming from an imprint of the father figure on a child's mind, which prevents a male child from directing his libido at his mother. A sense of entitlement and desire for plundering must be abandoned, and redirected in accordance with the societal rules represented by the father's image. If this has been successfully achieved, it is expected to be generalized to other aspects of functioning, thus allowing for compliance with societal rules and moral expectations at large.

The problem with such an interpretation of conscience and spirituality is its over-simplification in that the complexity of spirituality as a psychological regulatory system is reduced to dealing basically with a sexual drive. Campbell (1976) edited some of Jung's important papers, which offer a much broader perspective on human social adaptability by referring to the unconscious collective aspects of psyche that manifest as certain ubiquitous and timeless images and ideas that guide people's lives.

It is a central tenet of this chapter that whereas spirituality is in a dialectic opposition to instinctual drives, it cannot be reduced to the concept of super ego that is understood as an overseer and guardian of our instinctual life. It may be better understood in the broader historic, psychosocial, cultural and religious tradition as representing specific to humanity a separate regulatory system that involves the whole personality. The very purpose of spirituality is to provide relative freedom from instinctual demands, and an opportunity for progress by focusing and expanding on certain values, beliefs and astute judgments. This specific difference in understanding the role of spirituality (as contrasted to the role of the super-ego) is also reflected in a change of the therapeutic approach to dealing with self-punishing and guilt-producing internal dynamics which, according to psychoanalytic theory, result in neurosis. For this, the classic psychoanalytic answer would be in loosening the grip of the super-ego and removal of irrational guilt, enabling "normal" (more flexible) functioning. In contrast, recognition of spirituality as a regulatory system requires that the tension between instincts and spirituality be acknowledged as the necessary condition for personal growth and societal progress, and that the goal is their integration by referring to reason and wisdom.

Instinct and Spirituality: A Comparison

Spirituality is frequently contrasted with reason in that the former is considered as "irrational," and the latter as based on facts and logic. The position presented in this chapter is that the main function of spirituality is to be a regulatory system which is primarily directed at moderating the absolute demands of the instinctual needs by enabling us to act, while being inspired by values, reason and wisdom. Detailed comparisons between the characteristics of instincts and spirituality reveal that these two regulatory systems are addressing similar issues, but in a different way, thus offering vastly divergent perspectives on the self and its approach to reality. Table I presents the comparisons of the two systems from the point of view of their oppositional characteristics which allow for their dialectic relationships.

Therefore, it is evident that instincts and spirituality provide us with a different orientation to life and to ourselves while addressing the same life issues. Our instinctual life forces us to primarily focus on our survival and on satisfying our needs; for this, we intend to use as much control as available to us, so that reality yields to wishes and desires. Such a mentality may be attributed to a cave man, but also develops in prisons, concentration camps or poverty stricken social environments where people's attention is primarily concerned with momentary or daily survival.

Table 1. Comparison of Instincts and Spirituality

CRITERIA	SELF-REGULATION BASED ON INSTINCT	SELF-REGULATION BASED ON SPIRITUALITY
Behavioral importance	Setting priorities and goals	Setting priorities and goals
Consequences for others	Acting regardless of consequences	Acting responsibly
Desirable Outcome	Reduction of inner tension and adjustment	Satisfaction from connectivity with broader issues in life and with people
Awareness	Partially conscious but demanding action	Partially conscious but demanding action
Exploration	By trial and error	By sustained faith and commitment
Purpose	Survival as the utmost priority	Providing meaning and directions for life
Modus Operandi	Control	Transcendence, choice and creativity
Orientation	Individual pleasure	Benefits for humanity
Existence	Timeless	Timeless
Time Focus	Now or in the near future	Unlimited
Behavioral Expression	Always well-defined	Poorly defined implementation
Stimulus Trigger	Specific external or internal; emotional or physiologic needs	Crisis, deprivation, hopelessness or may not have or require specific trigger
When Blocked from fulfillment	Anger and Fear	Shame, guilt, sense of emptiness

The possibility that spirituality has ever developed may be attributed to the human species' ability to delay gratification due to the increased awareness of the motives other than one's own biological needs. Rather than relying on one's strength alone, perhaps gradual diversification in social roles, specialization in production of primitive tools and collective use of resources forced people to work together in some organized fashion that required from individuals postponement of their spontaneous reaction in consideration for others. In this context, there is also place for the psychoanalytic concept of the father figure who forced young sons to comply with the objective constraints and social demands by using his power over household affairs.

The argument I presenting here refers to the origin of spiritualty as associated with recognition of another individual and oneself as persons who enter in mutual relations and participate at the same time "in an actuality; that is, in a being neither merely part of him nor merely outside him"…"For as soon as we touch a You, we are touched by a breath of eternal life", as Martin Buber (1990, p. 118) pointed it out. By broadening of our awareness of others, spirituality offers a prospect of some freedom from absolute demands of instinctual fulfillment and reveals to people a different meaning of life (other than self-gratification and survival). By having a developmental momentum on its own it is a source of its own joy, fulfillment, satisfaction and connectivity with people; it also stipulates that doing the right thing is more important than getting any reward or personal satisfaction. Such a perspective on meaning and purpose of life places human beings in a unique position among species, as this enables people to exercise freedom and to choose how to direct the course of individual and social lives. In effect, the decisions are not only guided by basic needs or even a prospect of achieving specified outcomes, but rather by one's own images and beliefs in what is appropriate, and what represents a more complete understanding of the self, humanity's existence and awareness of the higher order of things. Such an orientation requires that we use wisdom (Targowski, 2011a,b) to combine instinctual drives with spiritual values and demands of reality.

In summary, spirituality is characterized by the ideas and values that are regarded as absolute, universal and eternal. They are also spontaneously or easily accepted as obvious (i.e. justice, truth) and as inspirational and motivating to the point of obsession or compulsion to do something that would express their meaning. They give people a sense of goodness and meaning of life which are rewarding in themselves. They unite us and synchronize our existence with the essence of Being that is larger than individual and with the collective which give people peace of mind due to an assurance that they are doing right things. Furthermore, spirituality offers a possibility of transcending with our thoughts, wishes and actions the daily pressures and obstacles thus empowering us to continue with our chosen activities or with an implementation of a plan in spite of the inconvenience and suffering that such an action may cause.

WISDOM AS A SPIRITUAL RESOURCE

Wisdom manifests a possibility of finding common ground for diverse or opposite perspectives, as it provides guidelines for finding solutions which would harmonize multiple aspects of reality. The wise judgement is recognized as having taken into consideration what an individual regards as important in his or her life (truth, beauty, justice, compassion, etc.). Wisdom should also allow us to decide, on one hand, to what degree we may accept lack of gratification and criticism from others, frustration from not achieving desirable results and a necessity to endure hardship. On the other hand, wisdom should also tell us to what degree we should continue putting forth effort in spite of obstacles by utilizing our faculties and resources, while being inspired by truth, compassion, justice etc. In essence, wisdom allows people to express opinions that may be contrary to the prevailing views, even if it may jeopardize their health or cause a loss of property, friends or even life. While St. Paul cautions us that "world's wisdom is foolishness to God "(St. Paul's letter: 1Cor.1:18-25), it probably means to be humble by knowing that no opinion and judgement is the final manifestation of Being and eternal wisdom. In this sense, we are also advised to transcend our usual concerns with accumulating or preservation of what is commonly regarded as important or valuable, as there are more important values to be continuously considered and searched for.

Let's imagine a situation of a person living in the 80's in one of the countries of the Central Europe dominated by the Soviet style Communist regime. For some people, it was foolishness to risk life or at least an ability to live a so-called "normal life" (as much as it was possible at that time), by discussing in public fallacies of the system, its corruption and oppression or even its economic mismanagement. Being "irrationally" motivated by hope that truth or at least common sense will prevail, could have been ridiculed by those who joined the government ranks or at least passively supported the system. When some years later, previously oppressed dissidents became well-known politicians, one could question who was wise and who was foolish, who had a sense of satisfaction and understanding of the laws of history and of human nature, and who was misled by appearances and a need for relative comfort.

A sense of freedom and understanding of who we are as human beings placed an obligation on us to acknowledge and to construct our own sense of truth about life and the value of our existence, and to visualize the way we choose to participate in the advancement of something good for us as individuals as well as for humanity at large. Spirituality manifests and makes a difference through steadfast adherence to certain values, beliefs and faith in its transformative ability. It spreads the message primarily through examples (for which sometimes personal sacrifices are necessary), as evidenced in the lives of the great leaders and teachers of humanity. Outcomes motivated by spirituality are sometimes ill-defined or not directly attributable to someone's deliberate action. For this reason, historic developments many times surprised those who regarded certain desirable societal changes as unachievable in a particular period of time and life circumstances. This is because spirituality does not use typical, coercive measures of control so that desirable outcomes can be achieved in a well-structured and predictable manner, but relies on the attractiveness of ideas and on some gradual momentum building which for a long time may remain less evident or suppressed by other concerns. Whitehead (1990) commented that "More than two thousand years ago, the wisest men proclaimed that the divine persuasion is the foundation of the order of the world, but that it could only produce such a measure of harmony as amid the brute forces it was possible to accomplish" (p. 206)

I will summarize the previous points as an answer to the question: why is it desirable to acknowledge, enhance and follow on one's spirituality?

- Individually, being grounded in spirituality provides the meaning of life that protects individuals from being primarily influenced by pressures of instincts and demands of a society or culture that sometimes clearly contradict what people wish to believe in on a spiritual level and what they are committed to manifest through their lives. The intrinsic reward from such a mental attitude is an endorsement of one's sense of freedom, satisfaction from being on the "right side", and peace of mind in spite of life circumstances.

- Collectively, if our behavior manifests solidarity with other people, compassion for suffering and intends to promote social justice, we have a possibility to achieve more trusting and mutually supportive relations among people that would promote social peace and enhance our global well being.
- Concurrently with cultural globalization that is associated with economic expansion should follow spiritual awareness of our common fate and destiny, and a responsibility to provide conditions for continuity and sustainable developments. Spirituality offers hope that we will manage to understand our challenges and find the way how to cope and resolve our problems.

SPIRITUALITY AND DYSFUNCTIONALITY

Table 1 presents the contrasting qualities of instinctual drives and spirituality, which are manifesting as the primary life orientations that need to be bridged by wisdom and reason. Analysis of the relationship between spirituality and other aspects of human nature reveals several types of dysfunctionality or psychopathology which are represented in everyday life, peoples' attitudes, philosophy, psychological theories and education.

Considering that spirituality is a partially unconscious but demanding force which punishes us with shame, guilt and a sense of inferiority, one of the most commonly known psychopathological manifestations is a tendency for *perfectionism.* In such a state of mind, obsessive pre-occupations with ones' own faults, weaknesses and inadequacy create a fear of failure that either prevents people from taking calculated risk or motivates them to compensate their feeling of inferiority. The latter case usually manifests an excessive focus on one value (at the exclusion of others) which then becomes the constant object of self-examination and obsession. In psychopathological conditions, this is reflected as an excessive need for order, cleanliness, punctuality, obedience and loyalty, honesty, sexual purity, etc. In such cases, the concept of the punishing super-ego is indeed particularly relevant and through psychological therapy it is possible to broaden the horizon and feel more at ease with one's own instinctual life, other perspectives on reality and oneself as an imperfect and fallible person.

A sense of not being able to measure up to the objective (cultural, religious and legal) standards may also result in *hypocrisy,* reflected in preaching one thing and doing just the opposite. This may be a way of life in certain communities, but is particularly evident in the situations where there are strict ethical codes and regulations formally expected to be followed, whereas it is only in private life that people have the opportunity to express their true feelings. In totalitarian systems, it was the common occurrence that people had public views and behaviors different than their private feelings and thoughts.

Relativism expresses a belief that because no one is able to fulfill moral or spiritual absolute demands they are to be modified according to the situation and one's own preferences.

Cynicism manifests as a more decisive expression of beliefs that what society imposes as morality or values is an unnecessary burden which prevents people from enjoying life and pursuing their self-interest, which is the only things that truly matters in life. Such beliefs and attitudes to life represent a human underdevelopment: it is an inability to see, acknowledge or feel anything valuable beyond one's own needs, either due to lack of emotional and intellectual maturity, lack of exposure to good examples or insufficient social nourishment. Therefore education and encouragement are needed to promote the view that an ability to transcend one's own narrow perspectives or instinctual demands is the necessary prerequisite to become fully human.

Fundamentalism is reflected in the literal understanding and implementation of certain articles of faith, metaphors or values which are then rigidly followed regardless of consequences. Can I lie in order to save somebody's life? Should I follow an advice to sell everything and give to the poor (Luke 18: 22) in order to document my commitment to values other than material possessions? Shall I, after selling and distributing all my possessions, accept as a real possibility that my Father in heaven will provide me with sufficient means to survive considering that birds of heaven don't plough or sow and survive? (Matthew 6:2). Should I cut off my hand (Matthew 5: 30) or take out my eye (Matthew 5: 29) if these are conducive to my sinful way of life? These are some examples of the most extreme ways in which values present themselves in their absolute form as commandments and sometimes painful obsessions causing that only few people can measure up to them, while the vast majority feels alienated, oppressed or persecuted. Fundamentalism is frequently associated with violence and attempts to impose totalitarian controls over people's minds (as was done in Medieval Europe by an office of Inquisition, and subsequently in the former communist and fashist countries and which continues in some theocratic societies). In fundamentalism, other values are neglected similarly as reason, individual wisdom and responsibility, and the importance of individual conscience.

One of humanity's spiritual achievements is the recognition that the self has the primary obligation to construct, in an educated, comprehensive and responsible way, meaning and value out of many discrepant perspectives so that we are able to achieve consistency and continuity of our behavior (Celinski and Gow, 2011). If people feel free to use their faculties to make sense of their lives, inevitably there will be divergent outcomes.

Nevertheless, as long as we are able to recognize in the views of others, some commonalities and dilemmas of human nature, we are at least able to tolerate perspectives different than ours. Those who refer to a divine origin of spirituality understand it as a reflection in individual's minds of longing for unity with a Supreme Being (King, 2001) who, as our Creator, best represents the essence of existence and interests of humanity. Another possibility is viewing spirituality as human creation reflecting deeper understanding of social developments or of the laws of nature. Fredrick Nietzsche (Stanford encyclopedia of philosophy, plato.stanford.edu/entries/nitzsche) was well aware of these dilemmas of the human mind while advocating that religious, but especially Judeo–Christian morality, needs to be rejected in order to make people strong. Victorious people are masters of their destiny and establish for themselves the guidelines which are an expression of their will to live and to power.

The 20th century Europe was the field test of these ideas as conventional morality stopped to guide the two totalitarian systems introduced in Germany and the Soviet Union. Depending on the interpretation of the historic, social or biological forces, ideologies may be created which offer people a missionary role to promote the supposedly finest achievements of humanity (for example such as embodied in Communism and Nazism) that would deserve ultimate sacrifices; whereas the former was presented as the liberation of the masses from oppression of the Capitalist system, the latter took inspiration from the idea of superior race and its mission to spread civilization achievements embodied in this race. Both ideologies collapsed; however, their existence left behind millions of victims from the war and concentration camps, and caused the destruction of Europe.

It would be gross misunderstanding of human nature to attribute these evil motives solely to German or Russian people. We have to remember that the pivotal point is in recognition of the origin of spirituality and morality: either as a product of human mind, which is therefore not absolute but relative and changeable over time, or as the objective values implanted in all human minds for the common good and indispensable, if we wish to continue fully human existence. While specific expressions of spirituality would change over time, if we remain faithful and persistent in our search, its broader and never exhausted meaning will be revealed to us.

CONCLUSION

To be fully human, one has an obligation to become aware and to integrate in one's conscience the regulatory systems which are instincts, spirituality, reason and wisdom. While doing this, people should autonomously exercise their freedom of choice and express the fullness of human nature, and their experience of "being- in- the world". In such a way, they become co-creators of social reality. Whereas instinctual drives and spiritual drives are clearly in opposition, their integration offers a more fulfilled way of life if a person intends to pursue such a goal. By contrast, an excessive focus on a "realistic" path dominated by "logic and reason" is deprived enthusiasm, passion and of "irrational" commitments while knowing they may never lead to tangible achievements in one's lifetime (as lives of some artists, musicians or freedom fighters document). Even being aware that some goals are not readily achievable, we should attempt to develop the best representation and expression of our personal truth about how to deal with life adversity; sometimes the only satisfaction and happiness is from being faithful to one's own "life mission."

It is quite natural that various interpretations of what represents the core of spirituality will lead to development of various religious denominations, cultures and lifestyles. The primary danger of formalized religions is to "privatize" their spirituality in order to feel righteous and to justify advancement of the self-interests through violence and oppression of others, as it happened many times in history. The very nature of spirituality enables us to enlarge our awareness in the service to the whole humanity. Such awareness leads to regard the essence of our existence as derived from a larger structure which is not fully understandable; however, rather than becoming discouraged or cynical about it, uncertainty and confusions should prompt our efforts to explore through faith and transcendence what lies beyond ourselves (i.e. our narrow views, beliefs and needs); while doing this, we reach out to other people with whom we share human destiny and the responsibility for betterment of our collective and individual lives. Preoccupation with the idea that happiness is the paramount purpose of life is contrary to progress, which requires that we continuously search for deeper understanding of spiritual values, persevere in spite of "insurmountable" obstacles and be prepared for enduring sacrifices.

Modern interpretations of spiritual values created cultures based on human rights, freedom and democracy, and developed technologies and civilizations that offer a possibility for almost everybody to live with dignity and opportunities for fulfillment of the best of human potential.

References

Bronowski, J. and Mazlish, B. (1960). *The Western intellectual tradition* (p. 495). New York: Harper and Brothers.

Buber, M. (1990). I and Thou. In J.Pelikan (Ed.), *The world treasury of modern religious thoughts*.(p. 118). Boston, Toronto, London: Little, Brown and Company.

Cambell,J . (Ed.), (1976). *The portable Jung*. New York: Penguin Books.

Campbell, J. (1990). *Explorations in the mythological dimensions of fairy tales, legends and symbols: the flight of the wild gander*. New York: Harper Perennial.

Celinski, M. J. (2011).The concepts of progress and regress in relation to civilizations. *Dialogue and Universalism, 21,* 123-143.

Celinski, M. J. and Gow, K.M .(Eds), (2011). *Continuity versus creative response to challenge. The primacy of resilience and resourcefulness in life and therapy*. New York: Nova Science Publishers.

Celinski, M. J. and Gow, K.M. (2008).Trauma clients: how understanding disintegration can help to restore resourcefulness of the self. *Australian Journal of Clinical and Experimental Hypnosis*, *33*,195-217.

Dawkins, R. (1995). *River out of Eden: A Darwinian view of life*. New York: Basic Books.

Dostoevsky, F. (1917). *Crime and punishment*. Vol. XVIII. Harvard Classics Shelf of Fiction. New York: P.F. Collier and Son.

Frankl, V. E. (2000). *Men's search for ultimate meaning*. Cambridge, Massachusetts: Perseus Publishing.

Frankl,V.E. (1966). *Men's search for meaning. An introduction to logotherapy*. New York , N.Y.: Washington Square Press.

Freud, S. (1961). *Civilization and its discontents*. New York: W. W. Norton and Company, Inc.

Fromm, E. and Xirau, R. (1968). *The nature of man*. Problems of Philosophy Series, Paul Edwards – General Editor. New York: The Macmillan Company.

Gleick, J. (1987). *Chaos: making a new science*. New York: Penguin Books.

Gow ,K., Separovich, B., Whitehead, A., Hii, B. and Gibbs, V. (2011). Religious orientation and its relation to well being and open–close mindedness across religious groups. In K.M.Gow and M.J.Celinski (Eds), *Way finding through life's challenges. Coping and survival* (pp. 41-162). New York: Nova Science Publishers.

Hall, C. S. (1954). *A primer on Freudian psychology*. New York: Mentor Books.

Heidegger, M. (1962). *Being and time*. New York, Hagerstown, San Francisco, London: Harper and Row, Publishers.

His Holiness the Dalai Lama. (2005). *The universe in a single atom: the convergence of science and spirituality*. New York: Morgan Road Books.

Kant, E. *Stanford encyclopedia of philosophy*, plato.stanford.edu/entries/kant-moral.

King, U. (2001). *Christian mystics. Their lives and legacies throughout the ages*. New Jersey: Hidden Spring

Mandler, G. (1997). *Human nature explored.* New York: Oxford University Press.

Miller, R. (1981). *Meaning and purpose in the intact brain: A philosophical, psychological and biological account of conscious processes.* Oxford: Clarendon Press.

Nitsche, F. *Stanford encyclopedia of philosophy*, plato.stanford.edu/ entries/nitsche.

Rachels, J. (1986). *The elements of moral philosophy* (pp. 114-17,122-23). New York: Random House, Inc.

Schwartz, B. (1986). *The battle for human nature: science, morality and modern life.* New York: W. W. Norton and Company, Inc.

Steiner,G.(1974). *Nostalgia for the absolute.* Toronto: Canadian Broadcasting Corporation.

Stevenson, L. (1987). *Seven theories of human nature.* New York: Oxford University Press.

Targowski, A. (2011b).Wisdom, awareness of life purpose , and happiness: the cognitive informatics approach. In M. J. Celinski and K .M. Gow (Eds), *Continuity versus creative response to challenge. The primacy of resilience and resourcefulness in life and therapy* (pp. 73 -92). New York: Nova Science Publishers, Inc.

Targowski, A. (2011a). *Cognitive informatics and wisdom development. .Interdisciplinary approaches.* IGI Global.

Tischne , J.(1984). *The spirit of solidarity.* San Francisco: Harper and Row, Publishers. *The New American Bible* (1971). Chicago: J.G. Ferguson Publishing Company.

Watson, P. (2006). *Ideas: A history from fire to Freud.* London: Phoenix Paperback.

Weil, S. (2003). *Letter to a priest* (p. 85). New York: Penguin Books.

Whitehead, A.N. (1990). The new reformation.. In J.Pelikan (Ed), *The world treasury of modern religious thoughts* (p. 206). Boston, Toronto, London: Little, Brown and Company.

In: Spirituality and Civilization Sustainability ...
Editors: Andrew Targowski and Marek J. Celinski
ISBN: 978-1-53610-729-6

Chapter 2

THE WORLD AND THE PLANET IN A GREAT CRISIS OF THE THIRD MILLENNIUM: WE NEED A NEW RENAISSANCE

Andrew Targowski*
Western Michigan University,
International Society for the Comparative Study of Civilizations
Kalamazoo, Michigan, US

ABSTRACT

The purpose of this chapter is to investigate the range of the crisis of civilization exemplified by the financial crisis of 2008. Beyond this type of crisis another 15 crises are characterized. In totality they define the Second Great Crisis of Civilization, which is taking place now in the Third millennium, while the First Great Crisis took place after the fall of the Roman Empire in 476 A.D.

The current civilization crisis is mainly caused by the crisis of ideas and morality and subsequent crisis of the ecosystem. A solution to the Great Crisis of Civilization may require long years, if not several generations. There may not be much time because of the negative dynamics of the Death Triangle of Civilization with its symptoms already felt, and which will strongly be felt by the middle of the 21st century.

The protection of the civilization that we know requires a Renaissance II. There must be change and new value to the role of the Internet, science, politics, business, technology, and the media along with other critical matters. Renaissance II requires leaders on the level of Leonardo da Vinci and must be supported by Enlightenment II, which will significantly educate and develop wise graduates, future professionals, and leaders. The future of civilization lies in a change from its present chaotic and self-destructive, fragmented course to a sound and sensible civilization. Is this possible?

* E-mail: andrew.targowski@wmich.edu

INTRODUCTION

The goal of this study is to define civilization's real state of crisis due to the Great Recession (2008-2012), developing after the financial crisis of 2008. This study strives to determine whether the crisis is cyclical and temporary, or structural and long term. If this crisis is of the second type, then what is the core? What is the character or structure of this crisis?

This study will include the analysis of sixteen smaller crises that together make up the real, current Great Crisis of Civilization. This crisis is actually the second great crisis of civilization. The first crisis occurred after the fall of Rome in the year 476 A.D. Not many understand the grave nature of the current crisis of our civilization.

Graphic models presented in this study will facilitate understanding of the relationship between these crises. Without these the analysis may be partial and incomplete. The conclusion will include results presented in the form of a composite road map recommending how this crisis may eventually be overcome.

THE SECOND GREAT CRISIS OF CIVILIZATION

Civilization has been developing for the last 6,000 years. During this time, there have been thousands of conflicts, battles, and wars (Reagan 1992). Civilization has endured one great crisis and is currently entering another great crisis in the 21st century. The First Great Crisis occurred after the fall of the Roman Empire in 476 A.D. and lasted almost 1,000 years up to the time of the Renaissance in the 15th century. Among the elements that led civilization, especially the West, toward renewed development was the invention of printing in 1453 and the dissemination of knowledge with the aid of printed material and books.

The dissemination and development of knowledge had a definite effect on the development of art, science, technology, literature, as well as politics and education. With the development of knowledge, civilization entered the Age of Enlightenment, a Social-Political Revolution in the 17th and 18th centuries, the First Industrial Revolution in the 19th century, the Second Industrial Revolution of mass production after the advent of the Ford assembly line, and the Scientific-Technological Revolution, with the invention of the radio, the television, the A bomb, radiology, computers, etc. Accompanying these were the Wave of Information Technology, the Wave of Virtualization, and the Third Industrial Revolution in the 21st century, based on the digitalization of the basic processes of manufacturing.

The fall of Rome I was due to the affluence of the ruling class with their diminished sense of morality and responsibility to society. The Second Great Crisis of Western Civilization, occurring since the beginning of the 21st century, is also attributed to the ruling class and their diminished sense of morality and responsibility for society, seen especially in the United States (Rome III) and in the developed European countries.

The fall of Rome I occurred after the intrusion of the so-called barbarian tribes of Central Europe including the Vandals beyond the Vistula. These tribes served the Roman Legions at the peripheries of the Empire, and as a part of the military, they rebelled and attacked the capitol of the people whom they served. The Second Great Crisis of Civilization has been caused by the transformation of Western Civilization into a Global Civilization accompanied by many internal crises in almost all the most important links in the chain of the world's great system.

Paradoxically, the Second Great Crisis of Civilization cannot be seen by the naked eye. We have no world war, no great epidemic, no great climate catastrophe on the planet. But this crisis does exist, because practically every one experiences it and has some idea of its cause. This is especially true since developed societies are well-educated and their elite are even better educated and capable of independent evaluations. So too, the elite class and even the middle class live in abundance, and do not feel the challenges of this great crisis that exists and gradually permeates the consciousness of those who are affluent and those who are very affluent. Only the elites believe this crisis is transient and not the Great Crisis of Civilization.

Another paradox has resulted from the rapid, fantastic development of the Internet in the 21st century. A great flow of quick information among almost all individuals, and certainly among diverse groups of people from different nations and societies is overwhelming.

The flow of information strengthened the role of individuals in providing information and reasoning. At the same time, however, we have seen a type of chaos, fragmentation, and misinformation together with radicalism and populism coming to voice, with the disappearance of practical wisdom. This is in contrast to the role of print that led to decreasing chaos in knowledge, information dissemination, and social-political life.

Let us analyze more important individual crises, as the sum of several simultaneous crises qualifies the above diagnosis of the world's state. The synthesis of these crises will be directed by the degree of their importance and entry, in the chain of the Second Great Crisis of Civilization.

THE CRISIS OF OVERCOMMUNICATION

The development of the Internet caused "the death of distance" (Cairncross 1997), and the phenomenon that the distance between individuals and organizations is unimportant and communication is immediate due to the speed of propagation of electromagnetic waves in which various types of computers and smart phones operate.

In the new e-communication, business in the developed countries profited the most, taking production to Asia within the same company that opened its offices outside of headquarters. So-called "outsourcing" resulted in the transfer of 40,000 factories from the U.S. to China and does not slow down the production cycle in the processing of information and communication. As a consequence, several million American workers lost good-paying jobs. This caused the elimination of the middle class and a structural economic crisis in the years 2008-2012. In response, the demand for goods collapsed, even the cheap goods produced abroad with very cheap labor.

The Internet has resulted in the development of the global economy, which increases the standard of living in developing countries and lowers the standard of living in developed countries. Enormous profits are derived by global corporations that develop new market outlets in Asia and Eastern Europe, but encounter strong social criticism from their mother countries. An example is a movement of the outraged, Occupy Wall Street, formed in the fall of 2011, addressing the growing income inequality in the U.S. between the wealthiest 1% and the remaining population of 99%.

The increase in information communication with global operations has been accompanied by an increase in the role of the individual who has access to the world reservoir of information and knowledge. Taking advantage of this are millions of various users who open up small businesses in places where both living conditions and business conditions are most conducive. The role of the English language has been strengthened as the worldwide language in social, business, scientific, and other forms of communication. The line of division between the workplace and the home is diminishing, as millions of workers choose to work at home and e-communicate with the workplace. The difference between large and small firms is also diminishing, especially in the area of services. Thanks to e-business and e-communication, small companies are able to offer services that previously only large companies could offer.

Speaking of users in Western countries, strengthened by the Internet, users support globalization and dispute any attempts to control the Net, not knowing that economic globalization adversely affects their standard of living. Although slowly, they are noticing, the destructive role of economic e-globalization, and we see them using the Internet for organizing themselves and protesting. In the fall of 2011, Internet users organized a simultaneous protest in 1,000 cities worldwide, against capturing the effects of globalization by 1% and even 0.1% of the wealthiest business people. Similarly, the so-called Arab Spring was put into motion by the Internet in 2011, with the goal of overthrowing a succession of dictators.

The development of social networks like *Facebook* and *Twitter* develops virtual social groups that constantly communicate with each other and organize their operations. In Europe a virtual social network inhibited real governments from confirming the international agreement of the Anti-Counterfeiting Trade Agreement, by a petition of 2 million signatures, which can fairly quickly be accomplished today through the Internet. ACTA had the goal of intellectual ownership on the Net, restricting what kinds of information users would have access to. For example, copyright holders would be helped if users watch a trailer on their favorite website, and the studio that distributed the trailer could shut down the website and force everyone to visit the studio's own site to view the trailer. ACTA would protect intellectual ownership on the Internet and trace the owners of servers that publish false information about people and organizations.

Without fail, the development of virtual societies inevitably leads to the substitution of representative democracy with direct democracy. This will lead to widespread radicalism and extremism as well as chaos. Unfortunately, although the invention of print lessened information chaos in the last 500 years, the Internet, with its many advantages, in specific areas of operation, increases informational-social chaos. Most Internet users, not being well-educated, are unable to distinguish between false data and information and that which is accurate. They become info-maniacs that make poor assessments and choose poor solutions.

Undeniably, a fault of e-communication is a growing number of lonely people. Yes, these people have even hundreds of e-friends, but these relationships are quick and on the surface, without any obligations or responsibility. Much valuable time is taken up through communication by computer or the computer-telephone, like the *iPhone*. The result is the lack of time to communicate face to face with the members of the family, neighbors, or real friends. So the Internet user isolates from real friends and acquaintances and may fall into depression and lack of enthusiasm for life. Thus the "machine" is no substitute for life.

The crisis of over-communication deepens, with the characteristic of dependency on electronic gadgets that sequential generations introduce to the delight of youth and companies, seeing in their networks a better form of marketing.

THE CRISIS OF SUPER OPPORTUNITIES

The great financial successes of the 1% elite and the success of internet firms comprised of young people have a strong influence on the imagination in society. This is especially so when political leaders believe "the sky is the limit". At the same time there is virtually high unemployment reaching about 10%. Of this percentage, almost one out of three young workers is unemployed and in Spain, one out of two. Engineers are encouraged to retrain as nurses and university graduates are offered unpaid positions, even by very prosperous Wall Street firms that can afford to employ these young graduates. But why? Money can be made on these too.

Of the ten jobs with the highest demand in the USA as of 2012, in first place is the care of the elderly at home. Of these ten types of jobs, six require higher education: teaching, information technology (IT) with hardware maintenance, IT software maintenance, IT systems analyzer, IT Webpage creator and maintainer, and pharmacologist. The last four jobs comprise the work of nurse, medical assistant, rehabilitation specialist, and the salesperson. These are not such highly specialized jobs that a superpower like the USA would need 2, 774 universities and colleges and 1,700 career technical schools.

Of course for people with big money, "the sky is the limit". For example, 25 directors of very speculative, so-called "hedge funds" have annual profits exceeding one billion per director. At the same time, general directors, CEOs of the largest corporations are compensated at a level of $15,000/per hour, or 1,500 times more than the average hourly wage of their employees (as with Walmart and Home Depot). The work of the director is not worth the large amount that is paid but is approved by the board of directors, composed of other general directors to whom the recipient will reciprocate by voting for similarly a high salary.

These kinds of people continue to look for new ways to make money. They buy politicians and pay a smaller percentage of their income on taxes than do their secretaries. Apparently they reinvest their profits and create new places of employment. It is true that they reinvest their income, but beyond the borders of their mother countries. For those investments they want tax relieves at home countries.

As the possibility of new great profits is attainable by the 1% elite, for the rest of the 99% of taxpayers, this kind of possibility is increasingly unattainable.

THE CRISIS OF BUSINESS

A business crisis is taking place in the sphere of role, ethics, and strategy. The great success of global corporations in development of income, as in the case of Apple, is measured by cash reserves of 100 billion dollars. The result is that society is to serve business, not business serving society as we have regarded its role thus far.

In the area of ethics, business uses the criterion of achieving its goals at any price. Greed is the driving motor of business, where the general directors capture the dividends of shareholders in the form of large bonuses.

The smartest and maybe the brightest individuals rally in the financial sector, which employs in the USA in 2012, the largest percent of the labor force – 12%. In this sector, bankers and financiers utilize a strategy of maximizing profit in very short terms, usually monthly, and at most quarterly. Their strategy depends upon speculation on funds comprised of customers' savings, entrusted to banks for trade and investment. If they are able to earn a profit, then they capture these in their entirety. If they experience losses they pass these on to their customers, burdening those who have entrusted them with their money.

As a result, Christian values that directed Western Civilization from 1,200 years have been submerged by the new religion of Global Civilization. Business has become religion, not subject to any critical assessments of politicians, especially the media. Business and the wealthiest businessmen set the tone for discussion in society, in the media, and in state and federal legislatures.

The result has been that business is gearing for its downfall, for example in the United States. In 2012, the factual symptoms have included the closing of 50 of the large department stores of Best Buy that sells computers, televisions, telephones, camera and other equipment, turning its focus to sales in smaller stores. This is happening due to the lack of affluent clientele that would adequately cover sales in their large department stores.

From the time the global corporations began eliminating the middle class in their mother countries, revenue has been diminishing and as a consequence, there is decreasing demand for their products and services, which is the main cause of the economic crisis from 2008-2012. The services market is too weak to promote economic growth and inconsequential are the accusations of business, putting all the blame on "big government". Even if pressed to intervene and the government applies various forms of Keynesian demand stimulation, the result will be production growth in China and not the USA. This obvious truth is not analyzed in the media, for which every business strategy is the final revelation and prognosis.

The Crisis of Religion

Because religion is not in a position to oppose the religion of business, it is in crisis. Mainline denominations themselves became businesses within a particular division of the market. In addition, organized religions are entangled in their own, internal crises of a moral-ethical nature. Evidence of this are the numerous lawsuits brought against the Roman Catholic Church in the USA and Western Europe, along with very high compensation awarded to victims. At the same time, the religion of Islam entered into open conflict with other religions, with the goal of promoting its own morality, apparently the only correct one, despite the damage incurred to societies. Not only is there the war on terror, controlled by Islam, but also there is the open religious war in Africa between Islam and Christianity.

Since the time that societies are better and better educated, it is more difficult for the clergy to maintain their prior high level of authority among the faithful. For this reason, the Roman Catholic Church is returning to mysticism and encourages the celebration of the Mass in Latin. The strategy is for the people to not completely understand what is being said in prayer, and that they show respect and fear of God. The better societies are educated, the better organized religions will be able to cope in a crisis. Currently, they are not in a position to adjust their approach to new social challenges.

The Crisis of Population

The population crisis is the result, among other causes, of the crisis of religion that opposes all forms of birth control. In 2012 the world population rose to exceed 7 billion people. If the current trend continues, then in 2050 there will be approximately 9-10 billion. The capacity of the ecosystem can only sustain 8 billion people. Only China is carrying a policy limiting its population. The remaining nations do not control their population growth, especially, as in Western and Eastern Civilization; the Christian churches oppose any type of birth control.

The Crisis of Ecology

A result of overpopulating the Earth is the degradation of the natural environment and climate warming. A specific crisis has grown from the lack of drinking water. It is estimated that every third inhabitant of the Earth has an inadequate supply of drinking water, and every fifth person lives in territories, where there are shortages of drinking water. While only 2.5% of all the water on the Earth is suitable for drinking, from this only 30% is accessible to people. The remaining drinking water is found in Arctica and Greenland. Driven by civilization, the secretion of excessive amounts of carbon dioxide from the combustion of fuels contributes to global warming and an imbalance of water on Earth. With the melting of snow and ice in Arctica, the level of the oceans is rising and the balance of water is changing to the disadvantage of the Earth's inhabitants. Much water evaporates from the rivers and reservoirs as a result of global warming. The consequences include the elimination of the elements necessary for the plant life of cultivated lands and increased demand for irrigation systems. People must learn to better conserve water, which leads to the development of policy for privatizing water systems, given this policy will supposedly help conserve water. Examples of this policy in practice are found in Latin America, where foreign companies offer their solutions or operate. This practice is met by the widespread, outspoken protest of those opposed to foreign companies drawing profits from their water-saving, related to a national resource.

The Crisis in Natural Resources

It is nonsense to continue the current economic strategy of achieving annual 3% growth to provide employment for a steadily growing population. A greater supply of goods not only promotes employment but also stimulates the number of births in families with the necessary income. This strategy repeats the proven strategy of the Industrial Revolution, regarding the relationship between economic development and population growth.

Table 1. If China and India develop like the USA (2005 figures)

COUNTRIES	Population in Millions	% of the World's Natural Resources Expended	American Way of Life % of the World's Natural Resources for Expending
USA	298	27	27
CHINA	1,300	5	117
INDIA	1,100	2	99
REMAINING COUNTRIES	3,700	66	66
TOTAL	6,465	100	309

Source: Pocket World in Figures, The Economist, 2008 and the author's estimate.

Table 1 presents the Planet's situation if China and India develop in the same manner as the USA.

From the data presented in Table 1, there is a need for three planets like Earth, to reach the standard of living *a la American Way* – to the people of China and India, assuming that the rest of the world or 50% of the total population will continue to live in poverty just as they do today. If these poor also wanted to live like Americans, we would need six planets like Earth, to assure this style of life or move 5 billion people to other planets. All this seems impossible.

Summing up this hopeless situation for civilization, we can quote the opinion of Lester Brown (2001):

1. If the Chinese ate as much beef as the Americans, they would need to actuate 343 million tons of grain each year, which is the annual production in the USA.
2. If the Chinese ate as much fish as the Japanese do, they would need to consume 100 million tons of the "fruit of the ocean", the same amount that is counted in the world for half a year.
3. If the Chinese had two cars per family, they would use 80 million barrels of oil daily, which is currently equal to the amount of worldwide extraction. They would also need to increase parking space for these vehicles by 31 million hectars, land on which they currently produce 132 million tons of rice, their basic food staple.
4. If the Chinese desire better education, they will need to increase the use of paper from 35 to 342 kgm/resident, the amount currently consumed by Americans. This is more paper than is counted in annual worldwide production.

These calculations, leading to the absurd, apply only to China. In comparison to India, the range of new requirements will be on the same scale. Commonly known estimates indicate that for the next 40 years civilization will have an adequate amount of oil, for the next 50 years enough natural gas, and for the next 40 years enough uranium to drive nuclear power plants. The traditional source of energy, coal, may last until the year 2300 (Targowski 2009).

We can deduce from these estimates an obvious result. The Civilization of Earth, if it is to endure, requires a new political-economic system.

THE CRISIS OF FOOD

The food crisis of the 21st century is the result of four main causes: 1). The production of biological fuel requires more areas for the production of corn and sugar cane. 2). The increase of meat consumption in the developed countries and also China and India requires greater production of feed. To produce one kilogram of meat , seven to eight kilograms of feed are needed like corn and soy beans. 3). The deregulation of foreign trade in food in the late 20th century led to destabilization of production, reserves, and food consumption in most countries. 4). Monopolization of agricultural production.

The monopolization of agricultural production is practiced by American companies in particular. For example, in the USA four companies captured control of the majority of agricultural business, leading to bankruptcy by many local farmers. At the same time, large companies supplied the market with unhealthy and tasteless food, while local producers supplied food that was not only healthy, but also good tasting.

In the USA, 81% of the beef market is supplied by four companies (Scharplatz 2003). Cargil, Inc. controls 45% of the world's grain crop, Archer Daniels Midland controls 30% of the world's agriculture processing (Lawrence 2004). Four international firms control over 70% of the liquid milk production in the USA, and an Ohio company supplies 3 billion eggs annually (Schmidt 2003). One firm in Utah raises 1.5 million pigs annually and has a problem with waste similar to that of the large city of Los Angeles (Halweil 2004). One large pig farm in North Carolina generates more waste than do the states of California, New York, and Washington combined (Imhoff 2003). The average bite of food that an American consumes will travel around 2000 kilometers from its origin to the place of sale. To supply a box of breakfast cereal to the store requires seven times more energy use, than which supplied the contents of the box (McKibben 2007).

For the sake of increased production and efficiency, agricultural farms arise comprising 200,000 acres of land that are overseen by a single manager and a few workers running automated machine systems. This concentration of agricultural production for the sake of greater efficiency is the cause of 6 million Americans becoming ill each year because of poor nourishment, including 300,000 hospitalizations, and 5,000 deaths (Pretty 2002).

In Western Civilization, in almost every country this type of concentrated agricultural production exists. The result is the low price of food, but with this local farmers are going bankrupt. In the same way, the environment is experiencing erosion from such a great scale of production and wastes that are difficult to dispose of. Certain regions in rural America are called "*the food desert*", with the churches and main streets empty. While concentrated agricultural production is effective for global firms, small farms are continually more efficient in food production per hectare, whether measured by tons, calories, or dollars, not to mention better quality. The success of the balanced development strategy depends upon the support of small and middle size farms, not giant ones. Small and middle-size farms are able to manage well with sufficient water and energy, and waste disposal. Super-farms of this scope have huge problems that effectually depreciate the environment and degrade civilization.

The food crisis may be systematically characterized by the growing cost of food in measurable terms. The cost of grain rose from $127 per ton in the year 2005, to $397 per ton in 2008. So in three years the price rose by 200%. But during this same period the price of rice by ton rose by 250% and cost $962 in 2008 (Winders 2011).

The food crisis caused many demonstrations from 2007-2012 in countries such as: Argentina, Mexico, India, Italy, Bangladesh, Egypt, Somalia, Tunesia, Algeria, and Morocco. Instead of decreasing, the number of hungry people increased from 800 million to one billion in 2009 (Winders 2011).

We arrive at the question, will there be enough food for all people if the population is nine billion in 2050?

THE CRISIS OF TECHNOLOGY

The development of technology had its practical place in Western Civilization before the Industrial Revolution in the 19th century and during this time, as well as currently, although to a different extent. From the time Western Civilization began to take production to Asia, regression in the development of technology began.

The greatest portion of technical innovation is now marketed where there is production, or beyond the developed countries. The measure of this occurrence is not the indicator of patented inventions. Americans patent the largest number of inventions, but market the largest portion of these beyond the borders of their own country, where they took their production. The second largest number of patents is held by the Japanese. Similar to Americans they produce where there is cheap labor, not in Japan. The Chinese patent about three times fewer inventions than the Americans, but put to use not only their own patented inventions, but also American, Japanese, certain German inventions, and also those from other countries.

The main emphasis on the development of technology has its place basically in the beginning of the 21st century in the scope of the development of computers and digital search and access to information like e-newspapers and e-books as well as the digitization of manufacturing. To the disappointment of readers, about half the operating newspapers using paper in the United States was substituted by e-newspapers. At a peak time, there were about 1,500.

In the publication and distribution of books, there has been a battle between electronic companies like Amazon, Apple, and Microsoft, and traditional publishers. Electronic companies would like to eliminate the publication of paper books. This a big attack on the culture and humanism that developed positively, supported by the traditionally published book for over 500 years. Already we hear the criticism that legal publishing achievements on electronic media are gradually being lost. Stored publications on electronic media are no longer readable, or there is a lack of machines for registration and reading.

By contrast, it is interesting how the manufacturing technique has been developing the use of print in three-dimensional space (3D). Instead of cutting machine tools to produce the specific detail of the machine, the powder of composite materials is printed, layer upon layer, according to specific measurements. On this same line of production, it is possible to produce the details for various final products, as for example, automobiles. Volkswagen has a new production strategy, *Modularer Querbaukasten* (MQB), which through far-reaching standardization will make possible the production of various models of cars on the same production line. This will be possible thanks to so-called production flexibility, controlled by software.

The system of modular production in conjunction with robotics based on a recognizable vision was introduced by Nissan in a factory in Sunderland, Great Britain. This system dramatically increased the productivity of workers. In 1999, this factory produced 271,157 automobiles by 4,594 workers. After implementing the new strategy, in 2011 there were 480,485 automobiles produced by 5,462 workers. Thus, productivity increased from 59 cars/worker to 88 cars/worker, or by 149% (*The Economist*, April 21, 2012, Special Report, pg. 4).

The digitalization of production is even called the Third Industrial Revolution, which should presumably result in the return of production to developed countries. Of course, this would depend upon the underutilization of these new forms of production by China.

Since the economies of the developed countries became economies of services, technical progress is concentrating upon the strategy of lowering the operational cost of services. Unfortunately, this depends upon the automation of customer service, and eliminating personal contact with the customer, substituted by an expert system. In practice, this leads to the death of client services and dispute from customers.

The technical development of nanotechnology is leading to the production of textile materials with a thickness of one atom (GraphExeter). These can be clothing, a type of computer, a smart telephone, an MP3 player, etc. Or the one-atom chemical material can be coated with insulating equipment, such as for medical protection against bacteria in hospitals. For the purpose of properly evaluating this type of innovation, there arose the Nano Impacts Intellectual Community, examining the ethical, legal, and safety impacts of nanotechnology at the University of Notre Dame.

The development of computerized purchase is spectacular. The buyer at *Starbucks Café* in the USA pays with the aid of his telephone that he brandishes at the cash register. You can bet that cash and the debit or credit card will vanish from the circuit by the year 2020, substituted by smart gadgets. Even in Africa, the system called *M-Pesa*, with *pesa* referring to the Swahili unit of monetary value, will transfer money between persons who do not have bank accounts but use electronic brokers. In England, the customer pays the seller for items bought using the system called *Square*, giving his last name. The customer's photo then appears on the seller's screen, assuring him that the buyer has sufficient funds. As the system *Pay Pal* is popular, so too *Google Wallet* has the same ambition. The latter one did not gain the popularity the firm had expected. *Pay Pal* launched its system in 2,000 Home Depot stores, where the telephone and pin number suffice to pay for goods.

Technology may develop a paying system that allows the customer to be recognized as soon as he enters the store, without reaching into a pocket or purse , or using a personal identification number (PIN). The customer will not have to physically visit the store. The seller will have an analysis with an enormous amount of data about the buyer, determining what is important to buy today, and will automatically make the purchase. This can occur with the regulation of claims and ensure the delivery of purchases to the home. Should we progress to this innovation because it is technically achievable?

The technological crisis is caused primarily by its unexamined use. Technology's first priority has been the substitution of human labor through the use of machines. Has this goal carried through to a priority of eliminating human labor because it is too expensive? It has been forgotten that the cost of human labor is a great success of civilization. Work fulfills man, leads him away from poverty, and enables him to have choices.

None of the business people or politicians consider the elimination of human labor as it causes the loss of consumers who are now dependent upon the government for financial assistance to make ends meet. The strategy should not be the elimination of human labor by technology, even the most brilliant. The goal of technology should be the steady, balanced support of human labor to assure full employment. For example, in the USA, the labor force totals 150 million workers and in Poland, the total is 18 million. It is assumed that full employment is achieved with only 4% unemployment, since a certain amount of fluctuation is inevitable. These kinds of indicators were evident in Western Civilization in the late 1960s. Currently, these countries are experiencing structural unemployment that will not return to a level of 4% without the application of a political solution.

The technology crisis has resulted not only from "*outsourcing*", but primarily from the goal of eliminating the "costly" worker. The consequence has been the goal, among others, of the structural crisis of the economic world that we have seen from 2008.

THE CRISIS OF SCIENCE

The scientific crisis is felt mildly since the scientific sector is developing spectacularly by measure of the number of scientific workers, the number of scientific periodicals, and the number of scientific conferences. Unfortunately, the quality of results from the large class of scientists is low. In the area of information technology for example, there are several tens of scientific periodicals in the world, but none of them are read by practicing information technologists. In this case, what is the societal usefulness of this type of science?

The greatest crisis is felt in the science of the economy, where economic theory is insufficiently developed regarding the global economy. The absence of this theory is leading to societal and political disruption with unemployment, and poor decision-making regarding development.

The strength of the theory of the "invisible hand" of the free market is inadequate for the actual situation, when the role of the monopoly is increasing and not decreasing. This is especially true, since the unabashed race for the greatest productivity triggers an increase in supply but also population increase along with depletion of essential resources like water, oil, natural gas, uranium, and non-ferrous metals. The result is an open, growing crisis of the civilization.

The theory of supply stimulation by the government, according to the principles of John M. Keynes does not work in the open economy because it stimulates imports and not domestic production. In the area of supply stimulation for example, by wealthy investors with the goal of lower taxes, this theory is not confirmed in practical application by Republican presidents like Ronald Reagan (1981-89), George H. Bush (1989-1993) and George W. Bush (2001-2009).

The data confirms the theory, that after lowering the budget deficit, periods of recession followed in American and European economies. Conversely, after periods of government stimulation, for example the increase in defense, periods of economic increase resulted (Krugman 2012). The policy of tighter belt-tightening in Great Britain introduced in 2010-2012 by conservative Premier David Cameron led the country into a significant recession. Governments supporting this kind of policy in Europe lose trust and fail, as in Holland,

France, and Greece in the spring of 2012. Unfortunately, economists are quiet on this subject, while conservative politicians keep promoting this ineffective economic policy, as if it has been positively tested. The policy has become doctrine, the worldview of those who stand to profit by it and cannot reconcile themselves to the facts of its impracticality.

It is commonly believed that the Great Recession of 2008-2012 showed diminished purchasing power by consumers and business, and that theoretically speaking; the solution lies in stimulating business with new ability to create jobs, resulting in stronger purchasing power. But this stimulation cannot be the result of the American Republican Party that in 2011-2012 has urged drastic budget cuts and lowering the purchasing power of consumers and businesses, taking advantage of administrative orders. This political policy is not supported by past data but arises from the doctrinal agenda of several billionaires that financially support this party. Thus, solving economic problems demands political resolution (Krugman 2012a) to limit the number of sponsoring funds that are unlimited currently, by a decision of the Supreme Court. To illustrate, Sheldon Adelson dedicated 100 million toward the Political Action Committee of Newton Gingrich in 2011. Gingrich then promoted the political opinions of this billionaire from Las Vegas. The social sciences and especially sociology, say little about the results of globalization such as the diminishing middle class and the rise of poverty in the wealthiest countries. Little is said about the marketing of society, where everything is for sale and should primarily serve the consumer, and not the common good, that is "too costly" to support. Sociology has completely misunderstood multi-culturalism, as a necessary diversification of societies since they depend on the processes of globalization within the scope of the inevitable movement of people. This has led to the transformation of the nation into political societies, organized into ethnic ghettos and groups interested mainly in their own benefit and not the good of the general population in which they live. Multi-culturalism needs to be considered from the viewpoint of human and civil rights, which leads to the treatment of each person with respect, regardless of the color of their skin or culture. The political sciences continue to appraise the time of the Cold War (1947-91), when capitalism triumphed, but with a human face, because there was competition with the Soviet system. Currently in the 21st century, capitalism has moved into the phase of turbo-capitalism and social Darwinism and should be subject to serious verification. Outraged at Wall Street, they are demonstrating on the streets, as 99% of citizens oppose the capture of the fruits of their labor by 1% of citizens. In the sphere of philosophy, we should activate the positive and think about ethics, especially in careers and business. The spark for this is the ethical crisis of the financial sector, especially in the USA, where the development of speculation strategy led to a financial crisis in 2008 and is still present. Philosophy, the cradle of knowledge is very important for people, directing us how to live and why. To be of real help, philosophy must leave its Ivory Tower and get close to everyday affairs. To accomplish this, philosophy must enter the mainstream and cease addressing the periphery of human wisdom. People need practical wisdom to know how to live and how to survive the current crisis. In the sphere of the natural sciences, the 20th century was an age of physics and the 21st century is predicted to be an age of biology. The function of the cell awaits new discoveries with nanotechnology and information processing. The mastery of rapid DNA sequencing and the use of powerful microscopes give hope for increasing knowledge about how cells function for better treatment. This should also contribute to the functioning of computers, which borrow from the human system, information processing in the brain at the cellular level. The mechanisms of consciousness may be discovered. The genetic maps of individuals should allow us to recognize the genes that indicate the human, and not, for example, the ape. Of course, of primary importance will be to determine in a specific person, which genes should be present so that the person is healthy and lives a long time. Also important will be the recognition of genes responsible for feeling like you, not to mention those responsible for cooperation, dedication, and sacrifice. The biological research noted here will need to be directed in cooperation with ethical and legal considerations, and well-planned strategy. Should human cloning be allowed? Is prolonging human life a good thing on an overpopulated planet? In contrast, research on Great Science, or the discovery of new laws of nature began slowing down in the USA in 1992, when Congress rejected funding for building the Superconducting-Super-Collider (SSC) in Texas for an estimated sum of 40 million dollars. This sum financed five months of war in Afghanistan in 2011. A smaller collider, called the Large-Hadron-Collider (LHC) was put into use in CERN, the European Organization for Nuclear Research in Geneva, in February, 2012, after resolving some problems that appeared after its first startup. This example indicates that American politicians do not assign much value to the development of basic research. This is contrary to tradition and history that the greatest number of Nobel prizes in physics were awarded to American scientists. Connecting research with the future of the world and research on the human cell may lead to an epic discovery about how human life began and how it can be reproduced in the laboratory. But does the discovery of this type of mystery make sense? What kind of influence would this have on civilization? The answer to this question requires well-balanced research and discussion. Every answer to this question will be of a critical nature for man, who has never encountered these types of challenges. Cosmological tests give hope that the discovery of new strategic resources on other planets will lead to places to relocate other than the overpopulated Earth. But is man able to overcome the speed of light to travel in a reasonable amount of time beyond Earth?

THE CRISIS OF ADMINISTRATION

The administration crisis is manifested in several forms that are systematically expressed below:

1. In terms of ideology, in democratic systems there is a sharp clash between the ideas of large and small government. Practically speaking, this discussion pertains to the USA and England, and the remaining Great Eight of Japan, Germany, Canada, Italy, France, and Russia. Successive governments prefer their own ideas of government, and continually destabilize administration with reorganization.
2. On the issue of developing a dual administration, the exterior administration is subject to the control of parliament, and the interior, more hidden administration is independent of this type of control and implements social policy such as through tax relief (Mettler 2011). The hidden administration has a goal of developing the safety net for people with low incomes. But the greatest benefits have been derived by people with high incomes, since tax credits are minimal for people with low incomes and high for wealthy taxpayers after converting the same percentage of the absolute numbers.

3. Regarding the issue of the budget deficit, the crisis of administration is a result of the structural economic crisis that began in 2008, with a decrease from business taxes since business is in a recession. In 2012, 37 of 50 states are practically speaking, bankrupt and the federal deficit is almost equal to the amount of the national annual income. The political strategy to reduce the deficit seems to be a product of healthy reasoning, but has led to a negative spiral, increasing and prolonging the recession, and thus further increasing the budget deficit.
4. With regard to corruption and not counting the costs, no matter what party leads in a democracy, corruption has developed in the commissioning of contracts. An estimated 3% of the combined income of the world's nations' falls in the hands of corrupt politicians and officials. In nations without a democratic system, this percentage is significantly higher. In addition there is carelessness in the use of public funds, with frequent participation in national and international conferences in the best hotels, inviting star entertainment to enhance the attractiveness of the conferences. This type of approach was discovered with an American administration in 2012. With one conference organized by the General Services Administration in 2010, the expenditure was close to one million dollars.
5. With administrative efficiency, it is evident that public administration is no longer in a place to offer free schools and subsidized colleges, nor assure an effective battle against crime. These administrations strive to remedy the situation by incurring more loans, lowering school budgets, lowering the wages, retirement pay of teachers, police officers, fire personnel, and others employed in administrative services. Some governors (Wisconsin, Ohio, Pennsylvania, Michigan) are pushing for state laws that prohibit government employees from joining trade unions. This is leading to great societal discontent and societal crisis.
6. In an effort to make the management of public services more efficient, public administrations are putting into the hands of business the management of schools, prisons, communication, parks, the supplying of water, trash pick up, and these types of services, causing the access to these services to be limited to those can afford to pay the fees. This causes the development of marketing in society where there is departure from the common good, and provision for the limited good.
7. With nations where a mafia operates, the criminal network not only bribes politicians, but also reaches even officially for those in government administrative positions. Countries of this type include: Bulgaria, Gwinea-Bissau, Montenegro, Myanmar (Birma), Ukraine and Venezuela. In Mexico the federal government sharply battles with the drug mafia warlords. But in the case of the independent states and cities of the Mexican Federation, the mafia rules and subjugates the police. It is increasingly difficult to differentiate between the geopolitical calculations of these countries and the profit motives that direct the mafia. Mafia-influenced countries operate with the speed and efficiency of international criminal networks, guaranteeing mafia members legal protection and diplomatic privilege that in prior times were only afforded to those governments (Naim 2012).

The crisis described above is difficult to overcome. As we can see, the bureaucracy is very inert and effective in maintaining the status quo.

The Wars of Wars

From millennia, wars have been incorporated into civilization. On one hand they destroy and on the other, arms build-up also leads to the development of new civilian technology. There are many examples. The global position system (GPS), now popular in vehicles, demonstrates one example. The GPS was first discovered for defense designs, and then carried over into civilian projects and applications. For a long time, war has involved battles between large masses of soldiers. In World War II, 85 million soldiers took part. Specifically, on the American side there were 16 million soldiers, 29 million from the USSR, and 20 million who fought on the German side. Military tactics and strategy were adapted to the Great War machine.

During the Cold War (1947-91), tactics and strategy were adapted to the atom bomb, which did not demand such great masses of soldiers. Astute politicians on both sides of the conflict effectively worked to prevent the use of the atom bomb. From the time of September 11 in the United States, war entered a new phase in civilization, between the classic military forces and the forces of terror. This reflects the fight between the elephant and the fly, and the fly can inflict serious damage. Terror is the war strategy of the weaker side that is able to engage in battle with the stronger side.

In the 21st century, civilization began practicing an even newer category of war called cyber warfare. This warfare uses computers and the Internet, and other measures with information storage or dissemination of information to carry out attacks on enemy information systems. Cyber warfare, not to be confused with info-communication, differs from classical warfare by the setting of the field of battle, which are the systems and networks of telecommunication. In this kind of war, the attacking side with minimal materials is in a strong position to paralyze the key infrastructure or economy of the enemy country, based on a sufficient number of computer systems. Cyber warfare is to a large degree asymmetrical, which allows weaker countries to wage war of this type against stronger countries. Thus, this leads to yet another kind of warfare based upon cybernetic terror.

Countries like China, Russia, and the United States specialize in leading cybernetic warfare. The enemies are hard to detect, but effective. For example in 2007 Estonia was attacked cybernetically by a Russian student on Russian terrain with a communication of *Distributed Denial of Service* (DDOS). The attacked server refused to accept new messages, clogged at the *Botnet* network which controls the attack of the computers. The country's most important national plans were paralyzed for several hours. The incident that instigated the attack was the transfer of a bronze statue commemorating Soviet soldiers from the downtown area of the city to a place at the military cemetery. The night during which the country was attacked was called *The Bronze Night*. In 2003 the United States became cybernetically attacked by China and Russia, and the attacks are being repeated. At the same time the United States in 2011 most probably attacked the nuclear installations of Iran, which slowed the development of Iran's atomic bomb. An attack against Iranian computers, not connected to the Internet, is being prepared.

The crisis of war lies in the fact that cybernetic warfare cannot be controlled within the existing international institutions. The greatest amount of cybernetic aggression is led by cybernetic criminals and they cannot be caught in the process of downloading, but they can be apprehended when they are in the process of future cybernetic aggression.

Countries are organizing various administrations and the command responsible for defense against cyber wars, crimes, and espionage. This process is quiet slow and is being activated from crisis to crisis. War strategy with cybernetic attacks should remind us of the strategy used in the Cold War, when it was understood that a nuclear attack would be met with another nuclear attack. Thus it is necessary to design Internet Protocol (IT/IP), so that the structure includes the last name and place of origin, and design the information infrastructure for defense against cybernetic attacks. Then the attacker will know he cannot pass the fire wall, and will get a cybernetic response that may end his work.

Currently there is lack of political resolve to implement these kinds of solutions. Cyber warfare is not visible to the naked eye and is not directly felt by politicians and their constituents.

The Crisis of Media

The media crisis in Western Civilization is the result of dependency upon business advertising. Issues that are uncomfortable for the business world are bypassed. Discussions on peripheral matters are conducted for the common good. The celebrities and the same journalists are asked to participate in the talk shows, and these do not bring any important thoughts or solutions to the discussion. The media conduct programs in tabloid style, capitalizing on sensation and scandal for increasing the number of viewers.

Taking this strategy, they have ceased to hold the politicians accountable and provide feedback, so that the system is less than democratic.

When it comes to the state of the media worldwide, conditions are poor. According to the World Press Freedom Index 2012, (Reporters without Borders – http://en.rsf.org/press-freedom-index-2011-2012,1043.html), this is the situation:

1. A state of free and independent press exists in 30 countries, including Scandinavia, Switzerland, the Netherlands, Ireland, Hungary, Portugal, Germany, the Slovak Republic, Lithuania, Poland, and others.
2. A satisfactory state of the media exists in 38 countries, including Australia, France, Israel, the USA, and others.
3. The media exists in a problematic state in 29 countries including Brazil, Argentina, Malaysia, and others.
4. The media is operating in a difficult state in 62 countries including India, Ukraine, Egypt, Singapore, Russia, and others.
5. A poor state of the media exists in eight countries including Saudi Arabia, Iran, China, Burma, Cuba, Eritrea, Turkmenistan, and North Korea.

Countries that lead in democracy, Great Britain and the United States are found way down on the index list, at the 28th and 47th place, respectively. A complete parody has been procured in South Africa, where a journalist must receive a permit from the Media Tribunal for investigating corruption in the administration. The person being investigated, protected by law on state secrets, may sue the journalist for operating aggressively and present a road block to the journalist's work. The law that permits investigation into corruption was confirmed by the parliament in Nov., 2011. This law is being challenged in the Supreme Court, but its confirmation by parliament reflects the attitude of those in authority who do not want to be controlled. This is evident in South Africa, where there was suffering for many years under the discriminatory policy of apartheid (Gordimer 2012). It is evident that power corrupts, and even yesterday's revolutionaries for freedom and equal rights. A similar situation exists in Russia and Ukraine, where totalitarianism has been eliminated, but the privileges of the ruling class retained and guarded from the media.

If we accept as conclusive the findings of this index, then we know that from the 167 countries researched, that in only 30 or 18% of the countries, the state of the media is satisfactory. This situation exists in smaller countries that do not have a great influence on world policy, with the exception of Germany. While Great Britain belongs to the group of countries in which the state of the media is good, the affair with Robert Murdoch and scandal uncovered in 2011, questions the high level status of the media in this country.

The media crisis contributes to many other crises, since the public is not well-informed about its function and cannot make informed decisions with effective correction. The media crisis supports the political and business crises, and these reinforce the crisis of the media.

The Crisis of Politics

The current political-economic system is characterized by solutions that were good for the 19th century, but are not good for the 21st century:

1. The policy of continued economic growth for the goal of guaranteeing new jobs for a growing population, that supports this policy, is growing in an upward spiral, leading to overpopulation and a tangled, self-destructing civilization.
2. The policy of continual improvement to the efficiency and effectiveness of agricultural and industrial production is the basic paradigm of modern business and schools of business. The consequence is a huge, senseless concentration of companies, automation, robot systems, and information technology systems along with virtualization, that decrease employment in a situation where the hands for work are increasing.

The above assessment of the state of civilization will not be reflected in any political party policy currently at the forefront or those in active opposition in developed or developing countries. Up to the current time, it has been accepted that in democratic systems, the political process leads to rational solutions for the common good.

In the 21st century, we have a total of 195 countries across the world, in which 64% or 125 practice the democratic system. In the countries of Western Civilization, democracy is pseudo-democracy because the actual authority, behind the scenes, is conducted by the global financiers. What is worse, several billionaires push their doctrines as the ultimate in solving social and economic crises. The political parties financed by them adopt these doctrines as their policy, and a multimillionaire can become president. The political process now depends on how quickly a party can get to power and how quickly its leaders rise in affluence during the discharge of duties. Of course there are many countries, especially the Scandinavian countries, where these practices do not exist.

After assuming power, the parties forget their platforms and accept the policies pushed by the lobbyists and sponsors of the primary elections, whose donations are no longer limited, by the Supreme Court decision in the USA. In Europe, the political process is still comparatively good in appearance, but is actually less effective. This situation is worsening and there are no indications that there will be improvement soon.

THE CRISIS OF CULTURE AND TRUST

Culture is comprised of the values and symbols controlling the patterns of behavior in society. Culture is expressed in the state of behavior in language, television, the media, tourism, sports, art, fashion, music, film, etc.

Massive access to the media, the Internet, movie theaters, and musical concerts has transformed the 19th century culture of the elite into the 21st century mass culture or pop culture. From the perspective of mass culture, this is a useful process. But in the mass process, the quality of culture has been lowered in order to satisfy the simplest tastes.

Culture has become a terrific business, especially in the film industry, music, sports, and fashion. To attract many viewers, the standard of film and music has decreased significantly, catering to the popular tastes of youth fascinated by crime, catastrophes, and science fiction. In music, popular are scenes of half-naked soloists, singing rather badly, but moving terrifically, especially with convulsive-type movements.

Fashion is promoting clothing or rather lack of clothes, especially among young men, with an open shirt and no tie. Following this are even politicians with the president, showing up for a ceremony of naval officers (dressed in elaborate, official uniforms), wearing a shirt with no tie, as if coming out of the bathroom and getting ready to dress. This style, accepted by people even in official positions supposedly identifies them as "cool". Instead of leading and giving example of style, they submit to a vulgar form, furthering the process of vulgarizing culture.

In the language sphere, the English language is commonly accepted as an international language, and this simplifies communication among people around the world. Unfortunately, this language has also been submitting to a vulgarizing process, especially among the youth, whose language expression and communication is limited to a few words like "good, exciting, cool, fun, and f--k".

Of course, these vulgarized designers of "cultural behavior" are shaped by values of the Global Civilization, reducing everything to money and … "fun".

The effect of this type of mass culture is society's dulling of the motivation to meet the important challenges of civilization, with the solutions left to someone else. It is easier to have command over these people, as the authorities in totalitarian countries have been convinced, and where alcoholism is popularized.

Mass culture has been developing and there is no sign that rock musicians and scandalous actors will cease being the models of behavior in society. Intellectuals, writers, professors, outstanding engineers and doctors, or people of knowledge and discernment go unnoticed in this type of culture. Of course, no one takes the rock and Hollywood celebrities very seriously, or even the politicians that mimic the celebrities. So who can be trusted and respected by the average citizen?

THE CRISIS OF EDUCATION

The education crisis can be analyzed after describing fifteen other crises, since these have a deciding effect on this type of crisis. Conversely, this crisis has a deciding effect on these other crises. The crisis of education cannot be viewed by itself alone, as it is discussed in the media and in society.

Education's crisis is most closely felt in conjunction with the crises of business and public administration. The influence of the business crisis is high unemployment, and consequent lower tax acquisition, with the effect of limiting school and state college budgets. Consequently, there are fewer teachers, professors, and education programs, and the standard of education drops. Thus, the system of rewarding the best teachers for academic results cannot be arranged. At the same time, we cannot employ the best teachers since funding is inadequate.

A further consequence of the business crisis is the lack of employment opportunities for graduates, who are reluctant to leave the walls of the school or college, for fear of being unemployed. The motivation for education decreases, and the burden is real for families with unemployment or low income. As a result of the limit on funding by the public administration, the colleges raise the cost of education, which is already high for strapped families. The amount of outstanding graduate education loans totaled one billion dollars and exceeded the amount of outstanding credit card debt in 2012.

An intermediate cause of the education crisis is the breakdown of the family, in which the friendship of children and youth is rather bought with gifts, leaving the schools and colleges with the task of raising and educating. In the schools and colleges, the popular culture dominates. Instead of knowledge, pleasure is promoted, often accompanied by street drugs and continual parties. Very obvious is the crisis seen in young men, who come to college classes dressed sloppily, and are preoccupied with playing computer games on their electronic phones and notebooks. At the same time, college girls almost constantly talk on their cell phones. As a result, a true bond disappears with the students present in the classroom or in the same course of study.

In this situation, teachers and professors have very limited opportunities to fulfill the role of upbringing normally provided by the parents. In many instances, the parents themselves are the offspring of divorced parents or partner unions, where there may be a number of children from former unions.

The education crisis in further encumbered by the media that publish poor, shallow solutions to the crisis. For example, the strongly opinionated TIME magazine (May 14, 2012, 35-38) published an article, "Learning That Works". The article indicates that employment opportunities are more available with career technical studies and their congruent two-year degrees, than are opportunities with higher degrees.

The shallowness of this article is obvious with its lack of information about young people enrolled in four and six-year higher education programs. In 2011, this segment of college students totaled eight million while the figure for those attending two-year colleges totaled

3.4 million. The challenge of educating American youth in 2,774 major universities and 4-year colleges is not addressed.

If we depend on the studies indicated by the media, there is no need to educate eight million people in full academic, at least four-year degree programs, because there will be no jobs for them in the future. Thus, we might deduce that most of these institutions should close, since there is lack of reason or ethics in obtaining fees, often very high and totaling several tens of thousands of dollars, from students for whom there is no employment when employers can pay workers in Asia, Africa and other places far less. Of course the business sector wants to employ cheaper workers beyond the country. To whom will the goods be sold? Business has liquidated the middle class and the upper class is small and not interested in the cheap goods that the lower class cannot even afford.

Only now can we analyze the internal education crisis, especially in the sphere of curriculum development. In this respect, career schools, two-year community colleges are doing well. The careers that are taught are well-defined such as: dental hygienist, radiologist, nurse, mason, veterinary technician, physical therapy assistant, etc., and their educational methods are well-managed.

But in the universities, especially in the schools of business, there is a degree of confusion about the concept of education. This became very evident in the Great Recession of 2008. No one recognized, nor even now recognizes the need for a radically new profile in educational programs. We must ask ourselves, are students acquiring proper knowledge and business wisdom in the 21st century?

Our doubts arise when we consider:

1. The glorification of globalization as the only business strategy.
2. Attachment to maximum spending rather than sufficiency.
3. Infatuation with the shareholder's profit and not meeting the needs of the stakeholders, interested in the company's success.
4. Emphasis on a shallow economic practice instead of a far-reaching one, accounting for the costs of business, environmental, and societal costs.
5. Idealization of the supply chain as the main task of business that also supports the strategy of outsourcing.
6. Idolizing the pivotal role of business in society.
7. Working with business manuals that reflect the knowledge and business wisdom of the years 1960-1970, when Western business flourished, but is now outdated for the new state of business in the 21st century.
8. The focus of education on a small scale and a piecemeal perspective of the elements of greater systems such as "civilization", not to mention the lack of education in the sphere of practical wisdom, as the most important virtue and resource of the human person.
9. Cutting electives from curriculum because of funding shortage in poor school districts, blocking the road to higher education for graduates.
10. Moving away from the mission to benefit the public, educate students, and promote the common good of the community.
11. Emphasizing the primary worth of doing something as it benefits corporations or leads to profits.
12. Treating education as a commodity that can be bought like a hamburger.

13. The rise of out-of-control tuition that outpaces the cost of a new car, or at some more affluent universities, approaches the annual income of the typical American.

An additional problem is caused by colleges and universities that do not generate energy and interest among faculty and administration, and do not give direction for education programs. This author knows of missions that are not missions but strategies consisting of 50 sub-strategies that no one remembers, nor implements. New challenges like education in the field of knowledge about sustainable development are supported by the administration, but in the form of slogans. Their incorporation into education programs takes years, while this is the fault of the same faculty that directs the profile of the curriculum. The current ideology and academic practice indicates it is easier to relocate a cemetery than change the curriculum. So there is low probability for the inclusion of practical wisdom into curriculum theory and curriculum. An age-old problem is the existence of an agreement as to the scope of specialized training alongside the liberal arts. Centers for Humanity are arising in many secondary institutions, but they concentrate on making greater humanists out of those that are already humanists, when we should concentrate on making humanists of those students engaged in professional study programs such as business, engineering, medicine, and other sciences. The problem magnifying the education crisis is the growth of universities and their "managerial" management. In the resulting disconnection between faculty and the administration, students ultimately lose the most. The department heads are not interested in curriculum development and are focused rather on increasing the number of buildings which may eventually carry their name. The result is a permanent reduction in the budget for teaching, often amounting to less than 40% of the total school budget, with funding beyond the established mission and operation of the administration. Can the graduates of an education crisis solve the other 15 crises and others? I believe this kind of hope is illusive.

THE DEATH TRIANGLE OF CIVILIZATION

The Catastrophy

Since we are analyzing crises in civilization in the 21st century, we must also predict three crises will cause the death of Civilization as we know it yet in this 21st century, -- overpopulation, ecology, and expended natural resources. A three-fold increase in human population has resulted in using up energy resources like water and nonferrous metals, and the wear and destruction of the environment. To better visualize the seriousness of this situation, we will describe the concept of the "Death Triangle of Civilization", or the synergistic action of the Population Bomb, the Ecology Bomb, and the Natural Resources Depletion Bomb of around 2050, as Figure 1 illustrates, since the earth's population will reach 9 or 10 billion, or one to two billion too many for the ecosystem to sustain.

If anyone doubts these types of hazards to civilization, it is important to remember that in 2006 the peak of oil production surpassed capacity. Already in 2011 this was demonstrated by a sharp increase in gasoline prices and food, as farmland is being converted to biofuel crops. These symptoms will intensify in the first half of the 21st century. Another example is the war in Afghanistan, a war in fact over oil in this region.

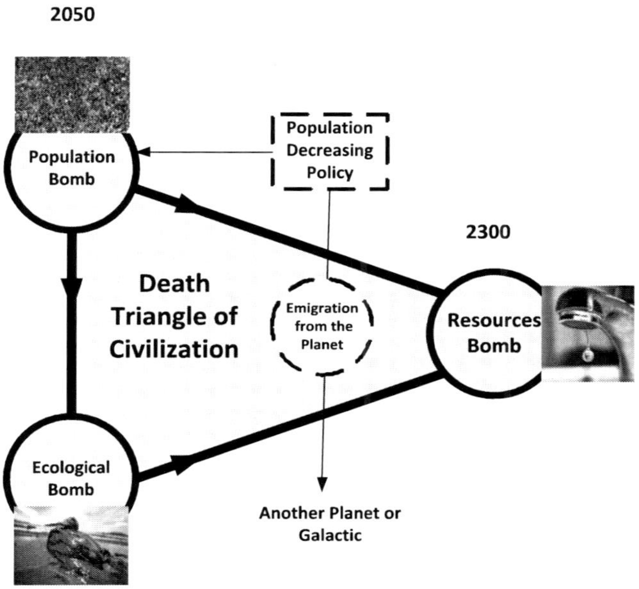

Figure 1. The Death Triangle of Civilization.

The facts surrounding the Death Triangle of Civilization speak for themselves and suggest a bleak future. Even more troublesome is the fact that none of the leading political, economic countries show concern over this threat. They are concerned about the environment, but progress in this field is rather small and inadequate for such a great threat. Environmental protection is truly in the hands of the non-governmental organizations (NGOs) and the involved, committed intellectuals of Western Civilization.

A Synthesis of the Great Crisis of Civilization in the 21st Century Road Map for a Path out of the Crisis

We analyzed 16 crises in civilization that make up the Great Crisis of Civilization in the 21st century. Evaluated together in Figure 2, they show the magnitude of this crisis. We are dealing with two categories of crisis: the crisis of ideas and morality and the crisis of the ecosystem. The crisis in the first category gives no hope for saving civilization, and the latter type of crisis threatens the physical, continued existence of civilization.

The situation is very poor. Can civilization be saved?

To answer this question, we must consider, where and how do we begin the repair? As seen in the map of crises of the 21st century and in the discussion presented thus far, it seems we must start from the simultaneous repair of four crises: the crisis of science, the crisis of global business, the political crisis, and the education crisis.

It is necessary to give a plan of economic theory for the global market that would give all the participants of the globalization processes equal opportunity, and would be recognized by the broad scientific, educational, professional, and political community.

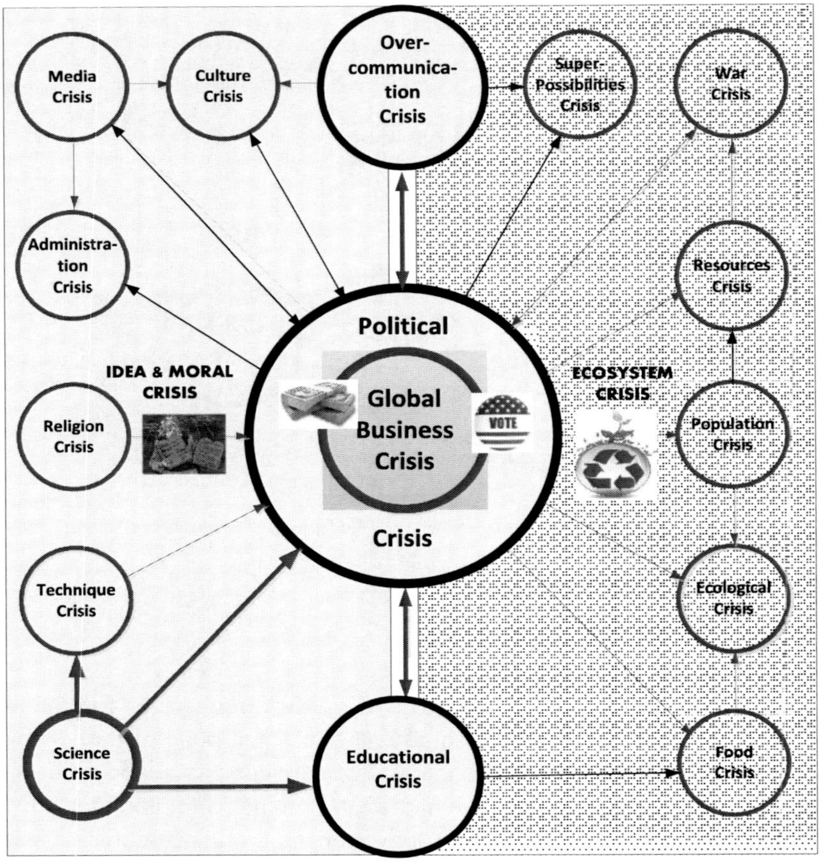

Figure 2. A Map of Great Crisis of Civilization in the 21st Century.

Further, the political community should be effectively free of business sponsors including lobbyists, and should undertake transparent decisions affecting the economy on the basis of the theory of an open global market. The political community should be accountable for understanding this theory to eliminate untestable doctrines and leanings toward narrow groups with financial interests. Schools and business colleges should immediately implement their curricula in alignment with this theory and begin to educate effective future business people and societal leaders. In the scope of this education, careful attention must be directed toward knowledge and ethical sensibility in business and public administration.

Science must guard further development of technology to support society, and not aggressively pursue the elimination of human work.

In the process of forging a new path out of the four major crises, a new orientation of the role of the media must take place in society, to serve the common good rather than narrow interest groups. The future of the remaining crises on the map will depend on the solved problems of the five crises, including the additional media crisis. The scope of this study does not include a discussion of the strategy for their elimination.

Can the model for an alternate road to the Great Crisis of Civilization be accomplished? It may happen, if the academic community will rise to the task and see its important role in the process of renewing civilization.

CONCLUSION

1. The Great Crisis of Civilization in the 21st century is a fact resulting from the mutual interaction of 16 large crises, mainly caused by the crisis of ideas and morality and subsequent crisis of the ecosystem.
2. A solution to the Great Crisis may require long years, if not several generations. There may not be much time because of the negative dynamics of the Triangular Death of Civilization with its symptoms already felt, and which will strongly be felt by the middle of the 21st century.
3. The protection of the civilization that we know, and the kind we dream about will require a Renaissance II. There must be change and new value to the role of the Internet, science, politics, business, technology, and the media along with other critical matters. Renaissance II requires leaders on the level of Leonardo da Vinci and must be supported by Enlightenment II that will significantly educate and develop intelligent graduates, future professionals, and leaders.
4. The future of civilization lies in a change from its present chaotic and self-destructive, fragmented course to a sound and sensible civilization. Is this possible?

REFERENCES

Brown, L. (2001). *Eco-economy*. New York: W. W. Norton and Co., p.17.

Cairncross, F. (1997). *The Death of distance*. Boston: Harvard Business School Press.

Gordimer, N. (2012). South Africa: the new threat to freedom. *The New York Review of Books*. May 24, 2012, pp. 43-44.

Halweil, B. (2004). *Eat here: reclaiming homegrown pleasures in a global supermarket*. New York: W. W. Norton and Company.

Imhoff, D. (2003). *Farming with the wild*. Healdsburg, CA: Sierra Club Books.

Krugman, P. (2012). How to end this recession. *The New York Review of Books*. May 24, 2012, pp. 12-14.

Krugman, P. (2012a). Plutocracy, paralysis, perplexiy. *The New York Times*. May 4, 2012, pp. A-23.

Lawrence, F. (2004). *Not on the label*. New York: Penguin Books.

McKibben, B.(2007). *Deep economy, the wealth of communities and the durable future*. New York: Times Books, Henry Holt and Company.

Mettler, S. (2011). *The Submerged State: How Invisible Government Policies Undermine American Democracy*. Chicago: University of Chicago Press.

Naim, M. (2012). Mafia states, organized crime takes office. *Foreign Affairs*. Vol. 91, nº 3, May/June, pp. 100-111.

Pretty, J. (2002). *Agri-culture*. London: Earthscan Publishing, Ltd.

Reagan, G. (1992). *The Guiness book of decisive battles*. New York: Abbeville Press.

Reporters without Borders - http://en.rsf.org/press-freedom-index-2011-2012,1043.html, Retrieved July 15, 2012.

Scharplatz, J. (2003).Weeding out the skilled farmer. *Prairie Writers Circle*, November 26.

Schmid, R. (2003). *The Untold story of milk*. Washington, DC: New Trends Publishing.

Targowski, A. (2009). *Information technology and societal development.* Hershey and New York: IGI Publishing.

Winders, B. (2011). The Food crisis and the deregulation of agriculture. *The Brown Journal of World Affairs*. Fall/Winter, pp. 83-96.

In: Spirituality and Civilization Sustainability …
Editors: Andrew Targowski and Marek J. Celinski
ISBN: 978-1-53610-729-6

Chapter 3

ARE WE OVERCIVILIZED? TOWARD (A) MORE SUSTAINABLE FUTURE(S)

Lech W. Zacher *
Kozminski University, Poland

"Unlike economists, most physical scientists recognize that growth within any functioning, bounded system has to stop sometime."

R. Heinberg, D. Lerch (2010)
The Post-Carbon Reader –
Managing the 21st Century's
Sustainability Crises

ABSTRACT

Civilizational change seems to be non-linear. Former expectations and visions concerning a universal progress for all have proved to be false. The present civilization of diversity requires new ideas and new approaches. It also requires transdisciplinary knowledge. No universalistic set of values and patterns of practices is appropriate for the differentiated and multicultural mankind. So all investigations and recommendations should be contextualized. Additional differences are created by a widening generational divide. Technological advances lead humanity to a hybrid stage – a techno-human civilization.

However the present goal of societies is to direct their development toward a broadly understood sustainability. There are many scientific efforts to introduce new ideas and concepts as e.g. sustainable citizenship, ethical consumption, knowledge democracy, resilient communities, sociability, ethic of care, ethic of flourishing, inclusive globalization, digital futures. These concepts can be instrumental for subsequent debates and research on sustainable trajectory. A new model of development based on principles of sustainability is needed to avoid a global crisis and possible Orwellian scenarios.

* E-mail: lzacher@kozminski.edu.pl

INTRODUCTION

Civilization is on the move, so no final conclusions can be valid and its dynamic is of a non-linear type. However, some fairly well grounded statements and observations may be formulated. The present civilization is a *civilization of diversity*. This diversity is multifaceted: it is connected with the state of the world, and the world is unequal and differentiated. One prescription for all involved – either the core or peripheries – will not be viable. Former expectations connected with some theories of modernization and some future visions that progress and imitation processes will allow all countries to catch up with leaders have proven false. Divides or gaps are still big and – some say – even growing. Present civilization, often called technological, is to a great extent technologically-driven, which creates opportunities, but also risks and gaps.

The diversity of the world – in spite of globalization based on rules of market economy – is even boosted by diversity within the societies of the world. Political systems, religions, culture, historical heritage, social life, patterns of consumption, education, etc. constitute *contexts* of peoples' behavior, attitudes, values, undertakings, and strategies of life. In spite of multicultural or cross-cultural efforts, it seems not feasible to propose any universal set of values and practices appropriate to all people. Additionally, there is a widening *generational divide* – due to present revolutions in science and technology (resulting in ICTs, biotechnologies, nanotechnologies). New generations ("born digital") already manifest their differences, especially as they transfer a big part of their lives to cyberspace, and display indifference to old traditions. To project or program a model of the future for the next generations (newly born and not yet born) could limit their choices and could violate their ambitions, expectations, aspirations, values, and goals.

There are also other issues preventing us from constructing an ideal model of the future, convenient for all people and all the planet, good forever. There are growing theoretical and political concerns on such fundamental problems as:

- the future of nation-states (and integration),
- the future of capitalism (flexible, post-liberal),
- the prospects of globalization (called corporate vs. inclusive),
- the fate of democracy under threat, conflicts (domestic and international), crises, natural catastrophes, mass unemployment, poverty, uncontrollable migrations, and climate turbulences.

Looking further forward, we should not overlook perspectives of increasing *transhumanism* connected with the artificialization of peoples' bodies, lives, and settings. Thanks to science e.g. bioscience, biomedicine, genomics, and technology, mostly medical and informational (electronic media, virtual reality), we and our lives will be radically different (inventors such as Kurzweil, Zey, and Rheingold predict radical changes at the turn of the century or even earlier). The *hybrid stage* of humanity and *technohuman civilization* will probably lead to further mechanization, technologization, automation, robotization, cyborgization and a totally new "brave" (to recall the term used by H. G. Wells) world – in prospect without real human creatures. Self-replicating intelligent systems will create their future without us.

Thus, there are serious obstacles to making ambitious long term projections and forecasts and to propose any ideal models or visions of the future as points of reference for the present thinking and activities. These obstacles are two-fold: one set is connected with the aforementioned *de facto* political uncertainties, notorious in the advancement of civilization and human development; the second set is based on the assumption of further revolutionary advances in science and technology and their mass applications (in the advanced world at least) and their impacts, radical and profound, and often unpredictable.

That is why – while not resigning from the struggle for survival and for civilization's sustainability – it may be wise to suggest an *improvement* as a viable method of human activity, including improvement in all dimensions – technological, economic, ecological, cultural, societal, personal, material, and spiritual. There is some potential (more than 7 billion people on the planet) to do it. *Yes, we can* – to paraphrase Barack Obama.

LOOKING FOR NEW IDEAS AND GOOD PRACTICES

A plethora of ideas, concepts, theories and also practical experiments and experiences exist and can be useful and can be applied widely, *en masse*. So there are some areas of rapidly growing understanding and knowledge and some promising initiatives; let us name a few exemplary cases. The important narrative, in fact the grand narrative, becomes as a *modus operandi for all sustainability* of human activities, not only for environmentally-oriented activities. The enlargement of this concept, making it as comprehensive as possible, generates studies, innovation, and applied proactive undertakings as elaboration of sustainable strategies and policies (on any level – from local to global), opens research areas, and promotes actions in the field of eco-innovations and eco-modernization. On the societal level a new term is coined – *sustainable citizenship* – instead of the more narrow *environmental citizenship* (Dobson, Bell 2006). There are ideas and investigations on de-carbonization and on eco-cities (*cf.* Bulkeley et al. 2011, Heinberg, Lerch 2010). Practical initiatives are in the making, e.g. The UK Carbon Transition Plan (2009) and Transition Towns. Movement, Urban gardening is the other, re-invented, innovation; transition management and the idea of transition are gaining popularity (http://www.transitionnetwork.org/) as a new key word. An important social innovation was the introduction of the European Union regulations called the *precautionary principle*. This concept also has wider meaning as a new orientation in production and use of technologies.

In the field of economics the neoliberal *business as usual* is criticized not only because of the financial crises of 2008–2009, but also because of the cases of Enron, Lehman Brothers, massive bailouts, and the Maddox case. Rethinking capitalism is timely (see the article "Rethinking capitalism from inside" by Ch. Freeland, International Herald Tribune, May 12, 2011). Bubbles and crashes of economies do not contribute to sustainability. The orientation of business should not be solely toward effectiveness and profitability, but to seek the common good. This society should organize business to be more effective for all (Freeland 2011, Martin 2011). The free market should be replaced by the *real market* and the economy must be driven by Main Street not Wall Street (Korten 2009). Moreover, empirical research shows that income inequalities are counter-productive from the point of view of economic development, and fewer disparities means better development (Cowen 2004). Perhaps there is a *new thinking* in economics? There is no possible return to the previous model, due to declining wages, increasing consumer debt, growing insecurity and especially growth based on cheap and abundant energy. A new economy is needed now, since crises are converging, interdependent and their scale and complexity and generated risks are unprecedented.

Consumption is another serious concern, not only in the context of the global environment (see e.g. Dauvergne 2008). There are calls for *ethical consumption* as a requirement of political rationality and global responsibility (Barnett et al. 2011). There is an ethical consumer movement and a fair trade movement (to avoid exploiting poor countries), and the idea of voluntary simplicity is rejuvenated. Ethical consumerism has become a political phenomenon. Consumers are economic voters. Market-embedded morality can be questioned. A market is a set of social relations between people and institutions they inhabit, not just a set of economic transactions.

Hopes are also raised by *science and research*. For example, further problematization of sustainability is needed now; research should be treated as the common weal; the mobilization of scientists for public engagement is crucial (Bauer, Jensen 2011); popularization of science (not only medical research) is important – science and journalism should not be "worlds apart" (Hartz, Chapell 1997). A feminist approach is useful not only in the ecological context (Cuomo 1997). Also such disciplines as *sociology of hope* and *sociology of gift* can be re-evaluated and re-used as new issues (Hayden 2007). All these can contribute immensely to the discourse on civilization.

Cultural theories are helpful when talking about modernization and improvement. Recent theories of cultural modernization, however widely criticized, have trumpeted the change of priorities of political values in modern societies. Traditional theories were based on postindustrial materialist values (hierarchical and authoritarian) concerned with political and economic stability and physical safety. In contrast, post-materialist values stress cultural and social matters, quality of life, ecology, feminism, pluralism, peace, participation, and collective actions. These classifications can be contested as characterized by having many limitations, including a growing scarcity of resources (e.g. water) and energy, mounting waste, and a rapidly increasing population. Anyway, these post-materialistic values played some role in political parties' programs in spite of their less than homogeneous commitment. Even among Greens there is a gap between idealistic beliefs and pragmatic policies. This incoherence should be "repaired," since the role of pro-ecological movements and parties is growing in politics.

Science, *knowledge*, and *democracy* constitute another valuable cluster of possible improvements and solutions working for political and social sustainability. New slogans appeared, such as *science in democracy* (Brown 2009), *knowledge democracy* (Veld 2010), *public participation* in science and technology decision-making or in politics of knowledge, saving public space. In other words, societies or at least large groups in them should be politically active and engaged in public life and decision-making. But proper legal conditions are necessary. It is not easy to elicit public involvement and to mobilize it to participate effectively in democratic processes. However, growing scientific literacy and new risky technologies may be good incentives to get out of civic apathy and disengagement. Legitimization of the knowledge policy will then enjoy public support, better choices can be made and responsibilities can be shared. Moreover, integrated thinking and replicable direct actions should be popularized by local leaders and grassroots organizers, especially in the context of sustainability. Community engagement and local projects will transform them into *resilient communities*.

It becomes increasingly clear that significant efforts by scientific communities must be made to construct frameworks and procedures allowing public deliberations and participatory governance, especially in the areas of new research and risky technologies (e.g., genetic). Some experience has already been gained (Braun, Schulz 2010, McLean, Burgess 2010). It would be of course naive to suppose that a committed *homo politicus* will be a model for all citizens, even in the Western countries with a long democratic tradition, not to mention in less developed countries and societies. A *dualistic type* of development, for many historical reasons (such as a late "take off," colonialism, wars, and dependency of peripheries) will probably not disappear. However, gaps – due to international efforts – may diminish and democratic experiences may be diffused, also in the context of debate on social justice and political participation on a world scale. International organizations (such as the UN) and institutions should support such a diffusion process with the help of local scientists and political activists. To facilitate such influences requires not only technical or financial aid, but also knowledge-enabling learning processes, debates and discourse-oriented policies. Sustainability as such is an emerging field of knowledge. The postulate was formulated that social sciences should take the lead in knowledge creation and in debates on sustainable development (see report of the conference supported by UNESCO – Becker et al. 1999). In opposition to the traditional approach to economic growth, a new more adequate term was proposed: "whole development" (Sachs, in: Becker 1999). It seems that one can use this term to characterize civilization development as well. Striving for such developments requires creating networks for sustainability, networks of scientists, engineers, managers, politicians, media and above all citizens, communities, NGOs, and others.

Returning to positive – new or rejuvenated – ideas, concepts, theories, innovations that may serve well and be functional to more humanistic and sustained development of civilization, one may give some interesting examples. To make social relations more empathic and human, the old concept *sociability* (used by Simmel, and later by Goffman) can be applied. Sociability allows closer relations and cooperative networks, all important to improve lives. For a better life in a setting of growing interdependence and increased risk, it is vital to propagate an *ethic of care*. This principle is very much connected with the feminist approach. In feminist narratives (crucial for science and for social practice since half of humankind are women) an ethos of care is not only taking on moral but also political and emotional overtones (de la Bellacasa 2011). If we expand the meaning of care, it can be stated that care is whatever we do to "maintain, continue, and repair" our world to improve our life as much as possible (Tronto 1993: 103). This care can be broadened to encompass even more: to maintain and repair the world to improve humans and non-humans living together as much as possible in a complex-sustaining web (de la Bellacasa 2011). So the care can also refer to domestic and wild animals and in the future to transhumans and posthumans (as e.g. human-machine associations and cyborgs). Another idea from the feminist perspective is an *ethic of flourishing* (Cuomo 1997). Resolving gender problems is important to create a better future, so we should strive for survival, improvement, and flourishing of everything on the planet (to paraphrase Cuomo 1997).

Perhaps we can contest the ideologies, theories, and social practices that associated civilization and development predominantly with wealth creation, consumption, and recently entertainment – based on greed, hedonism, egotism (because of competition and scarcity), individualism (self-sufficiency, autonomy and independence from others highly valued), and obsession with power and domination. If so, the discourse concerning the development of civilization would be different, stressing wisdom and identifying dysfunctionalities.

It should be acknowledged that recent publications undermine the old convictions that played an important ideological role. Interestingly, some books on this topic that will soon appear are reported in the world press (*International Herald Tribune* on May 20, 2011). According to the authors, altruism and cooperation are basic for people (see Nowak, Highfield 2011, Tomasello 2008, Keltner 2009, Haidt et al. *The Righteous Mind* – forthcoming 2012). So the new thesis is that competition and cooperation are entwined. The selfish-competitor model is perhaps one-sided and obsolete. Moreover, in case of competition within groups – it is said that the groups are internally altruistic, cohesive, and cooperative. So psychology and socio-biology support a less Darwinistic, more value-based model of human behavior. This trend indicates perhaps a different thinking about the role of values in economy and human life.

The most challenging area, however, can be – from the point of view of values and post-materiality in particular – *cyberspace*. This new social space "inhabited" by an increasing number of "internauts" (and many of their avatars) is still a new endeavor psychologically and socially, and also generationally. Shall we control it somehow, to protect our values such as intellectual property, privacy, intimacy, and freedom (understood as not being buried in spam, not being accompanied by thousands of "friends" every week, not being overwhelmed by triviality, not wasting our time budget)? There are more questions to be answered: Is communication our ultimate goal and the deterministic force in our behavior (compulsive talking, unimportant contents, participation in pseudo-communities, everyday blogging, substituting amateur versions of scientific knowledge, culture, art, and even entertainment for the genuine stuff? Do we – even young people – really need so much entertainment and non-stop music? Do we need new network gurus – inventors, smart entrepreneurs, but also hackers or plain criminals destroying information networks and data banks? Ideas concerning free culture, open sources, and free software are attractive. But something such as the Internet does not become democratic simply by being massive and common. So global networking is changing the world, it is creating a new space for all who are connected and is usually more or less influencing the rest (the unconnected). The human world has become a *hybrid* world. Which part – traditional or virtualized – will prevail and dominate the future and values? That is the question. What can be done now is "pumping" into cyberspace as many positive ideas, values, behavior patterns, lawful elements, initiatives, and undertakings as possible. Of course, the result will be uncertain. Anyway, cyberspace should also be targeted as an object to be civilized. And it is important to add that generally ICTs and their powerful new web-based tools are vital for human communication and activities to improve our civilization. Positive feedback is needed here. No doubts.

The narrative on "repairing" civilization turns to knowledge and for pragmatic reasons to its application – to social and individual practice (one can say that humankind is a "global community of practice"). The present knowledge results from reflexive studies and has been verified by research in the scientific community, not just from Wikipedia. This is to summarize the main findings and recommendations important and functional for improving civilization in crisis (or at risk at least): our civilization is at serious risk, its development trajectory should be promptly modified and finally changed, there is no return to the past, transition will be difficult and should be on time, new, transdisciplinary knowledge should be oriented toward the sustainability of humanity and the world (also cyberspace), there is a need for new thinking, new paradigms, innovations, new strategies, new leadership (in cyberspace as well), education and socialization, especially of the young, are a means to diffuse these new concepts, human values (of any origin) are indispensable if civilization is to be improved, peoples' activism at all levels, organizations, institutions, NGOs, households, and on the Internet is a *conditio sine qua non* of joint success (not certain of course).

These general recommendations should be a part of our *mindset* and our *Weltanschauung*. Critical moments need also other incentives to alert people, such as coercion, fear, and awareness that this is a point of no return. Since return to the past is not possible, all our efforts (scientific, technological, economic, political, individual, and social) should be future-oriented. Some efforts should be adaptive (e.g. adaptation to limits and to scarcity of resources such as water and fossil fuel); others will be knowledge-creating, e.g. while thinking in terms of limits – not viewing crisis symptoms in isolation but in their complexity, seeking intensively for alternative energy sources, developing post-carbon design of buildings and cities, trying to reduce waste (also e-waste), promoting ecological economics (in education, research, and media). It is *de facto* beyond doubt that the fossil fuel-based, automobile-centered, throwaway economy is no longer a viable model. New models should be carbon-free, with diversified transport systems, with a principle of reusing and recycling everything (Brown 2011: 183). Political challenges are serious as well: overcoming powerful vested interests (in the energy sector and transportation at least), eliciting international support and cooperation to build sustainable strategies of development, and elaborating policies of transition. In education, social life and mentality changes should be oriented toward promoting mass education (also by media and the Internet) for sustainability, to re-engineering our thinking about the position of humans in nature (and in our artificial setting), to stimulating personal and community undertakings and actions, to preparing people for uncertainty, and to changing our collective psyche – which was formed under other conditions – for "life after growth." So there are a lot of things distinct from what we have now at our disposal, in our minds and in our life.

It should be acknowledged, however, that the great hopes in science, research, knowledge, which are fully justified, require wide implementation, not only approval. It is usually taken for granted that knowledge diffusion (in information societies in particular) is not problematic. Empirical research indicates that so-called scientific literacy, even in societies calling themselves knowledge societies, is not high and profound. Moreover, transfer of knowledge through mass media is really marginal (out of 650,000 science papers between 1990 and 2001 in the US – fewer than 0.013–0.34% papers attracted mass media attention, and without health and medicine articles – only 0.01–0.005%; see Suleski, Ibaraki 2010). So the diffusion is mostly through education, which everywhere is weak and struggles to keep up with new knowledge. In the private (corporate) sector, research is financed, above all, if it pays. For example, in the pharmaceutical industry research for curing rare diseases is not sufficient, because the market is too small. Moreover, private property rights are executed and secured by patents, by companies, and protected by secrecy policies. So *knowledge sharing* – which is a fashionable slogan in particular in reference to the Internet – is limited but still possible. That is why there are new hopes in the Internet (free software, open sources, collective intelligence) and also in democratizing publicly financed science and technology research (public participation in decisions on agenda, directions, expected effects, risks). However, to engage the public and to organize the process of deliberation is not so simple (*cf.*

Braun, Schulz 2010, McLean, Burgess 2010, Zacher 2011). Nevertheless, experiments are promising. So more freedom (in the Internet) and democracy (in decision-making) can probably help, at least in the networked and democratic societies.

To sum up: There are plenty of new insights, innovative research, theoretical and policy recommendations (some are re-invented, and some are re-evaluations of their originals in the 1970s) which can be instrumental for improving our civilization. They just have to be included into the present grand narrative about *modern* (some would say-postmodern) *civilization* and its future. Also, they should be disseminated as widely as possible – in education systems, the decision-making bodies of government, businesses, international organizations and institutions, social movements, and NGOs, and should target as many people as possible. They have to be transformed into forms of social innovations ready for practical applications, and tailored to policy-oriented recommendations. Their wide use ought to be assured on all levels – from individual to global. The community level is of special importance. All changes are more or less politically, socially, and psychologically challenging. Good analyses, transparent implementation procedures, and accountability for their effects can bring wider acceptance. The changes should be socially acceptable and advantageous (e.g. energy use reduction or recycling e-waste).

Of course, even a problematization of such a comprehensive change is difficult. Approaching the problem requires articulation of human expectations, justification of policies, and methods of mobilizing all actors and stakeholders involved. Re-evaluating and re-thinking of past experiences and practices is a necessity. Politicizing and moralization of a way to sustainability can be helpful, too. It is rather evident that intellectual and practical "packages" of ideas, advice, innovations, and indications should be tailored to particular societies' potentials and needs. Cultures differ in their ability to adapt to change. And the heterogeneity of the world is immense. The leading affluent countries should express solidarity with the rest of world and help them in their transformations, because successful transformations are advantageous for all, for the futures of all.

WARNING: THE ORWELLIAN SCENARIO IS ALWAYS POSSIBLE

As indicated earlier, there are not only positive values and incentives that can encourage people and organizations to change toward sustainability. It is also important to recognize and indicate what should not be undertaken and practiced. The analysis of the diversity of risks to civilization gives us a number of warnings. A *consequentionalist approach* is instrumental while predicting and evaluating the future impacts of our past and present decisions and behavior as well as the impacts of existing recognized trends and tendencies.

Positive warnings can play a role in dystopias, doomsday forecasts, or negative "black" scenarios. There are many, not only in science fiction books and films, but also in scientific books and in scenarios prepared by international political bodies (e.g. Club of Rome) and intelligence agencies. These are usually neglected by regular people and by decision-makers in particular. They are being blamed for widespread pessimism, panic, and demobilization of social forces. Of course there is a red line which should not be crossed by scientists, politicians or the media. But on the other hand, a naive faith in perpetual progress (also technological) stimulates expectations, which are always rising, and makes us vulnerable and unprepared (at least mentally) for crises, big catastrophes, large scale natural disasters, social frustration, violent unrest and riots, international conflicts and wars.

It seems worthwhile to have in mind the Orwellian vision (or scenario) of the future. Global or sub-global collapse can be caused by many processes or events difficult to control, especially on a large scale. And scale here is significant. So the first danger is uncontrolled demographic growth (we have to remember that "population is the multiplier of everything else" – see Ryerson 2010). Stabilization of the global population is a touchy issue from a religious, political, or nationalistic standpoint. Even more controversial are appeals to diminish in some future human population to 1–2 billion people in order to assure a decent living for all (D. Meadows in the interview in 2009). The population bomb is dangerous from two angles: the planet's resources are limited and the "ecological footprint" of humans can surpass the regeneration abilities of nature; a rapidly growing population is dangerous because of radical changes in structures and proportions between races, religions, political systems, social customs, cultures, and so forth. Societies – carriers of the values connected with freedom, democracy, human rights (also called republican values) will be aging and losing power and influence. Civilization clashes (to recall Huntington) are already approaching .

Catastrophes, global or subglobal in size, may have a natural character. Climate change and turbulences, tsunamis, hurricanes, earthquakes, floods, volcano eruptions, rising sea levels, together with big material losses and mass ecological refugee flows can downsize GDP growth, diminish standards of living, and cause political and social tensions and conflicts. Exhausted natural resources, energy sources in particular, technical catastrophes (such as the Deep Horizon oil platform in the Gulf of Mexico or nuclear power plants in Chernobyl and Fukushima – remember almost all such plants are very old, and their use-expectancy has already passed) plus eventual nuclear regional wars and terrorist attacks with the use of weapons of mass destruction (chemical, biological, nuclear, and also logistic bombs in cyberspace) may empty the planet significantly.

There is also a danger of an economic and financial kind. The crisis of 2008–2009 was a sign of warning. A bubble economy (or "casino capitalism"), developing through crises will be unbearable for many countries and societies. Criticism is growing but radical changes in business behaviors are not seen whatsoever; instead, taxpayers' money is used to fund bankrupt companies (e.g. Obama's policy). Possible impacts on poor countries are not really being considered or discussed. A crisis trajectory of development (by the way, claimed by Marx already in the 19th century) may devastate national economies and global economies as well. An economic catastrophe could be just as dangerous as other catastrophes.

Other types of dangers, seen already, are those connected with *social structures* and *mechanisms* and with *individual lifestyles*. In many countries, even rich and democratic countries, the unemployment rate is increasing, and the numbers of low-income old people, the homeless, and beggars are rising. Crime and drug use are growing, and the number of prisoners is increasing. Flows of poor immigrants, who are not integrating with host societies, can get out of control. Strikes, civil unrests, poor people robberies (as in Haiti) are expensive and are demolishing social order. A growing phenomenon in some countries is soccer fans fighting among themselves and with the police. Economic disparities and big margins of socio-economic exclusion are disadvantageous for growth and development (this has already been proved by economists). Hopelessness, frustration, and social disintegration (a part of society is "fenced and guarded") generates distrust, hatred, and fear.

Two other risks can be assigned to social structures. One is connected with a consumption pattern that requires deep transformations and that may be unobtainable in spite of nice ideas like *ecological citizen* or *ethical consumer*. Global McDonaldization and Disneyization of societies, role model emulation geared by the mass media (to get ad money from business) may be destructive from the point of view of the survival of civilization.

Another social-type concern is connected with the process of *disintegration* of families, communities, and societies. Some ideologues deny it, but the rate of divorce confirms it. Moreover, young generations, especially those born "digital" (which we discussed earlier) are leaving real societies for virtual space. They find pseudo-communities, superficial contacts rather than social ties, as well as individuation and loneliness ("network loneliness"). Their identities are connected with the Internet, not with their nation-state or their own society as before, and they may have a monadistic life in spite of the accessible knowledge, information and ICT skills. Societies become *hybrid*. How they function and how to manage such aggregates, nobody knows yet. Besides hybridization, atomization, disintegration, and alienation can be a problem. Values, attitudes, and behaviors may be astonishing compared to traditional social structures. Many good and bad things will emerge and enter cyberspace – what will be their proportions?

Political dangers are multidimensional. Some are connected with *post-political* management of disintegrated and unstable societies, unemployment and uncontrolled migration, brain drain, a growing informal (or shadow) economy which is not taxed and is often tied to Mafia and other organized crime groups, some of which are international and established in cyberspace, too. There are already many such economies in many countries and worldwide. Can the phenomenon grow to become a serious national and international actor? The same question applies to governments and public authorities, which are often corrupted and connected with organized crime. The tipping point in this respect may be not far away.

Another political issue will be *democracy* – its lack and paradoxically – its excess. Authoritarian rulers try to keep as little democracy as possible (there are probably limits to this, as was illustrated by the recent Arab Spring). Democratic rulers often are not happy with the demands of participatory democracy, deliberation, and transparency. Some procedures are simply taking their decisive power away, prolonging decision-making processes, and making democracy rather anarchistic. Authorities should also learn how to rule via the Internet (not only by TV as before).

International political relations can be much more complex and complicated. Populous countries without democratic traditions of the Western type gain international power, not only economic and military, but also cultural and political. They may soon become main global players. What will be their influence on the old Western democracies and on world order? Various scenarios were elaborated, i.e. by the US National Security Agency; one of them is called global Caliphate. Earlier expectations of a more peaceful, cooperative, universalistic and intercultural world order appeared to be rather idealistic or simply wishful thinking. Still it seems that the affluent (yet hegemonistic) world underestimates such problems as international injustice, exploitation, neocolonial practices, developmental gaps, and the marginalization and exclusion of very large masses of people. It may be too late to prevent dangerous clashes in the future.

All these risks and dangers, some already well seen, can be associated with one more danger and this is the *ideological* one. It is not true that all people value freedom, democracy, human rights, and women's rights, and they are open, tolerant, and friendly to others. On the contrary, many demand a strong government power, more police and invigilation in the name of personal security, harsher punishment for criminals, unfettered treatment of terrorists (its legal expression was the Patriot Act passed during the second Bush administration). In countries with weak or short democratic traditions (e.g. Eastern Europe, Russia, China) more authoritarian rule is easily accepted, especially in a crisis situation – either domestic or international. This can be manifested in one-party rule (liberal or even communist), oligarchy and state capitalism. An ideological role is played by political organizations, parties, associations, and social movements. Quite often they are extremist (right or left), and populist. These trends do not mark the end of ideology (as predicted by Bell and Aron). Ideology is everywhere: on TV, in churches, advertising, education, politics, and civic movements. On the Internet, as well. However, it is difficult to measure the impact of these forces on people; these ideologies may effectively influence political choices as well as the decisions and behavior of governments, businesses, and citizens. The most dangerous ideologies are racist, fascist, extremist, militaristic, and hegemonic. They are all flourishing in cyberspace too. Perhaps young people will be more ideologically resistant?

In our turbulent world, while civilization is at risk and the future is uncertain, there are enough premises and assumptions for making an Orwellian-type scenario real in many parts of the planet. Authoritarian rulers, soft dictatorships or pseudo-democracies can dominate the political sphere and human values. That is why we can propose a slogan: "All democrats unite to avoid such a dire scenario!"

What could be worse than such a scenario? The possibility of the world without us, which would also mean the end of human civilization.

CONCLUSION

Alternative imaginings are also needed. The world can possibly be improved not due to imposed centralistic and universalistic models but by massive decentralized strategies, bottom-up campaigns, movements of many actors and stakeholders. Models of order cannot continue to be imposed by the world's leaders (i.e. the West) as radical reconfigurations of production, wealth, markets and power are emerging. A fundamental requirement for these strategies, policies, and activities is to obey conditions of a *sustainability trajectory*. Of course, possible coalitions, concerted efforts, coordination and cooperation are desirable since they can produce some synergetic effects. Also, international and global organizations and institutions can play an important role in organizing frameworks, initiating actions, providing top-down support , making various regulations and agreements, assuring peaceful solutions of conflicts, and observing implementation of various conventions and laws (e.g. human rights, humanitarian principles). There is no empty place in the world – there are already institutions and activities working this way. The answer is not to be submissive to corporate globalization and fully dependent on the world's big players, their choices and politics. Present possibilities of ICTs, of communication and networking can make life on the planet more human-centered and human-self dependent, not just fully relying willy-nilly on governments, corporations, and international financial institutions. A sustainability trajectory requires human counter-weight. Can we do it fast enough?

To sum up: the improvement of our civilization, now and in the future, the amelioration of *conditio humana* is not only about technology; however, technology may play a significant role, both positive and detrimental. It is about processes started long ago, about structures and mechanisms (economic, political, etc.), about vested interests and about inertia, convenient for all. It is also about mankind, about man himself and woman herself; so what is needed is self-reflection, a proper recognition of the world and its various limits, imagination and the will to change our present risky trajectory for a more rational, humanistic and sustainable one. Man is the only agent of change, sometimes helpless, sometimes powerful and wise. Can wisdom as a value and a mode of practice and decision-making save the civilization at risk? Let's hope for the best, since the future is always in the making.

REFERENCES

Barabasi, A.-L. (2003). *Linked*. New York: Plume.

Barber, B. R. (2007). *Consumed – how markets corrupt children, infantilized adults, and swallow citizens whole*. New York: Norton.

Barnett, C. et al. (Eds.). (2011). *Globalizing responsibility – the political rationalities of ethical consumption*. Chichester: Wiley.

Bauer, M. W., Jensen, P. (2011). The mobilizations of scientists for public engagement. *Public Understanding of Science* (pp. 3-11), 20(1), January.

Bauman, Z. (2000). *Liquid modernity*. Oxford: Blackwell.

Beck, U. (1997). *The Reinvention of politics – rethinking modernity in the global social order*. Cambridge, MA: Policy Press.

Beck, U., Giddens, A., Lash, S. (1994). *Reflexive modernization*. Cambridge: Polity Press.

Becker, E., Jahn, Th. (Eds.). (1999). *Sustainability and the social sciences. A cross-disciplinary approach to integrating environmental consideration into theoretical reorientation*. London – New York: Zed Books.

Bellacasa, de la M. (2011). Matters of care in technoscience: assembling neglected things. *Social Studies of Science*, 41 (1):85-106.

Berger P., Huntington, S. P. (2002). *Many globalizations – cultural diversity in the contemporary world*. New York: Oxford University Press.

Braun K., S. Schulz (2010), A certain amount of engineering involved: Constructing the public in participatory governance arrangements. *Public Understanding of Science*, 19 (4):403-419, July.

Brown, L. (2011). *World on edge*. London – Washington D.C.: Earthscan.

Brown M. (2009). *Science in democracy: expertise institutions and representation*. Cambridge, MA: MIT Press.

Bulkeley, H. et al. (2011). *Cities and low carbon transitions*. London – New York, Routledge.

Cowen, T. (2004). *Creative destruction: how globalization is changing the world's cultures*. Princeton, NJ: Princeton University Press.

Cuomo, C. J. (1997). *Feminism and ecological communities. An ethic of flourishing*. New York: Routledge.

Dankelman, I. (Ed.). (2010). *Gender and climate change: an introduction*. London – Sterling, VA: Earthscan.

Dauvergne, P. (2008). *The shadow of consumption: consequences for the global environment*. Cambridge, MA: MIT Press.

Diamond J. (2005), *Collapse of complex societies*. Cambridge: Cambridge University Press.

Dobson A., Bell, D. (2006), *Environmental citizenship*. Cambridge, MA – London: MIT Press.

Freeland, Ch. (2011). Rethinking capitalism from inside. *International Herald Tribune*, May 12.

Grin, J. et al. (2010). *Transitions to sustainable development – new directions in the study of long term transformative change*. New York – London: Routledge.

Haidt, J. et al. (2012). *The Righteous mind. Why good people are divided by politics and religion*. New York: Pantheon Books.

Hardt W., Negri, A. (2004). *Multitude*. New York: Penguin Books.

Hartz J., Chapell, R. (1997). Worlds apart: how the distance between science and journalism threatens America's future.

http://freedomforum.org/publications/first/worldsapart/.

Hayden, C. (2007). Taking as giving: bioscience, exchange, and the politics of benefit-sharing. *Social Studies of Science*, 37 (5): 729-758.

Heinberg, R., Lerch, D. (Eds.). (2010). *The post carbon reader – managing the 21st century's sustainability crises*. Healdsburg CA: Watershed Media.

Huntington, S. P. (1996). *The clash of civilizations and the remaking of world order*. New York: Simon and Schuster.

Keltner, D. (2009). *Born to be good: the science of meaningful life*. New York: Norton.

Korten, D. (2009). *Agenda for a new economy – from phantom wealth to real wealth*. San Francisco: Berrett-Koehler.

Laszlo, E. (1966). *The systems view of the world: a holistic vision for our time*. Cresshill, NJ: Hampton Press.

Martin, R. (2011), *Fixing the game: bubbles, crashes and what capitalism can learn from the N.F.L.* Toronto: University of Toronto.

McLean, S., Burgess, M. M. (2010). In the public interest: assessing expert and stakeholder influence in public deliberation about bio-banks (pp. 486-496), *Public Understanding of Science*, 19 (4), July.

Meadows D. (2009). Interview with US economist Dennis Meadows: 'Copenhagen is about doing as little as possible.'*Spiegel Online International*, 12/09/2009 http://www.spiegel.de/international/world/0,1518,666175,00.html.

Nowak, M., Highfield, R. (2011). *Supercooperators evolution, altruism and human behaviour or, why we need each other to succeed*. Edinburgh: Canongate.

Penna, A. N. (2010). *The human footprint: a global environmental history*. Malden, MA: Wiley – Blackwell.

Ryerson, W. N. (2010). Population: the multiplier of everything else. In: Heinberg, R., Lerch, D. (Eds.). *The post – carbon reader – managing the 21st century's sustainability crises*. Healdsburg CA: Watershed Media.

Sachs, I. (1999). Social sustainability and while development: exploring the dimensions of sustainable development. In: Becker, E., Jahn, Th. (eds.). (1999). *Sustainability and the social sciences. A cross-disciplinary approach to integrating environmental consideration into theoretical reorientation*. London – New York: Zed Books.

Searle, J. R. (2010). *Making the social world: the structure of human civilization*. Oxford: Oxford University Press.

Sovacool, B. (2008). *The dirty energy dilemma: what's blocking clean power in the United States*. Westport, Conn.: Praeger.

Suleski, J.and Ibaraki, M. (2010). Scientists are talking, but mostly to each other: a quantitative analysis of research represented in mass media. *Public Understanding of Science*, 19 (1):115-125.

Thomas, L. (ed.) (2004). *Religion, consumerism, and sustainability: paradise lost?* Basingstoke – New York: Palgrave Macmillan.

Tomasello, M. (2008). *Why we cooperate?* Cambridge, MA: MIT Press.

Tronto, J. C. (1993). *Moral boundaries: a political argument for an ethic of care*. New York: Routledge.

Veld in't , R. J. (Ed.). (2010). *Knowledge democracy. Consequences for science, politics and media*. Berlin/Heidelberg: Springer.

Zacher, L. W. (2010). Towards an information communication equity: challenge for the 21st century. *Transformacje*, 3–4:66–67 and 238-258.

Zacher, L. W. (2012). Toward democratization of science and technology spheres (some opportunities and problems). In: Getzinger, G. *et al*. (eds.). *IAS-STS* Yearbook 2011. Wien: Profil (forthcoming).

In: Spirituality and Civilization Sustainability ... ISBN: 978-1-53610-729-6
Editors: Andrew Targowski and Marek J. Celinski

Chapter 4

DIEU ET MON DROIT: SPIRITUAL SOVEREIGNTY AND THE DECLINE OF CIVILIZATIONS IN HISTORY

Stephen M. Borthwick*
University of Chicago, Illinois, US

ABSTRACT

The study of civilizations is largely motivated by a single question—what drives and defines a culture or civilization? In an effort to locate a civilization—or, in the case of this chapter, three civilizations—historically, perhaps the best way is to call this drive and defining quality the cultural "sovereign".

Historically, in almost every case, this sovereign takes on a spiritual and religious form in the earliest and most vitalized period of any civilization's lifespan. Conceptualizing civilizations in two phases, this chapter will seek to show that, as a rule, at some point this spiritual sovereign is usurped and replaced by a human and corrupted sovereign. This transition precipitates the decay of Civilization, first explored by Oswald Spengler, examined here with a focus on the point at which the original and eternal sovereign ceases to be the arbiter of moral and cultural questions, and the State takes over this sovereignty.

To understand "sovereignty", the chapter appeals to Schmitt; the sovereign is one who has the power "to decide the exception". In this way, the *ethos* of a culture begins as something in which no exceptions can be made by a human being—the point at which the eternal is sovereign.

As civilization declines, however, one witnesses human beings making exceptions, as morality ceases to be binding, social propriety becomes a luxury rather than a necessity, and religion becomes a fixture rather than the core of society. This state of collapse is highlighted in three separate civilizations—the Civic (i.e. Graeco-Roman), the Pharaonic (i.e. Egyptian), and the Ecclesiastic (i.e. Western). The viability of any project aimed at "revival" or "regeneration" is also examined and, the author hopes, soundly denied.

* E-mail: borthwick.sm@att.net

INTRODUCTION

The task of the historian is a question of increasing importance as humanity moves into the third millennium since the birth of Christ. It is ever more important because it is ever more felt; history no longer simply comes to be written: rather, it is scrutinized and studied, examined and dissected in an attempt to lay bare all its roots, all its causes, and all its drives. In 1944 Marc Bloch mused that "unlike others, our civilization has always been extremely attentive to its past" (p. 4).Indeed, he continued, but to what end? This question was the focus of what became his landmark work of historiography (albeit unfinished) *The Historian's Craft*, and it is still a question that concerns the historian today. Bloch proposes a number of answers in his text; he asserts that "in the last analysis it is human consciousness which is the subject-matter of history" and that the "faculty of understanding the living is, in very truth, the master quality of the historian" (pp. 151, 36). His conclusions are not so different than those drawn by Oswald Spengler, who wrote eleven years earlier that the historian's task is "to understand the actualities of his age and, using them, to sense the future, to indicate and to sketch out what will come, whether we desire it or not" (p. 14).

The historian, then, must show where humanity has been alongside where it is—where it has gone alongside where it is going. Inevitably, the historian's task is inextricably linked to the study of civilization—or, as this chapter will assert, of civilizations. The common belief that history is merely a study of the past neglects the relationship of the historian to the present, and the task of connecting the two. All good histories are of two types: the predictive and the comparative. Bold though the statement may be, it is neither wholly inaccurate nor wholly damning of those historians who do not actively relate their work to the present circumstances of the world. All who read history read it from their given place in time and their given historical moment—it is nearly impossible to avoid joining the past, in at least a small way, to the present. History's comparative aspect, though, seems to offer the most possibilities when it is deployed specifically, which most often means deployed in regard to the study of civilizations.

The historian is the teller of tales—to undertake *ἰστορία*, the "account of inquiries" from which the name "history" derives, there must be a basis for that account; there must be those things which make up a narrative or a story—plot, characters, conflict, context and scene. What is it that allows the historian to delineate and identify a civilization and to locate it historically? What is it that forms the soul of civilization and sets it essentially apart from all other civilizations? This is the fundamental question to the historian of civilization, because without it there is no *ἰστορία*. Oswald Spengler represents the first twentieth century effort in the project of identifying civilizations and comparing them, but he followed in the footsteps of historians who had been doing the same without knowing it for almost a century, from Gibbon to Burkhart. In turn, many came in his footsteps and either improved upon his work, like historian Arnold Toynbee, or pursued projects altogether their own, as with political scientist Samuel Huntington.

In all cases, the study of civilizations is a total study of history; it is a history that is impossible to contain in a small space and write about briefly—which is the root of the many shortcomings of this chapter. All that such a brief chapter can ever truly be in the realm of history is a proposal. As a result, the task of this chapter will not be the prediction of the future that Spengler undertook, nor will it be an in-depth analysis of the past. It will be, instead, an attempt to suggest a singular drive of civilizations, to illustrate that hypothesis with historical trends in some exemplary civilizations, and, ultimately, to propose what the result might mean for the future of the civilization in which the author and his readers exist.

Heraclitus seems to have captured the reality of the past when he said *ποταμοῖσι τοῖσιν αὐτοῖσινἐμβαίνουσιν, ἕτερα καὶ ἕτερα ὕδατα ἐπιρρεῖ.–* "upon those who step into the same rivers, newer and newer waters flow," or, more loosely, "one can never step into the same river twice" (Heraclitus, 1987, p. 16).To expand on the metaphor, the water, one might say, is the flow of human civilizations ever changing. The river bed, however, is constant and guides the movement of the waters. It is this river bed that the historian must find: the driving force and defining quality of a civilization. It must be a constant in human history that takes different form depending on what civilization flows over it: it must have been there since before the water, and will be there after the water has dried up or gone elsewhere.

Probably the most compelling constant, and really the only one that fits the rigorous demands just presented, is that of the notion of the eternal, the unchanging, the object of human spirituality—in short, the being or phenomenon that Western civilization has been accustomed to calling God. The means by which humans encounter, understand, and interpret this eternal—that which gives rise to the morality and ethics of a civilization, and by which humans seek to overcome their temporal nature and interpret and encounter those things beyond plain understanding—is religion. Religion is something that has been with humanity, most historians will agree, for as long as this species has walked the earth. Gilbert Murray (1955), phrased it quite well when he wrote that "man must have some relation toward the uncharted, the mysterious, tracts of life which surround him on every side" (p. 7).

It does not, thankfully, fall to the historian to define what exactly it is that religion seeks to identify and interpret—this falls to, and has baffled, the best and most learned of theologians and philosophers for millennia. The best the historian can do is confess ignorance of the object of religion—as Murray (1955) did when he asserted that "religion, like poetry and most other living things, cannot be defined"—and concentrate on its subject instead, thereby grasping how the unknown and unnamed constant shapes individual civilizations as a whole, and how it creates civilizations as individual historical phenomena and organisms (p. 4). As mentioned above, an exhaustive detailing of the several civilizations that have been born, lived, and collapsed since the dawn of humanity is impossible in so brief a chapter—indeed, it was barely accomplished by Toynbee in twelve volumes. What *can* be accomplished is to answer three questions facing contemporary civilization studies. First, can a declined civilization be revived?; second, what is the nature of global civilization?; third, what are the possibilities for civilization in the future? The first is can be answered by identifying, without exhaustive detail, three civilizations explicitly and their common life patterns with an explanation as to why these are so similar and why they all to terminate at such similar points.

The three civilizations with which this chapter will deal are named according to the prime symbol of their defining religion. Thus the ancient Egyptians find their civilization dubbed the Pharaonic, the Graeco-Romans the Civic, and the Western/European-American the Ecclesiastic. These symbols *indicate* the ultimate concern of the civilization in its religion, but they are not themselves this ultimate concern. Rather, the symbol is representative; the Pharaonic Culture finds its focus in the Divine Kingship, and the Pharaoh is the perfect symbol for this; likewise, civic duty and filial piety of the Classical Civilization make the *civitas* or *civis* its perfect symbol; finally, the monastic quest for Truth and anointed chivalry makes the Church the symbol for the entirety of Western religion. This chapter approaches the subject from the historical perspective; needless to say, in the view of the author, all of these have died and can be examined only historically. A Civilization can be said to be dying when it comes to a state of stagnation, in which it has lost its ability to shape and create life, and can maintain its presence only through artificial means—i.e. when it is preserved in stasis, i.e. as it was at its last moment of life, like an organ in formaldehyde or a pressed flower—usually by antiquarians. Such was Rome "preserved" by the Visigoths, Egypt by the Ptolemies, and the West by Traditionalists.

Civilizations As Life-Forms

Spengler has often been challenged for his assertion that Civilizations have lifespans just as plants and animals have lifespans; his so-called fatalism is at the root of Toynbee's difference with his work. Nevertheless, history does seem to indicate that civilizations die out, and that they all seem to reach their mortal limit at about the same point in their lifespan. For Spengler, this was critical; he was, after all, setting forth "to predeterminate history" specifically to determine "the destiny of a Culture which is actually in the phase of fulfillment" (Spengler, 1922, p. 3). His project is far vaster than that of the present chapter, but takes the same approach in the understanding civilization in two phases, calling *Zivilisation* "the organic and logical successor, the fulfillment and result of a Culture" [p. 42]. In order to approach the subject in this way, it is necessary both to embrace Spengler and turn from him; for to understand *Zivilisation* as the organic and logical outcome of a *Kultur* one must understand them together as a single organism that springs forth from the soil of time and returns thence in death after a more or less determined lifespan. Likewise, to take this understanding to its logical limit, it is impossible to rely so heavily, as Spengler did, on aesthetics and prime symbols derived therefrom, for these are too easily dismissed as subjective rather than eternal. The eternal, the permanent, the literally timeless is that which must drive and define Civilizations as life-forms in order for those life-forms to have meaning.

To delineate two separate phases of the development of a Civilization, one the living and one the crystallized, Spengler might suggest a biological metaphor, saying that the Culture is to the Civilization what a sapling is to a tree, for both are called, or can be called, a "tree". However, this does not assist with clarity, for one still does not know immediately what is meant by "Civilization" when it is used in this way. Better, then, is to seek different terms for this organism that matures in two stages. For substitute terms to describe a civilization's lifespan, a good source may be found in one of Spengler's predecessors, Ferdinand Tönnies, who first proposed these two phases in his landmark work of sociology, *Gemeinschaft und Gesellschaft* (1887), asserting that the connection between people can be "understood either as real and organic – this being the nature of the Communion – or in an ideological and mechanistic form – this being the notion of Association" and clarifying that, "All that is familiar, private, living together … is understood as life in a Community. Society is the public sphere, it is the World" (pp. 3-4). These two German words—*Gemeinschaft* and *Gesellschaft*—can be, and have been, translated in different ways: the prevailing translation is "community" and "society," but this fails to capture as accurately the difference between the German words. The English words "communion" and "association" better capture this disparity, and emphasize just how far apart a *Gemeinschaft* would be from a *Gesellschaft*.

Tönnies initially proposed that these were *Normaltypen* ("normal types") and would therefore only ever be found in degrees in actual applied sociology, since theoretical sociology and applied sociology belonged to two separate and mutually exclusive realms. Max Weber objected to this, proposing instead in 1904 that they were *Idealtypen*("pure types"), since sociology must necessarily work with abstract hypotheticals ("*Gedankenbild*") in order to approach the real world (p. 211)Spengler's *Kultur* and *Zivilisation* system falls closer to Weber if only because he does not use the terms with any Kantian sense of exclusivity between the real world and the conceptual world: "Culture" and "Civilization" are terms that describe historical realities and exist to help historians understand their subject matter. He differs only in that he does not consider them hypotheticals that do not exist in their pure form in reality; rather, they are terms that can be directly applied to historical reality. In this way, one might propose Spengler's conception of them as "real" as opposed to "normal" or "pure" types. Taking "Community" to refer to Spengler's "Culture" and "Society" to refer to his "Civilization" in the model here, not only can the link between Tönnies' sociology and Spengler's history be made more explicit, but the meaning of each category also becomes more explicit.

The community phase of the life-form called Civilization is one of rich vitality, of creative growth, and of a constant flowering of the driving force of that civilization. It is also, inevitably, the period in a civilization when its native driving force, its religion, still holds exclusive sovereignty. The religious experience of the people living in a civilization, therefore, indicates whether it is in the state of communion or a state of association. The lack of the native religious experience means that the eternal has lost sovereignty—i.e. both its inspirational power and its authority as arbiter moral and legal exceptions. This means religion has ceased to be the source of a community's ethics and morals. This is exemplified in Nietzsche's declaration "God is dead"—here Nietzsche is not asserting some sort of plain, vulgar atheism, but that the Christian God of his civilization has ceased to be morally compelling to that civilization, and its native *ethos* of has died (Welshon, 2004, pp. 16, 40). This is not a phenomenon unique to Nietzsche's Ecclesiastic Civilization; rather, it occurs at the same point in every civilization's lifespan. The death of the native *ethos* necessarily follows or is followed by the rise of a hitherto foreign *ethos*, as one sees perhaps most explicitly in the demise of Civic Civilization after Constantine's Edict of Milan in AD 313 and the subsequent Christianization of the Empire between his death in 337 BC and the rise of Theodosius I in AD 392. By illustrating this, the inevitability and irresistability of decline should become apparent.

Using examples such as Constantine, one can in fact pinpoint events and individuals as indicators of major turning points in the life and death of a civilization, albeit with varying degrees of precision. Civic Civilization, whose basis is Graeco-Roman civic piety, finds its death indicated by the death of Constantine I and the subsequent in-fighting among his descendants over various forms of Christianity (except Julian, whose apostasy was not only short-lived but treated with general ambivalence). Likewise, Ecclesiastic Civilization, defined and expressed in the Church community and mystical Body of Christ, falters at the death of Pope Pius X and the outbreak of the World Wars, in which the Ecclesiastic spirituality is finally conquered by technological advances and confidence in science—indicated by the empty overtures paid to God by the Allies and National Socialists alike that were coupled with active persecution of Christians by the latter and general decline in religious sentiment among the former. This reached its low point with the widespread mockery and derision of anything but skeptical agnosticism or militant atheism in popular culture from the AD 1950s forward, after which no trace at all of Ecclesiastic Civilization can be found.

This final death, however, should not be brought into focus without the understanding that it terminates a very long lifespan, drawn out over a millennium and a half in all those cases found here. Without the study of life, as Bloch (1944) asserted so firmly, there can be no true understanding of the history of a civilization. To give an overview of this life, the reader should refer to Figure 1 found at the end of this chapter; this is a simple, but nevertheless illustrative, outline of the long course of life each civilization follows. The dates are, as they must be, approximations, since a single moment in time is not at all the same as a single moment in history. History spans the ages, transcends them and conquers them. Time is the sequential organization of the day-to-day, of year-by-year events; it is a measurement for the politician, not the historian: it is a scale for the life of a specimen or a person, not for the life of a species or a civilization.

Working backwards from the final death, one finds another end which precipitates it. The end of spiritual sovereignty can be observed in the Pharaonic civilization with the death of Akhenaten, whose attempts to stifle the political power of the (quite human) Amonite priesthood suffered a reverse so drastic that one could easily say that the High Priest of Amon, formerly merely a servant of the representative of the gods on Earth (as Pharaoh was) wielded more social influence and political power than any subsequent Pharaoh as the head of what James H. Breasted (1912) called the “Amonite Papacy” (p. 319). Likewise, for the Civics the rise of Tiberius (AD 14) marks the end of any but an artificial religion after the Emperor deified his father, Augustus, thus founding the first (and last) enduring political cult in Rome (Wardman, 1982, pp. 51-52) In Ecclesiastic Culture, the end of religion’s sovereignty is contained in that great apocryphal declaration of the Sun King, *l’etat, c’est moi*, which captures the Absolutist form of rule perfectly. Aquinas and Augustine alike speak of tyrants as rulers who “lead their subjects to fall away from the perfection of virtue” and commit injustice because they are not themselves subjects of God (Aquinas, 1988, p. 20). After the seventeenth century, however, the King, and eventually parliaments and republics, are subject to themselves alone.

Each of these changes seems quite unique, but they are common to all three of the civilizations examined: that they take a unique s but again they do occur in three very different civilizations. What is in common among the three is the usurpation of a spiritual or religious sovereign by a human or political sovereign. For the Egyptians, the Pharaoh was understood in earlier times to be a sort of sub-god on Earth representing greater divine beings, and ultimately answering to The Creator: when his actual power in Egypt is usurped and the (quite human) Amonite priesthood gains in both reputation and power, one is witnessing the equivalent of a minister usurping Jesus Christ as the driving force of a modern Christian congregation. In Civic Civilization, the deification of the emperor fundamentally alters the peoples’ approach to civic duty: one is no longer paying duty to the state and the community for the sake of the gods: rather, one is paying duty to men claiming to be gods on Earth. In short, Divine power and State power become merged as one, or, better put, the State takes on a divine role. For the West, likewise, the King who was formerly intended to be a subject of God—though this was not always the case—now openly flouts this role without consequences, and becomes subject to none but himself, or, in the case of parliaments, looks downward to the people rather than upward to God for justification. In all cases, that which was formerly subject to the spiritual sovereign now takes on attributes of the sovereign, and in so doing usurps sovereignty.

Louis XIV, Tiberius, and Ackhenaten indicate only the final change after a process of decline, however. If they are the end-markers collapse of community and the rise of society, there must also be a beginning-marker, for such collapse does not happen in one man's lifetime. The period of decline is indicated by the rise of a great Reformer, hearkening back to an earlier time in an effort to reinvigorate the communion of a civilization before it shifts into mere association. This Reformer, however, cannot halt the movement of his civilization any more than one can stop a river from flowing: one can divert the flow or dam the river, but the water will always seek the sea. Historically speaking, this collapse is still quite sudden—only the space of a hundred to two hundred years. The common trait in all Reformers is both what they themselves see as well as what they indicate to the historian. The Reformer is one who lives in a time when decay is just barely noticeable: he is one who is more astute than his contemporaries, and acutely aware of the coming collapse of his Civilization. He is also one of supreme self-confidence and hope; he believes that he can prevent the end by revitalizing ancient forms from the earliest days of a Civilization. He also, as a rule, is a tragic figure, and in his effort to save his civilization actually accelerates its decay and, in many ways, causes the usurpation of the original sovereign.

The Reformer seems to arrive on the stage some hundred years before the final death of community and the rise of society. In Ecclesiastic Civilization, Martin Luther begins the Reformation in 1517 and dies in 1546, some ninety-eight years before the end of the Thirty Years' War. The War itself can be, and has been, directly traced to Luther's Reformation (though the famous monk of Wittenberg no doubt would be horrified by the war and its consequences). It is important to emphasize to what degree Luther has been called a "medieval man" by his premier biographer, Heiko Oberman (2006), who likewise emphasizes Luther's believe that he lived "in the shadow of the chaos of the Last Days"(pp. xv, 12).

Among the Civics, the Reformation takes on a political form under the direction of the Gracchi in 133 and 121 BC (roughly a century before Caesar). These men looked to the Athens of some three centuries before for their inspiration in a quest to restore the failing *res publica* with the long-past *πόλις*, the ideal of a more fully democratic republic—illustrated readily in efforts to prevent deposed public servants from being reinstated and establishing state control over the corn-trade (Scullard, 2011, p. 28).

While these minutiae are good illustrations, they belie the Greek education and admiration for Athens of Tiberius that drove his initial call for reform that would be put into action by his younger brother in these practical and legal measures. The Gracchi, fed by a fear of the collapse of the republic, desired a reform that would guarantee its survival indefinitely (Scullard, 2011, p. 20) Their own popularity, however, fed the political cult that would serve as the basis for the cult of Julius Caesar and, later, of Augustus, that marked the end of Civic community (Wardman, 1982, p. 51)

Finally, Thutmose III is the Pharaonic Reformer. "The first character of universal aspects," he sought to reassert both the power of the Pharaoh and belief in the ancient Sun-god with his Amonite Priesthood (Breasted, 1912, p. 314). It would, however, be the High Priest of Amon-Re and his "Amonite Papacy" that would challenge and eventually usurp the power of the pharaohs in the years following the death of Akhenaten in 1336 BC (Breasted, 1912, p. 319).

The lifespan of a civilization before it passes out of community and into society is much more vibrant and far less exact; this perhaps has something to do with the organic nature of a community contrasted with the regulated and artificial nature of society.

Before the rise of society, which is by its nature far more self-reflective and mechanistic than community, civilization experiences its birth and then several periods of distinct formation and growth that indicate cultural vitality. The birth of each civilization occurs roughly fifteen hundred years before its subsequent demise.[1]

For the Civics, all begins with the rise of the Dorians in c. 1200 BC and displays its first living indicators of civilization with the writings of Homer and Hesiod in the 850s and 750s BC. The Pharaonic Civilization is born from the sands of Egypt under the watchful eye ofPharaoh Djoser (the first Pharaoh of the Third Dynasty who began the building of Pyramids) in the c. 2600s BC and sees its first zenith with Dynasty VI (2345-2181 BC), immediately before the Egyptian Dark Age. Ecclesiastic Civilization is born with the merging of Germanic and Christian cultures, and must therefore begin with the missionary Ulfilas in the AD 340s, and experiences the first growth spurt in the time of Charlemagne in the 740s.

THE SOVEREIGN: CONCEPT AND APPLICATION

As mentioned above, the key to the shift from community to society is who holds sovereignty. It is unfortunate that the language here is so confined to a single civilization, since it is easy to confuse the political concept of the sovereign discussed by Aquinas, Hobbes, and Schmitt with what is meant here by "cultural sovereignty." Schmitt shall be the basis for the discussion of sovereignty here because of how compelling his definition is.

He wrote, "sovereign is he who decides on the exception" (Schmitt, 2006, p. 5). The language is somewhat clearer in the original: *Ausnahmezustand*, or the "state of being set aside," specifically refers to a legal standing in Schmitt—*i.e.* "the situation in which the law is set aside"— but one will find it also fits nicely to describe what occurs after religion ceases to be morally compelling and when the ineffable eternal is ousted from sovereignty. To this point in the history of a civilization, no exception can truly be made to the traditions and the laws of the community. Only in a society—i.e. where man is sovereign and the State assumes the religious mantle as arbiter of moral law and ethical conduct—can exceptions to moral laws be made without social repercussions.

Indeed, Schmitt's original conception of the sovereign is one that belongs strictly to society; it would be utterly foreign to the community. He describes the exception as "a case of extreme peril, a danger to the existence of the state, or the like," and further writes that "what characterizes the exception is principally unlimited authority, which means the suspension of the entire existing order… (but) because the exception is different from anarchy and chaos, order in the juristic sense still prevails" (Schmitt, 2006, pp. 6, 12). Suspension of the existing

---

[1] It is worth noting that this 1,500 year lifespan is an estimate, since from the Dorians to Constantine is 1,537 years, while from Djoser to Ramesses VIII is 1,580 years, and from Ulfilas to Pius X is 1,574 years, and there is reason to assume that a Civilisation might live as long as 1,600 years or as briefly as 1,400 years.

order is inconceivable to the community, which is self-sufficient and abiding rather than self-reflective and therefore anxious of its survival like the society.

Likewise, a legal concept like the sovereign, one "who is supposed to have unlimited power" and "produces and guarantees the situation in its totality" is something that cannot possibly exist in any community, where the eternal is the only thing that produces and guarantees anything in its totality (Schmitt, 2006, pp. 10, 13).

The question arises, then, if the concept of the sovereign can be extended beyond the realm of society. The chief reason for appealing to Schmitt is because his concept of "sovereign" is non-applicable to the community phase only in the eyes of society; in reality, in a communion-phase civilization, where the eternal is sovereign, that eternal *is* sovereign even by Schmitt's definition, and actually capable of making exceptions to rules.

That exceptions are never made is not something fundamentally important to them; indeed, it is ignored altogether or explained away, as one finds with questions in the young Ecclesiastic Civilization of why God does not cause miracles frequently.

Who, then, is sovereign? The sovereign should not be considered a figure restricted to the political realm; rather, the sovereign is the focal point of the entirety of a civilization.

In all civilizations, there is a focal point; regardless if the founder is recognized as a human being, an idea, an institution, a myth, or some other tangible or intangible thing, all civilizations revolve around what one might call a spiritual core. This core is the sovereign of the culture at its earliest stage, when it is still growing and producing and developing; when the core shifts, and a new concept or institution becomes sovereign, the civilization becomes as a tree ripped up by the root: it slowly begins to harden and die, eventually either rotting and returning to the soil or crystalizing into a fossilized state.

THE CIVILIZATIONS: PHARAONIC, CIVIC AND ECCLESIASTIC

This chapter has suggested that the symbol of each civilization—Pharaonic, Civic, Ecclesiastic—is directly related to the actual sovereign of that civilization in its community phase, but this does not give an answer as to who, or what, that sovereign is.

The task of truly uncovering the cultural sovereign, i.e. to describe the religion of each civilization, requires a look at each civilization specifically—not in the chronological sense, sketching out the life-span of each civilization, but in the cultural sense, actually examining what each civilization was.

The Pharaonic

The Pharaoh, one will find, is both "a being and an office, the former originally mortal and the latter always divine" (Silverman, 1991, p. 67). This can be a very confusing concept—indeed, one is almost tempted to call the statement nonsensical or mere platitude.

To understand how a single being can be both mortal, that is to say, profane, and divine, requires a brief discussion of the titles the pharaohs adopted as early as the fifth dynasty. At this point, during the height of the Old Kingdom when the famous Pyramid Texts were being composed, the Pharaohs took the name *S3R*ʿ, or "Son of Re," which would be adapted in the Middle Kingdom to*tjt- R*ʿ or "image of Re" (Silverman, 1991, p. 59).

That the Pharaoh conceptualized himself as the "son" of Re means that he put himself in a subsidiary position to the Sun-god and eternal Pharaoh,as Re (and Horus) was conceptualized (Breasted, 1912, p. 175). As son of Re, he took on the role of a son to his father and a servant to his master—indeed, the epithet *tjt- R*ʿmight almost be taken to emphasize the profane nature of the pharaoh rather than his divine nature, being the "image" of the god, an incarnation who is subject to the god and gods. Silverman highlights the obvious differences that accompanied this "Son of Re":

> A king had to earn his immortality, whereas a god was inherently immortal. The king's victories in battle were given to him by the deities…the monarch had to maintain *ma'at*[2]and to indicate that he was acting appropriately (p. 63)

All of this speaks plainly to the real role of the pharaoh as a man: he is a bridge between the divine world that the Egyptians worship and the profane world they inhabit. This divine world is discussed both in terms of "the gods" as well as "God"—for a disparity exists between those concepts to such an extent that there is active debate as to whether the Egyptians were polytheists or monotheists. Breasted (1912) attests to the fact that by "the beginning of the Pyramid Age, [the Egyptian] was already discerning the Sun-god… and made him the great arbiter and ruler of the Egyptian nation" (p. 12). Wallis Budge (1959) goes a step further, declaring that "a study of Egyptian religious texts will convince the reader that the Egyptian believed in One God, who is self-existent, immortal, invisible, eternal, omniscient, almighty, and inscrutable" (p. 17). These two giants—indeed, founders—of the field of Egyptology stand in opposition to their contemporary counterparts, however, like Byron Shafer (1991), who defies that "all but very few (Egyptians) were polytheists" (p. 3).

The conflict between the two is a conflict of two different understandings of religion taken from two different sources; Shafer is quick to assert that those textual sources upon which Budge and Breasted rely were written by and for an elite of Egyptian society, and therefore are untrustworthy to capture the true religion of Egypt (p. 3).

However, the religion contained in the Pyramid texts also speaks of many gods, but also offers strong evidence for the domination of one, as asserted by Budge. The answer to the controversy resides in what the Egyptians revered above all else: the Sun and Judgment, Re and Osiris. Re seems to be, like the Pharaoh, an incarnation of something greater—the Sun, that self-created Being. This indicates the real division of the world in the Egyptian mind: not the simplistic, Marxist vision of classes, but rather a long hierarchy that reaches from "humanity" to Pharaoh to the gods to the Creator. What one arrives at is several forms of henotheism[3] making the Pharaoh "high priest or first prophet of the god," though who that god "is"—i.e. what name he is called—finds itself disputed among Atum, Horus, Khepri, Amon, and the national god, Re (Silverman, 1991, p. 83).

Without a doubt, the great deity and the main focus of the Pharaonic religion was the Sun-god and all of his attributes and incarnations. It is the Sun-god who takes pity on Isis upon the death of Osiris and elevates him to his role as pharaoh of the netherworld,

---

[2] "Duty and preservation of order"; maʿat is similar to Hindu dharma, except that it applied solely to Pharaoh, not to Egyptians in general.

[3] Meaning, essentially, monotheism that accepts the existence of a multitude of deities.

"champion and friend of the dead" (Breasted, 1912, pp. 27, 37). This focus on both the Sun and on Judgment after death forms the entire impetus of Egyptian moral life, which means the impetus of Pharaonic Community.

At the height of Pharaonic Civilization in the Middle Kingdom, "people were morally accountable for their actions," albeit subject to fate, but judgment before passing into the afterlife is attested from well into the Old Kingdom period (Baines, 1991, pp.146, 151). Indeed, citing the Pyramid Texts, Breasted asserts that "the Egyptian of the Pyramid Age (the Old Kingdom) had already begun to look back upon a time when sin and strife did not exist, to 'the first body' of 'the company of the just'" [p. 166]. This shows clearly that the formation of Egyptian moral life and community begins early in the Old Kingdom and continues to develop in the Middle Kingdom; the role of the Pharaoh as arbiter becomes now especially important, for "the king is said to 'propitiate' rather than 'worship' the gods; he 'judges' humanity, setting them in order" (Baines, 1991, p. 128). As one approaches the New Kingdom period, however, the age of Thutmose III and Akhenaten, one finds that there is a growth in significance of *past* kings, though Baines (1991) insists that this is not a "royal 'ancestor cult'" (p. 128).

Further, the New Kingdom is the first place one begins to see doubt of the afterlife, which, since the Middle Kingdom and the "democratization" of funeral rites with the Book of the Dead, seems to have decreased in importance as it decreased in exclusivity (Silverman, 1991, p. 73). Baines points out "some New Kingdom texts doubt the value of provision for the next life, saying 'there is no one who has come back from there,'" sentiments that directly challenge the "potent moral presence" the blessed dead formerly needing placation from their living counterparts (pp. 151-152).

A need had arisen for a new birth of the old religion, and so Thutmose III asserted his Pharaonic power to merge all the priesthoods into "one great sacerdotal organization, at the head of which he placed the High Priest of Amon" (Breasted, 1912, p. 319). What had originally been an effort to reassert religious life and moral "fear of God," if such an anachronism is permitted, created the political institution that would seal the fate of Pharaonic civilization forever, ultimately putting the Pharaoh in the shadow of the priesthood of Amon-Re.

The "Amonite Papacy" would become the most "powerful political obstacle in the way of realizing the supremacy of the ancient Sun-god" in the time of Akhenaten [Breasted, 1912, p. 319]. In order, however, for Akhenaten, born Amenhotep ("Amon is satisfied") IV, to assert the Aten, the ineffable sun-disc, he himself had to take on powers and titles that earlier pharaohs would never have dared to touch.

He threw off the role he had as High Priest and First Prophet to the gods, as arbiter, and instead his "personal status was so high… that he rated his own First Prophet, as if he were a great god" and the new Pharaoh ordered images made of the royal family, portraying such intimacy as were formerly reserved only for mythical scenes (Silverman, 1991, pp. 83, 85).

It is at this point that the measures taken to ensure the old order ultimately fail: after Akhenaten's death, the Pharaoh retained his fully divine, rather than merely god-like, status, and the first prophet and High Priest of Amon-Re took on political powers like the pharaohs of old. This break-down of Egyptian society would continue only so long as there was asecure pharaoh, something that ceased to be after the death of Ramesses VIII and the chaos of subsequent reigns.

The Civic

The gods of Civic Civilization were not like those of Pharaonic culture, with the unspoken but pervading monotheism hidden behind a multitude of bestial idols. Rather, it is the numinous spirit as a type that occupies the Classical mind from the very earliest days. It is present with Varro when he asserts that the anthropomorphic gods were unknown to the earliest Romans (Wardman, 1982, p. 2). It is also present in Aeschylus when he writes that *εὐτυχεῖν* ("prosperity, the realization of success") is "both a god and more than a god" as well as in Euripides, whose Helen proclaims that "recognizing a friend is also a god" (Aeschylus,1884, p. 5; Euripides, 2002, p. 72). These gods of feeling, of sentiment, and of relationships represent a sort of noumenon at the very root of Greek religion that the statuary idols and great temples belie.[4] It is not just present in drama, either; J.E. Lendon (2010) comments that the focus of Greek competition was not material gain but for "honor or glory; worth," or *τιμή* (p. 7). This *τιμή*was "glory made palpable and somehow separate from its possessor. [It] was thought to have a real, almost physical existence in the world; it could...be taken from one man by another; it could be captured in war" (Lendon, 2010, p. 7). In Rome, the Greek noumenon was translated as *numen* and became something more specific—the numinous spirits that inhabited the world with the anthropomorphic gods, and were expected to "cooperate in the supreme task of civic polytheism, to protect and favor the city which has installed them and pays them respect" (Wardman, 1982, p. 3).

What of the Olympian Twelve, though? The immediate temptation is to look to Zeus/Jupiter, the chief god who held tremendous influence, and was the only god the others in his company truly feared, as the arbiter and focus of this noumenal religion (Murray, 1955, p. 45). After all, in Rome Jove stood as divine witness to oaths, and in early days bestowed on Rome the moral right to go to war. He gave justification to action and thought in the Classical world—but still he was a god, like all the Olympians, whose mythology is rife with flaws, inconsistency and injustice. The reason for this might be found in Murray (1955), who comments that the Olympian gods were "imposed upon a background strangely unlike themselves"; he points to the example of the Diasia, one of the three great festivals of Athens, in which Zeus was supposedly the patron, "though our authorities generally add an epithet to him, and call him Zeus Meilichios, or Zeus of Placation. A god with an 'epithet' is always suspicious... [and] in the rites Zeus had no place at all" (p. 13). John Gould, further, cites Heroditus to summarize his account of the Greek gods: "Divinity is envious and disorderly" (Gould, 1985, p. 32). The anthropomorphic gods, then, cannot be, with their constantly shifting loyalties, emotions, and lusts, a focal point for religion and social order.

One must, instead, look to the noumenon and numinous spirits that dominate the Classical religious mind. As early as Homer and Hesiod, the blossoming of Civic Civilization, already a sense exists of civic responsibility and right action (similar to Egyptian maʿat)—it can be found in Achilles and Hector, the former of whom is punished for his ὕβρις.

[4] Here we must consider the νοούμενονin its original sense, without Kant and his notion of the Ding-an-sich. Noumena are understood to be the opposite of phenomena, the latter of which belong to the realm of the sensual, while the former of which belong to the realm beyond or above the senses – Plato envisioned this realm as being the realm of the Forms, but it is not something unique to Platonic philosophy. To put it simply, the noumenon is something which is sensed rather than seen, though this simplification actually belies the complexity of those things sensed in the literal sense (i.e. by the senses) and those things sensed or detected by the mind with no input from the senses.

Indeed, if there is something to be found in common between the Romans and the Greeks to form a unified civilization, it is the fixation on civic responsibility to the πόλις and res publica. Maintaining ritual propriety not just in the temple, as in Egypt, but in absolutely all moments of life, was the duty not just of Greek and Roman leaders, but of all Greeks and Romans—and it was ultimately for the benefit of the city, be it the many πόλεις of the Greeks or the specific Urbs aeterna of the Romans. This is also at the root of the corruption of Civic Civilization, from the point when the civis—the citizen—is replaced by the State as the focal point of piety and virtue.

The cult of virtue was born, or at least put into words, with Homer and Hesiod, but it would reach its pinnacle in the time of the great philosophers in the fourth and fifth centuries BC. Plato would look to the form of the Good in his *Πολιτεία* while Xenophon would comment, "if you want virtue in a state, look for it in a good man, not in a speculative tangle of laws"; this "good man" is one who will "honor the gods, do his duty in the field, and practice obedience" (Murray, 1955, p. 83). Thus the eternal is encapsulated in a permanent presence that defines society: like the Egyptians had the ever-present, ever-reborn Sun, the Classics had their noumena of virtue. It was already failing, however, by the second century BC, when Cicero felt the need to reclaim it. He commented in his *De natura Deorum* that "if we wish to compare our people with foreigners, we find that... in religion, i.e. in the cult of the gods, we are far superior" (Cicero, 1890,p. 81).Grant (1957) writes that Cicero was supremely interested in bringing Romans to a more "philosophical" approach to religion, as the Greeks had pioneered; this is somewhat contested by the fact, which Grant admits, that Cicero "maintained an attitude of reserve... and criticism toward all schools of philosophy" (p. 59). Indeed, Cicero's chief function seems to be to combat the introduction of foreign influences on native Roman religion, a task he undertakes chiefly wielding the aspect of virtue known to him as *pietas*; he writes that one must "cultivate justice and a sense of duty (*pietatem*), which are greatly important as regards parents and relatives, but much more as regards the fatherland" (Cicero, 1826, p. 483). Augustine would later comment that it was the triumph of what Varro called "civic religion" over the religion of the philosophers that allowed Roman religion to degenerate into vulgar Emperor-worship; the Bishop of Hippo seemed to see the corruption clearly, but was unable to describe it historically (Augustine, 2003, pp. 234-236).

The Emperor-worship Augustine disdains arose with the deification of Augustus following his death and certainly had its roots in political cult, though perhaps not the same sort of civic cult that the Church Father condemned. Such political cults were not unknown before Augustus was deified; the Gracchi, the force of "Reformation" (with Cicero) in Civic Civilization and the reassertion of the *civitas,* were granted one in the first century BC, and while that cult ultimately failed, it was replaced by the cult of Julius Caesar and later by that the Roman Emperors.

Duty to the *civitas* became duty to the *Augustus*—the "venerable," the Emperor and the State he represented. While the sovereign was no longer eternal, however, the Emperor was still a Roman, and ultimately it was a corrupted and often abused civic piety that drove Civic Civilization until the Edict of Milan in 313, at which point civic piety began to break down in the face of Christian piety. By the time of Theodosius I, the latter had completely replaced the former.

The Ecclesiastic

There are two passages in the New Testament that represent Ecclesiastic Civilization; the first is St. Paul, "Now ye are the body of Christ, and members in particular. And God hath set some in the church (*ἐκκλησίᾳ*), first apostles, secondarily prophets, thirdly teachers" (1 Cor. 12:27-28); the second from St. Matthew, "And I say also unto thee, That thou art Peter, and upon this rock I will build my church (*ἐκκλησίαν*)" (Matt. 16:18). These are the entire basis for the interpretation of Christianity that would come to shape and form the Ecclesiastic world.

The formation of a Civilization based on the Christian community began as early as the fourth century AD with Ulfilas, the Arian missionary to the Goths, and was completed by the middle of the sixth century AD by Remigius, who baptized King Clovis in Nicene Christianity. These two moments are symbolic because they represent the coming together of Germanic warrior culture and the Christian culture of late antiquity in the formation of a new civilization.

The merger is found in passages of poetry and literature, such as the *Dream of the Rood,* which speaks of Christ as a "young hero" and "mighty king" who actively mounts the Cross, "bold before many" (Treharne, 2004, p. 111). The warrior ethos of the Germanics made its way early into Christianity, and while the imagery did not long find itself explicitly attached to the person of Jesus, it was an enduring drive for the *chevalier,* the knight, who waslegitimized in the service of the Church. It was the Crusadesthat "made knighthood, of which as yet very little good could be said, not only respectable, but glorious" (Southern, 1961, p. 54).

Knighthood, however, is not the sole expression of Ecclesiastic religion. It is joined by a the monastic quest for truth and knowledge. The monastery, founded as a means to seek God, became throughout the Golden Age of Ecclesiastic Civilization the chief fonts of knowledge and learning in Europe. They were the cause and the origin of almost all the writing done in the Ecclesiastic Community, a practice that defines civilization as it expresses its reality, and sets Ecclesiastic Civilization apart because of what it says about this Civilization.

Rather than relying on inferences as to what was political and cultural sovereign, the historian has the good fortune of having instructive books written for princes, like Aquinas' *De Regno* and John of Salisbury's *Policraticus* which outline it specifically.

Aquinas (1981) says of the King that he is "a shepherd seeking the common good of the multitude and not his own"; to prevent tyranny on the part of a king, he recommends that the king be "of such condition that it is improbably that he should become a tyrant," quoting the Book of Daniel, "the Lord hath sought him a man according to his own heart," i.e. a man who is first a subject to God (pp. 178, 188).

In regards to the removal of tyrants, the chief concern of John of Salisbury is that it should be done without "loss of religion and honor," and he condones the killing of tyrants "because it serves the cause of the faith, and fights in behalf of charity" (John, 1963, pp. 371,373). John also outlines the ideal knight, writing that the purpose of knighthood is "to protect the church, punish infidelity, reverence priesthood" and give of oneself to the point of death for others (PL 199, p. 600).

Thus all things are subordinated to serving God, a God unlike that in any other Civilization that has yet arisen. The Ecclesiastic conception of God allows for a combination of reason and mysticism on a level foreign to the Civic or Pharaonic Civilizations, because of the absolute nature of God. When Meister Eckhart (1979), for example, expresses the goal of his fellow monks as "always being born in God" and emphasizes again and again that "God is *one*," he is not an exception in Ecclesiastic spirituality, but a typical expression thereof (pp.118-119, 168).

The quest for God is absolute, penetrating, and permeating in Ecclesiastic civilization—the monastic quest for knowledge is a quest for God as Truth, the knightly quest is one for God in the form of redemption, the kingly quest is one to guide his people to God. This quest is understood by Spengler as reflective of Faust's tireless quest for knowledge—thus he calls Western Civilization "Faustian Civilization"—but in reality it has less diabolical origins than the name implies. When Martin Luther began his Reformation, it was a movement to bring Europe in general, and Germany in particular, back to God and Christ, and, just as other Reformers in other Civilizations, his shattering of a unified Christendom has effects which are quite the opposite of his goals.

The unintended consequence of the Thirty Years' War, and the subsequent turn from God that resulted, makes Luther's effort, like the Gracchi and Thutmose III, a direct cause for the result he feared worst of all.

It is likewise in the wake of the Thirty Years' War that the reaching quest for God becomes a quest for discovery and global conquest. Southern (1961) recounts that in 1095, Pope Urban II spoke of "this little portion of... ours is pressed upon by warlike Turks and Saracens... they have held Spain and the Balearic Islands, and they live in hope of devouring the rest" (p. 71). This distinctly defensive attitude of the God-fearing Ecclesiastic, begins to dissipate at the beginning of the sixteenth century and has all but vanished by the seventeenth, by which time the path to global domination by Ecclesiastic Civilization is already half-trodden.

It is important to highlight that insofar as these consequences are unintended, they are also inevitably part of the process of reform that brings an end to an *ancien regime*.

Ideally, reform should allow a civilization to begin anew with a blank slate, but a reformer can only destroy a corrupt institution; he cannot destroy the history that brought that institution to corruption. The creations of a Civilization can be reset, but the Civilization itself cannot be: it finds itself too old to create from scratch all that it created in its earliest days, just as an older man will never have the ability to heal broken bones or begin a new career with the speed or competency of a young man.

When Hobbes asserts in *Leviathan*, therefore, that the natural cause of religion is fear for the future, he is asserting something fundamentally original (p. 72). It is at this point when the Ecclesiastic Society is formed by breaking away from God; since true revelation cannot conflict with "natural reason" and human experience, suddenly human perception is elevated above God and science above revelatory religion, giving Hobbes' sovereign the same absolute control in politics as God enjoyed in Civilization (Hobbes, 1996, p. 247). Where God once was the arbiter of social ethics and cultural development, the State takes on this role in the form of Hobbes' absolute sovereign, either in absolutism or in parliamentarianism.

It is, ironically, Machiavelli who is most emblematic of this shift during Hobbes' time: for it is in Machiavelli that the Prince ceases to be a shepherd to his people, instead becoming chiefly concerned with social order and maintaining his own power. Machiavelli is not the cause of the change, however: he has, after all, only become popular since the 1600s and the age of Hobbes (Berlin, 1992, p. 206).

Nevertheless, when he writes that "I have often reflected that the causes of the success or failure of men depend on their manner of suiting their conduct to the times," he is making an emblematic statement about the temporal State as a replacement for eternal God in Ecclesiastic society (Machiavelli, 1992, p. 116).He, and those who worked from his foundation, introduces the earliest seeds of moral and social relativism that would come to fruition in Post-Modern philosophy and nihilism. The "Body of Christ" motif finally falters with the World Wars; proof of the end of the totality and sense of unity that defines the West can be found readily in Camus' hopeless declaration that "There is only one truly serious philosophical problem: that is suicide" (Camus, 1965, p. 99). One of the defining features of the dead West is this nihilism, as well as self-loathing. What is native is shunned, while what is foreign is glorified. Partially, this comes from a radical individualism, typified in Ayn Rand, but found in less pure forms more or less throughout the former West. This, the relativism that dominates post-modernity, and the unimpeded rise of militant atheist authors in recent times like Richard Dawkins and Christopher Hitchens, all speak to a chaotic state in which the reigning direction of Western civilization has ceased to exist. This chaos and disunity, the glorification of the individual and subsequently of relativism, has replaced the absolute nature of the Ecclesiastic Sovereign. While many have detected this, few have successfully recognized it as the repetition of earlier history; Orwell, Huxley, Bradbury, and the other dystopian novelists of the mid-20th century envision a world in which civilization as described here has ceased to exist entirely, replaced with a sprawling global artifice which keeps individuals controlled by eliminating empathy and feeling for one another. These visions of the future are insignificant except insofar as they speak to an awareness that something is not right, that what was taken for granted as a functioning social order no longer exists and is being replaced by something else—showing that in the wake of collapse, the self-awareness of the society phase is one of the few things to remain.

CONCLUSION

This chapter has attempted, briefly, to walk through three spans of 1,500 years and summarize the organisms that occupied that time. It is not by any means a completed project, but it is, the author hopes, a completed proposal. If the goal of the historian is to teach the present something about the past and, as a consequence, something about the future, the question remains, where does all of this leave the author and his readers? First and foremost, if there is any truth to the proposal at all, it is clear that the readers of this chapter are in the same position as many of their fellow men and women throughout history. Political order survives, to be sure, but it is without a doubt a false sense of calm—as Rome in the fourth century and Egypt in the tenth BC, Western Civilization has met its end with only passing notice. This does not seem a very hopeful message to gather, but, indeed, it is more hopeful than to declare that the West is "dying" or "declining"—indeed, it gives the readers a clean slate. Just as in the time of Valentinian and Theodosius, these are exciting and great times, for as one civilization fossilizes, another is readily on the rise. It is the distinct hope of the author, therefore, that he has left his readers with more questions than answers: who shall be, or is Ulfilas? Where is the next Benedict? Who plays the part of the Dorians, the Mycenaeans, the Germanics, the Christians?

Civilization		Pharaonic	Civic	Ecclesiastic
Spiritual Foundations/ Defining Features		Sun-God as prime mover; complex hierarchy of gods and men; *Pharaoh* as arbiter	Civic piety, duty to gods embodied in duty to *πόλις*and *res publica*; *Virtue* as arbiter	Tireless quest for knowledge/Truth, chivalric duty to Lord/Retainers; *God* as arbiter
Timeline				
Community/Communion	*Birth*	Pharaoh Djoser reigns c. 2691 – 2625 BC	Dorian Invasion, fall of Mycenean Greece. c. 1200 BC	Ulfilas' missionary work to Goths: AD 340s
	First Growth Spurt	Sixth Dynasty in Egypt c. 2345-2181 BC	Homer and Hesiod c. 850-650 BC	Carolingian Empire AD 742-877
	Reformation	Thutmose III reigns c. 1479 – 1425 BC	The Gracchi c. 162 – 121 BC	Martin Luther's Reformation AD 1516 – 1548
	End Community	Akhenaten (Amenhotep IV) reigns 1353-1336 BC	Reign of Caesar Augustus 27 BC – AD 14	Thirty Years' and English Civil Wars AD 1618-1651
Society/Association	*Begin Society*	Death of Akhenaten 1336 BC	Death of Augustus AD 14	Death of Cardinal Mazarin AD 1661
	"Last Gasp"[5]	Reign of Ramesses II 1279-1213 BC	Trajan's Roman Empire AD 98-117	John Wesley's Methodism AD 1770-1791
	Death	Death of Ramesses VIII 1156 BC	Death of Constantine I AD 337	Death of Pius X, WWI AD 1914

Figure 1. A Schema of Civilizations.

What two pre-histories will come together to form the next great historical organism? No historian can hope to know at this exact moment; being, however, in the post-historical (or pre-historical) period following the collapse of a Civilization, especially one so absolute and so far-reaching as the Ecclesiastic, puts the astute reader in the unique position to make predictions and become aware of trends that are repeating themselves now as they have dozens, possibly hundreds, of times in the history of human beings. If the history of civilizations briefly outlined here teaches anything, it certainly teaches that the birth of a new civilization is as inevitable as the death of the old, and the good fortune of coming from a civilization as absolute as the Ecclesiastic offers one the opportunity to perhaps detect, if not

[5] The "Last Gasp" is not mentioned in this chapter, but it is something that seems to appear in every Civilization as the last, and often late, reassertion of the original vitality of the Civilization in question. In the reign of Ramesses II, one finds some of the most memorable Pharaonic self-glorification after Akhenaten; likewise, Trajan stands out as the last Roman Emperor to engage in building projects to express the Roman religion in monuments to its civic greatness, including the ForaTraiani; finally, the expression of Western Ecclesiastical community captured in both German Pietism and Wesley's Methodism represent the final genuine development in Western Christianity. Ultimately, therefore, what defines these figures is the glorification of the "cultural sovereign" of each of their Civilization long after it had ceased to hold sway. All the other moments mentioned in the above table can be found throughout the chapter, and are described in detail save only for the "First Growth Spurt" which receives less attention than it likely deserves, since to describe all of the changes and creations going on in these major periods—the Sixth Dynasty, Homeric Greece, and Carolingian Europe—are so great that they deserve a chapter to themselves. It can suffice to say that during these periods, one sees for the first time definitive concrete expressions of a Civilization's sovereign—the monuments of the Sixth Dynasty, the culture of duty and timé in Homer and Hesiod, and the flourishing of monasticism, spread of Christianity to the Saxons, and birth of the Holy Roman Empire under Charlemagne.

shape, the coming of that new civilization. One of the greatest questions yet to be posed that surrounds the future of civilization itself and the viability of revival and resuscitation. It should be clear that these are both impossible. While it is too bold to proclaim who or what the next civilization shall be, it is at least certain that there will be no return of the West any more than there was a reborn Rome. The global nature of the West in its final phase seems only to emphasize that its death is inevitable and the Armageddon clash of the Western Gog against the Asiatic Magog is nowhere on the horizon. Indeed, the global influence of the West is the only evidence that Ecclesiastic Civilization was ever full of the vitality that defines its species' youth. Some may speak of the lingering influence of the West – but the historian may retort that Civic Civilization still exerts some influence on its successor today – there are few, however, who would say that Graeco-Roman Civilization still exists. In surrendering, as others before it, to the reign of non-native, non-spiritual sovereigns and the self-loathing such a surrender brings, the West died, and it is today a Civilization of ruins, whose influence is and shall remain residual at best. As said, it is too bold to make the claim that a proposal such as this or its author can dare to touch upon such predeterminations or such daring tasks as outlining the sovereign of a new civilization. That is not the task of the historian. Rather, by sketching out a rough image of civilization as an organism, the author has hoped to remind his audience of a truth expressed most poetically (if a little parochially) by Joseph de Maistre (1884):"*partout où vous verrez un autel, là se trouve la civilization*"—"where one sees an altar, there is Civilization" (p. 81). Find people who look skyward together rather than looking at one another individually, and there one will find a Civilization in its youth.

REFERENCES

Aeschylus (1884).*Choephoroi.*A. Sidgwick (Ed.) Oxford: Clarendon Press.

Aquinas, St. Thomas (1981).On kingship. In dicobigongiari (Ed. and Trans.), *The Political Ideas of St. Thomas Aquinas* (pp. 175-196). New York, NY: Hafner Press (Original work published in 1267).

Aquinas, St. Thomas (1988).*Aquinas on politics and ethics.* Paul E. Sigmund (Ed. and Trans.) New York, NY: W.W. Norton.

Baines, John (1991). Society, morality, and religious practice. In Byron E. Shafer (Ed.), *Religion in ancient Egypt: gods, myths, and personal practice* (pp. 123-200). Ithaca, NY: Cornell University Press.

Berlin, Isaiah (1992). The Question of Machiavelli. In Niccolo Machiavelli, *The Prince* (pp. 206-236). Robert M. Adams (Ed. and Trans.) New York, NY: W.W. Norton.

Bloch, Marc (1992). *The Historian's craft.* (Peter Putnam, Trans.) Manchester: Manchester University Press. (Original work published 1944).

Breasted, James H. (1972). *The development of religion and thought in Ancient Egypt.* Philadelphia, PA: University of Pennsylvania Press.

Budge, Sir E. A. Wallis (2008). *Egyptian religion.*San Diego, CA: Book Tree.

Camus, Albert (1965). *Essais.* Roger Quilliotand Louis Faucon (Eds.). Quetigny-Dijon: Gallimard.

Cicero, M. Tulius (1826). *De re publica.* Frankfurt-am-Main: TypographeoBroenneriano.

Cicero, M. Tulius (1890). *De natura deorum, libritres.* Boston, MA: Ginnand Co.

De Maistre, J. *Oeuvres completes.* (Vol. 4) Lyon: Vitte and Perrussel.

Euripides (2002).*Helen, Phoenecian women, orestes.* David Kovacs (Ed. and Trans.) Cambridge, MA: Harvard University Press.

Gould, John (1985). On making sense of Greek religion. In P.E. Easterling and J.V. Muir (Eds.), *Greek religion and society.* Cambridge: Cambridge University Press.

Grant, Frederick C. (1957) *Ancient Roman religion.* New York, NY: Liberal Arts Press.

Heraclitus (1987).*The Fragments.* (T.M. Robinson, Trans.) Toronto: University of Toronto Press. (Original work undated).

Hobbes, Thomas (1996). *Leviathan.* J.C.A Gaskin (Ed.) Oxford: Oxford University Press.

John of Salisbury (1963). *The Statesman's book of John of Salisbury.* (John Dickinson, Trans.) New York, NY: Russell and Russell. (Original work published c. 1159).

Joannis Saresberiensis (1855). *Patrologia Latina* (Vol. 199). J.-P. Migne, Ed. Paris: Migne.

Lendon, J.E. (2010) *Song of wrath: The Peloponnesian war begins.* New York, NY: Basic Books.

Machiavelli, Niccolo. *The Prince.* Robert M. Adams (Ed. and Trans.) New York, NY: W.W. Norton. (Original work published in 1532).

Meister Eckhart (1979).*Sermons and Treatises.*(Vol. 2). M. O'C. Walshe (Ed. and Trans.) Worcester: Element.

Murray, Gilbert (1955). *Five stages of Greek religion.* Garden City, NJ: Doubleday.

Oberman, Heiko (2006). *Luther: man between God and the Devil.* (Eileen Walliser-Schwarzbart, Trans.) New Haven: Yale. (Original work published in 1986).

Schmitt, Carl (1985). *Political theology.* (George Schwab, Trans.) Chicago, IL: University of Chicago Press. (Original work published in 1922).

Scullard, H. H. (2011). *From the Gracchi to Nero: A History of Rome 133 BC to AD 68.* New York, NY: Routledge.

Shafer, Byron (1991). Introduction. In Byron E. Shafer (Ed.), *Religion in ancient Egypt: gods, myths, and personal practice* (pp. 1-6). Ithaca, NY: Cornell University Press.

Silverman, David P. (1991) Divinity and deities in ancient Egypt. In Byron E. Shafer (Ed.), *Religion in ancient Egypt: gods, myths, and personal practice* (pp. 7-87). Ithaca, NY: Cornell University Press.

Spengler, Oswald (1922). *Der Untergang des Abendlandes.* (Vol. 1) Munich: C.H. Beck.

Spengler, Oswald (1933). *Jahre der Entscheidung.* Munich: C.H. Beck.

Southern, R.W. (1961) *The Making of the middle ages.* New Haven: Yale.

Tönnies, Ferdinand (1912). *Gemeinschaft und Gesellschaft: Grundbegriffe der reinenSoziologie.* Berlin: Karl Curtius.

Treharne, Elaine (2004). *Old and middle English c. 890-c.1400, An Anthology.* Oxford: Blackwell Publishers.

Wardman, Alan (1982). *Religion and satecraft among the Romans.* Baltimore, MD: Johns Hopkins Press.

Weber, Max (1904). Objectivity in social science. In Craig Calhoun, Joseph Gerteis, James Moody, Steven Pfaff, and IndermohanVirk (2007), *Classical Sociological Theory*(pp. 211-217)(2nded.) Oxford: Blackwell Publishing.

Welshon, Rex (2004). *The Philosophy of Nietzsche.* Quebec: McGill-Queen.

In: Spirituality and Civilization Sustainability ...
Editors: Andrew Targowski and Marek J. Celinski ISBN: 978-1-53610-729-6

Chapter 5

HUMAN AND SOCIETAL POTENTIALS FOR TRANSCENDING THE CRISIS OF CIVILIZATION

Lech W. Zacher [*]
Kozminski University, Poland

"There is much that we do not know about the future. But one thing we do know is that business as usual will not continue for much longer. Massive change is inevitable. ... Can we find another road before time runs out? ... How do we get from here to there before time runs out? ... We are in a race between political tipping points and natural tipping points. ... Mobilizing to save civilization means fundamentally restructuring the global economy in order to stabilize climate, eradicate poverty, stabilize population, restore the economy's natural support systems, and, above all, restore hope."

L. R. Brown (2009) Plan B 4.0
Mobilizing to Save Civilization

ABSTRACT

Civilization is at risk. Risks and dangers are local, national and global. Their nature is diverse – some are natural or technological, some are social, political, religious, axiological. What is desirable is not declarative discourse on various subjects as governments, corporations, churches, people but a real change of values, motivations and behavior. It is a very difficult task and, moreover, it requires a culturally differentiated approach since the world's societies are diverse. Human and societal potentials for transcending the coming crisis of civilization should be built. Many widely accepted assumptions and convictions have to be modified or radically changed: not only people's mindset and *Weltanschauung* but also human behavior needs re-engineering. Positive attitudes and values can contribute to a desirable change. Mastering technology is no less important.

[*] E-mail: lzacher@kozminski.edu.pl

INTRODUCTION: CIVILIZATION AT RISK

Civilization is at risk, endangered by climate change and climate turbulences, by tsunamis, floods, earthquakes, volcanic activities, forest fires, droughts, and the like. Non-naturally-driven dangers are also connected with civilization clashes (to recall Huntington's term), by political instabilities in many regions (e.g. North Africa, Middle East, and some parts of Asia and Latin America), by uncontrolled mass migrations, by epidemics like AIDS, by wars over resources, by big ethical conflicts, by possible use of chemical, biological, and nuclear weapons locally or by terrorists, by lack of drinking water for billions of people, and by rebellions of poor and excluded inhabitants of the globe. Drug trafficking and use in the rich countries is another concern, not to mention the growing mass unemployment, especially of young people (the Twitter class which led a revolution in North Africa exists in other countries, too). World reconfigurations are taking place (America's relative decline, new emerging powers – cf. Zakaria's book), the aging of many advanced (and democratic) societies, and changes in the proportions of races, religions, and cultures (multiculturalism appears to be unsuccessful e.g. in Europe). These risks and dangers are global or sometimes regional with wider possible impacts and tremendous costs. Also technical catastrophes should be mentioned, not just those in the past like Bhopal or Chernobyl, but recent ones like BP's Deep Horizon oil platform or the Japanese Fukushima Nuclear Power Plant.

The list of risks and dangers can be much longer. What is worth stressing is that if they come true (some already have) their destructive power can be immense, their span global or subglobal, their costs unbearable for the budget of states and households, their effects possibly surmounting ability to cope with, and moreover they can be very long-lasting. So, civilization is really in danger and may even be substantially devastated very soon if some detrimental events occur. Therefore, the risk to civilization is not a theoretical situation, but one in urgent need of intellectual and practical actions.

It is necessary to point out, however, that causes of the aforementioned dangers and risks are diverse – some are natural or technical, but some are political, social, cultural, religious and axiological. Spirituality (morality, values, culture) can work both ways, also generating hatred, intolerance, discrimination, and violence. Spirituality is not only positive, since it largely depends on context, place, and time.

Moreover, many dangers and risks are well known, even carefully observed and monitored (e.g. by satellites), but many unexpected "surprises" may emerge. So, we have to be prepared – technically, organizationally, financially – to cope with them. Strategic forward thinking is a must to enhance the future security of countries, societies, regions, the world, and humankind. However the problem is that perception of these dangers, risks and demanding requirements seems to be differentiated, not only from country to country, but also among governments, businesses, NGOs, and scientists. Risk perception is always due to some subjective evaluation. The situation gets complicated when scientists present what is typical and fully normal, that is,various opinions and views, when businesses (especially giant TNCs) and politicians play their own games, and when social movements and organizations are unable to unite. So the question appears: what values and procedures do we recommend in order to facilitate negotiations and consensus over risk perception and risk-diminishing remedies? Transparency, access to information, explicit stands and frank promises are difficult to achieve while there are contradictory interests, political adversaries at play and national security secrecy. It is so on any level – from local through national to global. Nevertheless, alerting, informing, educating, activating people everywhere can be helpful and can lead to their public engagement in support of risk agendas (in science, business, politics) and can facilitate their conscious participation in risk discourse and in decision-making processes (in democratic countries, institutions, and international organizations).

Highlighting the value-laden causes or circumstances of the present risks to civilization makes us more realistic. Political and religious declarations, often repeated for ages, concerning values such as responsibility, democracy, solidarity, humanitarianism, business ethics, and love hardly appear to be very effective in the prevention or abolition of poverty, slavery, exploitation, intolerance, racism, inequality, discrimination or violations of human rights. On the contrary, such anti-human attitudes and practices were often ideologically grounded and justified. Even now in many cases it seems that the present-day declarations of various subjects (governments, corporations, churches, people) are not really honest and trustworthy.

It is clear that in a *risk society* (and the "world risk society" – to use U. Beck's terms) a risk discourse is vital but should be honest and ethical. These values cannot be ignored in public debates. Analysis of the literature suggests that in such debates also other terms, such as responsibility, accountability, and prudence can help. Public engagements and public discussions – may elaborate other values and may lead to a well-constructed argument and consent solutions.

Assumptions, Convictions, and Clarifications

It is rather commonly assumed that our civilization is in a time of *crisis and change*. However, it should be remembered that such convictions or feelings emerged in the past. So perhaps growth and decline (crises) – together they constitute a change – are normal "behaviors" of civilization. It is naive to imagine an ever-growing trajectory of development without sinusoidal jumps and even discontinuities. The Enlightenment idea of progress – in spite of its elegance and mobilization force – should be treated in our technological civilization more carefully because of the experience gained, experience of not only positive ("progressive") effects and consequences of technology and most of its industrial applications (agricultural or military, of course, as well as related to sport, space, etc.), but also of its negative effects. So a more refined approach to civilization, its ups and downs, can be recommended. Moreover, the extended studies on civilizations (e.g. by Toynbee, Braudel, Needham) warn that civilizations can both live and die. There are many historical illustrations of this regularity. So there is no necessity that our present civilization should survive. However, it would be nice to continue. For this reason we need to re-evaluate, re-invent, and re-engineer our goals, strategies, policies, and behaviors. That is why the *idea of sustainability* (rather than progress, expansion or paradise) is so important. This is an extremely – even intellectually – hard task for the present and future generations.

One more clarification is needed. Talking in a very abstract sense about civilization is not enough, because civilization is embedded in *space and time*. So the use of this term in *plural* is justified. Alternatively, one can analyze parts or segments, also dimensions, of human civilization. The dimensions of space and time complicate the picture of the present times and impose a twofold strategy for survival – one local (not necessarily small) and one global, overwhelming. Moreover, such strategies cannot be effectively implemented in a short time, so they would also have a definite *generational dimension*. Any philosophical, educational, political, and ethical recommendations should not address the present generations of people on the planet only. It means that we assume some – not only moral – obligations to next generations (this factor is usually emphasized in sustainability studies) and we encompass their trajectory of development and limit their choices, patterns of life, behavior, achievements, etc. Some sensitive persons can ask whether we have a moral right to make these choices. Probably we do, since the survival of civilization and of mankind is at stake. We, present generations, were also limited and profiled by choices, undertakings, successes, and mistakes of our predecessors.

If we really wish to improve *conditio humana*, to make our civilization sustainable, it is necessary to seek a package of good innovative ideas, a set of general and concrete strategies, and to determine the means to achieve the goal, and a primordial condition is to find an *agent* (or agents) *of change*. Obviously, intensive pursuit of proper knowledge and various innovations (technological, economic, social, political, educational etc.) is necessary and should be timely (i.e., before possible global catastrophes undermine the prospect of sustainable development).

We cannot change civilization immediately, now, in a short time. So, debates on civilization should be *future-oriented*. Discontents of civilization (to recall Freud's old essay) have present and future dimensions. However, they can be traced historically, and they can be viewed as long-term tendencies, trends, or megatrends (to use Nesbit's term). Together with present human activities transforming the world and people's lives, these trends should be a subject of *consequentialist thinking* and *impact assessment* methods and procedures. It is therefore important to evaluate our past (if it has impacted our present situation) and existing trends, and their possible effects, especially if they are risky and detrimental. Adding to it our present activities, we define the state of things, i.e. of the civilization we live in here and now.

Important to the perspective being developed here is that any evaluation (as functional, wise, dysfunctional, etc.) assumes some criteria. Thus, in the case of civilization, there is a need to take a stand concerning its future vision; this vision can be a model, an ideal type or a scenario of a desirable future. Such a presupposition is not very promising, since it may be seen as advocating one final picture – finalistic, deterministic, teleological, or religious. The same can be supposed about a path to this final paradise. A contrasting approach can be an *open-ended* future which might emerge by evolutionary (sometimes revolutionary) processes (an array of events, emergencies, or bifurcations). Also, trajectories will be partly spontaneous, partly stimulated, controlled, steered, somewhat inertial, and chaotic. There is no final picture but, rather, many possible futures (in plural). A more *cybernetic-oriented approach* seems to be more adequate than a teleological one. Such a vision implies a different evaluation mode – not what is good or bad, functional or dysfunctional, but what *improves* human life on the planet (it is a kind of *meliorism*). Some boundary conditions which can be formulated will demarcate limits not to be surpassed. Thinking in terms of limits – especially in the case of civilization sustainability – proves to be very useful (e.g. see *Limits to Growth* of 1972 and its update published in 2004 – Meadows *et al.* – bibl.). So we seek not a final goal but rather a modest *mode of functioning* and progressing in time. Continuous improvement, social and individual, can be referred to as the Japanese idea called *kaizen*. Of course, such improvement can be measured (e.g. with quality of life indicators or a human development matrix) and monitored. Materiality and immateriality will constitute the quality of the improvement. *Process orientation* may prove to be more feasible and effective than goal orientation. The latter usually tends toward utopian thinking and as a result generates social frustration and political unrest.

As previously argued, a modest approach to shaping the future makes it open-ended. Limits, boundary conditions, and improvements are not closing this future. Civilization diversity is respected. Of significance are the occurring and expected risks. So again, the goal is not to construct a picture of the ideal future, but to make a persistent effort to prevent environmental and economic collapse. Preventive strategies can more easily be socially and internationally accepted (*cf.* Brown 2011). Such strategies should reflect not only a will but also abilities, obligations, and duties (e.g. ethical, solidarity type) of various actors and stakeholders (governments, corporations, international institutions, especially financial, social movement organizations, NGOs, and individuals). So, the strategies and actions they impose as projects, programs, and undertakings should be of material and immaterial nature. Although this type of thinking is well-known, implementation of the UN Millennium Goals has been delayed and does not seem very successful.

Perhaps more efforts on a local, grassroots scale might be more effective. Moreover, present possibilities of *networking* on all levels are unprecedented and make it possible to coordinate actions, build coalitions, and cooperate. Such possibilities are often underestimated or overlooked. Still a *state-dependent thinking* connected with anti-crisis interventionism (recommended by Keynes and performed many times, recently by Barack Obama), with experiences of the communist centrally planned economy, and in some countries with a political system of state capitalism, is still pretty strong, and even mentally difficult to discard. Hence more non-state governance is needed and should be learned and diffused widely. Through Internet networking such attempts are well instrumented. Again, some values here are important as well, such as the will of communication, consensus seeking, and cooperation.

Centralistic thinking was also, though not intentionally, promoted by globalists and their organizations (e.g. Club of Rome). Global thinking overlooked localities. A rather utopian idea of a world government, parliament etc. is still being called for. The centrally-driven actions of the UN cannot change the world. The new concept of *glocalization* looks promising but is still far from being well refined. Not only "think globally, act locally" but also "think locally to be effective globally" can be announced as a new slogan. Paradoxically, decentralizationist thinking can greatly contribute also at a global level.

There are more reasons not to mesmerize people by visions of a better future. Firstly, there is the old anecdote: "The better future already was." Seriously, many economists point out that there may be no return to the past (e.g. to cheap oil times). Secondly, societies are structured generationally; they are not in one bloc. People live longer, so there are even more generations living at the same time than before. The generations have differentiated needs, expectations, aspirations, and dreams, and also various evaluation criteria and propensities, e.g. to risk, or to wait for "better times." Finally, it would be arrogant – by the present decision-making generation – to plan and organize today the future world for next – yet non-existent – generations. We should only try to secure for them better conditions in general, larger areas of choice and fewer limits. Future choices – even not very distant – can be totally different than at present. Of course, changes of the conditions of choice cannot be precisely predicted, if at all. Moreover, not only the changed conditions will matter, but the next generations may have other priorities (e.g. less military spending or disarmament), too, and other evaluations than we now have of such things as GMO risks (e.g. due to high food deficit and prices). Let us grant them a right and a possibility to be free and rational – according to their own values and future conditions.

Anyway, convictions of many globalists and universalists prophesying *one ideal future for all* have proved to be naive. Our civilization of diversity will not accept such a simplistic solution because it is incompatible with reality. In spite of some universalizing tendencies, some market-driven imitations due to foreign trade and media, as well as some cultural, religious, and political effects of integration and imitation, there are no reports of any essential cohesion on a world scale. Alas, perhaps. But even immigrants in the host countries do not want to use a foreign language, even on the Internet. The defeat of a universalistic dream is a fact even though many particular ideologies or religions are declared as universalistic. However, the situation is not totally hopeless. What was thought as global can be decomposed and some general (global, universal) frameworks should be sought. These frameworks can be value-laden as well, e.g. peace, peaceful conflict resolutions, non-aggressive relations, looking for justice in international relations, for fair trade, openness, readiness to help in cases of crises, catastrophes, cooperative attitudes. And it is not really important by what motivations they are driven: religious, humanitarian, rationalistic or even a fear of uncertain future.

And finally what can be suggested here is properly funded research concerning the *problem approach* discussed above. Politicians, media, NGOs, social activists and enlightened business people should learn, propagate and implement it in their realms.

Gathering and analyzing real indicators of improvement (or of possible worsening) leads down to earth, to a real world which consists of states (nation-states), societies, political-economic groupings (as the EU), TNCs, international institutions, and organizations. This world is overwhelmingly differentiated in many dimensions such as politics, control, education, culture, socio-political systems or economic mechanisms. It is clear that strategies, policies, understandings – leading to improvement in the conditions of human existence – of various world actors and stakeholders will be correspondingly differentiated as well. Of course, the globalization discourse can be added here to indicate other important dimensions (and boundary conditions).

Toward a Positive Cultural Mindset of People

In spite of being in systems, groups and networks, people have their own individual *mindset* and *Weltanschauung*. They are loaded with knowledge, values, and attitudes of various kinds. For a better future world, sustainable and friendly to all people, a strong domination of positive features and mental and informational "inputs" is desirable and even necessary. However, this better world is not certain and does not occur by default. There is room for action and intellectual efforts in all fields of human activity to facilitate transforming people in a positive direction. People change individually and socially; there were many historical cases; however, some directions were not necessarily worthy of moral affirmation. People were mobilized by their various leaders to wars, conquests, hatred and aggression, to discrimination against other races, religions, and convictions, and they were encouraged to participate in ethnic cleansing, torture, and other atrocities.

The historical record of humanity is loaded with rather "bad stories." To mention a few examples: religious wars in Europe and crusades, the extermination of American Indians, conquest and colonization, the Inquisition, the genocide of Armenians, world wars, atomic bombing, the Holocaust, totalitarian regimes, neocolonialist conflicts and wars, jihad, exploitation of poor countries, etc. One could add to this list also the many inhuman rules and activities within particular countries and societies. So we are not starting from scratch but with a heavy burden of negative experiences.

Amelioration of human behavior can occur in dimensions of an individual, a group, a society and mankind. However, it is far from simple to describe this behavior in terms of propensities, attitudes, socialization impacts, cultural imprints and filters, values, etc. It is equally difficult to trace and explain their interactions, feedback or linkages. Many scientific disciplines work on that – psychology, psychiatry, sociology, biosociology, medicine, anthropology, law sciences and others.

Dimensions and acts of human behavior are interpreted in many ways. They are attributed to human nature, to biology, and there are also religious explanations; social embedding and political and economic systems are also blamed, not to mention illnesses, stress, traumas, poverty, hopelessness, disabilities, etc. That is why individual human behavior is hard to predict and to evaluate multi-dimensionally. Statistical behavior of a society is probably easier to forecast and investigate (e.g. by opinion polls). Nevertheless, while talking about the future of humanity a reflection – even if not deep or comprehensive – can be helpful. Transformative propensities, attitudes, moral and cultural values are of special importance. In spite of the above-mentioned difficulties, a general "map" of these behaviors can be sketched.

Good and bad values (anti-values that serve bad goals) clash. Throughout human history there are different origins, definitions and justifications of what is good and bad. Philosophic, religious, and political debates on this subject are well-known. If we want to get rid of bad values we cannot ignore them; we have to identify them first, and then fight them. Ideologies, religious, and political thought did it many, many times.

It may be worthwhile to sketch a list of bad values. The list below is certainly incomplete; rather, it is an array of frequently discussed examples:

- egotism, egocentricity
- greed
- extreme individualism
- hatred
- intolerance
- insensitivity.

There are also negative attitudes and behaviors and processes connected with bad values:

- anti-intellectualism	- mercenariness
- superficiality	- infantility
- hostility	- over-consumptionism
- aggressiveness	- escapism
- quarrelsomeness	- aggression
- narcissism	- disorder
- permissiveness	- suspiciousness
- irresponsibility	- discrimination
- distrust	- corruption
- racial and other prejudices	- infidelity
- dishonesty	- authoritarianism
- exclusivity	- betrayal
- fanaticism	- cruelty
	- social indifference

These lists are far from complete. Moreover, evaluation of their "items" may be not unanimous in all cases. For example, greed and egotism are considered as the most important motivations of economic activity (it is overlooked that A. Smith was not only interested in wealth creation but also in moral philosophy – see his "The Theory of Moral Sentiments"). Consumption, which may be treated by economists and business people as a driver of production, is in its present form called over-consumption (consumptionism was condemned not once by Pope John Paul II). There are also many other features, and convictions that cause controversies. e.g., how to classify the stupidity or primitivization of the hedonistic culture and low-level entertainment? Even in these questions there are value judgments. In some cases what will be immoral or sinful under specific conditions can be treated less rigorously (during a war or a revolution).

Evil behavior seems more clear to classify, when it comes to some cruel tradition such as the circumcision of girls (more than 100 million cases in Africa and some other countries), and it is more complicated since there are not many complaints. Another example is competition which is good in sports but can be rough and dishonest in business and politics. For example, neo-liberal capitalism is often labeled Social Darwinism.

Origins and expressions of evil will probably stay controversial forever. Of course, some theological and scientific analyses and insights (e.g. of Freud, Marx, Lorenz, Wilson, Dawkins, Zimbardo, John Paul II) are helpful for understanding the issue. Ideologies and religions have always declared the will to change man, to transform man into a morally superior creature. There is some significant progress here and there already, and there are many institutional, legal, and organizational changes, and there are international regulations, laws, conventions, treaties and agreements, not to mention social customs and habits. Democracy and human rights are good examples of improvements that are advantageous for all.

Probably to juxtapose a list of positive attitudes, values, behaviors would be more useful than criticizing bad characteristics of humanity. Again, without even trying to properly classify all people's characteristics, attitudes, behavior, expressions of good and their good impacts, one can mention such "things" as:

morality and ethics
spirituality
love
individual and social sensitivity
altruism
solidarity
honesty
trust
conviviality (to recall the term coined by I. Illich)
humanism (and eco-humanism)
mercy
compassion
social activism
stewardship
cooperativeness
peacefulness
nonviolent actions (e.g. Gandhi, Mandela, Martin Luther King, Wałęsa)
humanitarianism
respectfulness
tolerance
consolation
responsibility
friendship
brotherhood
openess
modesty
respect of law
prudence
accountability
reflexivity
wisdom

Of course, this list could be much expanded. All mentioned characteristics may work for peace, justice, equity, cooperation (from local to global level), for cross-culturalism, sustainability, culture of sharing and gifts etc. The potential for these values is great, and already in use, but not widespread and effective enough. This capability should be improved.

This is not a problem to be solved, this is a predicament of mankind to which we have to respond wisely and globally (individually and locally as well). Massive multilevel efforts, even limited in their strength, on a large scale can probably be a good response. Our networked and online world is an asset to this end.

So a recipe seems to be simple – in very general, abstract terms: one should limit, diminish, and possibly eliminate bad sides of man and his/her activities and in contrast – promote, teach, and reward good ones. This recipe is easy to prescribe, difficult to implement. Efforts are already thousands of years old in this respect. Are we civilized or overcivilized or perhaps undercivilized and in many areas just barbarians? Moreover, everything bad goes to a new social space which is cyberspace, where there are nasty hackers, there is bullying, stalking, hatred, primitivism, stupidity, aggression, manipulation, and so on. The biggest challenge nowadays – rather overlooked because of free-market liberalistic ideology – is to act for improving Internet contents (e.g. more knowledge and culture, more social actions, more mutual help and support, more education, values, spirituality, and less spam, info garbage, less criminal behavior, less pornography, less primitivity).

There are two political and organizational ways of improving the present situation in many countries and the whole world. One is to increase regulations, control, censorship, invigilation, more guards and police, prosecutors and judges, harsher punishments, more prisons and prisoners (also controlled electronically). Such an Orwellian type of governance is often supported by right wing, populist or authoritarian ideologues, politicians, political parties etc. We have never had so many security cameras, invigilation (even global as Echelon), guards, and prisoners before. This approach is extremely costly and not very effective.

A more sophisticated and comprehensive way should be recommended, though difficult and long-term. This is to be through education, knowledge, culture development, social activism and dedication, democracy, sharing responsibility, participation in debates and action, and also on a global scale. Of course, some ongoing activities of this kind are enriching social and cultural capitals (to use the jargon of management sciences). Such approaches and means can be instrumental in achieving social and civilizational sustainability. Good attitudes, values and patterns of behavior can be attributed to many historical and contemporary persons – philosophers, scientists, bishops, charismatic political leaders, international activists and many less known or unknown people. To make an exemplary list is a persistent temptation. The following list is not presented according to importance or influence but rather to time sequence (more or less). So, there are positive authorities, such as: Socrates, Seneca, Marcus Aurelius, Plato, St. Augustine, Kant, de Tocqueville, Jefferson, Kirkegaard, Sartre, Marcel, Mounier, Arendt, Fromm, Buber, Helder Camara, Jonas, Levinas, Galbraith, Peccei, Singer, Klein, Mother Theresa, Tutu. They formulated ideas which can be inspiring today. Let us name a few: from Plato's triad of truth, good and beauty to sanctity, from respecting otherness to freedom and democracy, from moral imperative to liberation theology, from environmental responsibility to animal rights, from the good society concept to alterglobalism. Another long list of writers and poets who deserve to be authorities and to be followed intellectually can be added, too.

Attempts were made in the social sciences to create an ideal or a model of man, a model that reflected their profile and general characteristics. So *homo sapiens* can be *homo oeconomicus, homo ludens, homo consumens, homo destruens, homo creator, homo technicus, homo globatus, homo politicus, homo universalis, homo rationalis, homo prudens, homo solidaritus, homo informaticus, netizen* and *global netizen* (to introduce a cyberspace dimension). These labels are the shortest descriptions of man's identity, profile, attitude, and sometimes conditioning. Obviously, these descriptors reflect a dominant characteristic. In reality man is an even more complex creature embedded in a certain culture, time, and space (also cyberspace). But what can be learned from this list is that, in these days, *homo sapiens is best characterized by* multidimensionality. However, to each of the models some constitutive features can be assigned, and not all are positive.

Role models to listen to, obey and emulate may be not only eminent individuals. These can be various institutions of religious, social, political, scientific or consumer nature, such as media. State agencies, courts, churches, concerned citizens, scientific associations, public interest organizations, NGOs, INGOs and transnational activists can be involved in constructing and promoting *sustainability values*. Both public and private, local, national and global, professional or lay citizen organizations can influence the government or companies, also via the Internet. Activism is what is needed.

Again, good values are not difficult to identify and find. They are found in philosophies, religions, and ideologies. Examples can be taken from, say, Judaism, Christianity, Buddhism, Islam, Taoism, Zen, Bahá' and Faith, humanism, eco-humanism, feminism, rationalism, atheism, socialism, globalism, alterglobalism and others. The origin of good is not important; good *per se* is what counts.

The more efforts made, the better chance to approach a sustainable trajectory. Some may strive for that, trying to construct a map of the "goals for mankind" (it is the title of E. Laszlo's report to the Club of Rome in 1977, gathering official documents and declarations) or Millennium Goals (UN), some prepare a kind of decalogue to obey (e.g. Coates), and finally some more practically oriented persons will suggest how to implement various recommendations (Heinberg, Lerch 2010). Values embedded in human minds should diffuse into their day-to-day practice. There is a chance for improvement of *conditio humana* if the posterity do not concentrate only on wealth multiplication, excessive consumption, and pop-entertainment.

Future generations will be probably quite different from us axiologically, psychologically, and socially. Their values, attitudes, approaches, and behavior cannot be predicted because we are in our own chains and because it is a long-term issue. Anyway, one can assume rather radical changes and, perhaps, surprises of unimaginable kinds. We can only imagine the future by observing present trends, those already established and those in their embryonic stage. However, conservationists and old people prefer to believe that the future will be similar, perhaps only incrementally modified.

There is much research showing that there are already significant changes. Some empirical experience already exists. To illustrate the changes introduced by cyberspace, some new terms were coined to label people. So there are "digital natives" (or "born digital") – very young users born and raised in digital setting, very skillful in use of ICTs. Older people, with some practical skills, but not fully dependent ("integrated") on computer and the Internet can be called "digital immigrants" (terms introduced by G. Small – a neurologist who investigated this issue). Of course, there is a class of the "digitally excluded," and, on a societal and international scale, this exclusion produces the so called *digital divide*. There is a pressing need to study how the digital environment (not only computers and the Internet but also all the popular electronics and gadgets such as mobiles, iPhones, game consoles, tablets and the like) influences these categories of people. Small's research showed that digital natives even have some brain changes, not to mention alterations in behavior (coordination with computers, Internet dependence or info-holism, difficulties with face to face contacts). Certainly the technology they use – not only hardware or software, but also network architecture, protocols, cyberspace and other users – composes a system, powerful and interactive. We cannot imagine its impact in the future when the digital only are born, i.e. the next generations of information society which is now emerging in advanced countries. New environments, new technical means and ambient intelligence may change people radically, also changing their attitudes, aspirations, values, and behavior. The virtual reality of cyberspace can become an "alternative home place," a parallel world, which enables disembodiment, dislocation, personal construction of identity (or multi-identity) and "makes traditional body codes, community, and geographic place irrelevant" (Opie 2008:10). "Placelessness" and overwhelming electronically-driven connectivity may cause the rise of indifference to the real and actual world. How then to debate the risks, challenges, and the future of civilization? Historically, territories created national myths of place and nation, national identity. What will be created by such placelessness and artificiality of computer worlds around? The real world was firm, durable, authentic, reliable. Cyberspace is not its "false replica," but seems to be a new world. So the human world will be hybrid. Its big part, growing and diffusing into the real world, already functions according to different rules, allows and even encourages (Zittrain 2008) "bad things" such as production and wide distribution of spam, online viruses, malware, phishing, and fraud. The problem occurs on a *scale* (even global) and causes *immediate impact*, never possible before. Cyberspace ideology praises such things as open collective intelligence, individual freedom, opportunities of self-expression, online collaboration, and a free culture. Additionally there are ideas and demand for free and open software as a collective technical system which "reconfigures knowledge and power" (Kelty 2008:3).

There are of course many more new and unexpected features of cyberspace inhabitants. Can we, the present "ruling" generation, program their lives and the future? They can ignore it or reject. Their aspirations and expectations may be totally different; the same refers to their ambitions and their moral authorities. Who will be their gurus – geeks or hackers like Mitnick, or inventors and businesspeople like Gates and Zuckerberg or Assange, the creator of Wikileaks or perhaps Internet pop culture celebrities (such as Lady Gaga)? In rather conservative expectations they may be – perhaps not all – good netizens, and also global netizens, showing some concern about the world and civilization. Some also believe in cross-generational "bridges" easing tensions and diminishing divides. Anyway visioning or programming the future for the next "digitalized" generations is a risky business today.

Societies or Socio-Technical Systems?

Civilization can be viewed as a material foundation of societies (some definitions include also culture as immaterial element). Anyway, technology is its dramatically vital component, asset and force. Technology became "a novel form of human power," embedded in the existing societies. It is not separate, abstract, or functioning outside all contexts. Technology consists of objects, machines, procedures, models, technological research, and skills, but what is important is that technology can be treated as a system, complex, intertwined, dynamic, generating a multiplicity of various (positive and negative) impacts. Moreover technology – especially in civilizationally developed societies – is interconnected with social systems. Members of such societies are technologically literate and equipped. They use technology (or rather a stock of technologies) in various ways. Technology becomes a *causal agent of change* in the opinion of many (see Marx 2010). However, technology demonstrates some autonomy (you cannot stop using technologies, or stop immediately all technical research, labs and universities, you cannot get rid of transportation, gadgets and the like. Also, some inertia develops in some "channels" that is difficult to modify or re-engineer. But a techno-system is dependent on social systems. Throughout history societies have learned how to use increasingly complicated technical systems; they invented and projected them, operated, modified, modernized them, and have been affected by them. In spite of feedback, there is a kind of asymmetry in mutual interactions of these two systems – technology and society. Talking about one socio-technical system, we can say that its components are not equally powerful over time. Since the middle of the last century the technological component seems to have become stronger. This strength is due in part to the sacralization of science and the deification of technology. Industrial societies have transformed themselves into technological ones; current versions of their names are: *e-society*, *information society*, *cyber-society*, *digital society*, *virtual society*. All these names are technologically driven. Thus it is not easy to reject the convenient temptation to accept technological determinism (at least for the present period and in the light and temporary form). Large complex socio-technical systems are places, or rather spaces of interconnected influences of both sides. People create, invent, exploit, modify, improve and apply technology to achieve certain social or human (individual) goals (military, economic, medical etc.). Moreover, they decide on technology: to finance technical research and innovation, to use technology and to what degree, to import machines, share know-how, to buy technical objects for household use and whether to play with new gadgets or not. Decision-makers are many: governments, corporations, universities, military, media and mass consumers. Demand for technological products is vital for the development of nations (all products are made with the help of technology or/and are technical objects plus instrumental knowledge). Of course, generalizations should be limited since the world's "technological landscape" is extremely differentiated. What is now called "civilization of diversity" also refers to technology, its level, stock, use, skills, effectiveness, and negative side effects. There are leaders who are world sources and repositories of technology, especially cutting edge technology. The rest of the world is greatly dependent. However, the new emerging powers (China, India, Brazil) can create a *multipolar technological world* rather soon. Technological acceleration – existing for years and centuries – makes technological gaps even wider. However, even technologically marginalized and excluded countries and their societies are what we can call passive users in the globalized and networked world. Additionally, they may be impacted by "dirty industries" or toxic waste exported to them. They are also impacted by global media and international politics (of G8, World Bank, IMF or WTO to name a few). They may experience more detrimental than positive effects of technology in service of their modernization. So some ethical recommendations can be formulated: do not destroy the environment, health, or the social life of the poor and dependent countries, do not capitalize on your bigger force, do not bribe their elites. Help them, instead, to develop technology, to assimilate new patterns of growth. Moreover, technologies for such countries, especially those which have large populations and low skills and no technical culture, should be tailored specifically to be appropriate to their real abilities (E. F. Schumacher four decades ago suggested the so-called intermediate technology and, later, the somewhat generalized "appropriate" technology). Technical assistance (done through UNIDO) should be accompanied by aid and cooperation – not by brain drain and making dependent. These recommendations are familiar to governments, business, and international institutions, but results are still not satisfactory. Perhaps the reason is that thinking and actions are subjugated to profit making and political game – not to values and ideals. There should be higher demands more from business people (not only CSR principles, which are often just a PR instrument), from politicians (preoccupied with local or country interests and the next election). But how to execute obedience to values in the world of competition, contradictory interests and growing political chaos? Media (public at least) should expose “bad practices,” condemn them and propagate “good practices,” through social movement organizations, NGOs, INGOs, churches, concerned scientists or the human *multitude* (to recall Hardt and Negri's term). Strengthened by ICTs and empowered as stakeholders, these can be quite significant local, national and global actors. So socially-oriented activism, openness, and cross-border cooperation are values to implement widely. This would mean a crucial psychological shift and progress towards enforcing human rights all over the world. Socio-technical systems are more than a social fabric. They try to integrate technological values (e.g. speed, precision, resistance, firmness, reliability, technological aesthetics) and socio-human values (described in the previous section). Material and immaterial values should co-exist and co-operate. The power of the social and socio-technical systems depends on value-assets carried by individual people and framing them – positively or not – through social rules, customs, networks, legal regulations, etc. To obtain sustainability, i.e. a stage (or rather a trajectory) “which can be maintained over time” (Heinberg, Lerch 2010), perhaps for centuries, but not forever, both “sides” of the system should make adequate efforts. Proportions and balance (a long term dynamic equilibrium) are important. Societies should not tame technology but stimulate it, and technology should serve societies well by not generating too much risk or too many negative side effects. So, there is a kind of co-evolution and co-production of technology and society (Jasanoff wrote in this sense on science and society; Jasanoff 2004), and of course science and technology at present are intertwined. Harmonizing the two subsystems – technology and society – implies wise mastery of technology (which is semi-autonomous and, through its connection with science, cognitively and practically oriented) and elaboration a societal strategy oriented towards sustainability. Building such a *societal potential* based on knowledge and values is a challenge for the civilization. The main characteristic of the world societies is their *heterogeneity*. Also, internally they are rarely homogenous. That is why there is no one good recipe for all, and that is why their future should be discussed in their plurality. The *world potential* for transcending the present crisis of civilization (partly ongoing, partly coming) will not be simply a sum total of the countries’ potentials. For the sake of all and of the global good, affluent countries and international institutions should try to coordinate individual efforts and support “weak chains” in order to reach a more sustainable state of the world. Flows of information, knowledge, technologies, technical assistance, financial aid, and political advice are indispensable. Therefore, the values needed are such as solidarity, global responsibility, cosmopolitanism, international justice and equity, cooperation and commonality. Also sustainability can be treated as a value, synthesizing other values and making them policy- and behavior-oriented. Observers of the evolution and transformations of the world societies, their directions, pace, and effects should consider not only their internal potentials and their capacity for change, but also international networking and possible synergies. Big disparities, divides, and exclusions do not contribute to the sustainability trajectory. So not only values and moral reasons but also pragmatic efforts should be involved.

Conclusion

Modern narratives concerning the many signs of the crisis of civilization have two dimensions: to indicate risks and to warn national and world actors and stakeholders of various kinds, and also to elicit some opposition to prevailing trends, patterns and activities (of business, governments, people) and to mobilize a counter-attack – intellectual, psychological, moral, civic and international. This offensive can be built around the concept (and value) of sustainability, which is a trajectory assuring (probably, if actions are massive and on time) the survival of civilization and a possible improvement of human life on the planet.

There is no *global society* (however the term is used frequently to mean networking and globalization). Still, societies function in nation-states, and people are in various structures, so there are social ties; there is a local level and people living in communities. People as individuals, living in families or alone in households, also have to be considered. Moreover many people "live" in cyberspace, in network communities, Internet tribes or they are cyber-nomads. Hybridization of technologically advanced societies is a fact, and so is increasing disintegration. Traditional societies of ties become *hybrid societies of contacts*. Present *e-societies* will be evolving in time even more (Zacher 2007). All this illustrates a complexity of efforts toward a sustainable path of development in particular societies, regions, and the whole world.

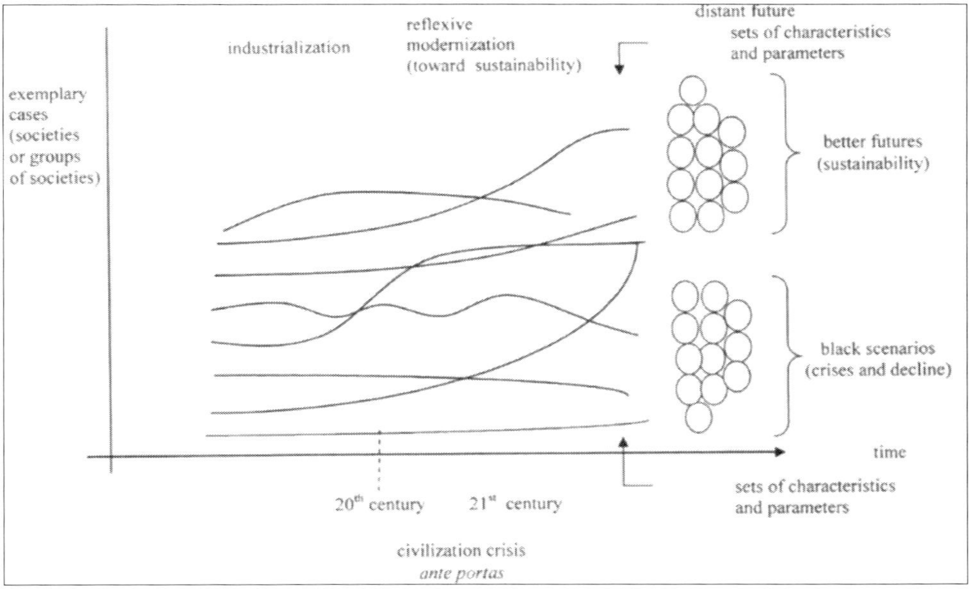

Figure 1. Hypothetical trajectories of civilizational development toward sustainable futures (a simplified model).

Rather than elaborate on utopian visions of the desirable future that can be enforced by would-be wisdom societies, it seems more rational to concentrate on the present state of societies, the leading ones and the rest, and offer them modest advice – act now more wisely and self-reflectively. Wisdom can be seen as a process based not only on knowledge but also on experience, practice, values, and imagination. So building a decent cultural ability for change toward a sustainable trajectory of civilization and reflexive modernization within such trajectory can prove more effective than any revolutionary moves. So the civilization trajectories can be modeled as in Figure 1.

REFERENCES

Barnett, C. et al. (2011). *Globalizing responsibility – The political rationalities of ethical consumption*. Chichester: Wiley.

Beck, U. (1999). *World risk society*. Cambridge, MA: Polity Press.

Beck, D. E., Cowen, Ch. C. (2006). *Spiral dynamics – mastering values, leadership, and change – exploring the new science of memetics*. Malden, MA: Blackwell.

Brown, L. R. (1981). *Building a sustainable society*. New York – London: Norton.

Brown, L. R. (2011). *World on edge*. London – Washington, DC: Earthscan.

Coates, J. F. (2007). *A Bill of rights for 21st century America*. Washington, DC: The Kanawha Institute.

De Nardis, L. (2009). *Protocol politics – the globalization of internet governance*. Cambridge, MA: MIT Press.

Dryzek, J. (1997). *The politics of the earth: environmental discourses*. Oxford: Oxford University Press.

Elliott, A., Lemert, C. (2006). T*he new individualism: the emotional costs of globalization*. London: Routledge.

Freud, S. (1962). *Civilization and its discontents*. New York: Norton.

Friedel, R. (2007). *A culture of improvement – technology and the Western Millennium*. Cambridge, MA: MIT Press.

Grundmann, R., Stehr, N. (2003). Social control and knowledge in democratic societies. *Science and Public Policy*, Vol. 30 (3):183-188.

Grunwald, A. (2010). *Technikfolgenabschätzung – eine Einführung*. Berlin: Sigma.

Gulbrandsen, L. H. (2010). *Transnational environmental governance – the emergence and effects of the certification of forestsand fisheries*. Cheltenham: Edward Elgar.

Hardt, M., Negri, A. (2004). *Multitude*. New York: Penguin.

Heinberg, R., Lerch, D. (Eds.). (2010). *The post-carbon reader. Managing the 21st century's sustainability crisis*. Healdsburg, CA: Watershed Media.

Hobson, K. (2002). Competing discourses of sustainable consumption: does the rationalization of lifestyles make sense? *Environmental Politics*, Vol. 11 (2):95-120.

Hughes, T. P. (2004). *Human-built world: how to think about technology and culture*. Chicago: Chicago University Press.

Illich, I. (2000). *Tools for conviviality*. London: Marion Boyars Publishers Ltd.

Jackson, T. (2009). *Prosperity without growth*. London – Washington, D.C.: Earthscan.

Jasanoff, S. (Ed.). (2006). *States of knowledge. The co-production of science and social order*. London – New York: Routledge.

Kelty, Ch. M. (2008). *Two bits: the cultural significance of free software*. Durham, NC: Duke University Press.

Klang, M., Murray, A. (Eds.). (2005). *Human rights in the digital age*. London: Routledge – Cavendish.

Lach, D., Sanford, S. (2010). Public understanding of science and technology embedded in complex institutional settings, *Public Understanding of Science*, Vol. 19 (2):130-146.

Laszlo, E. et al. (1977). *Goals for mankind*. New York: Dutton.

Leach, M., Scooner, I., Wynne, B. (2005). *Science and citizens. globalization and the challenge of engagement*. London: Zed Books.

Leone, R. C., Anrig, C., Jr. (Eds.). (2003). *The war on our freedoms – civil liberties in the age of terrorism*. New York: Public Affairs.

Leydesdorff, L. (2006). *The knowledge – based economy: modeled, measured, simulated.* Boca Raton, FL: Universal Publishers.

Lombardo, Th. (2006). *Contemporary futurist thought – science, fiction, future studies, and theories and visions of the future in the last century*. Bloomington, IND. – Central Milton Keynes: AuthorHouse.

Loorbach, D. (2007). *Transition management – The new mode of governance for sustainable development*. Utrecht: International Books.

Mack, T. C. (2006). *Creating global strategies for humanity's future*. Bethesda, MD: WFS.

Mack, T. C. (2007). *Hopes and visions for the 21st century*. Bethesda, MD: WFS.

Marx, L. (2010). Technology – the emergence of hazardous concept. *Technology and Culture*, Vol. 51(3):561-577.

Meadows, D. et al. (2004). Limits to growth – the 30-year update. *White River Junction*, VT: Chelsea Green.

Meadows, D. (2009). Interview with US economist Dennis Meadows: 'Copenhagen is about doing as little as possible', *Spiegel Online International*, 12/09/2009 http://www.spiegel.de/international/world /0,1518,666175,00.html.

Naisbitt, J. (1984). *Megatrends*. New York: Warner Books.

Naisbitt, J. (2006). *Mind set! reset your thinking and see the future*. New York: Collins.

Oehme I., Seebacher, U. (Eds.). (2005). *Corporate sustainability theoretical perspectives and practical approaches.* München – Wien: Profil.

Ogilvy, J. A. (2002). *Creating better futures – scenario planning as a tool for a better tomorrow*. New York: Oxford University Press.

Opie, J. (2008). *Virtual America: sleepwalking through paradise*. Lincoln, NB: University of Nebraska Press.

Rose, N. (2007). *The Politics of life itself: biomedicine, power, and subjectivity in the twenty – first century*. Princeton, NJ: Princeton University Press.

Sayfang, G. (2009). *The new economics of sustainable consumption*. Hampshire: Palgrave Macmillan.

Schudson, M. (2007). Citizens, consumers, and the good society. *The ANNALS of American Academy of Political and Social Science*, Vol. 611 (1):236-249.

Schumacher, E. F. (1973). *Small is beautiful – economics as if people mattered.* New York: Harper and Row.

Searle, J. R. (2010). M*aking the social world: the structure of human civilization.* Oxford: Oxford University Press.

Small, G. (2008). *iBrain: surviving the technological alteration of the modern mind.* New York: Harper/Collins.

Smith, A. (2000). *The theory of moral sentiments*. Amherst, NY: Prometheus Books.

Sykes, B. (2004). *A future without men – Adam's curse*. New York – London: Norton.

Voss, J.-P. et al. (Eds.). (2007) *Reflexive governance for sustainable development.* Cheltenham: Edward Elgar.

Wagner, C. G. (2008). *Seeing the future through new eyes*. Bethesda. MD: WFS.

Zacher, L. W. (2007). E-transformations of societies. In: Veikki-Antiroiko, A. (Ed.). *Electronic Governemnt: Concepts, Methodologies, Tools and Applications* (pp. 3754-3763). Hershey – New York: IGI Global.

Zacher, L. W. (2008). Some repetitive reflections on visioning the future. In: Sharma, S., Sharma, P. K. (Eds.). *Transformative Pathways: Attainable Utopias* (pp. 83-106). Jaipur: Prateekasha Publications.

Zacher, L. W. (2009). Information society discourse. In: *Encyclopedia of Information Science and Technology* (2nd edition pp. 1985-1993). Hershey: PA, IGI Global.

Zakaria, F. (2008). *The Post-American world*. New York: Norton.

Zittrain, J. (2008). The future of the internet – and how to stop it. *New Haven*, Conn.: Yale University Press.

PART B

THE ROLE OF SACRED SPIRITUALITY IN CIVILIZATIONAL DEVELOPMENT

In: Spirituality and Civilization Sustainability ... ISBN: 978-1-53610-729-6
Editors: Andrew Targowski and Marek J. Celinski

Chapter 6

THE ROLE OF RELIGION IN CIVILIZATIONAL DEVELOPMENT

Ashok Kumar Malhotra*
SUNY College at Oneonta, New York, US

ABSTRACT

In this chapter the question of what is the relationship between religion and civilization will be answered along with other associated questions. Two competing theories had been bandied about. The first one held by V. Gordon Childe states that it is civilization, which gave rise to religion. Through his most recent discovery of an ancient temple in Turkey, archeologist Klaus Schmidt theorizes the opposite view. However, both emphasize the importance of religion as a major defining force of civilization.

The history of the past 4,500 years reveals the influence of the great religions on their respective civilizations. The Indic religions of Hinduism, Buddhism, Jainism and Sikhism whose views range from polytheism to monism to atheism had created unique Eastern civilizations, different from the Western civilizations created by the monotheistic Abrahamic religions of Judaism, Christianity and Islam. A sample comparison of the Indic religions with the Abrahamic religions reveals the contrasting mind-sets that are fundamental to their theologies and belief systems. These mind-sets appear to be at the basis of conflict within the Abrahamic faiths and lack of conflict within the Indic faiths.

In the Indic religion of Hinduism, whose views range from a belief in many deities (polytheism), one deity (monotheism), an absolute principle (monism) or no deity (atheism) never used armies to clash with its parent religion of Hinduism or with each other. Instead, like a functional family, they got together to conduct public debates on issues pertaining to their unique faiths. They only fought intellectual battles through arguments and discussions that were well designed to convince the opponent. In contrast, Judaism as the source of the monotheistic religions shows major clashes between it and its offspring. Historically, Christianity has been at loggerheads with Judaism and Islam, whereas Islam in turn has been fighting endless battles against both Christianity and Judaism. These clashes are still continuing into the 20th and 21st centuries."

According to Radhakrishnan, *Spiritual Humanism* could become the bond between the Indic and Abrahamic religions. By bringing "together the Oriental Inwardness and

* E-mail: Ashok.Malhotra@oneonta.edu

Occidental Activism," it could develop into the hallmark of the 21st century where religions should make a move from monotheism towards monism i.e. from a belief in only one god, only one book and only one way towards one spiritual principle with infinite attributes towards whose understanding all the existing religions and their books would contribute their insights.

INTRODUCTION

What is the relationship between religion and civilization? What gave birth to whom? Two competing theories had been bandied about. The first one held by the anthropologists, states that it is civilization that gave rise to religion. V. Gordon Childe, the great proponent of this theory, believes that it was agriculture that provided "the necessary spark that led to villages and ignited civilization.

Organized religion began as a way of salving the tensions that inevitably arose when hunter-gatherers settled down, became farmers, and developed large societies...Though primitive religious practices...burying the dead, creating cave art and figurines...had emerged tens of thousands of years earlier, organized religion arose...only when a common vision of celestial order was needed to bind together these big, new, fragile groups of humankind" (Mann 2011:56-57).

However, through his most recent discovery of an ancient temple in Turkey, archeologist Klaus Schmidt theorizes the opposite view: "We used to think agriculture gave rise to cities and later to writing, art, and religion. Now the world's oldest temple suggests the urge to worship sparked civilization" (Mann 2011: 35). "The discovery of the Gobekli Tepe in Turkey, might suggest that 'the human sense of the sacred---the human love of a good spectacle---may have given rise to civilization itself'" (Mann 2011:40). "Twenty years ago, everyone believed civilization was driven by ecological forces;" Schmidt says, "I think what we are learning is that civilization is a product of the human mind" (Mann 2011:58).

At the various conferences of the International Society for the Comparative Study of Civilization {ISCSC}, different presenters had gone back and forth defending one or the other position regarding the origin of religion and civilization. Whether one upholds the view that the great civilizations produced great religions as their byproduct or the opposite that the great religions created the great civilizations, both are emphasizing the importance of religion as a major defining force of civilization.

The history of the past 4,500 years reveals that the great religions of the world have played a major role in molding their respective civilizations. The Indic religions of Hinduism, Buddhism, Jainism and Sikhism whose world views range from polytheism to monism to atheism had created unique Eastern civilizations, which are different from the Western civilizations that had been created by the monotheistic Abrahamic religions of Judaism, Christianity and Islam.

Religion provides a mind-set that is all pervasive in the life of the individual and the society leading to the creation of a unique civilization. Since the religion of Hinduism has had an all-embracing vision incorporating the other Eastern religions, we will take it as a paradigm for the Indic civilization. However, the Abrahamic religions of Judaism, Christianity and Islam that are monotheistic have had individualistic mind-sets that can be revealed only through their unique historical connection.

Religion and Civilization

"If there was no death, there will be no religion." (Bertrand Russell)
"Just consider how terrible the day of your death will be. Others will go on speaking, and you will not be able to argue back."

(Amartya Sen: The Argumentative Indian)

These statements are insightful and pertinent to our discussion regarding the role of religion in civilizational development. "All major religions strive to grapple with the issues of time and eternity; specifically with life, death and beyond. As the history of humanity indicates religions have had an all encompassing influence on their respective civilizations because they touch upon the major and minor aspects of people's lives singly and collectively.

Historically, religious beliefs, conventions and rituals have permeated into the life of an individual and the society so deeply that they have provided motives and intentions as reasons to go on with each day as well as throughout one's life. Those who follow the basic tenants of their specific religions, go through birth, growth, decay and death following the beliefs and rituals of their particular faith thus finding solace in them. Religions offer goal, purpose and meaning to the people's existence here and now while suggesting ways to build good credentials so that they would have a better life at present and beyond.

Religions are multi-tiered. At an intellectual level, they provide a philosophy and an outlook on life through which one could see connectedness among all human beings and unity in all existence. While interacting with others, this bird's eye view is conveyed through speech conducted in a dialogical fashion; transmitted through passion and compassion; expressed through sympathetic-empathy for others; and acted upon through sharing one's aliveness with others as well as by showing understanding, care, concern, respect and benevolence towards others.

At a social level, religions percolate and permeate by broadcasting themselves through the creation of painting, poetry, sculpture and music as well as through the construction of the churches, mosques, temples, shrines, cathedrals and monuments. Moreover, through their scriptures and belief systems, religions guide their followers so that they could live their daily lives with the awareness of a fundamental relationship between time and eternity as represented by a clock tower next to a church in the cities and towns of Europe" (Malhotra 2011).

In India, the words for religion, philosophy and civilization are *Dharma*, *Darshan* and *Sanskriti*. The word *"Dharma"*, which means religion, consists of a system comprised of a theology, a set of beliefs and a ritual practice that is to be adopted as a way of personal and social life by the followers. The word "*Darshan*", which designates philosophy, refers to a face to face or direct vision of reality. The immediate wisdom so gained is shared with others through a dialogical inquiry as well as put to a compassionate use to help humanity. The word "*Sanskriti*", which means civilization, is intimately connected to the word *"Sanskrit,"* the original language of India. It was through "*Sanskrit*" that India's scriptural revelations were grasped by the sages and through it their insights were imparted to the disciples. Since *Sanskrit* was regarded as the language of the gods, the word *Sanskriti* was used to designate civilization as the offshoot of the practice of the accumulated religious-philosophical wisdom.

Religion is what people practice whereas philosophy is what they aspire. However it is civilization that fuses the religious practice and philosophical aspirations by making them a way of life for its people.

Indic Religions and Civilization in India

In India, religion and civilization are so intimately connected to each other that to disconnect them would require as much power as that of splitting an atom. India has been the cradle of such Indic religions as Hinduism, Buddhism, Jainism and Sikhism! It has also provided refuge to the Abrahamic religions of Judaism, Christianity and Islam as well as to the religion of Zoroasterism. However, on the cultural side, India has amalgamated an assortment of civilizations of the Dravidians, Aryans, Greeks, Turks, Afghans, Persians, Moguls, Arabs, Portuguese, French and British that has made it more like a kaleidoscope!

India's diverse shapes and colors form a culture born of antiquity, but the picture is never static. Ever changing, ever growing, this ancient civilization throbs with life and energy. Yet with all this diversity, there is an unmistakable unity in the Indian civilization. It is this spirit of unity in diversity that mystifies and fascinates the inquisitive visitor or serious scholar of India.

The curious explorer might ask: What is India? Thoughtful reflection might reveal India to resemble a house with few walls and many open windows. Ideas from many cultures have lived in this house, coexisted with it, and ultimately have been absorbed by it. Still, this house continues to stand, a symbol of the tolerance for which India is justly famous. It is this capacity for open-mindedness that pervades various aspects of Indian life.

The inquiring voyager might ask: how is it possible for mystics to exist side by side with modern business people, for arranged marriages and joint families to coexist with singles cohabitating in Mumbai, for the 4,500 years old Vedic hymns to be chanted alongside Western rock music, and for yogis to become politicians, and philosophers "kings"?

A salad bowl of languages, a rainbow of people, an amalgam of cultures, a spectrum of religions, and the homogeneous heterogeneity of ethnic groups, India is a genuine study in contrasts.

How should one study India's kaleidoscopic diversity? How should one uncover India's grandiose multifariousness? How could one reveal India in its living colors? How would one delve into this mysterious unifying spirit of India? Though it appears to be a monumental task, a diligent effort might make it possible to uncover, grasp and display this unity.

How did India provide this unity to the diversity of religions and its concomitant civilizations? The answer might lie in the Indic religion of Hinduism that supplied the spirit of harmony in diversity and diversity in unanimity. What is this spirit of Hinduism that has made this unity in the diverse civilizations of India possible?

Hinduism: Unity in Diversity

Hinduism is the oldest and most misunderstood religion. It is older than the Western religions of Judaism, Christianity, and Islam, and the Eastern religions of Buddhism, Jainism, and Sikhism, which are its offspring. Hinduism originated in India in 2500 B.C. and has at present (2011) slightly more than a billion followers throughout the world.

It is unique because unlike the other major religions Hinduism has no single founder, no single scripture, no single deity, no single prophet, no strict priesthood, and no single way to reach salvation. Because it has numerous sages as spokespersons, scores of sacred books for open discussion and various paths available for enlightenment, it is liberal, tolerant of differences, accepting of other faiths, inclusive, and secular in orientation.

What gives Hinduism its unity is the belief that it is based upon eternal principles, which are stated in the sacred texts of the Vedas, the Upanishads, the Bhagavad-Gita and the Yoga Sutra. The quintessence of Hinduism is affirmed in the ancient text of the Rig Veda (2500 B.C.) as follows: "Ekam Sad Vipra Bahuda Vadyanti," which means: "There is one reality, the wise call it by many names or there is one truth, reached by many paths." This statement becomes the starting point of Hinduism and the Indian civilization.

The Hindu mindset views the sacred books of all religions including its own, as nothing more than limited human perspectives on the unlimited reality. Though each perspective captures an aspect of this truth, no single perspective is capable of conveying it totally. The ancient Indian story of the seven blind men and their limited perspectives on the elephant epitomizes this attitude. This is a clear example of Hinduism's tolerance of differences and acceptance of other faiths.

Hinduism uses the term "Brahman" for this single reality. Since Brahman is the source of everything, the plurality and divisions are only on the surface. Brahman permeates every aspect of existence ranging from inorganic matter to organic things, from plants to insects, and from animals to humans. Like our unique bodily cells, which while contributing to the development and sustenance of the various parts, are organically connected to the entire body, so are the different aspects of existence as cells connected to the body of Brahman. Though no single depiction of Brahman is capable of capturing its nature totally, Hinduism gives a partial description by identifying it with "sat-chit-anand" meaning "infinite blissful consciousness."

In Hinduism, the concept of a personal god is subservient to the notion of Brahman. A personal god is nothing more than the human attempt at conceptualizing what cannot be captured through the restricted categories of the limited minds. Since no single concept of god can confine the infinite spiritual depth of Brahman, Hinduism has no problem accepting many gods and goddesses (polytheism), a single almighty god (monotheism) and a single non-personal spiritual principle (monism). These deities or principles are nothing more than limited attempts of the human mind at revealing the innumerable qualities of the one all-encompassing spiritual principle. Moreover, these deities or principles are mere personal pathways through which one attempts to come in contact with one of the infinite manifestations of Brahman.

Brahman is unlike the creator in the Abrahamic monotheistic religions. It is not an artist or a sculptor that creates a painting or sculpts a statue and remains separate from its creation. Rather Brahman is more like a cosmic dancer (Nataraja Shiva), where the dance and the dancer are inseparably connected. The creator and its creation are inseparable from each other because there is no creator without the creation and no creation without the creator.

In Hinduism, another expression that comes closest to describing Brahman is "blissful creative cosmic consciousness." Brahman has been creating continuously the entire universe with its varied forms. It is more like an infinite circle whereas every object, animal, and human being is a concrete center of it. Each human being is a miniature fountain of creativity just like the blissful creative consciousness of Brahman. Hinduism asserts unambiguously that all life is a gift of this wonderful consciousness. The birth of a human being thus becomes an opportunity to get in touch with this joyful-creative-force that resides within.

Furthermore, this joyful-creative force is regarded as the divine spark in each human being. It resides in each of us as our conscience, which can act as our spiritual mentor. This conscience is our inner sacred spiritual space. Through the regular practice of meditation, one can gain access to one's conscience and can live a divine life on Earth. Moreover, this cosmic consciousness is available to anyone who approaches it with openness and without malice. Through meditation, this joyful-creative force can be made to descend into oneself to nurture and revive the conscience within and could be used for cosmic transformation of oneself and others. This viewpoint of Hinduism is a representative of the Indic religions. Let's now look at the Abrahamic religions of Judaism, Christianity and Islam.

Abrahamic Religions

Judaism is the most ancient of the Abrahamic religions and is the source of both Christianity and Islam. It is firmly monotheistic and based on three major principles of (1) a belief in one God-JHWH (2) who intervenes through historical events and (3) has chosen the Jews to be his representatives. The beginnings of Judaism lie in the story where God-JHWH called out to all humanity and no one else but Abraham listened to this call. JHWH then chose Abraham by forming a covenant with him to father a new nation and be faithful to this agreement. Later JHWH revealed the Ten Commandments to another prophet, Moses that led to making Judaism as the religion of the law and Jews as people who must adhere to these edicts. These ten laws defined Judaism as a monotheistic religion with JHWH as the only God; forbidding the creation of His images and taking His name in vain; observing Sabbath and honoring one's parents; forbidding killing, committing adultery, bearing false witness and coveting neighbor's property. Because the Ten Commandments were accorded absolute authority, they became the highest sacred laws for Judaism and the Jews that must be followed by the individual and the community (Hopfe 1983: 326).

Christianity started as a sect of Judaism during the first century AD, and has close to 2 billion followers as of 2011. Jesus and his supporters who constituted this group were all Jews practicing Judaism of that time. In its beginning stages, Christianity had modeled itself after Judaism by getting its inspiration from the Jewish scriptures, views on soul, life, death and beyond, mode of worship, and synagogue as a place of assembly.

The hostility between Judaism and Christianity commenced first when the Jewish religion did not accept Jesus as a messiah, and second when Christianity held the Jews accountable for the Crucifixion of Jesus. Other doctrinal issues contributed to a further schism. Judaism was a strictly monotheistic religion as stated forcefully in the Ten Commandments with JHWH as the only God who forbade the creation of its images! However, Christianity modified this stern monotheism by asserting that the Spirit (God) became flesh through Jesus, and salvation was possible only through the person of Jesus. Besides regarding Jesus as the only son of God, who was the messiah and the only way to salvation, Christianity regarded its own version of the Bible as the only book and its own methods of Baptism and Eucharist as the only ways to salvation.

This rupture was further widened when the Gnostic branch of Christianity "challenged the Jewish God and Old Testament by saying that the God of the Old Testament was not the true picture of God as found in Jesus. Theirs was the God of wrath and judgment whereas their own was the God of Love" (Hopfe 1983:392).

This bitterness turned into hatred when "the Gospel accounts placed responsibility for Jesus' death upon the Jewish leaders and crowds who were there for the Passover…thus laying the foundation for anti-Jewish feeling and persecution" that lasted for over two thousand years" (Hopfe 1983:383).

Consequently, throughout the history of Christianity almost all the Christian countries of Europe put restrictions on the Jews by making them wear badges, placing them in Ghettos, expelling them from their land and exterminating them through the most heinous means ever recorded in human history. A number of Jews who were able to save themselves through the Diaspora kept on moving from land to land for safety. This homeless wandering of the Jews for more than two thousand years finally ended with the creation of the country of Israel in 1948.

The systematic killing and domination of the Jews showed a total disregard for the quintessential teachings of Jesus' Sermon on the Mount, which had emphasized inwardness, meekness, mercy and non-violence as paths to salvation. This vile and violent mind-set adopted by the Christian crusaders and Christian monarchs of Europe perverted the Jesus' religion of love, kindness and compassion by turning it into "Christianity without Jesus."

Like Christianity, Islam was an off-shoot of the Abrahamic religion of Judaism. It started during the 7th century AD with a handful of supporters. At present in 2011, it has more than 1.7 billion followers throughout the world. Islam became the youngest, simplest and fastest growing Abrahamic religion. Similar to Judaism, it followed strict monotheism by holding that there was only one God-Allah, called by various names by other religions. Though God had revealed itself "incompletely to other prophets such as Abraham, Moses and Jesus," it was Muhammad, who received the "complete and final revelation," as contained in the book of Quran, "the word of God." Muhammad thought of himself as an ordinary man and never as divine.

There is noticeable contrast between the Christian view of Jesus and the Islamic view of Muhammad: "Unlike the image of Jesus in Christianity…who, as the Word of God; had existed since eternity and entered into history by becoming flesh"…Muhammad was just a human being. He was not the Word of God; he was a humble man touched by the Word of God…'I am only a human being like yourselves,' Quran ordered him to state. 'It is only revealed to me that your god is One God" (Mustafa 2011).

Muhammad was a charismatic leader. With the help of his dedicated followers, he offered the strict monotheism of Islam to the ordinary people in a simple and understandable language. This message was delivered through the five pillars of Islam consisting of the "recitation of the creed, daily prayer, almsgiving, fasting during the month of Ramadan, and pilgrimage to Mecca." Since these obligatory principles were presented in the simplest and easy to remember language, it spread Islam like a wild fire throughout the world (Hopfe 1983:446).

The creed of Islam involved only a few easy steps: accepting the Quran as the absolute word of God; reciting a simple daily prayer of 'there is no god but Allah and Muhammad is his messenger,' five times a day; an obligatory reciting of passages from the Quran at the time of birth, marriage and death; and believing in the promise of paradise on earth as well as in the principles of equality and freedom. Islam's use of simple, clear and easy language to reach the people infused the proselytes with an over-bubbling fanaticism that spread the message of Allah peacefully as well as with the force of arms to the far corners of the earth.

Christianity and Islam: Missionary Spirit

During the first century AD, when Jesus was born, the Roman Empire had reached its peak of expansion. By conquering the people of Europe, Asia Minor and North Africa, the Roman Empire had brought together the entire conquerable world of that time under the umbrella of an efficient administration of one government. Since the Roman Empire controlled all the major cities from Rome to Alexandria to Antioch to Damascus, it had joined them together through the best communication system by building cities and roads as well as large fleets of ships that could navigate safely through the waters of the Mediterranean Sea. This period could be dubbed as one of the first major attempts at bringing the world together through globalization. However, during the 1st century AD and the 2nd century AD, as the Roman Empire began to disintegrate, the Christian missionaries availed this opportunity to start broadcasting the message of Jesus by following the foot steps of the Roman Empire (Hopfe 1983:373).

Though Jesus was crucified and many Christian apostles were persecuted while others were killed by the Roman emperors, the able and shrewd missionaries took advantage of the downfall of the Romans by converting to Christianity a large number of people who resided in the big cities under the Roman control. During the span of the 3rd to 6th century AD, Christianity was methodically successful in taking over the entire world of the Roman Empire that was left in shambles because of the incompetent Roman rulers like Nero and others. By the end of the 6th century AD, the overflowing missionary zeal of Christianity led it to conquer the whole territory including all the major cities that was once the crown glory of the Roman Empire.

While the conquerable world of that time was basking in the glory of Christian missionary victory, Islam appeared on the world stage as the youngest of the Abrahamic religions. It hit the Christian hegemony like a hurricane. By the force of arms, it took from Christianity the major portions of the territory, which previously was occupied by the Roman Empire, thus destroying its supremacy. Driven by its youthful and extraordinary missionary zeal, and with its simple doctrine of one God-Allah and Quran as the absolute word of God, Islam expanded very quickly by spreading its message in the territories that belonged to the Christian world. From the 7th century AD onwards, Islamic armies kept on conquering most of the Christian cities, which were previously under the tutelage of the Roman Empire. Once the flood gates of its missionary spirit were flung open, and with the intoxication of success, Islam kept on extending its boundaries to the countries of the Middle East and Asia including those of China and India.

This clash between the Christian and Islamic missionaries was not without bloodshed. While millions of people were converted to Christianity and Islam, all those who refused and could not escape were taxed heavily or put to death. The egotistical crusaders of both religions, being high with their bubbling enthusiasm, presented themselves as the messengers of god in whose name they indulged in bloodshed. This blind passion of the missionaries pushed aside or left behind the meek and non-violent Christianity of Jesus and the peace-loving Islam of Muhammad avowing universal brotherhood. The Christian and Islamic fanatics converted their laudable religions into something very different from the way their founders had conceived them. By ignoring the original mission of the prophets of their unique religions, both the Christian and Muslim cohorts presented to the world only cruel versions of their faiths, by converting Christianity into "Christianity without Jesus" and Islam into "Islam without Muhammad."

MIND-SET OF INDIC AND ABRAHAMIC RELIGIONS

A sample comparison of the Indic religion of Hinduism with the Abrahamic religions of Judaism, Christianity and Islam might reveal the contrasting mind-sets that are fundamental to their theologies and belief systems. These mind-sets appear to be at the basis of conflict within the Abrahamic faiths and lack of conflict within the Indic faiths.

As indicated earlier, "the Indic religion of Hinduism is the source of Buddhism, Jainism and Sikhism whose views range from a belief in many deities (polytheism), one deity (monotheism), an absolute principle (monism) or no deity (atheism). Historically, Buddhism, Jainism and Sikhism never used armies to clash with its parent religion of Hinduism or with each other. Instead, like a functional family, they got together to conduct public debates on issues pertaining to their unique faiths. They fought intellectual battles through arguments and discussions that were well designed to convince the opponent with the quintessence of their world views and belief systems while tolerating differences. Instead of well-planned and meticulously organized armed raids against each other, these sibling religions used every ounce of their intellectual acumen and sagacity to defeat the challenger with the armamentarium of logic and reasoning. Each planned a calculated intellectual attack against the competitor by carefully constructed and finely honed logical arguments that sliced the opponents' defense, which led to their victory or defeat. No blood was ever shed during or at the end of these intellectual battles. When these logical skirmishes were over, the victors and the defeated would sit together for a further discussion while sharing their meals under the same roof" (Malhotra 2011).

Another item as an ingredient of their mind-set might have played a significant role leading to accommodation. "In the Indic tradition of Hinduism, Buddhism, Jainism and Sikhism, though the believers were convinced with the sacredness of their unique books, the exceptional qualities possessed by their prophets, the validity of their rituals, the genuineness of their conventions and the authenticity of their way of life leading to salvation, they were guided by the rational-integrative levels and less by the magical-mythic levels of consciousness as described by Jean Gebser[1], a European cultural anthropologist. This emphasis on rational-integrative plane of consciousness might have led them to adopt rational accommodation as a tool to resolve dispute pertaining to faith and doctrine. Intellectual up-

[1] According to Gebser, consciousness has developed through the five stages of the archaic, magical, mythic, rational and integrative consciousness. Civilizational differences/clashes/reconciliations are due to their unique emphasis on particular stages of consciousness. (See Malhotra's paper on Clash or Reconciliation of Civilizations for more detail, 2011)

man-ship through argument and debate might have helped them to view the other's position as a different approach to reaching the truth: leading them to accepting and tolerating the books and ways of salvation of different faiths other than their own" (Malhotra 2011).

In contrast, Judaism, which is the source of the monotheistic religions of Christianity and Islam, shows major clashes between it and its offspring. Historically, Christianity has been at loggerheads with Judaism and Islam, whereas Islam in turn has been fighting endless battles against both Christianity and Judaism. These clashes are still continuing into the 20th and 21st centuries."

One of the reasons might be the "way the Abrahamic religions assimilate, integrate and emphasize the various levels of consciousness as described by Jean Gebser. The Abrahamic religions of Judaism, Christianity and Islam, have created a mind-set consisting of religious beliefs, rituals, conventions and way of life that is guided more by the magical-mythic consciousness and less by the integrative consciousness structures. When and if there is any debate about the beliefs in the Abrahamic tradition, the believers utilize the magical-mythic mind-set by citing the miraculous birth of their prophets and books, their unilateral and one-sided relationship with their god, their book, their savior, their path, their way of life and their path to salvation. If one does not see eye to eye with their belief system, one might lose that eye. If one does not follow their way, one might have to flee to the high way to save one's life" (Malhotra 2011).

The history of the Abrahamic religions then attests to their being egotistical and territorial. To protect their unique territory, they limit their grasp of truth and salvation by believing only in their prophet, their book, their way, their doctrine, their god, and their outlook on life. If you are not with them, you are against them!

Radhakrishnan, a famous Indian philosopher and a comparative religionist, throws further light on egoism and territoriality as the basis of Abrahamic religions of Christianity and Islam. "In the Western religions, when the focus is on egoism, where the sense of I, my, me and mine becomes the all knowing judge, there is a tendency to ignore all others who might have similar needs and aspirations. This leads them to believe in the finality of 'their own religion, by trusting only in their own revelation and rejecting the claims of the rival creeds.' This being a child's view of nature, it is immature and belligerent...individualistic and intolerant...and therefore not conducive to inner realization."

Since both Christianity and Islam are missionary in spirit, they are marked with degree of intolerance towards each other and all other religions. Radhakrishnan believes that the culprit is the "Western emphasis on the mind as the subject (that) rejects anything higher than itself and thus negates the possibility of a soul or Atman. This leads to egoism and stratification of the panorama of life—thus sowing disconnection among all elements in nature and in society."

However, when looked upon from the Indic point of view, all this egoism is the expression of a "distressing immaturity revealing a bullying mentality...Where the ego is all mighty self, which provides the truth and then enforces it on others...Under the sway of the ego...instead of the true vision of the universal, we meet with attempts to universalize limited conceptions, with all the intolerance and unimaginativeness which it entails..." Aldous Huxley calls this attitude of Western religions as "theological imperialism." While concurring with Huxley, Lawrence Hyde, dubs this approach as "dialectical sinning," because the Western religions "convert what the Hindu thinks of as a Darshan—a point of view...into a dogma or a creedal definition." Hyde suggests that "to emancipate ourselves from partisanship and exclusiveness we must devote less attention to criticism and analysis and come interiorly into union with that Universal Self which is the principle behind all possible formulations." (p. 375-6)

Radhakrishnan offers a way out by pointing out that salvation is possible through the spiritual wisdom and not the creed because "the key to emancipation lies in knowledge of our true nature which is not the ego that has a particular point of view but the self that is universal and incorporates all other perspectives...It is called the power of seeing from the inside what is being accomplished within the souls of others...It is the transcendence of the egotism."

The reconciliation between the Abrahamic and Indic religious approaches is not only possible but can be brought about through Spiritual Humanism. Christian humility, which is at the core of Jesus' Sermon on the Mount, is similar to the Hindu, Buddhist, Jain, Zoroaster, Taoist and Confucian view on humility. In Spiritual Humanism, the emphasis is on inwardness, charity and tolerance as against outwardness, conflict and intimidation." Though the Western religions of Christianity and Islam have had this Spiritual Humanism as part of their faiths as propounded by their prophets, however during their historical missionary journey, this significant and original attribute was either ignored or pushed on the way side.

According to Radhakrishnan, Spiritual Humanism could become the bond between the Indic and Abrahamic religions. By bringing "together the Oriental Inwardness and Occidental Activism," it could develop into the hallmark of the 21st century where religions should make a move from *monotheism* towards *monism* i.e. from a belief in only one god, only one book and only one way towards one spiritual principle with infinite attributes towards whose understanding all the existing religions and their books would contribute their insights.

CONCLUSION

The 21st century could learn from the Indic religions of Hinduism, Buddhism, Jainism and Sikhism how to subdue the ego in order to tame it. Its motto might then become: "I am because of you." I and you together make up our society; our societies make up humanity; and humanity along with all other creatures make up the cells of this earth. The earth together with other planets make up the cells on the body of the solar system and our solar system in companionship with other solar systems make up the cells on the body of our galaxy whereas our galaxy in camaraderie with all other galaxies constitute the cells on the body of our entire universe. This reflective exercise might show the 21st century the way towards becoming more assimilative, inclusive, dialogical, tolerant and appreciative of many paths leading to the truth. By realizing this organic wholeness of the universe might offer this laudable opportunity towards a comprehensive vision of reality.

While the centuries of the past were designated as those of the discovery of the printing press, development of the gun powder, period of renaissance, age of industrial revolution, invention of the steam engine, creation of the airplane and the rise of great empires and wars, let's work together to make the 21st century as the century of peace where all humanity had come together to form a world government, a world spirituality and a world civilization not just for the white race or black race or brown race or yellow race but for the entire human race.

We need this kind of genuine globalization that would not be colonization and would become the real seal of the 21st century. It would aim at creating a one-world order where all races, all religions and all cultures would become part of the 21st Century Human Civilization. By living together in peace and harmony, all human beings will come to recognize that the ideal place desired by the diverse religions/civilizations, which had been called variously as Heaven, Kingdom of God, Fardosh, Bahisht or Swarg is our beautiful earth, our jewel, our home, our real Paradise!

REFERENCES

Ajaya, S. (1983). *Psychotherapy: East and West.* Honesdale, USA: Himalayan International Institute.

Ballentine, R.S. and Ajaya, S. (1976). *Yoga and psychotherapy: the evolution of consciousness.* Honesdale, USA: Himalayan International Institute.

Gebser, Jean. in *Wikipedia.*

Hopfe, L.M. (1983): *Religions of the world.* New York: Macmillan Publishing Co.

Malhotra, A. K. (1993): *On Hindu philosophies of experience: cults, mysticism and meditations.* New York: Oneonta Philosophy Studies Series.

Malhotra, A. K. (2004). "Toward a one-world culture: a philosophical perspective and a practical solution." *Common Ground*, Australia.

Malhotra, A. K. (2009). "Hinduism: one truth-many paths." *Civilitas, International Society for the Comparative Study of Civilizations,* November 30.

Malhotra, A. K (2011). Reflections on the clash or reconciliation of civilizations. *Dialogue and Universalism,* Vol.XXI, No. 1.

Malhotra, A. K. (2012). "Drama of consciousness: East West perspectives." *Forthcoming.*

Mann, C. "The Birth of Religion." *National Geographic*, June 2011.

Mustafa, A. (2011). *Islam without extremes: A Muslim case for liberty.* New York: W.W. Norton and Company.

Schilpp, P. Ed. (1952). *Philosophy of Sarvepalli Radhakrishnan.* New York: Tudor Publishing Co., The Library of Living Philosophers.

Sen, A. (2005). *The Argumentative Indian.* New York: Farrar, Straus and Giroux.

In: Spirituality and Civilization Sustainability ...
Editors: Andrew Targowski and Marek J. Celinski ISBN: 978-1-53610-729-6

Chapter 7

Potential of Christianity for the Civilization Revival in the Third Millennium

Anthony M. Stevens-Arroyo *
Brooklyn College, City University of New York, NY, US

"World history is the record of the spirit's efforts to attain knowledge of what it is in itself." - Hegel, in *Philosophy of History*.

"Late have I loved you, O Beauty ever ancient, ever new, late have I loved you! You were within me, but I was outside, and it was there that I searched for you."

St. Augustine, in *The Confessions*

Abstract

The division of Christianity into two: Orthodox Christian and Western Civilizations by Arnold Toynbee should be understood to describe not a difference of creedal belief but different spiritualities. Christian spiritualities are the animating forces for the material disposition of religious resources and the motivation that patterns individual behavior. The past offers many examples of how spirituality provides discipline to believers to overcome conflictive social pressures and follow doctrinal obligations. The monastic orders recast the evangelical counsel to holding material goods in common during the Middle Ages and groups like the Franciscans, Jesuits, Methodists, Quakers, etc. have performed similar functions. Despite the erosion of institutional resources since the Enlightenment and contemporary secularism, Christianity has produced various new spiritualities. For the III Millennium, it appears the two major characteristics of Christian spirituality include the discipline to "let go" that rejects the dystopia of contemporary society; and the embrace of an earth spirituality that extends respect for life to the environment and an equitable distribution of material resources.

* E-mail: stevensa@ptd.net

INTRODUCTION

As its distinguishing feature and the genesis of its name, Christianity is a belief system founded upon the incarnation of a spiritual God in the flesh and blood of a historical person, Jesus Christ. As affirmed in the Gospel of John, the basic belief of Christianity is that "The Word became flesh and dwelt amongst us." Christianity occupies physical space with its buildings that reach for the sky in steeples and domes, towers and obelisks. You can "hear" religion in its bells from cathedrals, organ fugues, in choirs and cantors of all types. You can "see" Christianity in robes, medals, bibles, and hats or veils to cover and uncover believers from head to toe. You can "touch" Christianity in rosaries, beads, the embrace of believers with the kiss of peace and in holding the consecrated host. The senses are brought into Christianity in ways that distinguish it from Gnosticism and Manichaeism in the past and other religions in the present that despise the human senses and contend that material humanity is contaminated. Yet it is Christianity's invisible force of faith and spirit that animates its material reality, much as the soul animates the body. It is a religion composed of people who are self-acknowledged sinners seeking sainthood. Their religion arranges them in complex groupings that promote equality while maintaining hierarchy; encourages love by turning the other cheek but permits violent wars of crusade; their faith fosters holding all material goods in common while it allows the church to amass immense wealth.

Over two millennia, Christianity has managed to meet the challenge of harmonizing materialized religion with idealized utopian aspirations promoted by theology. But, as claimed by St. Augustine, what is "ever ancient" is also "ever new." Christianity advocates *metanoia*, a change of mentality for both individuals and society, by projecting these changes, not as interruptions of past traditions, but as evolutionary improvements. Christianity affirms a need to retain fidelity to past belief while also modifying material behavior in accord with changing historical social circumstances. Thus, the religion that started as incarnational: spirit in flesh, maintains that balance by retaining the same spirit but also putting it into new material configurations.

The 20th century Marxist theorist, Antonio Gramsci (1971), marveled at the ability of Italian Catholicism, not only to reform itself, but to maintain the loyalty of the working class in the process. He observed this as a religious phenomenon in the sense that the rituals and symbols of Catholicism built a material link for ordinary persons to connect their moral behavior to abstract theological doctrines. Finding fault with the Marxism of his day that relied too heavily on a top-down instruction of the proletariat by Marxist elites, Gramsci extolled the power of Italian Catholicism to create organic intellectuals connected to grass-roots reality, but simultaneously guided by elaborate ideational systems. I believe it incumbent upon the civilizationalist to consider the religious spirit as a driving force from within civilization, especially in the case of Christianity.

Christianity makes its presence known in behaviors, both individual and collective. Unlike some religions where the spiritual is placed in opposition to the material, Christianity so values incarnation that faith without works is considered to be a dead faith (James 2:14-16). Christianity stubbornly refuses reductionism to either the purely spiritual or the purely material. This essay will examine the role of Christianity as civilizations have changed in the past, but as key to anticipating future trends in the III millennium. Throughout the analysis, the irresolvable tensions between the spiritual and the material will be reported dutifully, if not also apologetically.

Definition of Spirituality and Its Difference from "Religion"

In beginning, I think it useful to distinguish "faith" from "spirituality." Faith admits of definition as an assemblage of doctrines or teachings to be held by the faithful, upheld by a church hierarchy or elite as the basis for orthodoxy. Spirituality, on the other hand, has been used to describe the inner motivating force of faith among individuals and groups. Likewise, observance of ritual is a material measure of piety, i.e. "faithfulness to religious obligations," but ritual observance in and of itself does not require internal convictions. Christ contrasted a mere outward ritual observance with deep-felt interiority. Citing the Jewish prophet, Isaiah (29:13), Jesus (Mt. 15:8) noted that believers might feign rituals of prayer "with their lips" while their hearts were divorced from true commitment. In the Christian experience, spirituality has been a component to the ordinary "field of religion" because it motivates the habitual disposition for action (Bourdieu, 1991). Thus, while "religion" is construed as outwardly visible rituals and pronounced institutional beliefs, "spirituality" is a more subtle interior feeling that guides individuals in intimate behavior and the shaping of psychological motivations.

Spirituality, considered as "lived religion." has generated new forms of belief and religious behavior (Bellah, 1985). By aligning individual awareness with lofty goals and by establishing firm criteria as measurement of religious behavior, spirituality is a conscious exercise of a generalized religious feeling. Spirituality "thinks" for religion, in the sense that it reflects a purpose-driven behavior. For example, the earliest Christians shared all property in common, punishing with expulsion those who held back private possessions from community ownership (Acts: 2:45; 4:34-35; 5:1-10). Fittingly, history and theology describe this phase as "Primitive Christianity." Considered the earliest model for Christianity, the historical dimension nonetheless distinguishes this phase from all others in Church history. This is required to properly assess the changes in social form and organization from the initial decades when there was only a "Jesus Movement" (Blasi, 1988) and the later spectacular expansion of membership which eventually led to recognition of Christianity as the state religion in the 4th Century of the Common Era.

Routinization of Christian living from that of a sect into that of a majoritarian state-backed church forced a change in the approach to property. The communal ownership that originally had been imposed on all Christians was replaced. Taking its place was a theology of "evangelical counsels." Now, instead of an obligation to sacrifice the claims of private property in order to be a Christian, that surrender was a requirement only if a person wanted to be a "better" Christian. The majority of Christians were able to supplant their personal *surrender* of property with a more conventional almsgiving that allowed them to fulfill the obligation by *sharing* their property with others. This had been the long-standing practice of the religion of Israel into which Jesus and his earliest followers had been born. So while Jesus in his time had urged a special and new dimension in the practice of distributing wealth, some three hundred years later his special calling had been reduced in scope. Alienation from property that once had been imposed upon everyone was now only the choice of a few select followers.

This introduction cannot sufficiently detail the complex evolution of the vows of poverty within Christianity. However, one can conclude in most general terms that these notions evolved as social situations developed. As Christianity grew from a secret membership of Christ's disciples and was transformed into the institutional churches, East and West, of the Roman Empires after Constantine, the observance of poverty in monastic life also changed.

Importantly, the process of incarnational religion did not cease with the success of the medieval monastic models. With the creation of a European pre-capitalist economy in the late 12th Century, the ideal of evangelical poverty became the mission of the Mendicant Orders, especially the Franciscans. Today, in a contemporary global economy dominated by Late Capitalism, religion uses modern institutions like the Vatican Bank and the World Council of Churches and the network of charitable organizations operating worldwide in addressing calamities with sophisticated networks of distribution of needed supplies and medical attention. These resources are then translated into concrete acts of charity among the poor by volunteers like the sisters following in the footsteps of Blessed Theresa of Calcutta and lay missionaries of Bread for the World. Its contemporary forms may differ from its scriptural origins, but evangelical poverty continues to occupy a notable role among Christian believers.

The changes in material organization of Christianity to adapt the ideals to new social conditions did not occur in a vacuum, however. In order to motivate the achievement of Christianity's high ideals, guides to living and books on valued practices were produced for the faithful. In the case of monasticism, these guides became so detailed as to list activities and schedule them for particular times of the day. Such writings were formulated by the monastic groups as "Rules" and were considered to be authoritative pronouncements for how to incarnate the vital spirit of the Gospel for individuals living in particular cultures. A post-Reformation example of the same is found in Methodism, which the Wesleys, John and Charles, designed to guide those seeking greater holiness within the Church of England.

Such written materials contain the guiding principles of Christian spirituality. One noted church historian, Pierre Pourrat (1921-1930), wrote a multivolume work entirely on the power of spirituality in Christianity, studied diachronically, and much of the content below digests his exquisite treatment. Moreover, by examining the factors that shaped Christian spirituality in the past, the future can be better anticipated.

Christianity in Two Civilizations

The seminal civilizational analysis of Sir Arnold Toynbee describes an "Orthodox Christian Civilization," associating it with Russia and as heir to Constantinople, while Western Civilization is linked to Rome. But if there are two different Christian civilizations, that does not mean there are two different Christianities. Note that the separation between Rome and the Orthodox is self-styled as a "schism," meaning a split between two parts of the same whole. Each side in the schism recognizes the validity of the others' sacraments and the faith is held to be the same, with all Christians reciting the Nicene Creed as a basis for belief. The Roman West treasures the early writers of the Church like Cyril and Athanasius from

Alexandria, Egypt, and the Cappadocian Fathers: Basil and the two Gregorys, each of whom provided an effective marriage in theology between faith and reason.

Orthodox Civilization is different from Western Civilization, then, not because of faith and religion, but rather for spirituality and culture. Hence we have scholars like Jaroslav Pelikan (1974), who have pitched the Orthodox Eastern Christianity as more mystical in contrast to the rationality and sparse ceremony of the Roman West. It is my contention that what distinguishes Orthodox and Western Christianity is not creedal beliefs but different spiritualities. The common faith of Christianity manifests its adaptation to differing material circumstances by developing new spiritualities that enable practice of the religion in societies made distinct by time and events. Moreover, because the faith is common, the spiritualities can migrate. How else to explain the relative ease with which practices like the Orthodox "Jesus Prayer" can find acceptance in Western Christianity (Nichols, 1995)?

The Jesus Prayer is found in Jan van Ruysbroeck's poem "The Twelve Béguines", composed in the fourteen century and has its importance repeated in the current Catechism of the Catholic Church first produced after the II Vatican Council of 1964. This prayer exemplifies the key approach the Orthodox Christian spirituality which is labeled as "Apophatism," a form of contemplation upon divine transcendence beyond rational understanding (Axters, 1948). Christian Spirituality, I submit, transcends facile categories based on geography. The same might be said of the diverse spiritualities of Islam: Sunni, Shiite, Sufi. These produce differences as great as or greater than the difference between Orthodox and Western Christianity. As with Christianity, these forms of Islam adapt and change – perhaps not as rapidly or in the same ways – but enough to register that it is spirituality rather than creed that characterizes what is observable as civilization.

THE CHRISTIAN REFORMATIONS

It is impossible to speak of Christianity and overlook the Reformations in Europe with the onset of the 16th century (Fernández Armesto, 1996). I would say that the Protestant Reformation was a socio-political event with theological consequences, rather than vice-versa (Delumeau, 1971/1977). However, the changes correspond to the rise of new spiritualities fashioned to cope with social changes, such as the end of Feudalism.

Consider the case of the Low Countries of the Late Middle Ages and the resurgence of fervent piety, especially for lay persons, that included recourse to the Jesus Prayer. The socio-economic basis for this new spirituality was related to the shallowness of the feudal system in the Low Countries – today's Holland and Belgium – which were not kingdoms. When commerce had created a new urban class of self-sufficient merchants and urban workers in the Low Counties, the density of population and the industriousness of the population made the area highly prosperous, particularly with the textile industries of flax and wool. This newly generated wealth led to leisure for a non-noble class of burghers. New expressions of art and religion flourished, financed impart by the imitation of royal philanthropy in other countries.

The spirituality born in the Low Countries before the Protestant Reformation showed independence from existing forms that often depended heavily on the religious Third Orders of Franciscans and Dominicans. Instead, the new spirituality for lay persons emphasized slow reading of biblical texts, intense and personal prayer, and an inclination to mystic union with God – a concept borrowed from Orthodox Christianity known as "*theosis*" (Lossky, 1997). The Beguines for whom Jan van Ruysbroeck had written were lay persons who lived a communal life like nuns or monks, but without vows and only for stated times, being allowed permission to leave the order without reprisal for married life. Owning their own textile factories and sharing in the profits from their own work, the Beguines represented a new form of industry and the accumulation of wealth that was neither the feudal economy that had preceded it nor the capitalist economy that would follow.

To balance the acquisitive impulse implicit in their industry, the Beghard (men) and the Beguines (women) relied on teachings on meditation and interior life by writers such as the German Dominicans Meister Eckhart and his disciple, John Tauler. A century later, these experiences of communal life without vows for lay persons led to the popularity of the Brethren of the Common Life by Geert de Groote (1340-1384). The Brethren adopted an emergent spirituality called "Devotio Moderna," that emphasized the vanity of earthly endeavors, questioned the efficacy of sacraments taken without preparation, and eschewed the complicated tautologies of late Scholastic theology. The Brethren were not the predecessors of Lutherans or Calvinists, looked at from a doctrinal perspective. However, in terms of spirituality, there are several similarities. In fact, Luther cited Tauler in describing his own piety and the Lutheranism he suggested to his followers. Moreover, the institution of the "Brotherhoods / Bruderbund" became a fixture in Germany during the later Pietist Movements of the Mennonites, Amish, and Moravians and in the United States with groups like the Shakers.

Note, however, that spiritualities are not necessarily non-violent. There was not to be the easy replacement of Catholic authority with Protestant authority so as to maintaining a status quo society everywhere in Europe. Precisely because they set a pattern that conform material reality to the theological model for a blessed society, spiritualities can become militant. We work now to make God's kingdom come. This became the trajectory of Luther's separation of the individual's conscience from ecclesiastical control. He had protested against the dictates of the Catholic pope and Catholic lords; adopting his boldness, other movements claimed religious justification to also protest against Luther and Lutheran lords. This religious rebellion arose from the antinomian spirituality of Thomas Münzer and the Peasant War in Germany. It represented spirituality with no elite guidance at all and was succeeded by a tamer Anabaptist movement in Germany and the Quakers in Great Britain. Still, from the perspectives set forth in this analysis, one can see that antinomian spirituality within Christianity will sometimes justify a radical militancy that resorts to violence and oppression in the name of faith. In sum, religion generates not new ideologies, but new utopias (Mannheim, 1929/1936).

John Calvin preached a reform of Christianity that differed substantially from Luther, even though history links them for their cumulative impact on Catholicism in the "Protestant Reformation." Calvinism accepted the incarnation of Christ, the Word made flesh, but considered personal salvation a predestined event. The material world could be altered but those efforts at good works would be unavailing of changing the eternal decrees as to eternal destination. The spirituality of Calvinism was, as Weber (1930) suggested, "*weltfluchtig*" or "this world denying." It fled from ostentation, extravagance, emotion, affection, etc. The restraint required to deny so many natural impulses and delights permissible in virtually every other religion induced in Calvinism an inner discipline and devotion to duty that proved, as

Weber wrote, to be fundamental virtues for Capitalism. I would suggest, therefore, that when Weber wrote about the Protestant ethic and the spirit of Capitalism (1930), he was admitting the role and the importance of Calvinist spirituality upon world history and Western civilization.

The Jesuit Contribution to the Reformations

The Protestant Reformation impelled separation from the authority of Rome thus creating the divisions of Western Christianity. While Catholics were to claim continuity with the church founded by Christ at the dawn of the Common Era, in reality Catholicism had changed with the emergence of rival Christian denominations. There was a "reinvention" of Roman Catholicism. The continuing thesis of this analysis holds that spirituality accompanies changing social circumstances for Christianity, but (Maduro, 1982), the process produces conflicts. This is the context for the spirituality of the Catholic Reformation that was promoted by the Society of Jesus, commonly known as "Jesuits."

Founded by a crippled Spanish soldier, Ignatius of Loyola, who had "found God" after a life-threatening illness, the Society of Jesus utilized a form of organization inspired by Ignatius' military experience. The Jesuits skirted the dilemma of using religion to incite armed rebellion by focusing on education of lay persons who would be armed with ideas to combat the errors of the Church's enemies. Rejecting the previous paradigm of the Inquisition that refused to read the works of heretics by burning their books, the Jesuits instead made the works of Luther and Calvin part of their curriculum so that students would be prepared to refute in debate their rivals. This course of scholarly preparation was to continue when the works to be refuted carried the names of authors like Marx and Voltaire, Darwin and Huxley. Such "forbidden books" became the practice fields for a sharp Catholic critique about the errors implicit in both the premises and the conclusions of rivals. However, in debate with such public figures, Jesuit trained students absorbed what was valuable and acceptable in rivals, separating the good from the bad with logical precision. The Jesuits and their charges became so adept at this penetrating logic that their enemies invented the epithet "jesuitical" as an insult to their argumentative dialectic in finding truth.

The spirituality of the Jesuits that drove this sweeping redefinition of Catholicism and Catholic education (Caraman, 1981) was contained in the Spiritual Exercises of Ignatius Loyola. It was a requisite inner-self psychological examination required not only of members of the Society, but urged on their trainees who were formed in sodalities (like "soldiers") to be a fifth column for the work of the Church. There was a unique feature of the Exercises as meditations on the life of Christ that had only been hinted at in previous Catholic spiritualities, such as with the Benedictines and the Franciscans.

The Exercises called on adepts to create a mental image – not of themselves living alongside Christ in biblical times – but of the opposite: of Christ living alongside *them* in the contemporary world. Thus, for instance, instead of asking for meditation upon Christ's expulsion of the money-changers from the Temple in Jerusalem, the Exercises would request that one contemplate Jesus walking into a contemporary bank. The question of "What would Jesus do?" became newly explosive because the context for Catholic life and conformity with the Gospel was the real world in which one lived rather than in retreat to past times. This represented the intrusion of human psychology into spirituality.

Since the Jesuits and the decrees of the Council of Trent (1554-1563), Catholicism assumed a very different shape from the Medieval Church that had been tied to feudal conceptions of authority and territoriality, attempting to create sanctity for people locked into immobile social niches. In a world where Western Civilization was establishing colonies around the globe, the Jesuits developed a theology of natural law that restrained imperial powers in favor of self-determination among colonial populations that were afforded the political rights of nations. This missionary effort began to recognize the validity of religious rites and sentiment in the native religions (Stevens-Arroyo, 2003). Each culture was bestowed with status as a free nation, even if the state apparatus denied them sovereignty. As these outlying regions developed the infrastructure and the educated leadership capable of contesting sovereign rights within the existing political system, the Catholic imperial powers of Europe induced a papal repression of the Society of Jesus in 1754, a ban which lasted until 1773.

THE ENLIGHTENMENT AND SECULARISM

It is a familiar conclusion that the Protestant Reformation led to the Enlightenment (Habermas, 1990). It was the later movement which ended in Europe the definition of nation-states by the religion of the ruler, installed science as a counterweight to religious fundamentalism and began modernity by stressing the rights of the individual within the state just as Protestantism had stressed the individual liberty of biblical interpretation. Such linkage between the Enlightenment and Protestant Christianity, as frequent as it may be, overlooks the essentially conservative and anti-intellectualism of the Reformers. In fact, a case could be made that the Jesuits' approach was more in sync with the Enlightenment pursuit of a scientific method to find truth (Stevens-Arroyo 2006).

The patterns for spirituality within Christianity through the rest of the 19th century leading up to the first half of the 20th, developed against the background of secularization. The practice of religion tended to focus on immediate attention to poverty and sickness on an activist side and in searches for mystical religious experience on the other. Battered by Marxism, Socialism and Anarchism on the one hand, and by laissez-faire Capitalism and exploitative colonialism on the other, Christianity was nonetheless capable of producing new movements that addressed issues that governments could or would not. Whether it was the French Catholic creation of a St. Vincent de Paul Society to aid the poor or a Methodist outreach to the types of economic victims described in the novels of Charles Dickens, Western Christianity through most of the 19th century and leading into the 20th provided a "safety net" for those in need. Without dramatic change from already existing models of spirituality, religious persons dedicated time and resources to the creation and maintenance of hospitals, shelters, and schools for the underprivileged. They did this "at home" and abroad in foreign missions.

The ideological foundations for such types of church involvement were significant, particularly within Catholicism. Breaking from the reactionary mode of Catholic opposition to the secular state that had characterized the pontificate of Pius IX, Leo XIII created a "third way" for Christianity that traveled the middle ground between the two extremes of laissez-faire Capitalism on the right and Communism on the left. The landmark in this effort was the 1892 document *Rerum Novarum,* that was presented not only as an explanation of the Catholic opinions about economic conditions but also an invitation to non-Catholics to work for social justice goals such as the recognition of workers' rights in labor unions and for change through peaceful political participation.

The political aspects of religion surfaced from time to time by becoming a surrogate for nationalism. Thus, for instance, the effort of Ireland to throw off the British yoke appeared as a force urging restoration of Catholic rights. But religion was not always on the side of rebellion. In Italy, Catholicism was the reactionary force against Italian reunification led by the Red Shirts of Garibaldi. Christianity also choose sides along the Protestant-Catholic divide as for instance in Bismarck's Germany during the Kulturkampf. Notoriously, particularly for the Catholicism in Croatia, Slovakia, Hungary and to an extent in Portugal, Spain, Mexico, Poland and Germany, the church's identification with national identity also made it an ally of right-wing politics, particularly in the inter-war years from the 1920s to the outbreak of the II World War.

These ultra-conservative tendencies created spiritualities that bespoke a nostalgia for a less complicated world, one in which the "old-time religion" held sway. All were characterized by invocation of devotion to patron saints, especially the Blessed Virgin Mary (Zimdars-Swartz, 1991). The most famous of these was centered at Lourdes, a small French town at the base of the Pyrenees, when an uneducated girl reported speaking to the Blessed Mother in 1858. The devotion to Our Lady of Lourdes eventually became famous for miraculous cures produced by contact with an unexplained spring of gushing water suddenly welling up at the foot of the rock upon which the Blessed Mother was seen to be standing.

A little more than a half-century later there was a similar event with the reported appearance in 1917 of the Virgin to three shepherd children at Fatima in Portugal. These apparitions set the pattern for this brand of spirituality which was based on a warning about impending punishment to the world for the faithlessness that allowed the rise of atheistic socialism and included a list of secret prophecies disclosed only to the pope under orders from the celestial messenger. The same pattern was to be repeated in other appearances such as Sábana Grande in Puerto Rico and the more famous but now discredited apparition at Medjugorje in Croatia.

On the Protestant side of Christianity, the same period witnessed return to tradition, such as with the Oxford Movement that led Anglican divines such as John Henry Newman into the Catholic Church. The liberal Protestant equivalents included the Transcendentalist experience at Brook Farm and later, Fruitlands, under the inspiration of Ralph Waldo Emerson with followers as different as Henry David Thoreau, who inclined to a proto-Libertarianism; the Alcotts and their novelist daughter, Louisa May; Orestes Brownson, who became a Catholic Apologist; Nathanial Hawthorne, the novelist; Isaac Hecker, who became a Catholic priest and founder of the Paulist Fathers, dedicated to modern communications. None can doubt that Transcendentalism had Unitarianism, the ultimate form of Liberal Protestantism at its base (Dorrien, 2001). The movement was based on a spirituality that looked beyond the limitations of institutional religion and towards the more pure spiritual message that could be found in all religions, including Hinduism and Buddhism. Robert Bellah (1970) traced the same tendency in the 20th century Protestantism.

Protestant movements included various forms of Spiritism, such as the popular American forms: the Church of Christ, Scientist; the millenarian Jehovah's Witnesses; the Church of Latter Day Saints, or the Mormons; and the outgrowth of the "Holiness Movements" which include today's Pentecostalism (Chaves, 2004). Many of these movements within Protestantism began as reforms of existing denominations that had grown cold in fervor (Ammerman, 2005). Often, as with the Holiness churches, the effort was made within a denomination, only to be rejected and forced into creating a distinctly new "religion." Dodging any easy classification is the Salvation Army as a religious movement of aid to those in need. In other cases, as with the Witnesses and the Mormons, the new spiritualities carried with them some doctrinal teachings that were rejected as betrayals of the Christian tradition. The new spiritualities in each of the movements described above belong in any civilizational analysis that includes religious substance and change.

THE GLOBAL AWAKENING OF CHRISTIANITY

Civilization assumed a global mantle during the 19th century's extension of Capitalist driven colonialism. With due respect for the highs and lows in the process, by 1900, virtually all of Africa and large parts of Asia were under colonial rule from European capitals. Latin America had its political independence for each of 21 republics, but with the imperialist interpretation of the Monroe Doctrine, many of these countries were de facto "neo-colonies" of the United States. In fact, during the 19th century, the American Empire annexed two-thirds of Mexico and the major islands of the Caribbean.

Yet by the middle of the 20th century, an anti-colonial movement had been unleashed by the post-WW II institution of the United Nations. Initially, this anti-colonial movement was part of the Cold War which split spheres of interest between a supposed Capitalist West and a Communist East. The political face of such allegiances was combated by the Non-Aligned Movement that stressed the freedom of small countries in the periphery and of former colonies to trace their own path to economic and social development without dependence on the dictates of the super-powers. Almost simultaneously, the notion of common markets for certain regions of the world blurred the boundaries of the nation-state. The establishment of the European Union was the most significant of this regionalization of the globe. Rather than be seen as a force competing against the centrifugal pull of a global economy, such regionalization actually hastened the fusion of the world's economies into a giant network of compatible, if also rival, interests. Thus, for instance, the Andean Pact of Latin American nations trade more directly with China today without competing against each other in the pricing and supply of exports.

The signal religious articulation of these new contours in the world is reflected in documents such as *Pacem in Terris* by Pope John XXIII that embraces the role of secular political and aid organizations such as the UNESCO in supplanting strictly religious institutions that provide charity. *Progressio Populorum* by Pope Paul VI addressed international migration of both laborers and of investment capital, stressing the need for high ethical standards to assure that economic growth did not usurp the rights of human beings to better lives. Progress cannot be achieved at the expense of humanity, according to this document. *Centessimus Annus* was one of several such encyclicals on the new global order written by Pope John Paul II, to examine the results of the fall of Communism and the end of the Cold War. *Caritas in Veritate* by Pope Benedict XVI has applied ethical economic standards to issues such as climate change, environmental protection and power of international financial markets, stressing that only transparency enforced by governmental actions on an international scale will produce the kind of "truth" that can make economic progress into "love."

The application of these papal documents has parallels with similar pronouncements from Christian agencies such as the World Council of Churches. The sentiments are virtually the same despite the denominational differences. One tends to find in many non-Catholic organizations, however, a strong emphasis upon the rights of women world-wide (Díaz-Stevens, 2003) and the adjustment in economic development so as to enhance the role of women as they emerge from the shadows of ill treatment in traditional societies.

Admittedly, all these documents are for the most part "top-down" pronouncements from religious leaders. However, it would be a mistake to underestimate the Gramscian interchange between front-line engagement at the grass-roots level and the final articulation of these religiously inspired plans for human development. What is perhaps most important is to analyze the linkages from these trends to new spiritualities. Based on the notion that spiritualities are the spirit incarnated in the visible organization of institutionalized religion, several trends have been detailed above. In order to predict the next millennium, therefore, this review of the last two has served as introduction to speculation.

First, spiritualities have been presented as instruments within the Christian religion that fashion a socio-psychological discipline to enable believers to achieve the demands of the faith in a new social circumstance. Thus, each new challenge to Christianity has been met with some form of organized reform and renewal. More or less as with animal species, those that survive, do so because they "fit" the new circumstance (Robertson, 1985).

Second, spiritualities that are viewed as "new," generally claim origins in traditions of previous religious expression. They are new, of course, but more for their functions of meeting the challenges of social transformations rather than because they create new beliefs or doctrines. In effect, they "invent tradition" (see Hobsbawm, 1983). Occasionally, the new functions threaten the continued existence of the dominant model and the new spirituality results in a new Christian denomination.

Third, the new formulations that incarnate the existing Christian traditions over the centuries have become increasingly modern. Spiritualities in the modern era take in account theories of psychology, modern science, role of education, etc. Even when the spirituality is a vehicle for rejecting modernity and seeking return to a past era, it tends to justify itself in the language of contemporary science and society. The modernity of contemporary religion is often misunderstood (Carter, 1993). Thus, for instance, the Amish long ago rejected gasoline motors in the name of simplicity, while modern Benedictines reject cell phones to keep away distractions -- in the name of simplicity.

Fourth, adjustment to a new social circumstance for Christianity often experiences the simultaneous appearance of both forward-looking and nostalgic movements. Thus, at the very time in the 12th century that Franciscans abandoned the Benedictine model because it was too worldly, Benedictines themselves, such as the Sylvestrines, adopted a return to primitive austerity in order to preserve their model of spirituality.

These four qualities define the relationship between Christian spirituality and the civilizational process: 1) the function of adaptation to new circumstances; 2) the reinforcement of fidelity to tradition; 3) the inclusion of modern approaches to Christian life; and 4) the co-existence of both forward-looking and backward-looking variations (see Shils, 1981). It is to be anticipated that these characteristics will continue into the new millennium.

SPIRITUALITIES FOR THE III MILLENNIUM

Globalization in economics, culture, entertainment, and communications is the undeniable future for the world's civilizations. The issue is: "Who will control globalization?" One rival for control of globalization is corporatism. Like so many "-isms," corporatism is a bad word which has as many definitions as it has critics. It is easily equated with the profit motive of laissez-faire Capitalism that reduces all human beings and social interactions to commodities that can be bought and sold. But Communism had its version of corporatism that interpreted human differences and personal preferences to violations of good order. The thread that illuminates the central core of all corporatism is its depersonalization of the human being to serve ideological or commercial interests.

It is ironic that the internet, created with the personal computer, was a technology devised by corporatism to maximize profits by linking the world's markets into a single intercommunicative network. Yet it is the same global use of this technology through specialized websites, the social media such as Facebook and the video telephone that provides the tools to people opposed to the noxious effects of globalization. In its place is put a more localized control over resources and social processes. Moreover, just as corporatism uses this communications technology to supply its markets and depersonalize profit motives, the globalization opposition uses the same tools to create a nemesis network that opposes the depersonalization (see Castells, 1998). Thus, the effort to sell powdered baby-formula in remote parts of the world as a commercialized substitute for breast-feeding is helped by the internet, but also is opposed by international blogs that reveal the abuses that take place with such a substitution. This process can be seen in a host of issues: opposing genetic mutation in food by substituting organically-grown produce: banning hormone injection in livestock by preferring naturally grown beef, pork and chicken; preferring cotton cloth to synthetic fabrics in clothing. The list goes on in such issues and includes highly politicized matters such as access to clean water and pure air in spite of profit-driven forms of pollution and the use of renewable sources of energy rather than dependence on coal and petroleum.

Religious spirituality enters into these struggles because it has generally been a vehicle to provide individuals with the discipline to resist the seduction of more accommodating solutions to social living that nonetheless produce social inequalities. For example, avoiding chemically induced food ingredients and consuming only organic produce is generally more costly. Spirituality's function is to support this set of "harder choices" by faith, religious conviction and religious belonging.

There is evidence of this type of "return to simple living" that has characterized both Catholic and Protestant forms of Christianity. The Franciscans, the Shakers, the Society of Friends and the Catholic Worker Movement are such examples. Along with the tendencies listed above is the way that these previous traditions can be "modernized" to cope with new circumstances but retain the claim on the past. One can also see versions of a "left-leaning" anti-consumerism, anti-corporatism in this spirituality as well as politically conservative versions. Thus, as likely as some faith-based groups are to campaign for abstention from artificially generated vegetables and meat while adopting use of medical marijuana as a pro-life spirituality, one can find austere groups also invoking a pro-life spirituality to oppose abortion, artificial methods of contraception and research with stem-cells.

Spiritualities of "Letting Go"

All spiritualities in this III millennia of the Common Era will constitute some form of "letting go" of power and institutions (Neal, 1977). It is most obvious that ecclesiastical institutions have faded and continued to cede power and influence to governmental and public agencies. In some instances, such as in the United States, there are structures that allow taxpayers' money to be distributed to faith-based hospitals and universities while permitting retention of a religious identity. As the diversity of religious preferences has exploded, however, the premise that there was majority public bias in favor of Christianity has receded in the United States. One can anticipate a time in which the religious function of such public institutions becomes counter productive to the religious mission of the Christian church. For instance, doctrine may favor the formation of workers' unions while the "bottom line" for the hospital affiliated with the church requires attacking the formation of the union. As such contradictions of faith with practice multiply, it can be anticipated that the ecclesiastical institution will "let go" of such public agencies and return to a more pure promotion of entirely religious witness. While the notion that church and state are separated in the public forum has been a solid pillar of United States' democracy, there are new spiritualities that want to "let go" of this assumption. This is the trend predicted by José Casanova (1994) who envisions the public role of religion in the modern world as "critique" of the status quo rather than in participation in private-public partnerships. The nature of compromise with public process, he suggests, will be replaced by a church that works as gadfly against the imperfections of social institutions with the purpose of making such institutions responsive to ethical morality. Christianity, however, will not seek to substitute itself as provider of services.

There is, on the one hand, a real desire in some religious quarters to use such a critique to move in the opposite direction. They wish to reassert the primacy of the Christian religion over all other faiths would forestall legislation that is not in direct accordance with Christian teaching or allow the nullification of laws that contradict church teachings by civil disobedience. Thus, for instance, the notion that evolution of species is proved by science is held to be of lesser importance that a literal interpretation of the bible that the world was created in seven days. To be able to sustain this approach to science on evolution and host of other issues such as same sex marriage, the moment of conception, the personhood of the fetus, a spirituality that rejects modernity is a likely requisite.

Another aspect of the spirituality of "letting go" will abandon the consumerism and expectations of middle-class society to return to self-help projects of agriculture, communal sharing of income and forms of social participation that abandon public education for home-schooling, the use of automobiles, television and cell phones, etc. One may consider that this spirituality relaxes the religious impulse to establish utopias, to be content to denounce dystopias (Stevens-Díaz, 2006)

"Letting go" is not only a political critique: it may also invoke a spirituality that remains cool to ecclesiastical control or regularized religious practices. In Europe, as in parts of the United States, there is a public that has constructed a personalized spirituality around shrines and apparitions rather than churches and the commandments. In this scenario, individual believers fashion a personal creed, picking and choosing among doctrines and rituals, much as clients in a cafeteria pick and choose various entrees to their liking.

Earth Spiritualities

"Letting go" of old assumptions clearly implies putting something else in its place. Some choose, of course, to abandon Christianity and all religion to become some form of agnostic or atheist. The tendency to return to past tradition so as to negate modernity has been described above. A newly fashioned alternative that simultaneously "lets go" while also embracing simplicity might be what Fr. Thomas Berry (1988) called, "Earth spirituality." Owing a great deal to the Christian vision of Jesuit Teilhard de Chardin (1959/1964), earth spirituality supplants loyalty to institutions with loyalty to a protection of the environment as a worldwide responsibility. Earth spirituality provides the discipline and the vision to deny certain creaturely comforts of consumerism in order to protect material resources as the birthright of all humankind.

Earth spirituality is a critique of any so-called progress that violates the natural processes. It fosters renewable energy, along with the generation of clean air and water. The logic of this spirituality insists that if the earth is destroyed, humankind is destroyed because the earth is a God given organic reality and not a "thing" to be run by humans as a machine for their pleasure. Earth spirituality is the ultimate "pro-life" spirituality and the vision of Chardin (Stevens-Arroyo, 2011) has been recently resurrected by Pope Benedict XVI after decades of neglect from official church leaders.

Not only is earth spirituality ecological; it is also international because it places concern upon the globe and not just practices in one country or locality. By connecting places as parts of an integrated globe, it also locates humankind as a single species made up of individuals responsible for each other. Recognizing that Christianity has expressed limited appreciation of nature, earth spiritualities have incorporated elements from the other religions, "baptizing" them so to speak, so that they are acceptable within Christianity. Native American religions, Buddhist, Taoist and Hindu perspectives have resonance within earth spiritualities. In some cases, techniques for prayer and the like have been incorporated as helpful additions to the Christian tradition. Thus, Christian spirituality of the Earth has acquired a global appeal and represents the inculturation of the religion into the expansive reservoir of humanity's religious need.

Conclusion

Hegel addressed the civilizational process when he wrote: "World history is the record of the spirit's efforts to attain knowledge of what it is in itself." Christianity has a crucial role in the III Millennium of the Common Era by directed that knowledge of spirit towards new boundaries. Expect spirituality rather than clergy or institutional religion to be the bearer of this new dimension of civilization. The differing forms of Christian spirituality will not of themselves resolve the conflicts inherent in the development of civilization on the earth. However, spiritualities contain a universalizing effect that effectively transcend ordinary politics and stifling economics. Making humanity more conscious of itself and its responsible relations to material reality is a necessary dimension if the III Millennium is to be a civilized one.

REFERENCES

Ammerman, Nancy Tatom. 2005. *Pillars of faith: American congregations and their partners*. Berkley: University of California Press.

Axters, Stephanus. 1948. *La spiritualité des Pays-Bas: l'evloution d'une doctrine mystique.* Louvain (Translated by Donald Attwater as *The spirituality of the old Low Countries*, 1954. London: Blackfriars).

Bellah, Robert N. 1970. *Beyond belief: essays on religion in a post-traditional world.* New York: Harper and Row.

Bellah, Robert N., R. Madsen, A. Swidler, W. Sullivan and S. Tipton. 1985. *Habits of the heart: individualism and commitment in American life*. Berkeley: University of California Press.

Berry, Thomas. 1988. *The Dream of the earth*. Sierra Club Books: San Francisco.

Blasi, Anthony J. 1988. *Early Christianity as a social movement*. Bern and New York: Peter Lang.

Bourdieu, Pierre. 1991. "Genesis and structure of the religious field," *Comparative Social Research* 13 (1991) 1-17.

Caraman, Philip. 1981. *University of the nations: the story of the Gregorian University with its associated institutes, the biblical and the oriental*, 1551-1962. New York: Paulist Press.

Carter, Stephen. 1993. *Culture of disbelief: how American law and politics trivialize religious devotion*. Basic Books: New York.

Casanova, José. 1994. *Public religions in the modern world*. University of Chicago Press: Chicago.

Castells, Manuel. 1998, second edition, 2000. *End of millennium,* Vol. III. *The information age: economy, society and culture.* Cambridge, MA; Oxford, UK: Blackwell.

Chaves, Mark. 2004. *Congregations in America*. Cambridge: Harvard University Press.

Chardin, Teilhard de. 1959/1964; *L'Avenir de l'Homme*. Paris: Seuil. *The Future of man.* N.Y.: Harper.

Delumeau, Jean. 1971/1977. *Catholicism between Luther and Voltaire: a new view of the counter-reformation*. London: Burns and Oates. (First published in French, 1971).

Díaz-Stevens, Ana María. 1993. "The saving grace: the matriarchal core of Latino Catholicism." *Latino Studies Journal* 4:3(September)60-78.

Dorrien, Gary. 2001. *The making of American liberal theology: imagining progressive religion, 1805-1900*. Volume 1. Louisville: Westminster John Knox Press.

Fernández Armesto, Felipe and Derek Wilson. 1996. *Reformations: a radical interpretation of Christianity and the World (1500-2000)*. New York: Scribners.

Gramsci, Antonio. 1971. *Selections for the prison notebooks of Antonio Gramsci.* Translated and edited by Quintin Hoare and Geoffrey Nowell Smith. New York: International Publishers.

Habermas, Jürgen. 1990. *The structural transformation of the public sphere*. MIT Press: Cambridge.

Hobsbawm, Eric and Terence Ranger, eds. 1983. *The invention of tradition*. Cambridge: Cambridge University Press.

Lossky, Vladimir 1997. *The mystical theology of the Eastern Church*, Crestwood, N.Y.: SVS Press.

Maduro, Otto A. 1982. *Religion and social conflicts*. Maryknoll: Orbis Books.

Mannheim, Karl. 1929/1936. *Ideology and utopia*. International Library of Psychology, Philosophy and Scientific Method: Chicago. Published as a paperback, Harcourt Brace Janovich: New York.

Neal, Marie Augusta. 1977. *A socio-theology of letting go*. Berkeley: The University of California Press.

Nichols, Aidan. O. P. 1995. *Light from the East. authors and themes in Orthodox Theology.* London.

Pourrat, Pierre.1921-1930. *La spiritualité chrétienne*. Paris V. Lecoffre, 4 volumes. English translation : P. Pourrat, *Christian Spirituality,* Newman Press : Westminster, Md., 1953-55.

Pelikan, Jaroslav. (1974) *The Spirit of Eastern Christendom 600–1700.* Chicago: University of Chicago Press.

Robertson, Roland and JoAnn Chirico. 1985. "Humanity, globalization and worldwide religious resurgence: a theoretical explanation," *Sociological Analysis* 46:3 (Fall) 219-242.

Shils, Edward. 1981. *Tradition*. Chicago: University of Chicago Press.

Stevens-Díaz, Adán. 2006. "Dystopia and civilizations: comparison of social movements in the network society." *Comparative Civilizations Review* (55: 72-90).

Stevens-Arroyo, Anthony M. 2011. "Fire and force: civilization as noosphere in the works of Teilhard de Chardin" *Dialogue and Universalism* (Warsaw) Vol. XXI (2011) 1: 53-66.

Stevens-Arroyo, Anthony M. 2006. "Theologies of civilization: Jaime Balmes vs. François Guizot," presented at the annual meeting of the ISCSC, École de Hautes Études, Paris, France: July 2006.

Stevens-Arroyo, Anthony M. 2003. "Earth religions and book religions: Baroque Catholicism as openness to earth religions." *Comparative Civilizations Review* 49 (Fall 2003) 54-75. Second of two parts.

Weber, Max. 1930. *The Protestant ethic and the spirit of capitalism.* Translated by Talcott Parsons. London: Allen and Unwin

Zimdars-Swartz, Sandra L. 1991. *Encountering Mary: from La Salette to Medjugorje.* Princeton: Princeton University Press.

In: Spirituality and Civilization Sustainability ...
Editors: Andrew Targowski and Marek J. Celinski
ISBN: 978-1-53610-729-6

Chapter 8

THE CHINESE CIVILIZATIONS: DRIVING FORCES, IMPLICATIONS, AND CHALLENGES IN THE THIRD MILLENIUM

Bernard Han*
Western Michigan University, MI, US

ABSTRACT

Chinese civilization has lasted for more than 5000 years, the longest that has ever existed and never perished. Historically, Chinese civilization reached its climax in the Tang Dynasty (AD 618-907), and now it resurges again. Why did Chinese civilization last so long? In this chapter, a Three-Component Model, a revision of the TEM model by Targowski (2009), is used to explain the driving forces behind the Chinese civilization. In specific, the major factors in Chinese culture are detailed to expound the real causes that sustain Chinese civilization, which was deeply rooted in tacit values (i.e., family relationship, education-first concept) and excelled in peace-driven innovations and activities (e.g., compass, paper, Voyages of Zheng He AD 1405 – 1433). Nevertheless, the resurgence of Chinese civilization, especially under the leadership of the Chinese Communist Party, may imply some huge impacts in several areas including the world civilization, financial control, economic growth, and political federation. These impacts may not be harmful, but rather, could be very beneficial to the mankind if there is a smooth change in the leadership of the Chinese Communist Party, which is imposed by a few critical challenges resulting from the sudden resurgence of Chinese civilization. While China must cope with these challenges in order to prevent its downfall, in this chapter the author does provide some recommended actions to be taken by the West as a response to the resurgence of Chinese civilization to minimize unwanted clashes between the West and the awakening giant, China.

* E-mail: Bernard.han@wmich.edu

INTRODUCTION

The rising Chinese economy over the past 30 years, accompanied by China's active role in the international arena, has created hypes and hopes for many countries in the world, in particular, a few developed ones in Asia such as Singapore, Taiwan, Korea, and Hong Kong (China) to a great extent (Rawski 2011). In the meantime, many others in the West (e.g., USA, Germany, and Japan, etc.) have started to worry about if China's surge in the world platform will impose undesirable threats to their existing roles in world civilization. In other words, will the emerging Chinese civilization become dominant and replace the existing Western civilization created two hundred years ago after the industrial revolution in England (Coffin *et al.* 2011)? With a limited history of China and its unproven political maturity (Michelbach, 2011), it will not be easy to predict the future or draw a conclusion without making any mistakes.

As China marches into the fourth decade of economic growth, it does become a valid concern for many countries in the West to know if China will truly be the next superpower having the new world order (Jacques, 2009). If it does become the reality, how it will impact the current world order or human civilizations (Huntington, 1997). In this chapter, it will not be possible to offer all the answers, in particular, regarding whether China will rule the world (Jacques, 2009). However, our intent is to seek interpretations for our curiosity "Why a socialist democratic country like China (Stanczyk, 2008) can achieve such miraculous economic growth?" Or be more exact "Why a weak sleeping giant (Berher, 2010) suddenly woke up and seemingly created a 'new' civilization that overshadows the West?" A detailed examination, with a proper interpretation, this world phenomenon will help us obtain answers for many sub-questions such as "Why China bypassed the global recession in 2008-2009 (Dullien *et al.*, 2010)?" "Why China sustained continuous economic growth in an environment with limited human rights?" and/or "Will China's emerging civilization self-sustainable and provide positive impacts on the world civilizations?" While answers for these sub-questions are not provided in this chapter, it does address the implications of and challenges to the emerging Chinese civilization. As part of the research aims, this chapter does provide suggestions to the West to better prepare and develop strategic moves to work with China to pursue the best benefits of mankind and avoid preventable catastrophes resulted from political conflicts or human evil rivalry (e.g., genocide).

This chapter is organized as follows. The next section details the driving forces behind the Chinese civilization and offers some explanations about why it lasts so long. In fact, once upon a time Chinese civilization reached its climax in the Tang (唐) dynasty, which was 1,500 years ago (Gernet, 1999). To help us understand these driving forces, a revised Three-Element Model (Targowski 2009) was presented before the detailed explanation. The section follows discusses the implications of the resurgence of Chinese civilization. Our discussion is based on the author's understanding of the Communist Regime in China and the unique characteristics of Chinese culture. Will these implications fully crystalize in the coming years? Depends! The next section addresses the critical challenges currently encountered by the China's Communist Regime. Then, some recommendations are given for the actions that the West should take as a response to the rise of China (Jones, 2007). Finally, the chapter is ended with a concluding remark.

WHY DOES CHINESE CIVILIZATION LAST SO LONG?

Is it an illusion that Chinese civilization is regaining its world power? Of course not! (Jacques, 2009). It is amazing that China has 000 years of civilization, which has never been discontinued even China was conquered and temporarily lost its political power to two foreign races – the Mongolian led by Genghis Khan (成吉思汗) and the Manchurian led by Dorgon (多爾袞). The former created the Mongol Empire that covered both Asia and Europe and then withdrew to a country neighboring to the northern China, and the latter was fully assimilated into China as one of the fifty-five ethnic minorities (Poston and Shu, 1987).

Why did the Chinese civilization last so long without being destroyed? Will it recapture its power and become the new world order? Answers to these questions may be multiple. In this chapter, a thorough interpretation is provided based on the author's ethnic background and his in-depth understanding of Chinese civilization. Also, a graph model, similar to the one created by Targowski (2009), is used to point out the driving forces behind the Chinese culture. These driving forces (detailed later) are identified as critical factors essential to the sustainability of Chinese civilization.

To assist us in understanding the ramifications of these factors in Chinese civilization, a three-component model (**TCM**) is presented in Figure 8.1 to characterize Chinese civilization. Note that the TCM model resembles the three-element model (**TEM**) proposed by Targowski (2009) except some modifications are made to highlight the unique characteristics of Chinese civilization.

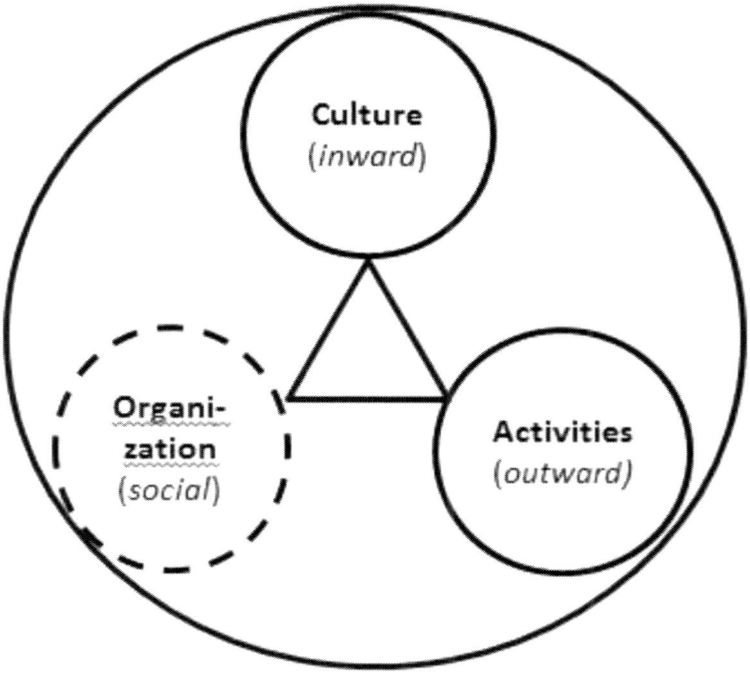

Figure 8.1. A Three-Component Model (TCM) to Express Chinese Civilization.

As shown in Figure 8.1, Chinese civilization can be analyzed based on three key components - *Culture, Activities, and Organization*. In contrast to Targowski's TEM model (i.e., *Culture*, *Entity*, and *Infrastructure*), a more general word *organization* is used to highlight the "weak" *infrastructure* in Chinese civilization. The *culture* component in our TCM model is somewhat different than the one defined in TEM. In TCM, *Culture* is confined to the "invisible (interior) belief and values" of Chinese thinking, and *Activities* represent all "visible behaviors and accomplished events" in Chinese society. A dashed circle is used to highlight the weakness of "Organization" as compared to the other two components - "Culture" and "Activities." With just a little study, it is easy to recognize that numerous "splendid footprints" have been left in Chinese history with respect to *Culture* and *Activities*. Some noticeable ones include Chinese philosophies, e.g., Confucianism and Daoism (i.e., the inward thinking), worldly known inventions, e.g., compass and paper (i.e., the outward accomplishments), and architectural landmarks, e.g., pagoda, palace, and the Great Wall (i.e., a mixture of both inward and outward achievements) (Thorp & Vinograd, 2001). Nevertheless, China has experienced more than two dozen of political struggles (i.e., be exact, 24 dynasties plus one democratic revolution) over the past 5,000 years. The average length of each dynasty is about 200 years, with the shortest of 15 years and the longest of 500+ years. Therefore, a dashed circle is used to highlight the instability of the *organization* in Chinese civilization. But, the interesting fact is that Chinese civilization never dies. Rather, it was expanded through merging and assimilating foreign peoples' cultures into one conglomerate civilization (Gernet, 1999). This phenomenon is quite unique and still true for the evolving Chinese civilization as compared to several extinct civilizations such as Roman and Maya. While more research is needed, it is clear that the "political" organization is not a critical component in Chinese civilization and it has little effect on the sustainability of Chinese civilization (Jacques, 2010).

What makes Chinese civilization immune to political instability? Because there are some unique characteristics in Chinese "culture" that create the "inherent stability" in Chinese civilization to wage against power (organization) changes and, furthermore, they become the driving force for Chinese civilization to assimilate other cultures. Indeed, there are some fundamental differences between the West and Chinese civilizations. These differences can be interpreted by a few factors that are indispensable to the survival of Chinese civilization and its resurgence in the 21st century. An elaboration of these factors follows.

- **Family-based Society**. Chinese culture is strongly family-based, and each family is an integral unit of the society. In contrast to the West, a number of human activities, from worship (of ancestors) to education (via home-based school) to discipline (by Home Laws 家法), are held in each family rather in a public place. Moreover, Chinese focus on financial help more through family members than from the public agency. It is very common to see a Chinese family composed of members from several generations along with relatives from their siblings. This unique characteristic becomes the grass root of Chinese culture, an influential component in Chinese civilization. It also becomes the very reason that Chinese society is relatively stable even there is no strong government and, in addition, is able to survive even there are financial hardships since most of the problems can be self-healed without exogenous help.

- **Self-motivated Altruistic Philosophy**. Nearly all Chinese have been educated with a strong focus of Confucianism, in which there is a fundamental teaching about the pathway of personal fulfillment. It can be identified by eight Chinese characters (格致誠正修齊治平), which becomes the "personal philosophy" and then materialized as the roadmap for each individual. The basic ideas of these eight characters are: focus your study of the environment (格物), seek your full knowledge (致知), purify your mind (誠意), straighten your heart (正心), improve yourself (修身), establish your family (齊家), govern your country (治國), and finally, universalize the whole world (平天下). This individual philosophy truly becomes the driving force for each Chinese to seek his/her best performance from working hard (self) to benefit the family (own offspring), the country (the people) and, eventually, the whole world. Due to this philosophy, poverty becomes a rare issue in Chinese society since most people carry the extra ability in helping others with a proud and voluntary heart. However, this philosophy does subtly internalize Chinese people's thinking and name their country "Middle Kingdom中國" (i.e., the Center of the World).
- **Education-first Value System**. Another discriminating force in Chinese culture is its value system that has been deeply-rooted in every Chinese mind. Unlike the Caste System in India (Pruthi, 2004), Chinese classify people into four groups: Intellectual (士), Farmer (農), Laborer (工), and Merchant (商), listed in an order of social status from high to low. Note that this value system motivates each Chinese individual to focus more on education (to become an intellectual, the highest) than on money-making (to become a merchant, the lowest). Also, the society gives more respect to farmers (i.e., self-employed natural producers) than to laborers (i.e., hiring hands by others), which fundamentally creates the foundation of stability as long as the society maintains its sufficiency via natural but essential productions (i.e., foods and other daily consumptions). Moreover, this value system is open to everyone and each individual has the opportunity to determine his/her social status, which is totally forbidden in Indian Caste System.
- **Little-Self vs. Super-Self Concept**. In Chinese history, the concept of "state" is very weak. Nearly in the first half of Chinese history (i.e., more than 2,100 years), there was no political structure or organization in China. Until 221 BC, China was united by Qin Shi Huang (秦始皇) and from that time point China entered a political system with the ruling of one emperor. However, the first "united nation," created by Emperor Qin, lasted only 15 years. While China becomes one country, there were more than twenty power changes (i.e., dynasties) during the subsequent 2500 years. As evidenced by the Chinese history, all these power struggles were led by civilians (not nobles) who were often illiterates such as monks, bandits, and famers (Keay, 2009). In history, Chinese intellectuals, the most prestigious ones, seldom showed interest in pursuing the emperor's position, though they did seek opportunities to serve as high officials (e.g., Provincial Governors (郡守) or Prime Ministers (宰相)) for the emperor. This special phenomenon originated from Confucius' teachings of "Heaven (天), Earth (地), Emperor (君), Parent (親), Master (師)," later transformed into a feudalistic notion of "Little Self (小我) vs. Super Self (大我)." As known, Qin

> Shi Huang (秦始皇) compared himself to the "Son of Heaven" (Qu, 2006) and, naturally, Emperor Qin represents the Super Self (大我). Given this, an intellectual is but a Little Self (小我), who, as a follower of Confucianism, shall of course respect his Master (師), Parent (親), and, most of all, the ultimate greatest – Heaven (天). This "feudalistic ideology," rooted in each intellectual's mind, provides the legitimacy for Chinese emperors, including today's communist government, to enjoy a total dictatorship since it is quite a noble deed for each "Little Self" sacrifices his benefits for the sake of the "Super Self" (犧牲小我成全大我). Clearly, from the viewpoint of democracy, it is a misfortune that Chinese people have given away their freedom and human rights as the modern West over the past few thousands of years. Nevertheless, Chinese civilization did weather through these power changes.

While our elaboration may not be exhaustive, the above four factors do provide a solid answer to "Why Chinese civilization last so long?" Simply put, Chinese civilization is hinged on a family-based structure, rather than on an external infrastructure such as well-organized top-down government. In particular, Chinese culture plays a pivotal role in Chinese civilization (see Figure 8.1). Families are the fundamental integral parts of Chinese society and most religious, financial, legal, and social activities occur within a family setting, which not only alleviates the function of an external government but also provides a strong self-healing power during unexpected financial crises or environmental chaos with a minimal level of social disorder. Moreover, Chinese culture values *education* and *self-motivated betterment* more than *business wealth* and *self-interest*. Since 500 BC, Chinese culture has been deeply influenced by Confucius' teachings, which were subtly exploited by Chinese political leaders (i.e., emperors) to create a new feudalism. Under this feudalistic Confucianism, Chinese were willingly giving away basic human rights (e.g., voting) and submitting to totalitarians with extra tolerance towards dictatorships as long as the environment provides essential and acceptable living conditions and resources. These resultant character changes in Chinese culture could be further exploited by the government to entertain its power or corrected by the West if democracy is effectively implemented in China. More discussion will be given in the following sections.

Implications of the Resurgence of Chinese Civilization

The resurgence of Chinese civilization resulted from China' fast economic growth over the past three decades that makes China the world's second largest economy in 2010, second to the United States. If China maintains its current economic growth, then, as forecasted, China will pass the United States as early as 2030 (Bardoza, 2010). No doubt, China has been the major driver of global economy for the past 30 years. China's continuous economic growth, on one hand, provides the Western capitalists ample opportunities to make unprecedented profit due to the low labor cost in China (Shenkar, 2005). On the other hand, many countries of the West, including Japan, become more and more anxious about the rise of China and deeply worry that China will create threats to the Western World (Callahan, 2005). Many of such concerns raised by the West can be easily dispelled if there is a certain degree of understanding about Chinese civilization, especially in its core component –

Chinese culture. However, if the West simply worries about China's economic growth or does not properly react to China's rise, then unexpected disasters may also happen. The implications of Chinese civilization's resurgence can be summarized as follows:

1. Civilization Impact: China will again become the world center of civilization. China has lost its spotlight since the beginning of the 19th Century. It is the common dream and the first priority for both China and its people to return to the world platform. Chinese civilization reached its climax in Tang dynasty (AD 618-907), which is 1500 years ago and then China was truly the center of world civilization. Since then, Chinese culture evolved through the teaching of Confucianism and many ethnic groups were assimilated by the largest ethnic group Han (漢). Today, the Han ethnic group accounts for 92% of Chinese population (i.e., 1.16 billion) and 19% of the world's total population. Of course, even today China is not quite a perfect democratic nation, most Chinese living in China and overseas would like to see the continuous development of Chinese civilization such that it will put China back onto the stage of world platform – the common wish of all Chinese by race.

2. Financial Impact: China will become the world resource center. The savings rate of China is high from many perspectives – historical experience, international standards, and the predictions of economic models. Furthermore, the average savings rate has been rising over time, with much of the increase taking place in the 2000s, so that the aggregate marginal propensity to save exceeds 50%. What really sets China apart from the rest of the world is that the rising aggregate savings has reflected high savings rates in all three sectors – corporate, household and government. (Ma & Yi, 2010). Historically, the Asian household savings rates are much higher than the West. In particular, due to the family-based Chinese culture, most Chinese choose to save money in a private mutual-saving system, which helps them gain higher interest without dealing with commercial banks or community credit unions. While there is a degree of risk that some members may not honor their obligation, by and large, Chinese retain their earnings with a high savings rate. This is a big contrast to the consumerism economy in the West. With Chinese high productivity and global strategies, China will continue to improve its economy and harbor its earnings through exports. As expected by the West, China will have no shyness to become the resource center for the whole world, though its GDP per capita may still way below that of the United States.

3. Economic Impact: The "Inland China" development will be the next project. Even though China has become the world's second largest economy, it is still a developing country. China's territory is about the same size as that of the U.S., but its population is not evenly distributed. In specific, 60% of Chinese population (i.e., 800 million) lives in 22% of its land, and most of them live in a band of 600 miles wide along the coast. The other 40% of population (i.e., 500 million) spreads over 78% of Chinese territory, the so-called Inland China. The sharp increase in the land value and labor costs in the coastal area has significantly reduced the competiveness and the growth of China economy in the global economy. Therefore, the Inland China development (i.e., China's *Great Western Development* project) will be the next economy project for China (and the globe) to maintain the economy growth in the coming two decades. It will of course provide job and business opportunities for the West to pursue corporate profits via talent sharing, low-cost manufacturing, and product consumption. As the world economy becomes more as one market, the Inland China development will possibly sustain the global economy.

4. Political impact: A pan-China Federation may be established through dialogues. To some extent, Confucianism leads to an "imperial thinking" (i.e., 格致誠正修齊治平) that has been deeply instilled into the mindset of every Chinese intellectual. This imperial thinking, different from the imperialism, will motivate Chinese to develop a nation that will assure a peaceful society for the common good of all citizens (i.e., 大同世界). This nation, often seen as the utopia defined in Socratism (Erdmann & Hough, 1899), may not be realistic from the global viewpoint. However, as China gains more global leadership, it will be very likely that some countries with Chinese as their major residents (e.g., Singapore, Taiwan) as well as countries having a strong influence from Confucianism (e.g., Viet Nam, Korea) to join with China in forming a federated country. In fact, a federated nation was created several times in Chinese history. The Han dynasties – East and West (206 BC – 226 AD) and the Tang dynasty (618 – 906 AD) are a few of such good precedents.

The above implications may or may not be fully realized, and they all depend on one condition – the continuous stability of the Communist Leadership and its government. Even there exists a great danger for the stability of the Communist Party in China, one thing for sure is Chinese civilization will not perish except it will sustain with discounted effects on the above implications. The potential challenges to Chinese civilization are detailed in the next section.

WHAT ARE CHALLENGES TO CHINESE CIVILIZATION?

It is miraculous that China has maintained an average of 8-9% economic growth continuously for the past 30 years. This outstanding performance has sharply improved China's role in global economy. Will this growing trend be continued for another two decades? The simple answer is "depends!" because there are a number of challenges that may cause significant impacts on the resurged Chinese civilization. As recently pointed out by the China's prime minister Wen Jiabao: "China must reform to maintain high levels of economic growth" (Lardy, 2012). What are to be reformed will be the key to identify these challenges to Chinese civilization. In brief, there are three major challenges: 1). How to maintain the stability of China's leadership? 2). How to keep high economic growths to justify the legitimacy of the current one party leadership (i.e., the dictatorship-like communist party)? 3).How to increase the openness of the political system (i.e., the so-called socialist democracy) in China? In fact, there three challenges are not independent of one and another. To understand the interactions among these three challenges, Figure 2 depicts their mutual relationships.

As seen in Figure 8.2, under the current socialist democracy in China, the legitimacy of the one-party (i.e., the communist party) leadership can be enhanced (i.e., a plus "+" sign) if China continues to generate high economic growth. In the meantime, due to the one-party leadership, the current government must have a tight control over other parties' different voices. Therefore, the stability of China's leadership will be worsened (i.e., a minus "-" sign) if the openness of political system is improved. In other words, the current China's one-party leadership (i.e., dictatorship) will be justified by the high economic growth and will be threatened if the political system becomes more open and transparent.

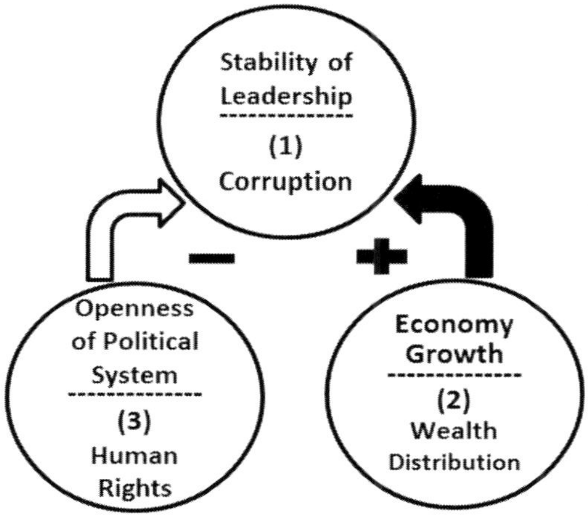

Figure 8.2. Major Challenges to Chinese Civilization.

Indeed, today's China is faced with these three steep challenges because there is a hidden concern behind each challenge. If each hidden concern is not effectively handled, then any of these three challenges may become out of control and subsequently generates domino effect that will collapse China's leadership, then its political system, and finally economic growth. Then, of course, the current progress of Chinese civilization will be hampered, though not destroyed. A brief highlight on the concern behind each challenge (see Figure 2) is given next.

- **Challenge 1:** How to maintain the stability of China's leadership? The key concern behind today China's leadership is corruption, which is prevalent from the bottom level (e.g., city mayor, county commissioner) to the top (e.g., provincial governors, party leaders) of Chinese government. It is recognized as the number one crisis that may strike down the communist party and crumble its leadership in China. Given the current condition of corruption, many experts as well as most intellectuals believe that there is no hope in Chinese communist party and its collapse is only a matter of time, which can happen anytime within ten years (Moses, 2012).
- **Challenge 2:** How to keep high economic growths to legitimize the current leadership? Maintaining high economic growths is still possible under the current China's leadership since the Inland China (i.e., the *Great Western Development*) Project will offer business opportunities to provide high economic growths. The real concern behind the high economic growth is *uneven wealth distribution*, which was pointed out that today China's success is built on 300 million people taking advantage of 1 billion cheap laborers. The unfair judicial system and the unfair distribution of wealth are making the challenges even greater (Lee, 2010). Similar to, but even worse than, the United States, 90% of China's wealth is in the hands of less than 1% of China's rich people, and 44% of the rich people indicate that they want to migrate to overseas countries. Such sharp uneven distribution of wealth could easily cause the poor to protest that may turn into a massive violence. In fact, China's leaders are aware of this concern and a reform plan is undergone. The problem for solving the uneven wealth distribution is it takes time and it will require 10 years (Xinhua, 2012). Will it be soon enough to avoid the next civil revolution in China? No one knows except there is a crystal ball.

- **Challenge 3:** How to increase the openness of the current political system while maintaining the current leadership? This is probably the most difficult challenge as compared to the above two. If China maintains its one-party leadership, then it is almost certain that there will be no way to increase the openness of the current political system. However, due to the strong influence of Confucianism on Chinese culture, Chinese people are willing to give away the "human rights" to trade for better economy and social stability. Thus, this challenge could be kicked aside by China if there is a way to keep a high economic growth as well as a better wealth distribution. Even this challenge is skillfully controlled, its hidden concern - *Human Rights* may turn into a hot issue that will force China to initiate political reform. If it happens, then it will be the beginning of the end of Chinese Communism.

The above three challenges to China may create huge impacts on Chinese civilization and each of them could cause the downfall of Chinese government if the hidden concerns (i.e., corruption, wealth distribution, and limited human rights) are not properly handled by the current government. To say the least, the downfall of China for sure will crash its economic growth, which of course is not what the West wants to see due to its detrimental impact on the global economy. However, the continuity of Chinese communists' leadership in China, with planned economic growth, may irrationally expand its military power at the expense of limited human rights could endanger the safety and benefits of its neighboring countries. Worse yet, the rise of Chinese communist party will become unavoidable threats to the "democratic" West, which currently suffers from poor economy but has full human rights and individual freedom. Hence, our next question will be "What should the West respond to the resurgence of Chinese civilization such that China can continue to maintain its economic growth while also improving its human rights?" Finding an answer for this question requires the West to develop some strategic moves. Some suggestions are provided below based on the author's knowledge of and insight into the communist party in China.

THE WEST'S RESPONSE TO THE RESURGENCE OF CHINESE CIVILIZATION

As pointed out earlier, Chinese civilization has survived after more than 20 power struggles (i.e., dynasties) in China history. One primary reason is the dominant component - *Chinese culture* in Chinese civilization as compared to the remaining two – *Activities* and *Organization* in the proposed civilization model (see Figure 1). As revealed in history, Chinese people are willing to trade human rights for the national stability (i.e., tolerate dictatorship for improved social stability), influenced by Confucianism and its resultant "Little Self vs. Super Self" concept. To avoid Chinese communist party's manipulation of Chinese people via leveraging stability for stronger dictatorship, the West should respond to the rise of Chinese civilization with the following actions:

1. *Open Arms to Chinese Civilization by accepting what is good for the West.* China has 5000 years of history and Chinese civilization plays a critical role in world civilization. Historically, Chinese civilization has significantly benefited mankind, in particular people in Asia, through culture assimilation (i.e., soft power). Its culture and accomplishments in many aspects have outreached at least one third of the whole world population (i.e., people in

China, Korea, Japan, and all countries in South Indo China). All these countries, except Japan, have never taken initiative to use hard power (i.e., military) to attack other countries. There are good reasons for the West to understand and learn unique components in Chinese civilization such as *family-based culture* and *self-motivated altruistic philosophy*. Over the past fifty years, the West made significant progress in science and technology to improve the materialistic aspect of human life. Nevertheless, less family value and reduced social moral have created an immense economic burden for the West and, subsequently, made the West an underdog in the global competition. It is time for the West to reexamine its weakness in culture and social values, which may be remedied by what is good in Chinese civilization.

2. *Introduce human right through open education channel.* Though Chinese civilization has surged and outperformed the West in the past three decades, in fact, it is still quite temporary and feeble. One primary reason that Chinese civilization rises is its huge but very inexpensive labors, for which the West shifted its financial capitals and resources (e.g., technology, factories, and management expertise) to China to seek a quick fix of competition against other competitors (e.g., Japan, Korea). This in turn provides China with ample opportunities to catch up its economic development. Therefore, the West entrepreneurs must be very careful since China does not share the same value system, ideology, and political infrastructure (i.e., democracy) with the West. Any economic opportunities offered by the West to China will solidify the communist party's tight control of human rights in name of improved national stability as well as legitimize the party's leadership by pushing China onto the world platform. As addressed in Figure 2, any improvement in human rights will increase the openness of the political system in China, which in fact is considered the most powerful way to challenge the current Chinese communist regime. Therefore, the West should max its power by wide opening its education to more Chinese intellectuals, who in fact are the cream of the crop in China. These intellectuals, once educated, will either stay overseas and be used by the West for economic advancement or later return to China to transform the communist party. In either case, this action produces a win-win for the West.

3. *Focus on self-improvement by making structural changes.* The West has made many progresses and enjoyed its wonderful civilization since 1900. However, it is also true that the West has been easy on themselves (i.e., relaxed in materialism) for more than 30 years. Since early 1980s, many Asian countries (e.g., Japan, Korea, Taiwan, Singapore, and Hong Kong) have worked extremely hard in education and economic development. Their economic growths have outperformed the West and their wealth and talents soon become the catalyst to speed up the economic activities in China. By comparing what have been consumed (i.e., both natural and derived resources) by the West to those by China, there is no reason or excuse for the West to point finger at China about its economic activities or production gains in the global market. As mentioned before, the Asian countries have relatively high savings towards their GDP as compared to the West. Today, while in significant trade deficits, most countries in the West is still in the midst (or myth) of promoting consumerism (or consumption). The West should not be scared by the prosperity of Chinese civilization. Rather, a structural change in economy activity shall be made by the West with respect to two major aspects: 1). the consumers should change their life style – balance the family (national) budget is the top priority. The rich's wealth (or national support) should be effectively used to help the poor. The best outcome is to minimize the overall deficit as close as possible to zero while engaging citizens in redefined economic activities. 2). the national economic should focus on activities that cannot be easily outsourced, which can be technology and innovation-based

such as health care products (everyone needs it) or bio-medical engineering (with high entry barrier). This implies that education modifications are required for all young generations, and all economic units such as families and communities should take initiative in deriving economic plans that are in line with the state and national strategic plan. Figure-pointing is an easy way to shift our own faults to others who are working hard. The following remark by Mitt Romney, the Republican Presidential Nominee, is a typical example to highlight a wrong and naïve response from the West towards the rise of China (Rapoza, 2011).

> "China is on almost every dimension cheating. We got to recognize that they're manipulating their currency and by doing so they're holding down the price of Chinese goods and making sure their products are artificially low-priced. It's predatory pricing. It's killing jobs in America."

The resurgence of Chinese civilization is not a surprise if the West understands the huge differences in labor costs and living standards between China and themselves. It is not really a threat to the West if proper responses are timely taken by the West to cope with own weakness in the past thirty years or to prevent unwanted political moves by the Chinese communist party in the global competition. The West should be willing to understand and learn the unique characteristics in Chinese civilization as a remedy to fix own weaknesses. Also, the West should stand firm in its civilization virtue – human rights and continue to provide such education approach to Chinese intellectuals for the sake of improving the political system in China. Moreover, the West should make a structural change to the economic activities that will promote new product development and manufacturing that cannot be easily outsourced or duplicated. In doing so, consumerism is not the key solution to solve the economic problems encountered by the West.

CONCLUSION

Chinese civilization has lasted more than 5000 years. Why did it resurge? In this Chapter, a three-component model (TCM) is used to explain why Chinese civilization survived after more than 20 dynasties (i.e., power changes). As compared to the West, Chinese civilization is dominated by the *Culture* component in the TCM model, not the development (i.e., activities) and the organization. The resurgence of Chinese civilization is truly expedited and influenced by the tacit values of the Chinese culture such as *family-based* society, *education-first* value system, and the teaching of Confucianism (e.g., *little-self* versus *super-self*). Given these unique characteristics of Chinese civilization, the recent rapid economic growth in China will cultivate an environment that justifies the leadership of the Chinese Communist Party in China while providing limited human rights to its people. Subsequently, the further development of Chinese civilization may create huge impacts on the world civilization, financial activities, economic growth, and a possible formation of a pan-China federation in Asia. These implications may not happen because the current Chinese Communist Regime is faced with critical challenges (or *concerns* be exact) that include *severe corruption* (from private to public), *uncertain economic growth*, and *restricted human rights*. Any of these concerns could easily cause the downfall of the current Chinese Communist Regime, which may not be the best for the West to see due to the dangling impacts from China's downfall.

Rather, the West should open arms to Chinese civilization by learning/accepting what is good for the West, continue to stand firm and promote human rights to China, and, finally, make structural changes in the national economy that are meaningful towards the global needs.

REFERENCES

Bardoza, D. (2010). China passes Japan as second-largest economy. *New York Times*, August 15.

Behrer, William H. (2010). China: a sleeping giant awakens. *The Real Truth*, March-April, 12-14.

Callahan, W.A. (2005). How to understand China: the dangers and opportunities of being a rising power. *Review of International Studies*. 31(04), 701-714.

Coffin, J., Stacey, R., Cole, J. & Symes, C. (2011). *Western civilizations: their history and their culture*, Volume 2 (17th Ed). U.S.A.: Houghton Mifflin.

Dullien, S, Kotte, D. J., Márquez, A. & Priewe, J (2010). *The financial and economic crisis of 2008-2009 and developing countries*. New York and Geneva: United Nations Publications.

Erdmann, J.E. & Hough, W. S. (1899). *A history of philosophy*. Volume 3, New York: The MacMillan CO.

Gernet, J. (1999). *A history of Chinese civilization*. (Second Edition). New York, New York: Cambridge University Press.

Huntington, S. P. (1997). *The clash of civilizations and the remaking of world order*. New York, New York: Simon & Schuster.

Jacques, Marin (2010). Understanding the rise of China. Retrieved on August 11, 2012 at http://www.ted.com/talks/martin_jacques_understanding_the_rise_of_china.html.

Jacques, M. (2009). *When China rules the world: The end of the western world and the birth of a new global order*. New York: The Penguin Press.

Jones, A. (2007). Responding to the rise of China. *Security Challenges*, 3(1) 7-17.

Keay, J. (2009). *China: A History*, New York, New York: Basic Books.

Lardy, N (2012). China must reform to maintain high levels of economic growth. Feb 3, 2012. Retrieved on August 30, 2012 at http://www.publicserviceeurope.com/article/1459/china-must-reform-to-maintain-high-levels-of-economic-growth.

Lee, S. (2010). China's unequal wealth-distribution map causing social problems. China Post, June 28. Retrieved on Aug 30, 2012 at http://www.chinapost.com.tw/commentary/the-china-post/special-to-the-china-post/2010/06/28/262505/p1/China's-unequal.htm.

Lin, J. Y. (2009). Economic development and structural change, Lecture at Cairo University, Cairo, Egypt, November 5.

Ma, G. & Yi, W. (2010). China's high saving rate: myth and reality. *BIS Working Paper* (No. 312). Basel, Switzerland: Bank of International Settlements.

Michelbach, P. A. (2011). Democracy as vocation: political maturity in Luther and Hegel. *Journal of Democratic Theory*, 1(4), 1-33.

Moses, R.L. (2012). The communist party's big problem? It's not Bo Xilai. *The Wall Street Journal*, Sept 6. Available at http://blogs.wsj.com/chinarealtime/2012/09/06/the-chinese-communist-partys-big-problem-its-not-bo-xilai/.

Poston, D.L. & Shu, J. (1987). The demographic and socioeconomic composition of China's ethnic minorities. *Population and Development Review* 13(4), 703-722.

Pruthi, R.K. (2004). *Indian caste system*. New Delhi, India: Discovery Publishing House.

Qu, L. (2006). The characteristics of the theory of history in ancient china. *Frontiers of History in China* 1(1), 1-18.

Rapoza, K. (2011). Romney says China is cheating. *Forbes*, November 21. Retrieved on August 30, 2012 at http://www.forbes.com/sites/kenrapoza/2011/11/21/romney-says-china-is-cheating/.

Rawski, T.G. (2011) The rise of China's economy. *Footnotes*, 16 (06) The Newsletter of FPRI's Wachman Center, Foreign Policy Research Institute.

Shenkar, O. (2005). *The Chinese century – The rising Chinese economy and its impact on the global economy, the balance of power, and your job*. Upper Saddle River, New Jersey: Pearson Education.

Stanczyk, M. T. (2008). Enter the dragon's lair: The new socialism and private property ownership in the People's Republic of China. *Journal of Civil Rights and Economic Development*, 22(3), Article 7.

Targowski, A. (2009). *Information technology and societal development*. (Chapter 1). Hershey, Pennsylvania: IGI Global.

Thorp, R. L. and Vinograd, R. E. (2001). *Chinese art & culture*. New York, New York: Harry A. Abrams.

Xinhua News (2012). China to solve wealth distribution issues in 10 years, Retrieved on Aug 30, 2012. at http://www.chinadaily.com.cn/business/2012-5/28/content_15403600.htm *People's Daily Online*.

In: Spirituality and Civilization Sustainability ... ISBN: 978-1-53610-729-6
Editors: Andrew Targowski and Marek J. Celinski

Chapter 9

THE POTENTIAL OF JAPANESE CIVILISATION: ITS RELIGIOUS CHARACTERISTICS AND CONTRIBUTIONS TO THE WORLD

Hisanori Kato*
Butsuryo College of Osaka, Japan

ABSTRACT

Although modern civilisation has brought about great technical achievements, mankind face various problems today. It seems that humans are endlessly pursuing economic development, and they often neglect the preservation of the environment. Japan is not free from this world-wide problem. However, Japanese civilisation would be able to offer an important paradigm for the future course of mankind. In particular, animism and tolerance towards religious differences seem to be vital elements for the betterment of this world. Religious tolerance in Japan also seems to be a crucial pointer to the future of this world. Shinto and Buddhism can set a model for religions co-existing with each other. We have to admit, however, that as Shinto and Buddhism are orientated towards polytheism, these two religions face relatively fewer obstacles in peaceful co-existence.

INTRODUCTION

Ever since Man's passage from the Lower to the Upper Palaeolithic stage of technological progress, the Human Race had been Lords of Creation on Earth in the sense that, from that time onwards, it has no longer been possible either for inanimate Nature or for any other non-human creature either to exterminate Mankind or even to interrupt human progress (Toynbee, Somervell, & Royal Institute of International Affairs, 1987, p. 320).

Japanese philosopher Michiaki Kobayashi believes that as economic development reaches its peak, a civilisation starts to lose its traditional values that hitherto played an important role in the process of consolidating the civilisation itself (Kobayashi, 2001). He

* E-mail: hisanorikato@hotmail.com.

also warns that due to the prevailing epicurean attitude and a weakened sense of morality the fate of today's world is showing closer resemblance to that of the Roman Empire. Yoshimichi Someya, a noted Japanese anthropologist, thinks that modern civilisation has reached a sort of dead-end and insists that we should create a civilisation whose creed is reciprocative rather than exploitative (Someya, 2010). Toynbee (1987) also notes that only mankind is able to determine the course of this world in the face of technological mastery, including the invention of the atomic bomb.

Epicureanism and materialism are also ubiquitous in Japan, where a long-standing civilisation exists. Various social problems, including disrespect for life, have been observed in this country, which is regarded as among the most 'modernised'.[1] How does Japanese civilisation fit in to contemporary society? Has Japanese civilisation already perished due to dysfunction? Further, is Japanese civilisation still able to play its role in mending the fractures characterising the world today?

GLOBAL PROBLEMS

Religious conflicts, economic inequality, destruction of nature, and violence caused by wars and crimes are major challenges that we – mankind – face today. We may still vividly remember the apocalyptic scenes in north-eastern Japan following the earthquake and tsunami of March 2011. In the wake of this disaster, a nuclear power plant in Fukushima prefecture was severely damaged. This is a stark reminder that modern technology, the hallmark of modern civilisation, has the potential to threaten the safety and welfare of humans.

We cannot deny the fact that modern technology has changed the lives of humans. Washing machines and microwave ovens have emancipated women from laborious house work. Aeroplanes and bullet trains have drastically shortened our travel time. Personal computers and multi-purpose electronic devices, such as mobile phones, have made communication among people miraculously rapid. Faster trains, greater convenience and more instantaneous communication are among the goals that modern humans have been obsessively pursuing. All these are unquestionably the result of the progress of civilisation. In a society that positively evaluates itself as 'advanced' and 'civilised', materialistic values are highly appreciated.

Western-originated materialism seems to have spread all over the globe, and non-Western countries also have followed the path which the West has paved. It is not an exaggeration to say that Western civilisation has now become a global civilisation. The most prominent attribute of the highly-advanced technological and materialistic society is mass consumption, which appeared in the middle of the twentieth century (Braudel, 1993). Simultaneously, mass production has emerged to meet the demand. 'Moreness' is greatly valued by the people living in this materialistic world. In order to realise 'moreness', a considerable amount of energy is needed. The life-style of urban dwellers profoundly depends on the stable supply of energy. However, we have to remember that nuclear power, which is the main source of

[1]For example, the total number of the case of suicide in Japan amounted 31,690 in 2010. Official statistics revealed by National Police Agency. http://www.npa.go.jp/safetylife/seianki/H22jisatsunogaiyou.pdf. The child abuse in Japan has increased lately with 380,950 cases in 2006 while it was 352,814 in 2004.Official statistics revealed by Ministry of Health, Labour and Welfare: http://www.mhlw.go.jp/bunya/kodomo/dv16/index.html

generating electricity for maintaining 'civilised' life in Japan, is never free from the potential of destruction on a global scale as shown by the Fukushima incident.

As Someya has already pointed out, the orientation of modern civilisation may have created an uneven circulation of wealth, which justifies the survival of the fittest (Someya, 2010). In the twenty-first century, many believe that the colonialism is defunct. Yet, according to Someya, we now encounter metamorphosis of this exploitative system that had functioned in the less developed or less 'civilised' areas in the world previously. Materialism has taken the place of colonialism and seems to be a powerfully dominant force in maintaining the law of the jungle (Someya, 2010).

Industrialisation with technological advancement, which has been the mainstay of materialism, is a European endowment. The U.S. is another great representation of this Western civilisation. Towards the end of twentieth century, Kenneth Clark wrote about the manifestation of this in one of the greatest cities in the U.S (Clark, 1982, p. 226):

> "Imagine an immensely speeded up movie to Manhattan Island during the last hundred years. It would look less like a work of man than like some tremendous natural upheaval. It's godless, it's brutal, it's violent – but one can't laugh it off, because in the energy, strength of will and mental grasp that have gone to make New York, materialism has transcended itself."

The process of technology-based industrialisation has been one of conquering nature. Descartes, Galileo, Newton, and Einstein have contributed to the explanation of scientifically 'mysterious miracles', which were hitherto believed to be the deeds of God (Clark, 1982). Scientific findings have undoubtedly played an important role in eradicating superstitions and 'uncivilised' beliefs in the lives of people.

In Christian tradition, which is the backbone of Western civilisation (Brunner, 1949/2000), God created nature and the laws of nature. It is correct to understand that nature itself has no other religious significance in Christian tradition. This view is also shared by Islam in that every phenomenon observed in this world is the manifestation of Allah's will.[2] There is no sacredness in nature, and thus people are enthusiastic to conquer nature without fear in both Christian and Islamic traditions. This attitude is highly pertinent to the progress of civilisation; industrial and material development require the establishment of various facilities on earth, neglecting the merits of woods, mountains, seas and other natural entities.

As the result of the consolidation of global or Western-originated materialistic civilisation, mankind now faces a serious environmental problem. On 22nd September, 2009, at the closing session of the Summit on Climate Change, Secretary-General of the United Nations Ban Ki-Moon stated that "Climate change is a defining challenge of our time. The opportunity and responsibility to avoid catastrophic climate change is in your hands."[3]

The conflict between religions is another serious threat to peace in this world. For example, there is a significant division between the believers of God and Allah. Although

[2] *Al-Quran* offers a clear explanation of this: "In the creation of the heavens and the earth; in the alternation of night and day; in the ships that sail the ocean with cargoes beneficial to man; in the water which God sends down from the sky and with which He revives the earth after its death, dispersing over it all manner of beasts; in the disposal of the winds, and in the clouds that are driven between sky and earth: surely in these there are signs for rational men" *(al-Baqarah*, 2:164, *The Koran*, Harmondsworth, 1995, p.26).

[3] http://www.mofa.go.jp/policy/un/assembly2009/sg0922.pdf

both Christians and Muslims make huge efforts to reconcile two religions through various activities, we have to admit that there is a tug of war between Christianity and Islam. It is unfortunate for us to witness violence resulting from the conflict between these religions from time to time; monotheism tends to justify itself and refuse to accept multiple deities.

FORGOTTEN JAPANESE TRADITION?

Since the Restoration of Meiji in the end of the nineteenth century, Japan has endeavoured to modernise its society. The slogan of Meiji reformers was *datsuanyuo* or "leave Asia and enter the West" (see for example Fukuzawa, 1995). Westernisation with modern technology was tantamount to bringing about modern civilisation, known as *bunmeikaika* in Japan. It is true that Japan has been under the influence of Western civilisation throughout its modern history. Pursuing modernity and technology, which the Renaissance and Enlightenment movements in Europe intended to realise in the eighteenth and nineteenth centuries, had become an essential goal for Japan. Japan had succeeded in creating an efficient and convenient society with various modern machineries in one hundred years.

In the process of modernising Japan, it is also true that the appreciation of traditional values has declined. An example can be found in education policy, which precludes religious studies, and on the basis of which teachers are not even allowed to discuss the issue of religion in public schools. Shinto and Buddhism, two popular religions in Japan, have therefore been excluded from formal education since the end of World War II. Given Japan's pre-war history, when the Emperor Hirohito was regarded as a living deity, it is understandable that the separation of church and state should be firmly maintained in order to prevent theocracy from emerging. Yet, this does not mean that the long-standing Japanese civilisation should be discarded; it still contains much potential to offer solutions to the problems we face today.

In ancient Japan, animistic worship of nature was dominant, and later developed into Shinto. The sea, sun, wind, thunder, trees, mountains, waterfalls and even lightening were objects of worship (Craig, 2003). The worship of any natural entity is common among Japanese people. For example, Japanese classical literature shows this disposition of Japanese people.[4] A prominent Buddhist monk explains that the quintessential Japanese attitude towards deities is very simple: that there is a supernatural and sacred existence with much power in nature (Miyazaki, 2007). Mt. Fuji is also an object of worship, and it is a common practice for the Japanese to climb the mountain, believing that the sacred mountain purifies all of their senses, including vision, hearing, smell, taste, touch, and consciousness. They chant a specific incantation, *rokkonnshojo*, or purification of the six senses, while climbing Mt. Fuji. Miyawaki points out that the woods surrounding Buddhist temples and Shinto shrines, known as *chinjunoori* (forest of the guardian), have been cared for by the Japanese, and they have become spiritual sanctuary for the community (Miyazaki, 2007). Yoshinori Yasuda, a Japanese anthropologist, depicts animism as the civilisation of "beauty and compassion" that has existed in Japan throughout its history (Yasuda, 2006, p.180). In the

[4] *Manyoshu*, the anthology of classical poems compiled in the seventh century, contains some works that personalise nature.

world of animism, any existence, whether animate or inanimate, is shown a great deal of respect out of the spirit embodied within it.

This spiritual orientation, however, has been diminished in post-war Japan due to the supremacy of materialism, and a rationalism which regarded animism as superstitious and unreasonable (Yasuda, 2006). After the devastation brought by the war in 1945, the essential goal of Japan was to restore the country to stable economic growth. In this respect, Japan has achieved great successes. Such economic development required the expansion of industrial sectors, and consequently created heedlessness towards nature, which hitherto was deeply cared for and appreciated by the Japanese. The establishment of nuclear power stations, which would damage nature and would threaten the safety of residents nearby, is one of the examples of this supremacy of modernisation. It is true that development was given priority over the preservation of nature in modern Japan.

Having said this, Yasuda believes that Japanese people still maintain their civilisation's virtue and that they constantly search for the means of co-existence with all living creatures as their ancestors did (Yasuda, 2006). The fact that no riots or looting took place after more than 500,000 people lost their homes in the time of Hanshin-Awaji Great Earthquake in 1995, according to Yasuda, is a clear indication of the legacy of the civilisation of 'beauty and compassion' (Yasuda, 2006). Yasuda's theory is reaffirmed after the great earthquake and tsunami hit Eastern Japan in March 2011, in that the victims of calamities orderly and patiently queued up while waiting for the distribution of emergency food supplies. An American researcher said that "I am not even sure if there's a word for it that is as clear in its implications as when we hear 'looting'".[5]

Apart from materialism and rationalism, another burden was thrust upon Japanese animism-oriented civilisation after the Meiji Restoration in the late nineteenth century, namely, imperialism. Japan's invasion of Asia and its cruelty to 'other human existences' during the Pacific War clearly showed that the civilisation of 'beauty and compassion' was completely forgotten and dysfunctional. During this time, Shinto, which had originally sprung from animism with its appreciation for nature, was transformed into State Shinto and headed by a living God or the then Emperor. State Shinto functioned as a political tool in order to rationalise Japanese imperialism.

HARMONY IN RELIGION

While primitive animism, which is discordant with monotheism, is a distinctive feature, another notable aspect of Japanese civilisation is its syncretistic tendencies with respect to religions. Two major religions in Japan, Shinto and Buddhism in fact have never experienced an ideological clash in their history, except in the time of the establishment of State Shinto in the late nineteenth century.[6]

Shinto and Buddhism have been closely associated with the lives of Japanese people throughout history, and the characteristics of these religions are essential in order to maintain peaceful co-existence. S.N. Eisenstadt (1996, p. 235) explains that:

---

[5] *The Week*, 15 March, "Why is there no looting in Japan?" This article is available at: http://theweek.com/article/index/213154/why-is-there-no-looting-in-japan

[6] After the enforcement of *Shin ButsuBunriRei* (Order of the separation of Shinto and Buddhism) in 1869, some Buddhism temples were the target of assault, and some of them were physically damaged.

> "A central aspect of the syncretistic process was that no sharp demarcation of the symbolic boundaries of the religious collectivism (in this case of the Buddhist one, but the same could apply to Confucianism) and of the theological domain of doctrine developed."

The amicable relationship between the two religions could be already observed in the eighth century. It appeared as the establishment of Shinto-Buddhist combined temple known as *jinguji*.[7] One of the earliest *jinguji*s is Tado *jinguji* in Mie prefecture of present Japan. According to historical records dated 788, the Shinto deity or *kami* in Tado shrine confessed that he desired to leave his godhood and convert to Buddhism (Yoshie, 2008).

The conversion of *kami* known as *shinshinridatsu* frequently took place in the eighth and ninth centuries (Yoshie, 2008). Yoshie points out that the conversion of *kami*, who is supposed to be the guardian of aristocrats, was politically-oriented as Buddhist local warriors was gaining more power, and the Shintoist aristocrats had to capitulate to the new power. Although *shinshinridatsu* may have been facilitated for political reasons, it could never have been realised without polytheistic feature of Shinto and Buddhism, which also values harmony and detests friction.

The relationship between Shinto and Buddhism further developed in subsequent centuries. The belief that *kami* is the emanation of *hotoke* or Buddhist deities known as *honjisuijaku* became popular in the twelfth century onwards. Therefore, it is common that *kami* and *hotoke* are worshipped in the same vicinity in present-day Japan. Japanese people in fact pay little heed to the distinction between *kami* and *hotoke* as they utter both names when they make a plea to divine being. Sato also affirms the closeness of two kinds of divine beings (Sato, 2003, p. 113):

> "Of course, even in the medieval period many deities were clearly defined as either kami or buddhas, and there were ways to distinguish between the two. However, we must not lose sight of the fact that there was a large divine realm that was not so easily categorised."

It is correct to understand that two kinds of divine beings have harmoniously co-existed in the Japanese religious scene while being equally appreciated by the people.

Kukai, the founder of Shingon sect in the ninth century, played an important role in the process of consolidating these harmonious relations. Kukai, popularly known as Kobodaishi, went to Tang of China to learn Buddhism in 804 and established a monastery at Mt. Koya of the Kii mountains in the Western part of Japan after his return in 816. The monastery Kukai founded is based on *Shingon* doctrine of which the literal meaning is "true words" or "mantra" (Craig, 2003). The Koyasan or Mt. Koya is thought to be the centre of syncretic relationship between Shinto and Buddhism. The area has been listed as a World Heritage Site by UNESCO on the following grounds:

"Criterion (ii): The monuments and sites that form the cultural landscape of the Kii Mountains are a unique fusion between Shintoism and Buddhism that illustrates the interchange and development of religious cultures in East Asia.

[7] *Jing* means Shinto shrine while *ji* means Buddhist temple.

Criterion (iii): The Shinto shrines and Buddhist temples in the Kii Mountains, and their associated rituals, bear exceptional testimony to the development of Japan's religious culture over more than a thousand years.

Criterion (iv): The Kii Mountains have become the setting for the creation of unique forms of shrine and temple buildings which have had a profound influence on the building of temples and shrines elsewhere in Japan.

Criterion (vi): Together, the sites and the forest landscape of the Kii Mountains reflect a persistent and extraordinarily well-documented tradition of sacred mountains over the past 1200 years."[8]

The mythology on how Kukai found the site of monastery at Mt. Koya is rather symbolic of the amicable relationship between the two religions. When Kukai was wandering around the Kii Mountains, he met a hunter who was with a black and a white dog. The hunter led him to a mountain and introduced him to the Shinto deity, *Niutsuhimeookami*. This Shinto deity then agreed to lease the area to Kukai for his Buddhist propagation. Kukai, with much appreciation, decided to honour both *Niutsuhimeookami* and *Takanomikooomikami* (in fact the hunter) who led him to see his father *Niutsuhimeookami*. (*Kishyuwakayama Prefecture Official Handbook, Koyasan Kumanokoto*, 2007; Oyama, 1975). That was the beginning of his monastery at Mt Koya.

Kukai's Shingon school teaches a form of esoteric Buddhism, and its magical and mysterious rituals attracted people (Schirokauer, 1993). Kukai put more emphasis on worldly matters that people were concerned with rather than philosophical and metaphysical questions in Buddhism. Kukai in fact was a master of art, calligraphy and poetry. It would be reasonable to assume that Kukai employed a cultural means of interchanges among people in order to bring about harmonious and peaceful co-existence of religions. Even now, Buddhist monks in the tradition of Kukai at Mt Koya chant Buddhist sutra daily at Shinto shrines of *Niutsumyojin* and *Takanomyoujin*. Even some Buddhist rituals are conducted by Shinto priests (*Kishyu Wakayama Prefecture Official Handbook, Koyasan Kumanokoto*, 2007; Oyama, 1975). These facts, according to the head priest at *Miutsumyojin*, epitomise the spirit of the Japanese that appreciates co-existence with other entities, including nature. In sharp contrast with Islam and Christianity, Japanese religion lacks any absolute claim over people (Sato, 2003).

TRADITIONS OF CONFLICT AND CONQUERING NATURE

Islam and Christianity, in fact, are never able to share ideological common ground, although there have been numerous efforts to bridge these two religions by the followers of both religions. For Muslims, Jesus Christ was merely one of the prophets while Christians steadfastly believing that Jesus Christ was the son of God. These religious convictions often lead both Muslims and Christians to political disagreement and even to physical clashes, all with the aim of safeguarding their only God. We have to admit that both religions emphasise a vertical relationship of humans with God. What is important in this relationship is the 'I' who corresponds with God. What does count is how 'I' am judged by the One after leaving this world.

[8] Available at: http://whc.unesco.org/en/list/1142

With regard to the human's attitude towards nature, the two religions share similar perspectives. We know that 'I-ness' has contributed to the development of the concept of human rights. Western tradition, in its appreciation of the conveniences of life, has surely made the lives of humans much easier by conquering nature. In Christian tradition, according to Brunner, technological development is highly valued. As he explains (Brunner, 1949/2009, p. 173):

> "Technics in itself is no problem for the Christian man. As long as technics is subordinate to human will, and human will is obedient to the divine will, technics is neutral, and as a means of goodwill is itself good. From the Christian point of view, there is no reason to condemn the machine and to return to the spinning-wheel."

'I-ness', which has brought about modern civilisation with technological development has at the same time a tendency for disregarding the relationship between humanity and its environment. Muslims also put less emphasis on the cordial relationship between nature and humans as for them nature is merely a sign of divine will (Nasr, 1978). Again, what does matter for Muslims is to follow the will of Allah. In both Christian and Islamic traditions, self-assurance of faith is a very primary concept, which creates the sense of supremacy in their faith, if not the denial of others. We should also remember that the salvation of humans is emphasised in Christian tradition, and there should be punishments for any irreverent acts of humans that have occurred among humans, but not for any acts conducted between humans and things, such as nature (Yoshie, 2008). In this paradigm, 'things', including nature, are merely regarded as the objects that have no substantial relationship with humans. However, as Shuntaro Ito has already pointed out, because humans are in fact are part of nature, there should be a balanced co-existence between nature and humans (Ito, 1990).

Conclusion

As demonstrated above, some notable characteristics of Japanese civilisation include a deep appreciation of nature, which we might call animism, and a tolerance towards religions, especially between Shinto and Buddhism. These tendencies epitomise the appreciation of 'otherness' rather than 'I-ness' as Someya points out (Someya, 2010).

It is obvious that the environmental problems and ideological conflicts posing a major threat to today's world have been created by a self-centred mentality, one that refuses to accept other existences, and which simultaneously prioritises one's own interests over all others. Needless to say, the prevailing modern civilisation is associated not only with this mentality but has led to improved medical treatment and emancipation of women from laborious work. We also know that there have been enormous efforts to narrow the gap between religions.

Having said this, it seems that all humans face a sort of dilemma. As has been mentioned earlier, the Great Eastern Earthquake in March 2011 in Japan has revealed the vulnerability of modern technology. The devastating tsunami severely damaged Fukushima Daiichi Nuclear Plant, and the leakage of radiation has caused serious environmental as well as health problems in the area. In the wake of Fukushima incident, the operating ratio of nuclear power plants in Japan plunged to 26.4% in August 2011.[9] The shortage of electricity in Japan forced Japanese people to return to a more primitive lifestyle on scorching summer days.

Such inconvenience, however, offered an opportunity for the Japanese to remember their traditional wisdom of simply living with nature and appreciating every existence. It is the reality today that a 'convenient and comfortable' lifestyle realised by modern civilisation has become such a paramount value. Mass production and mass consumption have been dominating this world. Modernity is almost tantamount to creating 'moreness'. However, pursuing this value requires sacrifices, such as reckless development of land, risking human lives with exposure to radiation, disregarding morality, the greed generated by materialism, and so on.

Animism, on the other hand, is still useful for creating an alternative value in life. As both living and non-living entities are thought to have actual life in animism, people would refrain from above-mentioned negative human deeds. In this tradition, 'I' tend to care for 'others'. Rather than emphasising benefits only for humans, people need to care for the benefits for other entities, including the earth.

Religious tolerance in Japan also seems to be a crucial pointer to the future of this world. Shinto and Buddhism can set a model for religions co-existing with each other. We have to admit, however, that as Shinto and Buddhism are orientated towards polytheism, these two religions face relatively fewer obstacles in peaceful co-existence. Yet, their rather syncretic tradition is still valid as a model for eradicating religious conflicts. As the case of Mt. Koya shows, two religions have co-existed with mutual respect and modesty. Kukai, a leader of Buddhism, in fact 'borrowed' his premises from Shinto deity, and Buddhist monks and Shinto priests have been conducting inter-faith activities for centuries. Should monotheists also share Kukai's paradigm, there would be a more open-minded attitude towards other faiths.

In other words, the earth will be annihilated, if 'moreness' based on the mentality of 'I-ness' persists. Thus, Japanese civilisation should be reaffirmed, and it is important that the wisdom that embodied in Japanese civilisation should be exposed to the other parts of the world.

REFERENCES

Braudel, F. (1993). *A history of civilizations*. New York: Penguin Books.

Brunner, E. (1949/2009). *Christianity and civilisation*. Cambridge: James Clarke & Co.

Clark, K. (1982). *Civilisation*. London: Penguin Books.

Craig, A. M. (2003). *The heritage of Japanese civilization*. New Jersey: Prentice Hall.

Eisenstadt, S. N. (1996). *Japanese civilisation*. Chicago: The University of Chicago Press.

Fukuzawa, Y. (1995). *Bunmeron no Gairyaku [Summary of Civilisational Theory]*. Tokyo: Iwananmi Shoten.

Ito, S. (1990). *Hikakubunmei to Nihon [Comparative civilisation and Japan]*. Tokyo: Chuokoronsha.

Kobayashi, M. (2001). *Fuanna Jidan, Soshite Bunmeino Suitai [Era of unrest and the decline of civilisation)*. Tokyo: NHK Books.

Kumanokodo K. (2007). *Kishyu Wakayama Prefecture Official Handbook*. Tokyo.

[9] http://www.fepc.or.jp/news/__icsFiles/afieldfile/2011/09/13/hatsuju20110913.pdf

Miyawaki, A. (2007). *Chinju no Mori [Forest of the guardian]*. Tokyo: Shinchosha.

Nasr, S. H. (1987). *Science and civilization in Islam*. Cambridge: The Islamic Text Society.

Oyama, K. (1975). *Shinbutsu Koshoshi [History of the interchange between Shinto and Buddhism]*. Kyoto: Rinkawashoten.

Sato, H. (2003). Wrathful deities and saving deities. In M. Teeuwen & F. Rambelli (Eds.), *Buddhism and Kami in Japan: Honji suijaku as a combinatory paradigm*. New York: Routledge.

Schirokauer, C. (1993). *A brief history of Japanese civilization*. Fort Worth, Texas: Harcourt Brace Jovanovich College Publishers.

Someya, Y. (2010). Bunmei mo Mata Kanryuno michiwo [Civilisation goes to recurrent path]. *Comparative Civilisation*, vol. 26.

Toynbee, A. J., Somervell, D. C., & Royal Institute of International Affairs. (1987). *A study of history: Abridgement of Volumes VII-X*. New York: Oxford University Press.

Yasuda, Y. (2006). *Isshinkyo no Yami [Darkness of monotheism]*. Tokyo: Chikumashobo.

Yoshie, A. (2008). *Shibutsu Shugo [Amalgamation of Shinto and Buddhism]*. Tokyo: Iwanamishoten.

In: Spirituality and Civilization Sustainability ...
Editors: Andrew Targowski and Marek J. Celinski ISBN: 978-1-53610-729-6

Chapter 10

ISLAM IN THE FORTHCOMING MILLENNIUM: POTENTIAL FOR REVIVAL IN THE THIRD MILLENNIUM

Norman C. Rothman*
University of Maryland University College, Adelphi, MD, US

ABSTRACT

Islam is the second-largest religion in the world and is a global force in economic, social and political change. This paper takes a look at the present state of the Islamic religion and the nations which it populates. Demographic trends are analyzed, including the steeply rising number of technically-literate young people and the ever-increasing empowerment of women in a region where many outsiders think women are oppressed chattel. The paper also studies the economics of the Islamic world, how Islamic beliefs have influenced economic growth in the past and what Muslims are doing now to reconcile the differences between their beliefs and the necessary tools for economic growth. Lastly, the paper examines the social and political changes that have been rocking the Muslim world, and the potential of a revival for the religion, and even the possibility of it soon becoming the largest religion in the world.

INTRODUCTION

The Islamic world now includes large parts of two continents and has congregants in all six continents. By 2025, it is estimated that it may pass the position currently held by Christianity as the world's largest denomination. It has assumed critical mass, and its change-ng demography, economic structure, social configuration, and political evolution will inevitably affect global sustainability including the spiritual element which it embodies. This chapter will examine the role that the above elements of demography, economics, social, and political change play in the process. Its ongoing development including its revival as a central

* E-mail: ncrothman@aaol.com.

participant in global affairs makes Islam a critical segment in the future of humanity. Is there a potential for a revival that would rival the period between 750 and 1100 C.E/A.D. when the Muslim Middle East and adjoining areas in Asia, Africa and Europe were a center of arts, sciences, and culture?

DEMOGRAPHY

When discussing topics of population related to the Islamic world, it is well to recognize that it is a global phenomenon. The Arab Middle East, which is not wholly Muslim, is the home of perhaps 15% of the world's Muslims. A number of African countries such as Gambia, Mauritania, Senegal, Burkina Faso, Ghana, Mali, Niger, Chad, Sudan, Nigeria, Cameroon, Ethiopia, Djibouti, Somalia, and Tanzania have a majority or near majority of Muslims. The Balkans in Southeastern Europe contain large numbers of Muslims as does the European segments of the former Soviet Union in the Caucasus and along the Volta River and Ural Mountains as represented by the Tatar, Bashkirs, and the Chuvash. India alone has over 100 million Muslims while Central Asia is entirely Muslim. The largest Muslim concentrations in the world are in the Southeast Asian nation of Indonesia and the South Asian nation of Pakistan with Muslim populations approaching 200 million and over 150 million people respectively. It is estimated that by 2025 the Muslim population will reach 30% of the world's people and will challenge Christianity as the world's largest denomination (Hakim (2011).

The characteristics of the population indicate that it is not just the quantity but also the nature of the population that will affect change including the potential for sustained revival. The biggest bulge in the population is that of those under thirty. Most Muslim countries have for some time been in the second stage of the demographic transition where, because of greater advances of health, deaths have declined while births remained high, so that it was not unusual to have the population double in less than 25 years. This has begun to level off in a number of countries as the realization has set in that in a post-agricultural or less agricultural era and an increasingly urbanized and post industrialized era too many children can be an economic liability. Nevertheless, due to the echo effect as large numbers of young adults will continue to reach reproductive maturity, it will take one to two generations before the bottom heavy concentration of people begins to decrease (Rostow 1960).

What are the implications for change from the above? Between 1990 and 2010, it is estimated that the labor market grew 50% in Arab countries as young people entered the labor market. It has been estimated that 91% of these youth were literate many with college educations (Feiler 2011). The economies of these countries had not grown sufficiently to absorb these young people, many of whom had modern technical as well as literary skills. The result was unrest, especially as these countries were urbanizing. The unrest that currently besets the Middle East in the demand for social and political reform is, to a large extent, caused by frustrated young people who must deal with stagnant socio-economic and political conditions. The access to global communications including availability of world-wide satellite, the web, and social networking only added to the frustration as it provides access to other parts of the globe with examples of young people who were applying their skills. Historically, population growth along with urbanization has led to unrest, and ultimately revolution, such as the revolutions that affected Europe and Latin America between 1789 and 1848. A young population usually brings a dynamism and energy that has the potential for constructive or destructive change.

The increasing ability of Muslims to effect change and progress on a global scale is evident for shifting balances of population in Africa and Europe. If demography is destiny, the destiny of these continents may be preordained. Islam is on the march in Africa south of the Sahara, as the proselytizing zeal of Muslims has led to the spread in such previously and traditionally non-Muslim areas as Ghana and Ethiopia - the latter of which is on the verge of a Muslim majority. This is especially striking in Ethiopia as much of its traditional culture and identity is based on its Christian Orthodox traditions which date back to the 4th century A.D./C.E. The ruling groups have been first the Amhara speakers from the central highlands and then the current ruling group - the Tigreans from the northeast highlands (Murad 2011). The late nineteenth expansion into Muslim-inhabited Oromo, Sidamo, and Somali-speaking areas has now come full-circle so that the census is now a political document. The spread of Islam can work both ways as undue pressure from a Muslim population can lead to reaction such as the recent separation of Christian and animist Southern Sudan into its own nation after half a century of resistance to Islamic domination.

Due to a combination of Muslim immigration and stagnant or declining home populations, Europe feels that its culture and society is under threat of displacement. Different groups of Muslims have gone to different areas—Pakistanis to Britain, North Africans to France and Italy, Turks to Germany, Muslims from former colonies in Indonesia and the Congo to the Netherlands and Belgium, Kurds, Palestinians, Bosnian Muslims, and Albanians to various places, and Muslims from the Caucasus and Central Asia to Russia proper. The shifting balance of population has been so great (due in part to a higher birthrate of Muslims) that population figures reflect this trend. It is estimated that 95% of population increase along the Mediterranean was along its southern North African shore, not its northern European shore. It is now estimated that 10% of European's population will be Muslim by the year 2020—a figure already in sight in a country like France. Macedonia—due to the differential between the Muslim Albanian population and the current majority Slavic/Bulgarian Orthodox population could become Muslim in 20 years if present birth rates hold true. Today it is the second largest religion in every major European city on the continent. In Brussels, the administrative center of the European Union, over half of the babies born in the last two decades have been Muslim. Last year Muhammed was the single most popular name for neonates in the United Kingdom (Murad 2011).

The disparity of increases between Muslim and non-Muslim has had political ramifications in Europe. The discrepancy is often cited as a contributing cause for the implosion of the Soviet Union. From the 70's, Muslim population grew 24% while that of Great Russia only 6.5 % (it has until recently been declining in the post-Soviet period).

The rate of annual increase in Central Asia was 2.9% in Tajikistan, 2.6% in Uzbekistan, 2.5% in Turkmenistan, and 1.9% in Kirghizia (Murad 2011). The presence of immigrants from the Caucasus and other Muslim groups inside Russia proper is quite evident in major cities such as Moscow and St. Petersburg. There have been continuous struggles in the Caucasus Mountains in Dagestan, Chechneya, Inguishteya, and other areas between Christians and Muslim as well as outbreaks of Islamic separatism. Elsewhere, in Europe, there have been demonstrations and protests in France and Italy over immigration, especially Muslim immigration. Anti-immigrant movements have gained political support in France,

Italy, the Netherlands, and Austria. There have been protests from the other side as many young immigrants feel a sense of discrimination in terms of employment, especially in France. Europe has been ambivalent as it simultaneously is afraid of displacement, but needs young immigrants for necessary labor that an aging indigenous population will not do. It passes anti-discrimination legislation yet at the same time in places like France outlaws the wearing of the veil (although for purposes of political covering it includes all religious garments) (*Hurryet Daily News* 2011). The basic issue is, unlike North America and the Antipodes, European societies have historically not been immigrant societies, so that there is a lack of integration that has reinforced Islamic separateness. So deep is the divide that there are some areas where non-Muslims do not go. Given current trends, however, Muslims will have to be part of the future of Europe (*Hurryet Daily News* 2011).

When one looks at the potential for revival, there are three criteria to be considered—numbers, skill sets, and attitudes. We have already reviewed the critical mass that the global Muslim population has assumed in terms of both numbers and age distribution. We have noted (and will note in later sections) that the overwhelming percentage of young people is literate (virtually 100% in places like Malaysia and Turkey) with a large segment college educated and technically proficient (Inside Islam 2011).[9] There remain attitudes, however. The PBS series "Inside Islam" has examined Muslim attitudes. It finds that only 7% support terrorism as a means of seeking progressive change with a very small percentage supporting violence. The group that were inclined to extreme solutions were no more religious than their co-religionists so that "Radical Islam" is really those who seek political change and progress in a drastic fashion are preeminently political radicals not religious radicals. The major goal of Muslims is to improve their lives through better education and a better standard of living for themselves and their children. Their use of the term Jihad, often considered the sixth pillar of Islam, is not for war against non-Muslims but a crusade for a better life against poverty, corruption and other factors that prevent the attainment of these goals (Inside Islam 2011). Therefore, the potential is there.

Economics

In many Muslim nations, the economies are between traditional and pre-take-off conditions in their economic development. The economies still have a large agricultural sector and much of the trade is local. Nevertheless, the money economy is spreading as more and more people with higher education and modern skills go into the industrial and service areas. Inevitably, with the green revolution in countries such as Bangladesh, agricultural production has become more efficient so that more people are free to engage in other occupations and working on the land is no longer as essential for survival, as agricultural surpluses enable cultivators to go beyond subsistence and engage in export trade beyond the local level. Communications and infrastructure are also developing. Nevertheless, at the beginning of the millennium, most Muslim countries had a per capita income below other developing countries (with the exception of the oil-producing states) (Hunter 2005). However, several countries are now in the take-off stage, including Turkey, Malaysia, and Indonesia (it is hard to generalize in this area as the Muslim world is so vast, encompassing at one end the European inhabitants of the Balkans and the other end the emerging states of the sub-Sahara).

An examination of the Malay Muslim states of Malaysia and Indonesia demonstrates that, with the proper conditions, Muslim countries can emulate Brazil, India, and China in economic development. Malaysia is an example of a Muslim state that has basically reached take-off and crossed the line between developing and developed. By 2001, 42% of its population was engaged in services and 49% in industry leaving just 9% in agriculture. The illiteracy rate for all youth between 15 and 24 had been reduced to 2% due to the institution of universal public education. The figures were virtually the same for male and female (another factor in development is the reduction of inequity between men and women). By 2003, the literacy rate for all adults was 92% and 84% for males and females respectively (Hunter 2005). By the beginning of the millennium it had the highest per capita income in Southeast Asia after the oil-rich Muslim Sultanate of Brunei and the emporium city-state of Singapore (World Bank 2003).

After Malay riots in May, 1969, the government embarked upon the New Economic Policy which set up an affirmative action designed specifically to benefit Malays through state subsidies, scholarships, job quotas, preferential licensing for various commercial, fishing, farming, and general commercial purposes. Companies were set up with the purpose of ensuring a minimum of 30% Malay ownership. Funding was made available as well as tax concessions to encourage companies to set up modern enterprises. As further refined and enunciated in 1984, Government put the emphasis on private enterprise with five goals in mind: reducing the public deficit; promoting competitiveness, efficiency, and productivity by exposing public agencies to market forces; deregulation and liberalization of the economy; reducing the role of government in private enterprise; and subsidizing ethnic Malays in business (Milner and Mauzy 1986).[14] This last provision has caused ethnic and communal tensions and engendered recent controversy when the current prime minister suggested phasing out preferences that were supposed to be temporary (an argument familiar to other societies which have instituted affirmative action programs) (Milner and Mauzy 1986).

It is in the fields of communications infrastructure that Malaysia approaches full scale development. By the beginning of the third millennium, there were 158 people per newspaper. It already had 126 personal computers per 1,000 and 6,500,000 out of a population of 21,000,000 of internet users. The corresponding figures for telephones were 196. The figure for mobile phones was particularly impressive as it amounted to 314 out of a thousand (Hunter 2005).

The other major Muslim country in the region (and the largest Muslim country in the world) is Indonesia. Although its income and communications infrastructure is relatively low compared to Malaysia, it has made substantial strides in other fields. By the early part of the decade its illiteracy rate for men and women was 2% and 3% for young adults 15-24, and overall illiteracy for all adults was 8% and 17 % respectively. In the period between 1881 and 2001, employment in agriculture decreased from 54.5 % to 16%, as opposed to 47% and 37% for industry and services (the former had tripled in the same period). Moreover, the discrepancy between haves and have-nots so often huge in societies at the traditional stage of economic development had decreased so that the upper 20% consumed only a little more than 40% of income (Hunter 2005).

The strides that Indonesia has made are certainly due in part to its large amount of natural resources as well as its educational cadre. However, it is the positive climate that has produced results. Indonesians support Islam in society but not necessarily an Islamic state. Successive governments have supported modernization. More importantly, the two major

Islamic organizations have supported economic development. Both the traditionalist NU with over 40 million members and the modernist Muhammadiya with over 20 million members and branches overseas have for decades espoused a pro-growth agenda. As these social service organizations operate thousands of clinics, hospitals, libraries, orphanages, and schools throughout the country, their influence is incalculable (Lubis 2004). The NU has affirmed in spite of Koranic proscriptions against usury that banking interest can benefit customers and society as a whole (Lubis 2004). The Muhammadiya has supported the use of banking services (Lubis 2004). Over the past two decades. Indonesia has established thousands of Muslim banks. The Muhammadiya has maintained that its members have a right to establish economic and cooperative foundations along the lines of the *waqf,* or traditional religious foundations. Its traditionalist counterpart has gone even further and argued that modern banks do not fall under *riba* or usury regulations (as the Qur'an prohibits the charging of interest) (Lubis 2004). Following this point of view, the NU has established about 2,000 People's Credit Banks in Indonesia. Each bank has seed money approved by private donors and gives money to the smallest and neediest recipients. In this respect, the Islamic banks are more forthcoming than their secular counterparts represented by the BMI (the National Banking Association) and other private counterparts including Chinese-run banks (the Chinese were the traditional moneylenders in colonial Indonesia) (Lubis 2004).

Does Islamic theory provide theoretical leeway for economic progress and revival that goes beyond case studies of individual Muslim countries? Doctrinal passages suggest it does. The Quar'an, Sharia, and the Haditha all suggest that earning one's living is not only lawful but a virtue. One's place in the hereafter is earned by how productive a person is in this world. Human needs, according to Muslim writings, can be divided into three categories. The first is defined as necessities, which includes wealth. Wealth is not an end in itself; it is a means by which one realizes well-being. The second category refers to those needs that must be met to alleviate hardship. The third category refers to those needs that go beyond basic needs and refer to the process by which one goes beyond the requirements of law such as giving additional assistance beyond *zakat* (one of the major pillars of Islam). The Qur'an has many verses that refer to economics. It prescribes and describes appropriate attitudes that govern work, savings, poverty, trade, and spending. In the last twenty years, the government has regulated *zakat* and the *waqf* (charitable foundations often supported by *zakat*) (Lubis 2004).

What has held Islam back in regard to economics? The first is the attitude to banking. Medieval Europe only turned toward commerce and modern banking after 1600 when it rid itself of the idea of the just price and the prohibition of usury (excessive interest) and the recognition that profit was not impious. Banks in the Islamic world have been moving to this end during the past half-century. Secondly, until recently, Muslim revival has been retarded by the lack of capital. The discovery of the New World led to the availability of specie after 1550 that quite eclipsed the specie available to the Muslim world. Simultaneously, European technical mastery disrupted both the Indian Ocean trade and great Silk Road that had been major conduits of trade. First, through joint stock companies after 1600, and then colonies after 1700, through mercantilism, and then through the imperialism of free trade (both considered non-European regions as sources of raw materials the profits of which went to Europe) led ultimately to the European monopolies of commercial and financial outlets. The collapse of this system after WWII with the end of European overseas empires and the increasing acquisition of capital by the Muslim world via control of raw materials (oil, rubber, copper, tin, etc.,) and development of new sources of wealth through manufacturing of goods at competitive prices for export has altered the situation (Graham 2006). As these trends develop, the revitalization of the Muslim world in the economic sense should accelerate.

SOCIAL CHANGE

As indicated in the demography section, the addition of a vast new generation of greatly educated young people have brought a whole new subset of people open to and skilled in various forces of globalization via Telstar, Internet, and social networking has opened the Muslim world to new ideas. Concepts of openness, universal human rights, and individual rights and equality have found their way through agencies such as you tube. Slogans reflecting these ideas have been present in demonstrations sweeping the Middle East as well as Malaysia (in the latter case, ethnic rights) (Shboul 2004).

The issue of whether Islam is inimical to social change has been at least partially vitiated by countries such as Turkey, Malaysia, and Indonesia that have combined traditionalism based on Islam with secularism. Social change does not seem as marked in some other Islamic countries (for example the role of women and the young). Yet there are exceptions even within this generalization. In Iran, for example, women are represented at the higher educational level in large numbers and in the professions. In Afghanistan, they were often in the majority in such professions such as teaching and medicine (before the Taliban) (Yasmeen 2004).

The concept of social change is often defined by the construct of modernity which is based on rationalism, secularism, and pluralism. The teachings and practices of Islam have accommodated all three sub-components. The rational school of Islam with the emphasis on analysis of text, insight, and introspection has long existed along with the revelation school in Islam. The Golden Age of Islam when the Muslim Middle East was at the forefront of intellectual discourse in the arts and sciences was in part based on the rational spirit of inquiry existent in ancient Greek and Indian classics which Arabs and Persians adapted between the 8th and 12th centuries. Although the Muslim world recognizes that there is a single *umma*—a political/legal community of believers, there has always been a separation of church and state. The Turkic and Malay Muslim states had both religious leaders—caliphs/imams—and political leader—sultans. The Shia states of Islam, especially Persia/Iran always differentiated the political leaders—the shahs—from the religious leaders—the ayatollahs. From the beginning, the Qur'an included Christians and Jews as People of the Book even though non-believers. When Islam spread, non-believers were tolerated if they paid a non-believer tax with the exception of differentiated systems of taxation, criminal, and civil jurisprudence (Son 2005).[27]

In contemporary times, the communications revolution has led to a proliferation of social movements across the Muslim world as elsewhere. These movements include minority/indigenous rights, environmental issues, free speech, and rights of children and women.

It is the issue of gender rights or equality of women's rights that is often a harbinger of social change. In this respect, there has been measurable progress in the areas of employment and education. The rate of female participation in the workforce has ranged from 24% to 76%

as of the beginning of this millennium—all of which showed a great increase over 15 years. Female literacy for adults was near or over 50% at the end of the last millennium with the exceptions of Egypt, Bangladesh, Pakistan, and Yemen. In addition, Muslim countries such as Bangladesh, Pakistan, and Indonesia have had female leaders and representation in Parliament has increased for women in many Islamic countries (Moghadan 2005).

Women's organizations are now active in many Muslim countries. The Arab Women's Solidarity Association, The Magreb-Mashrek Gender Link Information Project, Women Living Under Muslim Laws, and Sisterhood is Global Institute are examples of transnational organizations. Some specific women's organization operating within particular Muslim countries include Women for Women's Human Rights in Turkey, Women's Action Forum in Pakistan, and Revolutionary Association of the Women of Afghanistan in Afghanistan. From these and similar organizations, there has been an overflow to other related issues. These include domestic violence, family planning, women's health, female genital mutilation, honor killings, child custody, and the trafficking of women (Yasmeen 2004:170-172).

As both a cause and result of movements for gender equality, educational attainments among women have risen. By 2003, more than 50% of college students in Bahrain, Iran, Jordan, Kuwait, Lebanon, Qatar, and Saudi Arabia were women, and over 40% of students in Libya, Morocco, Palestine, and Tunisia were women. Certain subjects traditionally male were now attracting female students. They include commerce, computer studies, engineering, finance, law, mathematics, and medicine. With these new credentials, educated women entering societies are coming to the fore. With them have come new causes such as agitation against early marriage, child labor, and punishment by stoning (Moghaden 2004:105-107. There have been demographic consequences in terms of family size so that by the middle of the first decade of the first millennium, the fertility rate of women was 2.3 children in Iran, Lebanon, and Turkey (Moghaden 2004).

Ethnic minorities have been a bit less active but there are organizations that seek to represent the Copts in Egypt, the Berbers in Algeria, the Chinese in Malaysia, and the Kurds in Turkey. However, the most active movements for change in addition to women have been student and youth groups, especially in Muslim countries with high rates of education such as Indonesia and Malaysia. These often combine a desire for a purer Islam with advocacy of social change to assist the poor. Examples of these types are AKIM (The Islamic Youth Movement of Malaysia) and PMII (the Indonesian Islamic Movement) (Milne and Mauzy, 1986: 74-75). The recent and current upheavals in Southwest Asia and North Africa as were earlier upheavals in Indonesia were led by educated youth.

With a huge population bulge of people under thirty and largely literate as well as plugged in to new forms of information and communication such as the internet and social networks, the potential for new actors who agitate for social change and societal revival is huge. A segment of the population—a new generation—has asserted itself and is no longer bound by the dictates of elders or patriarchs who were the arbiters of society and tended to support the status quo. In a society run by aging leaders often guided by cronyism and an economy not growing fast enough to generate sufficient jobs to absorb a huge number of literate and skilled college graduates, frustration has grown. The potential for a dynamic social change will be great as such a large percentage is both youthful and unable to find a position in society.

POLITICAL CHANGE

Although there have been periodic calls for a new Caliphate (to replace the one abolished in 1923/1924 by Kemal Ataturk) (Bulliet 2004) or a universal Islamic state that would consist of all members of the *umma,* or all Muslims, only a small percentage of Muslims have supported this concept. With the establishment of independent states after WWII, political reform has come from within Islamic states. Even though Malaysia has had a functioning democratic government since 1957, Turkey has had a democratic government since 1946, and Bangladesh has had democratic government since it split from Pakistan in 1971 (both Turkey and Bangladesh have had brief periods of military rule), most Muslim countries have had autocratic rule. They have taken the form of absolutist or near absolutist monarchies, military dictatorship, and one-party rule. Elections have often been shams, and there has been consequent unrest as the losing side has called foul. The current wave of revolutions that have convulsed the Arab world appear to herald a new democratic wave. Currently, Indonesia has had a functioning democracy since the fall of Suharto and Pakistan since the departure of Musharraf, while Morocco and Jordan are moving to constitutional monarchy, and Nigeria (which has the largest Muslim population in Black Africa) had a recent basically fair (if controversial) election (Associated Press 2011). These document that the prospect of democracy for a majority of Muslims now appears possible.

The major debate is whether democracy as understood in modern society will develop in most Muslim countries in the forthcoming millennium. Many traditionalist theorists argue that sovereignty derives from God and not from parliaments and political leaders. Even today, in the Islamic republic of Iran, the elected parliamentary representatives are supervised by a council of guardians appointed by the supreme religious leader, the grand Ayatollah. Indeed, the concept of parliament making laws was considered blasphemous. For over 1,000 years, there was no participating representation, no commons, no estates, and no assembly (Halleq1997).

Some theorists had grouped modernization as synonymous with liberal democracy. This has not always been borne out. Modernization sub-processes such as urbanization, industrialization, secularization, mass education, and mass communications do not necessarily bring with them liberal democracy. Indeed, totalitarian societies such as Nazi Germany and Communist Russia used both mass education and mass communications as agents of propaganda to crush dissent and popular protest. This was the situation with the Baathist regimes in Syria and Iraq.

The colonial regimes established in the 19th and 20th centuries by England and France were authoritarian. Although democratic slogans were used, in practice rule in Muslim states during the colonial period was basically autocratic. After independence, the rule of autocratic monarchs, one-party states, and military leaders were seen as a continuation in spite of the nominal fig leaf of democratic forms such as constitutions and universal suffrage. Often, the military that recruited from all segments of society and had training programs was seen as an agent of equality and social mobility. In some cases, countries such as Egypt, Pakistan, and Kirghizia had democratic regimes that were seen as corrupt and/or at the service of only one segment of the population (Ibrahim and Picard 2005). In the past two decades and until possibly the present time, advocates of theocratic Islamic rule have argued that theocracy is supported by the masses as opposed to elitist and minority middle class interests (McAmis 2002).

Among the other factors that lead to non-democratic outcomes was the artificial character of some Muslim states that were either put together in colonial times or after WWI or WWII. Mauritania, Sudan, Lebanon, Jordan, and Pakistan were not based on historical legacy or ethnic homogeneity. Consequently, Islam was more of a unity factor between Punjabis and Pashtuns in Pakistan than ethnicity or Bedouins and Palestinians in Jordan. In other instances, there were communal tensions between Christians and Muslims in Mauritania, Lebanon, and Sudan (Ibrahim 2004: 211-213). As identification with the nation state is weak, quite often outside powers were involved in propping up unrepresentative regimes.

On the other hand, modernists and some traditionalists (who believe that Islam must accommodate modernization when necessary) have argued that Islamic belief is not incompatible with democracy. Early writings by Muslim thinkers in addition to the Qur'an and Haditha have numerous sections devoted to individual and civic liberty, including certain Muslim concepts such as justice (*'adl*), right (*haqq*), consultation (*shura*) and equality (*musawat*). They maintain that democracy and rule of freedom consist of imparting justice and right to people who help determine a country's destiny (Voll 2004).

Contemporary Muslim theorists go as far to say that it is from early texts that the ideas comes that Muslim culture is intrinsically democratic. Moreover, pluralistic parliamentary democracy is the ideal to implement Sharia law as it ensures that no single individual or class can exercise sovereignty. A number point out that Qur'an commands that the Muslims conduct their affairs through mutual consultation (*shura*) and recommends the use of representative agency (*khilafah*) for the entire community or *umma* rather than one group of people. Therefore leadership chosen by *shura* and *khilifah* is based on the free will of the people (Voll 2004).

There is thus a doctrinal argument for democracy in the Islamic World. What about recent history and contemporary support for the thesis? One must admit that there are other factors in this equation so that it is not an either/or proposition. Realism indicates that there will be hindrances to democracy in Muslim states even should democratic forms such as a parliament and an independent judiciary exist. Multi-ethnic states such as Burkina Faso or Guinea or Mali or Nigeria will have potential bars to a fully functioning democracy. Great powers will continue to be ambivalent about democracy in a country where the strategic interests of the concerned great power are felt to be at stake as in the case of Yemen or Pakistan, or where important minerals exist as in the case of Saudi Arabia and Kuwait. A number of countries have complicated internal factors. Syria has a Sunni majority but significant Alawite, Christian, Druze, and Kurd minorities. Nigeria has over 200 separate ethnic-linguistic groups. Chad, Niger, and Somalia have clan and regional disputes greater than Islam. The United States and Japan would still be interested in Saudi Arabia and the Gulf States if they were Christian.

There is evidence that in fact there has been a movement toward liberal democracy for some time. It can be gleaned by looking at the record of certain Muslim states from the 19th and 20th century. The 19th century definition of liberal democracy placed the emphasis on individual economic, political, and religious rights. It believed in laissez-faire in economics, free trade, rule of law, and tolerance. The emphasis was placed on elections and the overall process. As part of this process, civil organization began to appear with the rising middle class such as the Chamber of Commerce and the League for Good Government. These groups gave citizens practice in organizing, debating, and compromising as a prelude for representative government. They began to appear in the more commercial states such as Egypt, Turkey, and Tunisia, in the latter part of the 19th century (Ibrahim 2004:210-212). In 1864 Egypt ratified a constitution followed by Turkey in 1876. Although the Egyptian democratic interlude ended with British occupation in 1881, the Turks continued with a parliament –although a rather limited parliament—until the Kemalist Revolution of 1920. Kemal Ataturk was a great modernizer but not a proponent of liberal democracy (Rothman 2007). After 1920, semi-independent countries such as Iraq and Egypt did have parliaments and other Muslim countries such as Lebanon, Jordan, and Syria did have organizations like welfare societies, freemasons, and benevolent societies based on the historic religious foundations or *waqf*. As both political organizations and civil societies were based on a rather thin sliver of society—the educated middle class and bourgeoisie—they could not withstand the rise of nationalism after WWII, aggravated by the Israeli-Palestinian conflict which led to the rise of autocracy in various forms—military, monarchial, party dictatorship, theocracy (Ibrahim:210-212). The current wave of pro-democracy demonstrators in the Middle East and North Africa involves educated and web-savvy youth who represent a huge slice of the population.

Even before the current wave of pro-democracy youth, there were 100 million plus Muslims living in democratic economically booming India about one/third of the world's Muslim population and three Muslim states with a Muslim population approaching 300 million (about one quarter of the world's Muslim population) who have demonstrated that a country can advance in modernization, enjoy economic progress, and continue on the road to political democracy. The Islamic states in question are Turkey, Indonesia, and Malaysia.

Turkey has had a rather tolerant attitude toward non-Muslim groups for much of its history (with the exception of the pogroms against the Armenians in the early part of this century which ultimately led due to civil strife and starvation to well over one million deaths and which was conducted during the waning days of the Ottoman Empire and during the ascendancy of the Young Turks-ultra-nationalists who ruled between 1908 and 1918) (Rothman 2007:35-38). During its heyday, the Ottoman Empire had established semi-autonomous administrative unit (the millet system) for different groups including non-Muslims. At one time, Turkey proper was multi-ethnic and multi-religious as it contained large communities of Armenians before the pogroms, Greeks before the mass deportations in the early 1920's during an exchange of populations with Greece, and Jews before most left Turkey to join the world-wide Diaspora. As such, many converted Christians held administrative positions and were military commanders. As Turkey held most of the Balkans, interaction with Europe was constant. As early as the 18th century, fearing it was falling behind Europe and influenced by the Enlightenment, Turkey embarked upon a series of reforms designed to streamline its governmental system and introduced technical training. After 1800, a modern school system was introduced so that by 1900 the majority of both boys and girls were attending state-supported public schools. The greatest period of reform came during the Tanzimat Period of 1839-1876 when a modern bureaucracy was created as was a civil service chosen on merit. Basic rights and liberties of all subjects of the Ottoman Empire (Muslim and non-Muslim) were recognized. The period climaxed with a constitution promulgated in 1876 (a subsequent one was written in 1908) and the beginning of a parliament (Rothman 2007:27-34).

Further steps in modernization with an emphasis on secularization came after the foundation of a republic in 1923. An independent judiciary was established. Secular commercial, criminal, and family codes were initiated. A written constitution was enacted which guaranteed basic rights and liberties to all citizens. Women were given equal civic and political right and equal opportunities in education and employment.

Today public schooling is coeducational as are the 53 public and 23 private universities. Elections have been held since 1946, and the country has been ruled by an Islamist party since 2002. The party has not interfered with most of the structures it inherited and both bureaucracy and judiciary remain secular. Islam has made a comeback as Sufi brothers and Islamic schools are now permitted (Toprak 2004). Nonetheless, there is no movement for an Islamic state, and Turkey today has a thriving modern economy and nearly complete literacy among its youth.

Malaysia has had democratic government and basic democratic political processes since its independence. It profited from the British colonial experience that developed a westernized secular service. Its ruling coalition dominated by the UMNO has included ethnic minorities as well as non-Muslims. It has a functioning federal system with the central government and various states each having assigned powers, although the balance was at one time threatened by the dictatorial Mahathir (1981-2002), the three branches along with the federalized system have survived. By paying lip service to Islam such as identifying religion (Malay) with Muslim and making symbolic gestures such as the establishment of an Islamic Bank and allow individual states to use Sharia in domestic matters, it has outbid the opposition Islamic (PAS) party. It enjoys almost universal literacy for both genders and has a modernized economy (McAmis 2002:77-90). Indonesia, since the end of the Suharto era has had three free elections.

Islamic parties have contested these elections, but they have never totaled more than 18% of the vote. Many Muslims support the role of Islam in society but not an Islamic state. Indonesia has a tradition of syncretism with animism, Buddhism, Hinduism, and traditional beliefs commingling with Islam so that there is a general cultural tolerance (McAmis 2002). This tolerance is exemplified by the first democratically elected president, Dr. Abdurrahman Wahid (1999-2001).

Dr. Wahid was the long-time leader of the traditionalist Muslim organization, the NU. Wahid is an advocate of liberal democracy, a supporter of minority rights, and a proponent of religious tolerance. His position is not unique among Muslim leaders (Effendy 2003). As in Malaysia, leeway has been given to local governments to institute Sharia for domestic cases if they so choose. Since democracy came to Indonesia, the country has achieved substantial economic expansion as it modernizes its economy. Literacy has increased exponentially so that it is almost universal (hooker 2004).

The phenomenon of spreading democracy is not limited to the countries just described. The monarch of Morocco, Mohammed VI, submitted a new constitution to his subjects in July 2011. It was approved by 98% of voters. It gave more power to an elected parliament and established an independent judiciary. It gave equal protection to women and minorities under the law. These developments fell on fertile ground as Morocco has had political parties and labor unions since independence in 1956 (Ginsbertg 2011).

SPIRITUAL VALUES AND INTERCULTURAL AND INTERFAITH COMMUNION

The spiritual aspect of Islam, especially its tolerance and acceptance of other faiths and cultures, has been evident since the first days of Islam in the form of Sufism. Sufism is widespread in the Muslim world particularly in the areas outside the Middle East that constitute the majority of the world's Islamic population. It is the mystical devotional side of Islam, dating from the 8th century. It was this form of Islam that reached the average individual outside of the Middle East. Trade and force of arms might have influenced the merchants and rulers around the globe, but the average person was often introduced to the faith by Sufi missionaries whether it was Sub-Saharan Africa or Southeast Asia or South Asia or the Caucasus or Central Asia. It played a substantial role in the formation of culture in the Ottoman Empire and in resistance to external imperialism (Godlas 2012).

Historically, Sufism was and has been a reaction to the materialism and emphasis on worldly politics of the Islamic world. There is some evidence that it was influenced by mysticism from other faiths such as Buddhism, Christianity, Hinduism, and Judaism which preceded Islam (Godlas 2012).

As constituted, Sufism concentrates on one's personal experience with Allah. Acolytes of Sufism study under a teacher who reports to an overall master. Since the 13th century, Sufi-run institutions have been supported by *waqfs* or religious foundations. Many philosophers and poets have been Sufi. Sufis are organized into various brotherhoods; the largest of these are the Naqshabandi, Qadiriyyah, and Chisti. Quite often these Sufi orders are very active in providing essential services to the people through hospitals and schools (Godlas 2012).

Essentially, Sufism emphasizes the common message of appealing to God through the heart. It has proclaimed throughout the ages that all religions are the same whether it proclaims this message in Arabic, Malay, Persian, or Turkic dialects. Sufis have always maintained that all religions have the same purpose in the carrying out of God's wishes. According to Sufi teachings, the almighty can be found everywhere, whether it is the church, mosque, synagogue, or temple. The stress is not just on the relationship with God as in orthodox texts but in the relationship with other human beings and the correct actions toward others in this world.[55]

Sufi orders can be quite ecumenical as well as global. In India and Europe, non-Muslims have joined Sufi organizations. The largest organizations are global and can have members who are Azeri, Uzbek, or Malay. They are also non-sectarian as they often have both Shia and Sunni members. Due to the universality of both its message and membership, Sufism has often formed a barrier to fundamentalism that would establish a strictly Islamic state under Sharia law to the exclusion of non-Muslims. It is able to do this for three major reasons. First, the fundamentalist sects, whether the Wahhabis from Saudi Arabia or the Salafis from Egypt, are relatively recent in creation with the former originating in the 18th century and the latter dating from the late 19th and early 20th centuries. In contrast, the Sufi movement has existed for over a millennium.

Fundamentalist sects are comparative newcomers to the Muslim world outside of the Middle East. The degree of their acceptance often depends upon economic or political dissatisfaction. This brings us to the second reason for the Sufi advantage—its mysticism. Sufi orders which emphasized personal communion and the worship of saints and the use of shrines often fits in with local traditions and beliefs. In contrast, the fundamentalists exclude these practices. Economic and political grievances cannot be underestimated, but traditional beliefs and customs extend from cradle to grave and beyond. In sum, the Sufi version of Islam has acquired an indigenous quality which the newly-arrived fundamentalists do not as yet have. Finally, the latitude of Sufi beliefs including tolerance and acceptance of non-Islamic customs and practices encourages syncretism with local culture in the worship of ancestor worship and aspects of nature as links to the almighty (Godlas 2012).

CONCLUSION

The last two decades have seen new agents of change as communications have brought global currents into the Muslim world. Al-Arabiyya and Al-Jazeera are now viewed by hundreds of millions. When one adds the overwhelming presence of the internet and social networking, which played such a great part in the Egyptian revolution of February 2011, it is quite obvious that change and revival in the forthcoming millennium is here to stay. It will be sustained because demographically, the huge bulge of technologically literate youth—the forthcoming generation—cannot be denied. Economically, the onset of industrialization and services is on the way. With greater education leading to greater social mobility, the changing social structure is an accomplished fact. The role of women and resulting alteration in family size and family structure created by new educational opportunities and related modernization processes such as secularization and urbanization appears irreversible. It should be noted that there is a practical process of crypto-secularization underway, as there has been an introduction of Sharia in various places but it is limited to family law and family courts—a great narrowing of the concept of Sharia as the supreme law of the land. Finally, the spread of constitutions in conjunction with greater modern education and greatly increased literacy combined with employment in the modern sector in the economy inevitably means that the ordinary citizen will feel a greater stake in future of the country and act accordingly, thereby assuring the spread of democracy. The genie is out of the bottle, and it cannot be put back. Nonetheless, there are aspects of Islam such as Sufism which have always been open to external factors and change.

REFERENCES

Associated Press (2011) Amid rioting Nigeria's President declared. Edited by Jon Gambrell, April 19, Boston.

Baktiar Effendy, B. (2003). *Islam and the state in Indonesia.* Athens, Ohio: Ohio University Press, pp. 120-126; 131-133; 201-209.

Bruce Feiler, interview by Fareed Zakaria, , *GPS CNN*, 3 July, 2011.

Bulliet,R.W.(2004). *Case for Islamo-Christian Civilization.* New York: Columbia University Press.

Ginsberg, T. (2010). Morocco Constitution approved. *Comparative Constitution. Retrieved on* July 3.

Godlas,A.(2012). Sufism's many paths at *http://Islam.uga.edu/Sufism.html* Retrieved January 31.

Graham, M. (2006), *How Islam created the world.* Bellville Maryland: Ariana Publications, pp. 170-175.

Halleq,W.B. (1997) *Islamic legal theories.* Cambridge: University of Cambridge, chapter 4.

Hooker, M.B. (2004). Perspectives on Sharia and the state: The Indonesia Debates. In V. Hooker (Ed). *Islamic perspectives on the new millennium* (204-205). Singapore: Institute of Southeast Asian Studies.

Hunter, Sh. (2005), Introduction in *Modernization, democracy, and Islam* (p.4). In Sh. Hunter & H. Malik. Westport, CT: Praeger, p.4.

Hurryet Daily News (Turkey), "Muslims in Europe face growing hostility." May 10, 2011.

Ibrahim,S.E. (2005). Arab liberal legacies full circle. In Sh. Hunter & H. Malik (Eds.), *Modernization, democracy, and Islam* (205-220). Westport, CT: Praeger.

Inside Islam: What a Billion Muslims Think. PBS series. Retrieved 5 July, 2011.

John Voll, J. (2004). Islam and democracy: is modernization a barrier? In Sh. Hunter & H. Malik (Eds.), *Modernization, democracy, and Islam* (p.84). Westport, CT: Praeger.

Lubis, Nur Ahmad Fadhil (2004). Financial activism among Indonesian Muslims" in *Islamic perspectives on the new millennium* (Singapore: ISEAS), p. 94.

McAmis, R.D. (2002). *Malay Muslims: The history and challenge of resurgent Islam in Southeast Asia.* Cambridge: Eerdnans, pp. 72-80.

Milne, R.S. and D. K. Mauzy (1986), *Malaysia: trade, modernization and Islam.* Boulder,Colo: Westview, pp. 40-47; 132-141.

Moghadan, V.M. (2005). Gender inequality in Muslim Society: a barrier to modernization and democratization. In Sh. Hunter & H. Malik (Eds.), *Modernization, democracy, and Islam* (pp. 102-109). Westport, CT: Praeger.

Murad, A. H. (2011). Islam and the new millennium. *Barak Institute.* Retrieved, 30 June,; also available at http://www.sunnah.org/audio/millen.htm.

Picard, E. (2005). The role of the military. In Sh. Hunter & H. Malik (Eds.), *Modernization, democracy, and Islam* (pp. 117-132). Westport, CT: Praeger.

Rostow, W.W. (1960). *Stages of economic growth.* New York: Cambridge University Press.

Rothman, N. (2007). *Three faces of Islam.* Charleston, S,C.: Amazon, pp.38-41.

Samira Yasmeen, S. (2004). Muslim women and human rights in the Middle East and South Asia: occupying different spaces. In V. Hooker, *Islamic perspectives on the new millennium* (pp.161-182). Singapore: Institute of Southeast Asian Studies, 2004.

Shboul, A. (2004). Islam and globalization: Arab world perspectives. In V. Hooker, *Islamic perspectives on the new millennium* (pp.43-70). Singapore: Institute of Southeast Asian Studies.

Sonn, T. (2005). Islam and modernity: are they compatible? In *Modernization, democracy, and Islam.* Sh. Hunter & H. Malik (Eds.), *Modernization, democracy, and Islam* (pp. 74-75). Westport, CT: Praeger.

Toprak, B.(2004). A secular democracy in the Muslim world: the Turkish Model. In Sh. Hunter & H. Malik (Eds.), *Modernization, democracy, and Islam* (pp. 279-288). Westport, CT: Praeger.

World Bank and United Nations Development Program (2003), *Human development report.* New York: Human Development Program.

In: Spirituality and Civilization Sustainability ...
Editors: Andrew Targowski and Marek J. Celinski
ISBN: 978-1-53610-729-6

Chapter 11

POTENTIAL OF BUDDHISM FOR RENEWAL OF CIVILIZATION IN THE THIRD MILLENNIUM

Walter Benesch*
Department of Philosophy & Humanities
University of Alaska, Fairbanks, AK, US

ABSTRACT

One of the challenges of philosophy is the understanding of and experiencing of the dynamic syntheses of *self* and *environment* as *processes* and not just as static identities that are often associated with abstract terms. Increasingly, understanding the synthesis of *self* and *world* is reflected in evolving developments and theories in social and physical science, e.g., as in physics in quantum mechanics in biology as in the nature/nurture approach to genetics and human behavior in neurobiology. The implications of in process views of experiencing are clearly expressed in physicist John Wheeler's *participant/spectator view of the universe:* "...in the quantum principle we're instructed that he actual act of making an observation changes what it is that one looks at. It is in understanding the *situational nature of physical and mental processes* that Buddhist Philosophy can make a major contribution to spirituality and sustainability in civilizations in the third Millennium.

In traditional Indian and Greco-European subject and object philosophies and logics, it is assumed that one or more constant essences transcends immediate experience of the world. This assumption is fundamental to the sciences and religions and value systems that evolve in these traditions. In the Indian traditions of the *Vedas, Upanisads,* and Orthodox Vedic Schools, the ultimate essence is 'consciousness' which was the source of the world as manifestation of *Brahman* and *Atman* as manifestation of *Brahman* in the individual. The logics that originated in the various Indian treatments of consciousness then relate levels and states of consciousness and awareness. In the subject logic of the Jains, the object world was knowable only by the individual consciousness (or J*iva)* relatively from points of view. For the Jain, jiva and a-jiva , i.e. *'self* and *non-self'* are the six basic *substances* or ultimate 'givens'. Buddhism , however, developed a view in which the constant was not an essence, but rather the changing, '*now*' as ***'moments of***

* E-mail: wbenesch@alaska.edu

experiencing'. In Buddhism in general, *mind* functions as *momentary attending* and *intending (attentions* and *intentions)* in situations. It is the purpose of this paper to indicate the applicability of various Buddhist *situational assumptions* to the continuing evolution of science and technology, religion and philosophy, as well as national and international political and social institutions in the new Millenium.

INTRODUCTION

Perhaps Buddhist interpretations of the immediate, situational nature of experience might best be illustrated with the story of Gautama's (app 560-480B.C.E.) own search for understanding and enlightenment. Like all Indian philosophers, he was deeply concerned with the nature of consciousness, its role in suffering, and the possibility of its conservation in the transmigration cycles of Samsara as determined by Karma.

According to accounts of Gautama's life, his father, who was the king of a small state in Nepal, wanted to shield his son from contact with the poverty, sickness, old age, violence, and death outside the palace. The king landscaped a beautiful park around the palace and surrounded it with a high walls. Gautama was free to wander anywhere he liked within the palace and park but was not to leave them. The accounts of his life relate that one day while wandering in the park, Gautama had four visionary experiences: He met an old man bent with age, a sick man afflicted with sores, fever and pain, a dead man whose corpse was being carried on a stretcher to the 'cremation grounds', and a monk who seemed to radiate a sense of peace and harmony. Whether these experiences were illusionary or not, Gautama realized that the 'meaning of life' could only come from experiencing both the pleasant and the terrible that were the two faces of meaning. He left the palace and like the monk set about trying to understand aging, sickness, and death. During this period he deliberated with teachers and other philosophers, none of whom could provide the meaning he was seeking. He also practiced an extreme form of asceticism---starving and ignoring his physical body until he collapsed and was presumed dead by his fellow ascetics . He was not dead and gradually in the care of friends he recovered his strength. Asceticism had proven itself as useless as the doctrines of the various schools, and he abandoned it too.

Finally, after meditating for 49 days under a Bo tree he attained the understanding which was the source of his the *Four Noble Truths* and the *Eight Fold Noble Path.* These are the basis for Buddhist *situational logic* and are central to Buddhism everywhere. Gautama realized that 'life' was only an abstract concept, a word but was not *living*. However, he was *living, seeing, hearing, tasting, touching, smelling, thinking*---but, the things seen, heard, tasted, touched, smelled, thought were concepts, words, interpretations memories but not *conceiving, speaking, interpreting, remembering.* This dynamic *awareness of being aware* as opposed to 'objects of awareness' is also basic to Buddhism around the world.

EXPERIENCING AS ATTENDING AND INTENDING CONTINUUM

In order to understand Buddhist views of human awareness and then to understand and apply the 'situational logics' that the Buddhist philosophers developed, one must also understand the two basic insights that occurred to Gautama meditating under the Bo Tree.

The first insight that Buddha attained is referred to as anatman (*anatta* in Pali) which means *no self* or *no soul.* The Buddha in a radical empirical review of being conscious, living, desiring, acting, etc., found he could identify five basic *skandhas* or *aspects* of his living and being: *sannna,* i.e., perceiving and sensing*; vedana,* i.e., feeling; *rupa*, i.e., physical body; *samskara,* i.e., predispositions and preferences from past impressions and experiences; *vijnana*, i.e., consciousness. Apart from these five aspects of being and experiencing he could find no basis for an empirical 'self'. He concluded that 'self' was a term, an abstraction but not an empirical 'owner' of the situational aspects of being. For example when one exclaims "I cut myself" – the hurting is an experiencing aspect, but the "I" is only a term, and abstract expression.

The second insight Buddha attained under the Bo Tree is referred to as anitya (*anicca* in Pali) which means *impermanent* or *no constant unchanging identity.* Just as Buddha in his self analysis discovered no constant and unchanging owner of situational being and consciousness, he realized as did the Pre-Socratic Greek Philosopher, Heraclitus (6th-5th Century BCE), that change seemed to be the only 'constant' said that 'one cannot step into the same river twice'. (Wheelwright, 1986) As the Buddha pointed out, one of the sources of suffering is the human desire to 'stop change' i.e. to make the world or a set of circumstances to 'stand still.' One of the most important implications of situational consciousness in a changing in a changing world *(anatman + anitya)* is the enlightened perspective that 'human beings are individually and collectively impermanent *aspects* of a dynamic world of aspects. Both the Indian Jains and the Buddhists saw this '*aspect view*'of self and the world as the only solution to the violence that plagues human beings---their religions, politics, interpersonal relations – and that hinder their intellectual and compassionate growth and development.

From a Buddhist perspective, personal awareness then seems to consist of an unbroken attending/intending process of innumerable particular acts and objects of attention and intention, e.g., sensations, concepts, feelings, etc.. The terms 'attention' and 'intention' come from the Latin root *tender*e whch means *to stretch.* From this root which we also derive *tendon* which makes physical stretching possible. Thus 'attention' is 'stretching outward or toward' and 'intention' is 'stretching inwardly at meaning' or 'concentrating'. The possibility of attending is never exhausted in any particular attention just as intending is not limited to any particular intention, and knowing is a synthesis of focusing upon specific attention and intention aspects of an attending/intending continuum of observations, emotions, physical processes combined with perspectives which provide the meaning and significance of their relationship contexts. It is the perspectives within this *aspect continuum*, which enable us to change our 'minds', to emphasize questions over answers, to shift thinking 'levels' in interpreting events and other experiences, to withhold judging for the sake of further inquiry.

To rephrase this position, I would suggest one might define human consciousness as the *possibility of attending/intending*, and describe specific experiences and their interpretations as *possibilities for consciousness as attentions and intentions.* Experiencing is a synthesis of '*of*' and '*for'*. We encounter an excellent example of this synthesis when we seek to explain and/or define 'self' or 'world'. Any explanation, interpretation, definition, etc., is an attending/intending flow with at least five perspective aspects: 1) The 'explainer'; 2) the 'explained' or experienced object which is the context to which the explainer refers; 3) the process of 'explaining'; 4) the 'explanation' that emerges from 1-3; and 5) the 'awareness' of and ability to distinguish the preceding four aspects of this continuum and to focus upon them individually and collectively, assigning each significance and value. It is within this fifth aspect that perspectives occur on the other four and upon number five itself. Every aspect of this continuum provides a vast number of possibilities for consciousness, while consciousness as the possibility of the totality is not reducible to any particular aspect, and is the source most clearly reflected in the fifth aspect. In practice, or course, individuals and societies, emphasize times and places. Particular cultures and civilizations will emphasize particular possibilities for consciousness and may select a particular emphasis or set of emphases to the exclusion *of* the 'totality'. For example, it would seem that this emphasizing has been one of the most important characteristics of dogmatic *monotheistic* religion in the West. [1]

This five aspect continuum seems to me implicit in all subject—object—process—language—understanding relationships. The challenge is to preserve the totality of 'consciousness as possibility while utilizing and/or emphasizing particular aspects within it as possibilities for consciousness. Otherwise, we confuse the aspect with the whole or perhaps adopt the 'perspective of no perspective'. It is the processing of 'consciousness as possibility' that is the source of exploring, explaining, defining—the possibility for *theorizing, theologizing, biologizing, cosmologizing, psychologizing*. And it is the processing of 'consciousness as possibility' that discusses the 'possibilities for consciousness' in the contexts of the sciences, arts, and humanities.

In applying *anatman* and *anitya* to the modern world with its conflicts one might begin to stress this Buddhist 'aspect/perspectve' view rather than the absolute dichotomies which seem to characterize economic issues, international relations, theological institutions. I might add that this approach has characterized much of the revolution in the physical sciences over the last two to three hundred years – culminating in modern theories of *incompleteness, uncertainty, participant-spectator views of the world.* I would suggest one might define human consciousness as the possibility of attending/intending, and describe aspects of experiences and their interpretations as possibilities for consciousness as attentions and intentions. Experiencing is a synthesis of 'of' and 'for'. We encounter an excellent example of this synthesis when we seek to explain and/or define 'self' or 'world'. The context of all claims 'to know' consists of at least five aspects:

Aspect # 1 The context of the 'knower-observer':... What experiences, intentions, assumptions, and potential interpretations from levels II and III do we as observers bring to an event or object, which will influence our intentions and attentions. Are there personal intentions and conditions that are relevant, for example, our attitudes toward race,. gender, profession, etc.? How aware are we as observers of our theories and concepts and how these can influence the 'conceptualizing' that arises in our observations.

Aspect # 2 Context of the 'known-observed'... Since every event or object represents emphasis and focus upon limited aspects within a totality of potential characteristics and causes, what were or are the relevant and irrelevant aspects and characteristics of the observed that we take into account or reject? Under what conditions and in what

[1] ***Consciousness'*** is a combination of 'com' = 'with', and 'scire' – 'to know'. These two terms combined in the way in which they are used here imply the 'possibility of knowing with knowledge of one's knowing. An excellent example of this meaning is implied with the term 'conscience' which mean in moral and ethical matters, not only knowing what one is doing, but also knowing the ethical implications of ones actions and, coupled with 'potis' and 'esse', implying both the possibility of choosing and the possibility of responsibility for choices. Such bowing our awareness suggests the ability to pose on one level questions about one's views and actions on another level – to remain aware of attending/intending beyond specific attentions and intentions.

circumstances is/was the observed event or object experienced? What was included or excluded in terms of circumstances and characteristics....and why? Are there relevant connections to other observations which are being considered or ignored? For example, one of the Buddhist theories of observation is that 'one sees what one sees by *not seeing* that which surrounds what one sees. The focus of the observer or knower is limited, but it is critical that one remember that these limits are arbitrary.

Aspect # 3 Context of 'knowing-observing' processes... In addition to the senses, what techniques, methods, instruments are employed in our observing and how do these affect our observing. For example, to measure a phenomena means to introduce some sort of measuring device, whether as instrument or statistical method. A class being tested is not a class 'not being tested'. What limits to observing are incorporated in or determine the act itself? How do direct versus indirect knowing and observing relate? Which is given preference? The problem with distinguishing. It is with this aspect of the knowing and observing process that one must be aware that distinguishing creates distinctions and not the other way round.

Aspect #4 Context of the 'knowledge—observation product': Since it is the knowledge as 'observation' or 'explanation' that is symbolized and communicated, it is important to consider what our linguistic, categorical and/or cultural constraints are that will determine the expression of the observation. This aspect is a categorical and/or conceptual synthesis of #1,#2 and #3. This level combines syntax, semantics, and pragmatics. To what degree is the ego of the observer included or excluded in the symbolized and verbalized observation? Is the observation to be expressed in a combination of natural and artificial languages and if so, how will the languages used and their structures inter-relate and influence what is said or written---this question is particularly relevant to the uses of statistics and polls. What are the purposes of our observations and to whom are they to be communicated? As Albert Einstein cautioned: "As far as the propositions of mathematics refer to reality, they are not certain, and in so far as they are certain, they do not refer to reality." (Herman, 1949)

Aspect # 5 Context of the 'perspectives' upon #1-#4. It is as this stage where the scientists, theologian. Philosopher, politician must first of all know how to doubt" in order to reflect and question, for "People who do not doubt simply have not devoted themselves to concrete practice. If they have concretely practiced, there must be some doubts." (Chan 1967) With the fifth aspect , the knower, observer, and/or interpreter, begins reviewing the inter-relationships of the first four aspects. For example, does the 'observed' take priority over the 'observer'? Does 'observing' alter the 'observed' and thus the 'observations' How do the observations verbalized and conceptualized relate to the observed and influence observing? What was included or excluded in observing? What was included and or excluded in symbolizing the observation? How do name and named relate in their origins? What are the most important definitions involved in stating the observation? What terms remain indefinable in stating the observation? What pre-conditions were placed upon observation by stated and unstated assumptions of the observer and/or the condition and circumstances of the observed? The function of the fifth aspect of the knowing process is to provide an understanding of the basic perspectives and questions at the level of situational and immediate experience so that we begin to discover and understand the experiential paradoxes and problems of the human intellect as both spectator and participant in the world. Here we become aware of the priorities that we accept and or assign and the influences that these have in turn upon our claims to knowledge and understanding.

The Danish Physicist, Niels Bohr, with his profound insight into process philosophy, would seem to have summarized most effectively the critical function of this level with its five aspects: "Scientific research in many domains of knowledge has indeed time and again proved the necessity of abandoning or remolding points of view which because of their fruitfulness and apparently unrestricted applicability, were regarded as indispensable for rational explanation" (Bohr 1987). The French Anthropologist, Georges Devereux, in his *Ethnopsychoanalysis*, would seem to have had the same objective in mind in the social sciences: "The simple fact is that a human phenomenon which is explained in one way only is, so to speak, not explained at all ...and this even---and, in fact, chiefly---if this phenomenon's first explanation has made it perfectly comprehensible, controllable and foreseeable in terms of its own specific frame of reference" (Devereux 1978).

Every aspect of this continuum provides a vast number of possibilities for consciousness, with consciousness the possibility of the totality is not reducible to any particular aspect, and is the source most clearly reflected in the fifth aspect. In practice, or course, as individuals and societies, we emphasize times and places. Particular cultures and civilizations will emphasize particular possibilities for consciousness and may select a particular emphasis or set of emphases to the exclusion of the 'totality'. For example, it would seem that this has been one of the most important functions of dogmatic *monotheistic* religion in the West.

This five aspect continuum seems to me implicit in all subject—object—process—language—understanding relationships. The challenge is to preserve the emphases on *aspect* and *perspectives upon aspects*. Otherwise, we confuse the aspect with the whole or perhaps adopt the 'perspective of no perspective' of the 'dogmatist and his/her revelations. It is the processing of 'consciousness of aspects as possibility' that is the source of exploring, explaining, defining—the possibility for theorizing, theologizing, biologizing, cosmologizing, psychologizing, and it is the processing of 'consciousness as possibility' that discusses the 'possibilities for consciousness' in the contexts of the sciences, arts, and humanities.

Buddhist Logics of Aspects and Perspectives

The term logic is derived from the Greek 'logos' which is often translated as 'reason'. However it also meant speech, law, word, divine wisdom, and essence---especially in reference to 'nature' or the universe, e.g. Heraclitus' theory of change which is ordered by the logos.

> "Although this Logos is eternally valid, yet men are unable to understand it – not only before hearing it, but even after they have heard it for the first time. That is to say, although all things come to pass in accordance with this Logos, men seem to be quite without any experience of it" (Wheelwright, 1985).

Logics as 'thinking in orderly and related sequences', whether in natural or artificial symbolic languages, have a purposive function in philosophical systems where they are employed as methods in knowing processes. Knowledge, in turn, is a synthesis of metaphysics and epistemology and so systems of logic are inseparably linked to the history of this synthesis in the traditions in which they occur.

I would suggest that logics and their traditions can be understood in terms of four metaphysical/epistemological emphases: an object emphasis, a subject emphasis, a situational emphasis, and a process emphasis. For example, in 'object approaches', the object world and object knowledge are seen as more basic than the experiencing, interpreting subjects who experience objects. Here the emphasis may be upon the conservation of matter. In 'subject approaches', the knowing subject as consciousness is stressed over the objects of knowledge. Here the emphasis may be upon the conservation of consciousness as in rebirth and transmigration. In 'situational approaches', the situational contexts of subject/object encounters are stressed over either subject or object in isolation. Here the emphasis may be upon conservation of situationality, as in the Buddhist views of 'anatta' (no self), 'anitya' (impermanence), and 'pratitysamutpada' (dependent origination I believe that referring to consciousness as the 'possibility of possibilities' preserves the dynamic of thinking and perceiving (*minding*) without limiting this dynamic either affirmatively or negatively by restricting these processes to a specific possibility or interpretation. This is an approach that will permit discussion beyond the dichotomies of 'something/nothing' 'emptiness/non-emptiness' (*sunyata/asunyata)*. This is a view quite in harmony with Nagarjuna's own position in the *Mulamadhyamakakarika*: "'Empty', 'non empty', 'both' or 'neither' – these should not be declared. It is expressed only for the purpose of communication."

Any distinguishing between possibility of and possibility for generates a number of paradoxes'. For example, as the source of explaining, defining, interpreting, we cannot reduce ourselves as explainers and definers to our explanations, definitions, or interpretations. The Spanish Sufi philosophy, Ibn Al Aarabi said that when one looks into a mirror and claims "I see myself." This statement is paradoxically both 'true' and 'false'. Just as the 'liars paradox' "I always tell lies" is false is it is true an true if it is false. This does not mean that we cannot talk about ourselves. It does mean we are not our statements. It is the nature of a paradox that understanding it requires an intuitive leap beyond the terms employed in its expression – a leap beyond language and often beyond rational analysis which occurs within clearly delineated systems of thought. A simple example might be the mental shift that is involved when I formulate two questions, using the same words but changing their order: "What time is it?" vs. "Time, what is it?" Clearly, more than a linguistic exercise is involved here. These two questions occur on different levels or in different contexts. In responding to the first question, one might look at one's watch, the sun, or call a telephone time service. The second question, however, points beyond the perception of the watch, or the position of the sun. It reflects an 'inside/outside' puzzle implicit in most such attempts to universalize and conceptualize experience. For example, any answer to "what is time" would be about time from within some particular questioning context.

The consequences of this attending/intending paradox becomes more obvious if one tries to establish that one's concept of time is non-temporal, that is, defines the nature of time beyond any and all relativity to particular times or to time concepts that are historical or personal, i.e. a definition which would be *timeless*. Where the first question focuses attention/intention upon some device for measuring time, the second question focuses attention /intention upon thinking beyond a measuring device. How different the levels are becomes apparent when one begins to wonder about judging the accuracy of any answer to either question.

Gautama realized that 'consciousness' was' *being conscious'*. Once he had realized this distinction between the *NOW* of sensing and interpreting and the concepts and words that flowed in and out of thinking, he no longer confused 'thinking' with particular thoughts, 'seeing' with particular sights, hearing, with particular sounds, smelling with particular smells, tasting with particular tastes, desiring with particular desires, and words with particular meanings. An excellent illustration of this understanding that the seeing is not the seen nor seer, is the Buddhist theory of 'not seeing'. When we see or recognize an object in front of us---a vase, a cat a car,, if we reflect upon our seeing, we realize that we see the object by *not seeing* everything else in front of us. This means we can try to see what we did not see in our initial seeing. This changing seeing is a very important aspect of the history of science----for example, looking at the heliocentric versus geocentric sky.

BUDDHIST SISTUATIONAL LOGIC I NAGARJUNA'S CATUSKOTI

Using the *Four Noble Truths* and the *Eight Fold Noble Path* as an introduction to Buddhist situational logic, one can see that such a logic is used to facilitate *reflexive self awareness*, and this occurs in two different but related systems the first of which was Nagarjuna'a '*four step Catuskoti* or *Tetralemma logic.* Th*e* second system was the five part *Syllogism* of Dignaga (450-520 C.E.). Little is definitely known about Nagarjuna (250-320 CE) apart from the fact that he was born in Southern India in a Brahmin family. He entered a Buddhist monastery as a young man, perhaps a teenager, and studied all of the Buddhist texts that were available there. Nagarjuna was the founder of the Madhyamika school of Buddhism and his texts were the central texts in China, Japan, and Tibet around which Chan and Zen evolved.

Nagarjuna is often called the 'Second Buddha'. In his text, the M*ulamadhyamakakarika,* we encounter a series of related radical dichotomies that Nagarjuna believed were particularly important to understanding *reflexive self-awareness.* These are dichotomies that we found in the initial discussion of 'sensing' vs. the 'sensed'---'seeing/seen', 'hearing/heard/, 'smelling/-smelled'/, 'tasting/tasted', 'touching/touched, and 'thinking/thought'. These dichotomies then become 'word vs. meaning' when we try to express 'experiencing' in language and other symbol systems. In Buddhism being aware of these dichotomies is particularly important because mistaking sensing for the sensed, desiring for the desired, words for their meanings, or mistaking the car one drives, the titles one has, the possessions one has acquired, or even one's body, moods, and emotions for the '*meaning of life* is the source of much of the suffering referred to in the first "Noble Truth" of Gautama. "Living is suffering". Anyone who is familiar with the ways in which attitudes and desires can influence an individual's sense of peace, understands the point Nagsrjuna was making.

Nagarjuna uses two ideas that will help in understanding suffering as well as the situational logic of the *Catuskoti.*

- The first idea is *emptiness (sunyata).* For example the utility of a bowl is its 'emptiness'. We may put rice, or ice cream or coins into the bowl, but the basic emptiness of the bowl as container is its nature, regardless of the different things we may put into it.
- The second idea is *thusaess (thatata).* This refers to the immediate *now* of the moment of sensing, or cognizing---before one recognizes, interprets, names, or even

conceptualizes what one has sensed. This is just sensing, before the sensed is placed in a context.

Catuskoti or Tetralema

The Logic: This is the four step logic of the catuskoti: Sarvam tathyam na va tathyam, tathyam catathyam eva ca, naivatathyam, naiva tathyam, etad buddhanusanam. Everything or anything is 'such', 'not such', 'both such and not such', and 'neither such nor not such'.

Examples. This catuskoti can be applied to 'cognizing' (such), and 'recognizing' (not such), or it can be applied to any synthesis of attending with object of attention, intending with object of intending. In could also be applied to any attempt to distinguish 'real' and 'apparent', or locate a 'true definition of truth' or relate conceiving to 'self as concept' or name to named to naming. Since each step on the Catuskoti affirms or denies an aspect of experiencing and thinking, to treat one step as final would be to treat an 'aspect' as an 'absolute'. The logic consists of four statements, each of which expresses an aspect of reflexive self awareness on the nature of experiencing in which one is seeking to relate the dichotomies that experiencing entails without confusing the seeing with the seen, or experiencing with the experienced. This is the difference already discussed between experiencing as the *possibility of attending and intending* as other than the possibilities *for attending and intending (attention and intention).*

One might start with any one of the senses:

- I see/recognize 'myself' in the mirror. This is attending within a context based on memory and past situations where I have looked into mirrors(affirmation).
- I do not see 'myself' in the mirror.) 'I' and 'self' as possibility of seeing is the realizing that there is seeing of a reflection but not seeing of that which is doing the seeing. (negation)
- I see myself in the mirror and I do not see myself in the mirror)This combination of attending (seeing) and attention lets me make sure my hair is combed without mistaking uncombed/combed hair, black eye, or other facial deformities, with the possibility of seeing. (Affirmation and negation).
- I neither see nor do not see myself in the mirror. This negation of both attending and not attending, seeing and seen frees/separates attending and intending from attention and intention and objects of attention and intention.

Buddhist Situational Logic II

The *five part syllogism* of Dignaga (450-520 CE), like Aristotle's *three part categorical syllogism,* is used in the pursuit of knowledge using reasoned arguments composed of premises and a conclusion. There however, the similarities end for the emphasis in the five-part syllogism is upon identifying and verifying the situational source of the *reason (hetu) that is used to relate the subject and predicate in the conclusion.* Given the limits to and relative nature of experiencing, naming and conceiving that are entailed in the *Catuskoti*, the situational syllogism incorporates and affirms these limits in all empirical reasoning based on specific experiences. The syllogism requires that the thinker identify the previous situations that provide the context for the conclusion to the line of reasoning. Look at the sequence in the following line of reasoning relating 'fire' and the 'mountain'.

1. Thesis: There is a fire burning on the mountain.
2. Reason: Because there is smoke on the mountain.
3.Examples:
Affirmative Situation Example: As is the case of smoke and fire in a burn barrel.
Negative Situation Example: As is not the case with a lake and fog which looks like smoke but where there is no fire.
4. Application:
Affirmative Application: The smoking mountain is similar to a smoking burn barrel.
Negative Application: The smoke on the mountain is not similar to fog on a lake.
5. Conclusion: There is fire on the mountain.

In this example of a situational syllogism, notice there is no reliance on *definitions* or the *universal "A" and "E" propositions* of Aristotle. (*EXPLAIN*) The line of reasoning connects a sequence of situational experiences in order to draw its conclusion. And these

Situational experiences and applications are both affirmative and negative. Although the sequence may seem quite complex, it actually reflects the way in which we reason from past experiences to present situations.

A Situational View (The Buddhist)

Assumptions: Three assumptions are basic to almost all Buddhist schools: 1). The idea of no self' or anatta. The individual consists of empirically verifiable aspects or aggregates (skandas): body, sensation, feelings, dispositions and inclinations, consciousness and memory. However, there is no 'owner' of these aspects. 2). The idea of 'no fixed, static, reality or anicca. Everything changes from moment to moment. Theravada Buddhism sees the world as infinite point instants or moments all inter-related. Mahayana and Madhyamika see constant change as flowing aspects of an unnamable totality. Both stress the situational nature not only of life and the moment, but of all statements and knowledge. One may seem to transcend situations with concepts, but these are constantly changing. 3). The idea of pratityasamutpada or causality - this is expressed in the phrase 'this arising that arises'.

The basic view of consciousness and its possibility in Buddhism would seem to me to be the view of the world as a continuum upon which or within which the human being is an 'attending/intending' aspect - which is expressed individually in intentions and attentions. From this basis one can then explain the idea of suffering (there is suffering but no sufferer as a form of identity crisis in three senses). (1) With 'anatta' (no self) the identity crisis relates to the suffering one encounters when trying to identify some 'internal' essence - asking what am I, viewing ones self as contaminated by 'original sin' or plagued by wrong 'intentions' or conflicting 'intentions' e.g. paradoxes and contradictions, the uncertainties of death, problems of the 'meaning of life' chances of rebirth, when one applies them to ones self. (2) with

"Anicca" (no permanence or essence apart from change), the identify crisis consists of trying to find ones self or ones meaning and value and significance in the non-I - the empirical or external world – believing one is the titles and honors and slurs and slanders that are given and applied to one. We are the cars we drive, the stocks we own, the child of ours who has become president of the U.S. (3) With pratityasamutpada universal causality and interdependence, the identify crisis centers around the exclusive belief in the 'uniqueness' of the individual. It consists of attempts to separate the individual or 'things' out of the totality of relationships where everything is connected and inter-related. This is frequently a problem when one juxtaposes rights over against responsibilities.

Each of these views alleviates suffering by negating a spurious positive, i.e. anatta negates atman or self or soul, anicca negates permanence of external unchanging essence, and pratitysamutpada negates the non empathetic/sympathetic uniqueness of the individual seen as being separate from other beings.

Conclusion

Perhaps the best conclusion to and summary of the *potential of Buddhism for the civilization revival in the Third Millennium* is to be found in the observations of the great philosophers, scientists, and humanists who see and seek to transcend the absolutes and dogmas---both theological and scientific---of our time and to open the world around to renewed enquiring minds and to renewed perspectives and worldly dialogues on every front. Such perspectives can be the sources of human creativity in all fields. As human attention focuses upon ever more technically refined experiencing and the puzzles and problems involved in relating actual experiencing, an increasingly relativistic world in philosophy, logic, and the sciences emerges: 'parallel lines crossing in curved space', 'incompleteness theorems', 'uncertainty principles' 'fractals and chaos theories' in a 'participant—spectator universe.'

References

Bohr, N. (1987). *The philosophical writings of Neil Bohr.* (Vol. 2, pp. 67-68). Woodbridge, Conn: OX Bow Press.

Chan, W. (1967). *Reflections on things at hand.* (p. 85, 94). New York, NY: Columbia University Press.

Devereux, G. (1978). *Ethnopsychoanalysis.* (p. 1). Berkeley, Ca: Univ of California Berkeley.

Herman, W. H. (1949). *Philosophy of mathematics and natural science.* (p. 135). Princeton, NJ: Princeton University.

Wheelwright, P. (1985). *The presocratics.* (p. 69). New York, NY: Collier Macmillan.

Wheelwright, P. (1986). *The presocratics.* (p. 71). New York, NY: Collier Macmillan.

In: Spirituality and Civilization Sustainability … ISBN: 978-1-53610-729-6
Editors: Andrew Targowski and Marek J. Celinski

Chapter 12

HINDUISM: A COLLECTIVE TRADITION IN THE THIRD MILLENIUM

Satish P. Deshpande[1]* and Samir S. Deshpande[2‡]
[1]Western Michigan University, Kalamazoo, MI, US
[2]Kalamazoo College, Kalamazoo, MI, US

ABSTRACT

The purpose of this chapter is to get a better understanding of Hinduism and its relevance in today's world. Hinduism is a collection of religious traditions and practices that originated in the Indian sub-continent. It is the oldest religion in the world and is followed by more than one billion people. The purpose of this paper is to get a better understanding of Hinduism, its relevance in today's world, and how it impacts business ethics. The paper first examines how Hinduism is different from Christianity and Islam. It then traces the origin of Hinduism, its philosophy, and its code of conduct. This is followed by a discussion on specific topic like the role of yoga in Hinduism, the Hindu caste system, and the Ayurvedic form of medicine. The stand of Hinduism on issues like the environment and business ethics is discussed. Finally, the paper examines the changes taking place in Hinduism and its role in the new millennium.

INTRODUCTION

Religion plays a very important part in our lives. It explains our existence, the history of our culture, provides us with a code of conduct, instills moral principles, and is the essence of our civilization (McFaul, 2006). In addition, suggested benefits of religiosity include strong marriages, increase in mental health, and a stable family life (Fagan, 2006). In order to be relevant in modern times any religion must make its social and ethical message available for solving the problems of modern civilization (Niebuhr, 1927). It is common to see the influence of religious institutions on public policy throughout the world (Hefner, 1998,

* E-mail: satish.deshpande@wmich.edu
‡ E-mail: sdeshpande102@gmail.com

Micklethwait and Wooldridge, 2009). Religion can help the society by providing a vision of human life living in dignity and inculcating a high level of virtue in the population. In fact a growing number of people turn to religion to answer many of the problems they have to face (Newell, 2009). Over the years we have seen that religion also has an impact on international relations (Fox and Sandler, 2004).

Major Religions of the World

While many religions exist throughout the world, nearly two out of three people practice Christianity, Islam, or Hinduism. Christianity and Islam trace their origin to Abraham, identify a superior divine being (e.g., Jesus, Muhammad) and believe that god and universe are separate. Hinduism on the other hand has many gods and suggests that god and universe are one. The Hindu religious text *Rig Veda* in 1:164:46 states *"Truth is one; sages speak of it variously.* "The *Bhagavat Gita* in 9:23-31 reinforces this by stating *"there are different paths to God.* "The *Upanishads* reinforce this by stating that all cows of different colors produce the same white milk. Since Hinduism assumes that there are many paths to the truth, it has an array of deities and rituals. It is also more accepting of the beliefs and faiths of other religions. In addition, unlike Christianity and Islam, Hinduism does not owe its origin to a prophet (Singh and Singh, 2009; Spinner-Halev, 2005). It is a collection of wisdom accumulated over generations. While Christianity and Islam are spread throughout the world, Hinduism and its offspring religions like Jainism, Buddhism, and Sikhism are concentrated in the Indian subcontinent. Table 12.1 shows countries with a major Hindu population.

Table 12.1 Hindus as a percentage of population

Country	% of Hindus
Fiji	30%- 33%
Guyana	28.3% - 33%
India	80.50%
Kuwait	12%
Mauritius	48% - 50%
Nepal	80.6%- 81%
Sri Lanka	7.1%- 15%
Suriname	20%- 27.4%
Trinidad and Tobago	22.50%
United Arab Emirates	21.25%

Source: http://en.wikipedia.org/wiki/Hinduism_by_country#By_country. Accessed February 22, 2011.

Origin of Hinduism

Many believe Hinduism is the oldest religion in the world and its origin may date back to 6500 BC. Its name is linked to river Indus which today flows from north India into Pakistan. In olden times, the river was called Sindhu, but Persians (today's Iranians), called the river

Hindu and the civilization that existed in the Indus valley as Hindustan (land of Hindus). Accordingly, the religion followed by the Hindus was labeled Hinduism. Hinduism was originally known as *Sanatana Dharma (eternal laws of the Spirit or* actions/practices that promote happiness and realization of God). Hindus believe that Brahman or the ultimate spirits composed of three powers; Brahma the creator, Vishnu the preserver, and Shiva the destroyer. Hinduism is a very diverse religion. There is no single spiritual authority or founder. There are various denominations (e.g., Vaishnavism, Shaivism, Shaktism, and Smarta), each with its distinctive features, deities, rituals, and doctrines. Each denomination may further have various schools of thoughts. For example, Vaishnavas, the largest denomination of Hindus worship Vishnu. Under Vaishnavism_tradition, there are schools of thoughts focusing on different incarnations (*avatar*) of Vishnu like Krishna and Rama. It is typical to find that many Hindus do not align themselves to one tradition or school of thought but follow all of them. To an outsider, some of the aspects of Hinduism may seem unconnected, but to a Hindu they are all branches and leaves of the same tree. Table 12.2 differentiates between the major Hindu denominations.

Table 12.2. Major Hindu Denominations

Denominations	**Deity of choice (incarnations)**	**Nature of god**	**Favored doctrine**
Vaishnavas	Vishnu (Krishna or Rama)	Loving and pleased by devotion	Personalists
Shaivas	Shiva	Loving and compassioned	Impersonalists
Shaktas	Shakti/Devi (Parvati, Durga, Kali)	Both kindhearted and enraged	Impersonalists
Smartas	Vishnu, Shiva, Devi, Ganesh, and Surya	Believe in universality of Hinduism and no specific deity	Impersonalists

Source:http://hinduism.iskcon.com/tradition/1200.htm;www.hinduismtoday.com; www.ganesh.us/hindu_denominations.html, Accessed March 5, 2011.

It was at one time believed that the development of Hinduism was influenced by Indo-European or Aryan invaders from Europe and Central Asia. But this was later proven to be untrue. In addition, astronomical references in Hindu texts and archaeological findings suggest that the Indus Valley civilization existed as early as 3500 BC (Frawley, 1991).The primary texts of Hinduism are the four *Vedas*: the *Rig Veda* (the book of mantras), *Sama Veda* (book of song), *Yajur Veda* (book of ritual) *and Atharva Veda* (book of spells and charms). These books are one of the oldest religious texts in existence and provide a unique look at the life Indians lived at that time. While we are not sure when the Vedas were composed, we speculate that the *Yajur Veda existed* around 2500 BC. This is based on astrological references in it. The other important texts of Hinduism are the *Upanishads*. They were written around 800 BC and are an extension of the Vedic beliefs. These texts explain how through meditation and the aggregate of a person's actions (Karma), one's soul (*Atma*) can be united with the ultimate truth (*Brahman*).

HINDU PHILOSOPHY

All Hindus believe that life is a cycle of births and deaths. In addition, every action or deed has consequences (*Karma*) which can affect future births. This understanding along with the belief in reincarnation makes Hindus appreciate the fact that the human soul will have many opportunities to grow, develop, and mature. Through good deeds one can be reborn at a higher level and ultimately be a part of the ultimate spirit or *Brahman*. The ultimate goal of all Hindus is to escape the endless cycle of births and death and achieve *Nirvana* (freedom from suffering). In addition, a basic cornerstone of Hinduism is *Dharma* or obligations and duties that God has created for us. Dharma changes as one goes through different stages of life. The *Mahabharata* and *Ramayana* are two major Hindu epics that illustrate the conflicts and problems that arise in following Dharma. The *Bhagavat Gita* is the most important part of the Mahabharata. In this narration Krishna (incarnation of Vishnu) provides his disciple Arjuna, with advice on how to lead a moral life and also the logic for just war. Krishna stresses that one should act according to Dharma not for its pleasurable fruits but because it is the right thing to do (Rinehart, 2004).

HINDUISM CODE OF CONDUCT

The Upanishads and other holy books of Hinduism have 20 ethical guidelines for its followers. It consists of ten restraints called *Yamas* and ten injunctions, or *Niyamas*. These guidelines help followers of Hinduism control negative waves and thoughts and enable Hindus to live a life of contentment and fulfillment. The ten Yamas are Ahimsa (non-injury and non-violence), Satya (to be truthful), Asteya (not to steal), Brahmacharya (abstinence when single and faithful in marriage), Kshama (patience), Dhriti (firmness of character), Daya (compassion), Arjava (honesty), Mitahara (moderation of the appetite), and Shaucha (external and internal purity). The ten Niyamas are Hri (remorse and modesty), Santosha (be contented with what you have), Dana (give generously), Astikya (faith in oneself, religion, and gurus), Ishvara Pujana (devotion through worship and meditation), Siddhanta Shravana (listen to the wise), Mati (develop spiritual will under guidance of guru), Vrata (embrace sacred vows), Japa (chant holy mantras daily), and Tapas (practice penance and sacrifice).

Yoga

Yog (or yoga for Westerners) is the practice to attain the state of enlightenment or oneness with God. Yoga is a disciplined path to enable us to purify our mind and get rid of our attachment to our objects, emotions, and worldly form. There are various forms of yoga (see Table 12.3). For example, Karma Yoga is the spiritual path to realize god through selfless work and denial of the fruits of actions both performed as offerings to God. Bhakti Yoga is the path to God via devotion. Raja Yoga is using meditation to discipline the mind to communicate with God. Jnana Yoga is the process used to realize one's real divine nature. While some believe that each yoga can help us reach salvation, others believe in the amalgamation of different forms of Yoga (Shivananda, 1997).

Yogi Swatmarama, a sage of 15th century India, used principles of Raja Yoga to introduce Hatha Yoga, which is primarily aimed at body control and regulation of breath. The objective of Hatha yoga was to prepare the body for higher levels of meditation. It includes breathing exercises, poses, and purification of body. Hatha Yoga has becomes very popular in Western countries as a way to improve physical and mental health. Unfortunately some Christian and Jewish religious leaders contend that those who do Yoga are practicing Hinduism and are betraying their own religion.

Table 12.3.Types of Yoga, Source: Sivananda (1997)

Type	Path to God	Temperament
Karma Yoga	Selfless work	Moral discipline
Bhakti Yoga	Intense Devotion	Self surrender to god
Raja Yoga	Discipline of mind	Concentration skills
Jnana Yoga	Spiritual insight and Knowledge	Philosophical

Caste System in Hinduism

The caste system is one of the most controversial aspects of Hinduism. The doctrine of Karma or deeds in previous life dictates which caste one is born within. One remains in his/her caste till one dies. The Hindu society is divided into four *varnas* or caste groups: Brahmin (priests), Kshatriya (warriors), Vaishya (traders), and Shudra (laborers). Thus the caste system shaped levels of economic activities and ensured division of labor among the population. Every individual has the privilege of salvation through the performance of the social duties that came to his/her lot.

Only the first three castes come to age religiously by performing the thread ceremony. This ceremony entitles one to learn Sanskrit and participate in Vedic ceremonies. There is also a hierarchy within each caste called Jatis. A fifth group called the Dalits, Harijans or "untouchables" are considered inferior to the other four castes. These groups were limited to work that nobody else wanted to do like leatherwork, butchering, cleaning sewers and toilets, and garbage collection. They also faced social isolation and enormous poverty. Many of them converted to Buddhism and Christianity to escape the social stigma of being a Dalit. Untouchability was abolished and its practices were forbidden under Article 17 of the Indian constitution. In addition in 1950, a system of affirmative action was created under the Indian constitution where space in schools and colleges, jobs in government agencies and departments, and seats in Parliament and state legislatures were reserved for those identified as scheduled castes and tribes by the Indian constitution. Subsequently, a number of members of this group have risen to powerful offices including the President of India, Chief Justice of India, Deputy Prime Minister of India, and Chief Minister of various Indian states. Table 12.4 provides more information on the Vedic caste system.

Table 12.4. The Hindu Caste System

Caste	Typical Occupations	Traditional Duty	Thread Ceremony
Brahmin	Priests	Faith, wisdom, serve dharma	8 years
Kshatriya	Rulers, Warriors	Courage in battle, dispense justice, protect social order	11 years
Vaishya	Merchants, Farmers	Trade, agriculture	12 years
Shudra	Serfs, Servants	Service to upper three classes	Not applicable
Outcasts/ Untouchables	Hunters, Butchers, professional cleaners	Tanning, scavenging, clean human waste	Not applicable

Hinduism and Ayurvedic Medicine

India's traditional system of medicine called Ayurveda (science of life) has its basic roots in Atharva-Veda. Ayurveda focuses on disease prevention through herbal preparations, natural therapies, yoga, and lifestyle changes. It also focuses on the balance between mind and body. Ayurveda is widely used in South Asia. It is the first known documented medical system in the world (Ganesan, 2010). Like allopathic physicians, Ayurvedic physicians in India also go through rigorous training in government recognized medical schools. Research studies have shown numerous beneficial effects of practicing ayurvedic treatment methods. In 1995, California College of Ayurveda became the first Ayurvedic college in the United States. Dr. Deepak Chopra is one of the leading proponents of ayurvedic medicine in the United States. Currently, there are a number of peer reviewed medical journals that focus on Ayurvedic medicine.

Meat Consumption and Hinduism

One misconception about Hinduism is that it bans the consumption of meat. In Western countries people chose to be vegetarian primarily for concern over animal rights or health reasons. A large proportion of Hindus, especially those from South India, tend to be vegetarian. All priests are vegetarian. While there is no specific injunction against meat eating, most of the holy books recommend a vegetarian diet. For example, the Laws of Manu Chapter 5: 48 state that since meat is obtained by causing injury to living beings, eating it is detrimental to the attainment of heavenly bliss. The Yajur Veda (12.32) states, "You must not use your God-given body for killing God's creatures, whether they are human, animal or whatever." According to Hinduism, violence or pain against another being can impact your karma. Thus it is recommended that one not eat living things.

Role of Cows

Another misconception about Hinduism is that the cow is worshipped. Hindus consider the cow as a symbol of tolerance, dignity, and self-less service. It was also very central to the life of an average Hindu in an agricultural society. It provided a number of products for its owners including milk, butter for food and lighting prayer lamps. In addition its dried dung was a common source of fuel for fire. The bull-progeny served to draw carriages, and to plough the fields. In ancient times, a cow was a typical gift given to Brahmans (high-caste priests). The cow is closely linked with Lord Krishna who appeared as a cowherd. It is respected because it asks for nothing but gives a lot to the common man. It is considered the mother of human beings. Thus the cow holds a special place in the hearts of a Hindu but is not worshipped.

Hinduism and the Environment

Various Hindu religious books make strong statements on environmental protection, excess consumption of resources, and natural balance. The Vedas recognize the importance of maintaining a balance between earth and man to ensure effective functioning of nature. For example, the Atharva Veda states that Earth was created for all mortal creatures and not humans alone. The Rig Veda has a prayer to Varuna (head of solar deities) to protect the Earth from dangerous rays and radiation from outer space. The Bhagavad Gita 3:12 is very clear that we are stewards of natural resources and warns against excess consumption. It states that those who take supplies from God, and are immersed in a materialistic society, and give nothing in return are thieves. The Rig Veda 10:97 is a hymn in praise of the healing power of herbs. In addition, the Rig Veda 6:48 warns of the danger of pollution if trees are cut. The Bishnois in India consider cutting trees and killing birds and animals blasphemy. The Chipko and Appiko movements in India used religious beliefs to protect trees from loggers. Today many of the modern Hindu movements like the Ramkrishna Mission and the International Society for Krishna Consciousness (ISKON) stress that the only way to achieve environmental sustainability is to break the desire for worldly things via spiritual development (Haigh, 2010).

Hinduism and Business Ethics

Lack of ethics and corporate fraud has resulted in a general distrust towards the business world. Companies such as Enron and WorldCom are synonymous with corporate greed. In 2008-2009, illegal and abusive lending practices of the financial-service industry resulted in the worst financial crisis in the world since the Great Depression. Many managers in India and abroad are now turning to the Bhagavad Gita for lessons on business ethics and leadership (Parekh, 2008; Roka, 2006).

The Bhagavad Gita has many verses that can guide corporate executives in ethical decision making. One of the most popular verses of Gita 2.47 states that an individual should not be motivated by the results or fruits of one's actions while performing one's duty. Anxiety, disappointment, and stress are inevitable if we focus on anticipated outcomes. It adds that those who work for their own self-interest and not the good of everyone are sinners (Roka, 2006). This suggests that corporations should not undertake strategies that only benefit their shareholders but all their stakeholders. The Gita 18:16 also stresses that one should not take complete credit for ones actions. Always share credit with others. It describes different types of work cultures and recommends a divine work culture that is absent of greed, pride, blaming, and egoism. The Gita 10.4-5 states that the qualities of a good leader include forgiveness, truthfulness, nonviolence and charity. Only leaders with these traits inspire others to do the right things.

Changes in Hinduism

The colonization of India by the British had a significant impact on Hinduism. Internal reform started with the formation of Brahmo Samaj in 1828 by Ram Mohan Roy as a reaction to conversion of low caste Hindus to Christians by British missionaries. He stressed that the Upanishads are the true essence of Hinduism. Swami Dayanand Saraswati founded the *Arya Samaj,* and argued that the Vedas were the true essence of Hinduism. His book, Satyarth Prakash (Light of Truth) written in 1875, was a major impetus to the Indian independence movement. Swami Vivekendanda was another influential Hindu reformer who founded the Ramkrishna Mission in India. He focused on introducing Hinduism in the United States and Europe and spoke at the Parliament of the World's Religions at Chicago in 1893.

Another progressive reformer was Mohandas Karamchand Gandhi, also known as Mahatma (great soul) Gandhi. He advocated the ending of discrimination against the untouchables and tolerance of other religions. He used the Hindu concept of *ahimsa* (nonviolence) to advocate resistance to oppression by the British through mass civil defiance. This philosophy of nonviolent resistance had a major impact on Nelson Mandela in South Africa and Martin Luther King, Jr. in the United States in their efforts to fight social injustice and discrimination.

Hinduism in the New Millennium

In the last few decades, many Hindus from India have immigrated to various parts of the world in search of better opportunities. The first major migration took place in the late nineteenth century when indentured Indian workers were sent to the Caribbean countries, Fiji and East Africa by their British colonial masters after the abolition of slavery. Most of the migration to Western countries and the Middle East took place after World War 2. This has helped raise awareness of Hindu philosophy in all corners of the world. Hindu community is now the richest and the most educated community in developed countries like the United States. Hindu temples and Indian grocery stores have spread rapidly in Western countries. Many Westerners follow Hindu practices such as Yoga and meditation.

In recent years, Hindu gurus (spiritual leaders) such as Maharishi Mahesh Yogi, Swami Satchidananda, Swami Muktananda, and Swami Prabhupada introduced Hinduism to many Westerners. Ayurvedic medicine and herbal medicines are now widely accepted by many Westerners as a part of alternative therapy. Many Westerners have also become vegetarian to avoid eating another living being, and also have a positive impact on the environment. In addition, there has been a steady increase in the number of Westerners believing in reincarnation. Clearly, sacred elements of Hinduism have found a willing audience in the West. Also, in the last decade, India and a number of Western countries like the United States have found themselves targets of Muslim extremists. This has resulted in an unprecedented cooperation on the political and defense front between India and these countries against a common enemy. This has raised the positive perception about Hinduism in these nations.

Conclusion

Hinduism is a collection of religious traditions and practices that originated in the Indian sub-continent. It is the oldest religion in the world and is followed by more than one billion people. It is not rigid or dogmatic. It is flexible to incorporate changes without compromising its core values. It is caste based religion but lacks a central authority. While it suffers from various stereotypes and misconceptions, certain aspects of Hinduism like yoga and Ayurvedic medicine has been widely embraced in the West without understanding its true significance. Immigrants have enabled Hinduism and its core values to spread throughout the world. Hinduism has gone through a lot of reform over two decades and has survived and adapted to both internal and external challenges to its existence.

References

Fagan, P. F. (2006). Why religion matters even more: the impact of religious practice on social stability. *The Backgrounder*, No. 1992, Heritage Foundation, Washington DC.

Fox, J., & Sandler, S. (2004). *Bringing religion into international relations*. New York: Palgrave Macmillan. pp. 163-179.

Frawley, D. (1991). *Gods, sages, and kings*., Salt Lake City, UT: Morson Publications.

Ganesan, U. (2010). Medicine and modernity: The Ayurvedic revival movement in India, 1885-1947. *Studies on Asia*, vol.4, n° 1, pp. 108-131.

Haigh, M. (2010). Education for a sustainable future: strategies of the new hindu religious movements.*Sustainability*, vol.2, pp. 3500-3519.

Hefner, R. W. (1998). Multiple maternities: Christianity, Islam, and Hinduism in a Globalizing Age. *Annual Reviews*. pp. 83-104.

McFaul, T. (2006). Religion in the future global civilization. *The Futurist*. pp.30-36.

Micklethwait, J. & Wooldridge, A. (2009), *God is back: How the global revival of faith is changing the world*, Penguin Press, London, England.

Newell, S. J. (2009). Trends in religious belief and the role of religious in future world affairs. *39th International Conference of the International Society for the Comparative Study of Civilization*, pp.284-290.

Niebuhr, R. (1927). *Does civilization need religion? A Study in the Social Resources and Limitations of Religion in Modern Life*. New York: The Macmillan Company.

Parekh, S. (2008). The crisis and emancipation of the modern corporate executive: how the Bhagavad Gita reinforces Edward Freeman's stakeholder theory. *The Michigan Journal of Business*, vol.1, pp. 7-34.

Rinehart, R. (Ed.). (2004).*Contemporary Hinduism: rituals, culture, and practice.* Santa Barbara, CA: ABC-CLIO.

Roka, P. (2006). Bhagavad Gita on effective leadership. New York: iUniverse.

Singh, A. N. and Singh, P.(2009). What can international law learn from Indian mythology, Hinduism and history? *II Jeail,* vol. 1.

Sivananda, S. S. (1997). *All about Hinduism.* Shivanandanagar, India: The Devine Life Society.

Smith, B. K. (1996). Re-envisioning Hinduism and evaluating the Hindutva Movement. *Religion*, vol. 26, pp. 119-128.

Spinner-Halev, J.(2005). Hinduism, Christianity, and liberal religious. Toleration. *Political Theory*, vol. 1, pp. 28-57.

In: Spirituality and Civilization Sustainability ...
Editors: Andrew Targowski and Marek J. Celinski
ISBN: 978-1-53610-729-6

Chapter 13

CURRENT SOCIAL AND POLITICAL ROLE OF RELIGIONS: THE PARTICULAR CASE OF JUDAISM AND OF CANDOMBLE

Pedro Geiger*
State University of Rio de Janeiro, Brazil

ABSTRACT

This chapter examines the role of organized religions in modern societal and political life, and deals, particularly, with Judaism and with Cabdomblé. Judaism was introduced in Brasil, since the beginning of the country´s colonization, by Jews and new Christians. Candomblé, was introduced by Africans brought to Brazil by slave traders. The origins, the fundaments and the evolution over the years of both religions are presented, as well, their influence in Brazil´s formation. In its new development, Candomblé presents signals of an increasing influence in Brazilian culture and in politics. Additionally, globalization creates better conditions for the international institutional encounters of the Brazilian African religions with the current African religions in African countries, and with those of African origin, in Cuba, USA and elsewhere.

INTRODUCTION

From the 19th century on, it seemed that religions would enter in a cycle of continuous accelerated decline, given the advances of modernity. Acting in this direction were, on one side, the increasing powers of science and technology, reacting to the monotheist religious creative explanations. On the other side was the development of the National State, supported by an increasing urbanization, introducing its own laic ethical and social codes (Marx, Weber, Durkheim, Bordieu). More recently, Henri Lefébvre introduced the expression "urban rights".

However, since the sixties of the 20th century, one sees a reversion in this movement. Not only there is an increase in the number of followers of religions, including young people

* E-mail: pedro.geiger@gmail.com

and new generations, but also the appearance of new forms of religious practices, new forms of syncretism between religions and the fact that some people are adopting more than one religious faith and practice.

Are all these facts representing an influence of the post modern principle of uncertainty? Many different reasons are brought by scholars to explain these new changes. It is not enough to think about the recent urbanization in less developed countries, multiplying masses of illiterate people, originating in the countryside. Religion is also increasing among middle and upper classes in urban environments of developed countries. Some relate them to the fact that, increasingly, one realizes that, apparently, science will never reach a final end in its search for the *real*. After each phase of discoveries and findings, the *real* presents a new set of questions and mysteries, in an infinite sequence. Some scientific personalities, such as Fritjof Capra, writer of *The Tao of Physics*, turned to mysticism. The effects of globalization are in other's accounts. Given the Nation State weakening in many aspects, globalization shifts the State to a 'local' position, giving religion the opportunity to retake former 'universal' characteristics. Traditional religion would assume a counter point position of criticism to some negative ethical aspects of current globalization (David Held).While on the contrary, as if following capitalist rules, one sees the appearance of new sects guided by charismatic personalities exploring the market.

The increasing geographical connections across the world are diminishing past views, about dividing religions between universal and particular flavors. The current means of transportation and communication are providing movements of greater integration between similar religious communities. Even among less hegemonic groups, such as those practicing African origin religions, in the Americas. One also observes the increase of different forms of syncretism among religions, especially in the more open societies. Postmodernism made it clear that people can hold many contradictory identities. It is common today to find people with multiple legal passports from different nations. In the same way, one finds people celebrating or following different religions today. Mixed marriages play a role in this. In December, around the world, numerous Jews celebrate Chanukah and Christmas.

The presented framework raises the question about the roles that religions can play in the current historical process. In this chapter, one will deal particularly with two religions: Judaism, which is spread over the world; and Candomblé, a religion of African roots, practiced in Brazil.

JUDAISM

The word Judaism has a double meaning. It refers to the Jewish people and to its cultural manifestations, and it refers to the Jewish religion. Actually, this makes Judaism a universal religion, because Jewish religion does not exactly belong to just only one ethnic group. It is Judaism that produces a unique people, as any gentile who converts to Judaism becomes automatically a member of the Jewish people, or 'nation' (nation in a sense of a preserved form, from antiquity, when national identity was equal to religious identity).

Thus, living in the Diaspora, when Jews acquired state citizenship in Europe, starting in France and England during the 19th century, under the influence of the Enlightenment, they appear as a postmodern prototype by holding two 'national' identities – as Jews and as state citizens. That posed an odd situation for Napoleon, who called an assembly to inquiry about the loyalty of the French Jews. A situation that still raises suspicions and prejudices, and that gave opportunity to the Dreyfuss' affair and to Zola's famous "*J'accuse*".

This Jewish brotherly feeling, linked to an idea of a biological ancestral father, Abraham, acted positively in favor of universal peace given the presence of Jews in any part of the World. A view on current Geopolitics shows Jews involved – as Jews –, in only a local war – that related to the existence of Israel.

Other aspects justify Judaism as a universal religion. For instance, being the first to produce a written "great narrative" (Lyotard, Jack Goody) – the Bible. No more in stone or brick, but on sheep skin, that can be presented in a form of roll, occupying a minimum of space, and easy to transport while reading. It started to be open and read for the people in the synagogues, and the Jews were called "the people of the Book". The Bible was written during the 5th century B.C.E., a time of lively cultural activities and exchanges among the regions around the Mediterranean. One can show the relations between the Talmudist and the Greek Stoic philosopher. Within such world of interchanges, of ideological diffusion, of social values, the Jewish religion gave birth to Christianity, and by the 8th century C.E., to Islam.

During centuries of existence, the Jewish religion, as other religions, underwent continuous transformations and division in different currents, due to inter-related forces acting both from inside and from outside. The chapter emphasizes the following passages of transitions: The shift from priests to rabbis, or from sacrifices to prayers, or from Temple to synagogue; the appearance of the Cabala, and its relations to the Renaissance; Maimonides and the influence of the Christian Theology. Baruch Spinoza, Mendelssohn, and the God of immanence, and the Enlightenment in one side, and Jewish Reform in the other side; the populist movement of Hassidism, its joy of living; its replacement of the figure of Messiah by a just man, the *Tzadik*; the continuous concert of the Earth, *Tikun Olam*; the diminishing of the me in face or the other (Martin Bubber, John Bonker); the Jewish religion in face of Zionism (Eban).

Heidegger, in "Being and Time" says that, although every knowledge or discipline has its principles, concepts, even foundations, but when subjected to temporal changes, in order to maintain its individuality, has, however, to hold some of its ontological foundations. Like a birth certificate. The Bible is a foundation of the Jewish religion. Essentially, the continuous building of this religion is to interpret and re-interpret this "great narrative" (sic). One can see this practice as a representation of the dialectic of human values. Their universal concepts change between different historical phases, but human values, as a category, stand permanently.

For example, the second of the three books of the Bible is called "Kings" in its English version and "Prophets" in Hebrew. One realizes immediately that the permanent question of power and morality lies in the texts, and that its contents still provide illumination for the future.

On a political approach, one observes the majority of Jewish religious institutions adhering to the current ecumenical movement. Jewish religion has no proselytism practices or an ideology of world conquests. Currently, for some institutional sectors, violence is admittedly used for justice or in defense of a local territory in the land of Israel.

The Jews of antiquity were astonished when looking at the stars, the Sun, the Moon, all moving in the sky, in an order, never colliding. They saw it as God's desire for harmony and peace. Until nowadays an important prayer, the *Kaddish* is repeated at significant occasions. It says "He who makes peace in His heights, He will make peace on us"...

CANDOMBLE

Candomblé is a religion developed in Brazil and based on faiths brought from Africa during the slave trade. Actually, Candomblé is one of the forms of the adjustment of past African religions in the Americas. In Cuba, they developed the cult of Voodoo.

It is common to see scholars defining African religions as local, either by considering them as magical beliefs or practices, or by considering geographical differences in their consistencies. It is true that these religions do not have written narratives, they have survived on the base of oral transmissions. Another reason is that they do not have pre-scripted commands about human behavior, as in the case of the Ten Commandments of Sinai. However, recently a large literature is being developed inclusively by people who are practitioners of this faith (Velho). When some consider the African religions as geographically local, or mere magical beliefs, one can see it is as a result of ignorance and prejudice against a non-hegemonic sector.

When the Europeans started taking slaves to America, the black African societies, other than the ones taken by Islam, were organized in local kingdoms, as the Marxian called *Asiatic mode of production.* They followed a common religion, but with differentiations between geographical localities. It was a frame facilitated by the fact that the religion admitted the birth of new gods from an ancestral god, and by the fact that there was not a central geographical or clerical power. As one can see, they are not dissimilar from the Greek model where gods give birth to gods, or from the current Jewish or Protestant models in regard to the absence of a hierarchical central institutional power. *Olumadure* is the name of the supreme god, or supreme *Orixá*, in Candomblé, who continues to generate gods, secondary *Orixás*. Each one of these gods is related to a given human activity, character, or locality.

As for the animal sacrifices practiced by African religions, they are not far from the sacrifices ordered in the Old Testament. What one sees in the African religions is the maintenance of very old religious forms, certainly due to the absence of written narratives. One may think that a written narrative stimulates new written narratives (see the diverse Gospels in the New Testament), and that they conduct to formal interpretations and transformations. The oral tradition of the African religion suggests about past relations with ancient Egypt, Jewry, and other cultures. There are even stories among some Yoruban tribes that tell about descending from past Jewish tribes. Recently, the London BBC reported on DNA evidence supporting the founding Jewish roots of the Zimbabwe Lemba tribe.

Recent decades show Candomblé spreading in Brazil, winning followers in the middle and even upper classes. The reasons are the same used to explain the general current returns to religion, the search for 'pure' old values. In this instance, 'pure' means that these values were not contaminated by involvement with current economic or political interests.

In its new development, Candomblé presents signals of an increasing influence in Brazilian culture and in politics. Additionally, globalization creates better conditions for the international institutional encounters of the Brazilian African religions with the current African religions in African countries, and with those of African origin, in Cuba, USA and elsewhere. Nowadays the role that religions of African origin can play for the future is the same as that of other religions. They can be shields against forces of domination of men by other men. They can be places to develop social identities outside from the currently imposed public institutions, as if they were never also authoritarian imposed institutions.

REFERENCES

Atkins, R. (1990). *Art speak, a guide to contemporary ideas, movements, and buzzwords.* New York: Abbeville Press Publishers.

Benesch, W. (2010). Religion versus the gods. *Civilitas blog*, ISCSC, March 29.

Bowker. J. (2000). *Concise dictionary of world religions.* Oxford, New York: Oxford University Press.

Buarque de Holanda, S. (1936). *Raízes do Brasil.* Rio de Janeiro: José Olimpio.

Buber, M. (1996). *I and thou.* New York: Touchstone.

Deleuze, G. (1969). *Logique du sens.* Paris : Les Éditions de Minuit.

Eban, A. (1984). *Heritage, civilization and the Jews.* New York: Summit Books.

Edward, P. (1988). *Inquisition.* New York: The Free Press.

Ezrahi, S. D. (2000). *Booking passage.* Berkeley, CA: University of California Press.

Farhat-Holzman, L. (2010). Was there an original human religion? *Civilitas blog*, ISCSC, March 26.

Harvey, D. (1977). Population, Resources and Ideology in Science. In R. Peet (Ed.), *Radical Geography: Alternative Viewpoints on Contemporary Social Issues* (pp. 213-242). Chicago: Maaroufa Press Inc.

Held, D. (1997). *Democracy and global order: from the modern state to cosmopolitan governance.* Cambridge: Polity Press.

Jullien, F. (2010) *O diálogo cultural: do universal ao multiculturalismo.* Rio de Janeiro,: Zahar.

Kam-tuck yip, A., Keenan, M. & Page, S-J. (2010). A sociological exploration of religious young people's sense of place and belonging. *Abstracts*, Session 1204, AAG Conference, Washington.

Lewin, H. (2005). *Identidade e Cidadania, como se expressa o Judaísmo Brasileiro.* Rio de Janeiro: Universidade Estadual do Rio de Janeiro.

Ortiz, R. (2001). Anotações sobre religião e globalização. *Revista Brasileira de Ciências Sociais*, vol. 16, n° 47, São Paulo.

Piveteau, J. L. (1995) Le Territoire est-il um lieu de memoire?, *L´Espace Geographyque*, vol. 24, n 2, pp.113-123.

THE ECONOMIST. (2010). A quantum calculation, *The Economist*, vol. 395. n° 8679, pp.81-82.

Vedral, V. (2010). *Decoding reality: the universe as quantum information.* New York: Oxford University Press.

Velho, J. (2010). An interview (by this writer), March.

Voeglin, E. (1958). *Israel and Revelation.* Volume I of Order and History. Baton Rouge: Louisiana State University Press.

In: Spirituality and Civilization Sustainability ...
Editors: Andrew Targowski and Marek J. Celinski
ISBN: 978-1-53610-729-6

Chapter 14

AFRICAN CIVILIZATION: THE RELIGIOUS DIMENSIONS IN LIGHT OF THE THIRD MILLENIUM

Tseggai Isaac [*]
Missouri University of Science and Technology, Rolla, MO, US

ABSTRACT

Africa prides itself in its ancient civilizations, but the celebratory value of those civilizations is overshadowed by the recurrent challenges of poverty, political and religious wars, ethnic strife, and unrelenting tyrannical rule. Of all these challenges, the inabilities of state institutions to reconcile religious and confessional divisions represent the hardest. Scholars on civilization have in recent years contemplated of operationalizing scientific thinking. The sense of nationalism that tends to look at civilizations as sacred attributes of societies is challenged by the secular features quantitative analysis. The expansion of global trade and commerce effectively facilitated by the swiftness of Information Technology (IT) provide opportunities for identifying across cultural and civilizational variables of peace and "wisdom". This analysis focuses on Africa's religious political experiences to state that Africa's problems are intractable even to the dynamic theories of IT and globalization.

"Nathanael wondered, can there any good thing come out of Nazareth? Philip said unto him, come and see." The Gospel According St. John, Chapter 1: 46.

INTRODUCTION

[*] E-mail: tseggai@mst.edu

The biblical quote above is a reflection of a locality, Nazareth of Galilee, inhabited by a people whose history and their self-worth was wrongly judged on the basis of biased and prejudiced assumptions. The "Prince of Peace," Christ, came from Nazareth, but it mattered little due to the negative perception against that community. The religious authorities of the time were content with their religious beliefs. They did not believe that the city of Nazareth or any important figure such as Jesus Christ deserved any level of recognition. This illustrates that religion and political legacies speak louder if the platforms from which they stand to affirm their parochial values are well managed and fortified with the requisites of political clout. At their respective evangelistic and jihad dispensations, Christianity and Islam promoted their teachings in Africa vigorously and managed to garner millions of followers. For the last two millennia, both religions forced themselves on the passive and hospitable societies of Africa, greater Asia, and the Middle East. The new religions provided their own paradigms and created new perceptions of their civilizations and of the world.

This study takes its theoretical basis from the techno-globalist disciplines. Scholars on Information Technology (IT) and on globalization have expressed optimistic views about the rise of global peace and understanding through the application of Information Technology (Targowski, A. 2009 and 2011). They state that the current political, military, and diplomatic endeavors that had counted on the "wisdom" and benevolence of the current world civilizations had not delivered an enduring peace. Their record on lasting human happiness is not satisfactory. Information Technology has the answer. With the dawn of the 21st century, post-modern Western civilization has discovered in "cognitive informatics and wisdom development" the tool with which to tame the destructive tendencies of secular humans. The integrative capacities of Information technology and their inherent efficiency can serve as the panacea for global crises. Civilizations can also be rejuvenated by IT to internalize globalist and comprehensive visions of humanity based on "wisdom" (Targowski 2009, Stigler 2003).[1]

These IT and globalist theories are visionary and highly refined. In the first place, they border on specialization. Their sharpness and focus orient them to interpret social science problems using mathematical tools. When they are transposed to the broad, but nebulous elements of global civilizations, their specialized and quantitative features leave out outlying civilizations that are less endowed with the globalization and IT resources. Second, they are result oriented as in mathematical computations providing specific answers to axiomized formulas. Hence they tend to be linear and tethered to the dictates of scientific discoveries that cumulatively add up to the rich harvest of computational sciences. Third, in their vertical analysis, these theories leave out the outlier civilizations that have not yet found their space in the IT landscape. These are the states and regions whose capacity to avail themselves of the bounties of information technology (IT) is marginal or nonexistent.

This analysis describes the African dilemma with respect to African civilization and religions. As the transition to the Third Millennium is well underway, the expectation that IT would contribute to the revitalization of African peace is remote. I argue that the ability of African states to harness IT and join the countries of Europe and Asia to institutionalize

[1]Targowski's broad theory of applying IT to define commonalties in civilizations is almost identical, but with an opposite focus, to that of Fernand Braudel. Targowski invokes IT and its attendant software products as possibly having unifying and edifying effect on civilizations. Braudel uses cultural elements and the tools of everyday life, such as household items, as the basis for commonalities of civilizations and societies. See footnote #4 for Targowski. Fernand Braudel (1992), *Capitalism & Civilization 15th-18th Century: The Structure of Everyday Life*, University of California Press, Berkeley, CA.

lasting peace, unity, and wisdom are negated by the prevalence of religious frictions, poverty, and tyrannical regimes impervious to civility or civilized means of governance. The analysis of the paradigmic context that outlines African political and economic trajectories will begin below.

PARADIGMS: SHIFTING OR OTHERWISE, STATIC IN AFRICA

The surge in religious revivalism in the second half of the twentieth century continues in Africa during the twenty-first century also. In theoretical terms, religion would be a fringe topic if it were not for the deadly effects that the religious competitions between Christianity and Islam brought to bear upon the march of civilization and the tranquility of civil societies. Many historical developments that enriched African civilization are based on robust African Christianity that flowered in North Africa and radiated to Europe (Isichei 1995: 13-74). Those are long forgotten with their civilizational legacies, such as churches, cathedrals, libraries, museums, monuments, manuscripts, and architectural relics reduced to ashes in the fiery sweep of Islamic conquest.[2]

For a long time in the modernist theoretical analysis, religious topics in their ecclesiastical renderings are looked at with suspicion as fables and imaginative stories. This is because religions as a basis for scientific affirmations of facts are disquieting to the historian as they are to the scientist who must deal with hard sciences. Historians are just as secular in their pedagogical focus. To the believer, offering hard evidence is not requisite for the fervency and absolute dedication to the faith. And historians are not humble believers of faith without hard evidence; they have joined the hard sciences in deifying rationality. Yet, without meeting the high standards of scientific objectivity, religions have aroused hateful controversies, tolerated bloodletting throughout the ages, and inspired dogmatic principles for which the believers are willing to sacrifice their lives for rewards in heaven. Some of the most holy or unholy brutalities took place in Africa. For this reason, the perceptions created by Christianity and Islam of other civilizations may bear little resemblance to reality. In the African landscape, both faiths have fought for supremacy and mostly, but not completely, one of the two, Islam, has won the battles.

THE TENSIONS BETWEEN SCIENCE AND RELIGIONS

Any faith that justifies its existence by denying the survival of other faiths lacks the scriptural strength to compete in the market place of religious and social ideas. Religions negate paradigms, because paradigms are contextualized by the expectations of rationality. Religions are not hospitable to paradigms to have the unassailable force of episodic objectivity until the arrival of competing paradigms to dethrone the previous ones (Khun1967). The scientific debates that are undertaken to resolve the clash of paradigms are settled by reaching a consensus among the competing advocates where the dominant paradigm is accepted as objectively right and correct as measured by proven scientific

[2] For a detailed description of the destruction of African Churches, see Edward Gibbons (1952), *The Decline and Fall of the Roman Empire,* Vol. II, No. 41, pp. 271-288.

criterion. Andrew Targowski observed this in his analysis of Aristotelian methodology and empiricism by stating:

> Aristotle valued knowledge gained from the senses and to a certain degree neglected the value of empiric data. . . . The Copernicus Revolution in the 16th century gave birth to a critique of the Aristotelian reasoning method [paradigm] and triggered a quest for a new [paradigm] method of reasoning (Targowski 2011:26).

This scientific procedure allows for ideas that are only proven, meritorious, honest, and faultless to prevail. Conclusions that are pseudo-objective are quickly jettisoned. In religion, the ground-rules for resolving paradigm conflicts are not based on scientific methods. They are watered and nurtured by visions, inspirations, and actions that are decidedly not open to rationality. The irrationality of competing sacred faiths when used to govern the lives of their followers falls short of objectivity because emotions are often rationalized as inspirations. For example, hate as emotion can be elevated to actionable religious programs and deadly missions such as holy wars and culture- and-faith-displacing evangelistic outreaches to enforce an outside belief on indigenous peoples and their faiths. The outside beliefs can also revolutionize cultures and enforce or persuade converts to accept the new religious system. Such is the epiphenomenon of African civilization. Its ability to withstand the onslaught of the 21st century challenges will be determined in light of Islamic jihad, Christian evangelism, and charismatic Christian revivalism. In light of religious revivalism, cultural parochialism, and predatory tyranny, the African political and social landscape appears unprepared for the benefits of IT based accommodations. Information Technology and its technical attributes to inject wisdom onto the scene are bound to be a difficult undertaking. The high optimism of scientists and scholars such as Targowski may be an admirable venture, but Africa is a difficult terrain to navigate even for those equipped with the best framed theories on civilization.

The reasons for this pessimism are two major cataclysmic events that had befallen Africa in the last eight hundred years, slavery and European colonialism. Slavery began long before the arrival of Europeans and was driven by Arab thirsts for capitalization and monetization of human beings. The practice wounded and scared the African soul and pride. Colonialism followed slavery and both practices resulted in the home-grown violent system of post-colonial and post-independence African authoritarianism and totalitarianism. Given these factors, Africa's role in the civilizational outlook for the third millennium is bound to be determined by the cultures of anger, victimhood, and dogmatism that Christianity and Islam are showing throughout the Continent.

If Christianity and Islam are to compete for the heart and soul of Africa, the *Cognitive Information and Wisdom Development (2011)* approach will have to account for its linear and salutary socio-cultural ideals. If twenty-first century Christianity prevails in the African landscape, will it be Christianity coming home to reclaim the St. Augustine mantle or to wear a new garb in the temper of Protestant fundamentalism? If Islam proves dominant in the African setting, will it be in its zero-sum expectations of proselytization where tolerance of other faiths is considered an Islamic anomaly or will it have the scriptural flexibilities needed in Asia and the Middle East? Will it shed its medieval habits that have long needed revisiting by its clergies?

Andrew Targowski's work of integrating culture, religion, and post-modern information technology to the proper orientation of societies for universal "wisdom" is optimistic in line with the idealist school (Targowski 2009; 2011). The realist school is likely to gaze at the current global alliances, realize how they are mostly inspired by unyielding religious and confessional visions, and negate the idealist perspective.[3] In the expectations of "Cognitive Information and Wisdom Development," the approaches that Targowski lists do not seem to directly apply to Africa as they may do to the rest of the world. I select the religious and political approaches to argue that the third millennium is bound to be less hopeful as the second had been for Africa. The African culture of opting for peace when peace can be had and forswearing destruction on the basis that peace is superior to the fervency and zeal that are easily ignited by religious beliefs (Targowski 2011: 53).

The African Perception of Africa: Africans see and imagine Africa in its geographical totality. They do not imagine the Sahara Desert as a demarcation line separating Africans into north and south. Africa is a whole Continent indivisible in terms of the civilizations that had originated in its soil and in the religious and cultural legacies that had touched its soil both in the Old and New Testament eras. Africa is a tapestry of cultures, ethnicities, languages, and hews of skin color.

To the religiously inspired African, ancient Africa is the first born in the family of God. As such, it deserves the claim that it also shares a common beginning with its sister civilizations in the Middle East and Asia (Davidson, B. 1970: 26-40). With the dawn of the 21st century, the determination by Christian and Islamic revivalists to affirm sectarian differences rages just as it did in the 20th century. Contemporary Africa finds itself as a focus of religious revival. Christianity and Islam compete for converts who can be expected to spread the religious banner to the vast Continent. The pattern of religious activism is a demonstration of the most fervent types of religious awakening. The Christians invoke revival and anointment of the Holy Spirit such as speaking in tongues, dreaming visions, prophesying, and healing of sickness. The Muslims use infiltration, monetary incentives, social pressures, and in their most ardent zeal, deadly force as in the case of the Boko Haram of Nigeria. As religious fervency attempts to make its mark in Africa, the African civilization that had given birth to the African cultural patterns of community, neighborhood, common cause, consensus and conciliation are overshadowed by faith and the fantasy of peace through religious sectarianism.

The Arab Perception of Africa: The driving force in the Islamic civilization is the commission given to the believer to extol Islam as a religious, political, and social guide. Scripturally, Islam is a path to submission as in totally rejecting other faiths and submitting only to the teachings of Prophet Mohammed (Lewis, B. 1994). Islam has fixed and irrevocable rules of faith that make it hard for its clerics to exercise judicial review on matters of legislation and adjudication. The conceptof "developmental wisdom" is heresy in Islam. The dictates of the first principles as given during the founding of the faith must govern all political and social life. Orthodoxy in raw faith, as it was scripturally ordered at the inauguration of the religion, must be observed without compromise to modernity. In order to stay true to this order, Islam is taught and propagated as a superior faith to other faiths. It is also taught as the only true religion. Other religions must surrender or submit to the first principles of Islam.

[3] For an in-depth analysis of the realist and idealist schools, see, Doyle, M. (1997). *Ways of War and Peace*, W. W. Norton, New York, NY.

Based on these religious principles, Islam rose up in Arabia and swept through the Middle East and moved on to Africa. In its advance, Islam presented itself as a religious faith that must be accepted and as a political system that must be obeyed by its adherents with submission.[4]

The European Perception of Africa: The topographical features of Africa have always been a major part of the historical and religious analysis of Africa. The divide between Western and African scholars is cast in a stark line of east-west dichotomy. Western scholars view Africa as comprising north and south. African scholars view Africa as one entity like Asia or Europe where topographical differences do not reflect demographical differences. The proprietorship of legacies as in Greece being considered as the fountainhead of European civilizations represents a straitjacket thinking and inside-out dogmatism that affirms robust European civilization undiluted by the legacies and sublime features of other civilizations such as that of Egypt or Mesopotamia.[5]

Biblical references are critical parts of African religious legacies, as are indigenous traditional faiths. What has become apparent in recent decades is the ability of the African Church to adapt and find common grounds between traditional faiths and biblical principles to enhance the favorable environment that Christianity is enjoying in Africa. The African Church managed to resolve the paradigmatic dichotomy between Christianity and traditional faiths by translating traditional faith as compatible with Christianity (Isichei 1995:338). Whether they are taken as foundations of faith or imaginative fantasies, the Apostolic Creed of Faith and the assorted practices and principles of the Christian faith are regarded as the heart of Christianity. Without the central features of the Christian faith, such as the Ten Commandments, the birth of Christ, baptism by water, and the Sermon on the Mount, the symbolic profession and the practical application of the Christianity would be meaningless. According to Merrills and Miller:

> The African Church was defined by its saints and martyrs, but was also shaped by its great theologians: Tertullian was prominent in the 2nd century, Cyprian and Arnobius in the third, and Lactonius in the Fourth. The tradition reached its peak with St. Augustine who was educated in the Carthage of the late fourth century, provided leadership as the bishop of the city of Hippo Regius in the early fifth and eventually died in 430 as the Vandals laid siege to his adopted home (Merrills& Miles 2010:3).

Theological arguments over these central features of Christianity left an impact on Africa. The equally determined and fervently zealous campaigns by Islamic fundamentalists and Wuhabists pose counter-balancing moves. Both, in their own strategies, are determined to achieve their prominence.

---

[4] The word Islam is a derivative of "*salaam*", a Semitic word meaning peace; it is an adjective describing a state of being at a specific time. Islam on the other hand is a noun meaning let there be peace now, indicating a change in the state of being now. For the definition of the word "Islam" see Bernard Lewis, "*The Roots of the Muslim Rage*", *The Atlantic Monthly*, and September, 1990. http://www.theatlantic.com/magazine/print/1990/09/the-roots-of-muslim-rage/4643/ (Viewed February 4, 2012.

[5]Targowski and other scholars on civilization, such as Toynbee, and Sorokin do consider Mesopotamian and Egyptian civilizations as the foundations of Western Civilization. American conservatives would rather emphasize the "Great Books" tradition, enumerations of Western thoughts and philosophical discourses as the basis of Western civilization (See Targowski, A. (2009) *Information Technology and Societal Development*, IGI Global, p. 48, Figure 2-1; See also Bloom, A. (1987), *The Closing of the American Mind, Touchstone Books, Chapter 1.*

THE AFRICAN PARADIGMS AND THE QUEST FOR WISDOM

Globalization, information technology and "developmental wisdom" have a long path to cover before their integrative features can be materialized in the African landscape. Traditional Christianity in the Abyssinian region and in Nubia, Catholicism in the broad expanses of West Africa, and Islam will be defined here to illustrate the untenable prospects for African respite through civilizational intervention.

The values of religious references and sectional differences bring deep convictions at the grassroots level. Overcoming the barriers of illiteracy, poverty, and rural isolation requires the basic rudiments of information delivery. The entities that can mobilize resources will have the upper hand, but their advantage will not be taken as an effort for enlightenment, but as an advantage for rampant proselytization.

Rationalizing religious proprietary claims, as was stated above, is problematic also from the point of view of empiricism and the hard sciences. In terms of cultural and ideological orthodoxies, even in their most ardent and emotional manifestations, they move societies to action whether for war or peace. As an example, the Abyssinians cherish their culture and ideology in a fervent temper regardless of the skepticism of outsiders who attribute far-fetched elements as being part of the Ethiopian belief (Budge1928). To the Abyssinian, devotion to faith, family, and to the state have inspired extreme levels of emotional commitment. This was translated to a type of nationalism that fused religion and a warrior-type of psychological state.

The Abyssinian plateau on the Red Sea coast has Old and New Testament religious and cultural characteristics identical to that Egypt, Nubia, Arabia and the Holy Land in general. It also stands apart from this region in its cultural resilience as a bastion of the Christian faith. In traditional Ethiopia, the state was sanctified by its cultural and political principles as referenced in the Bible. Ethiopian emperors from Emperor Ezana, the first to accept Christianity and declare it a national religion around 335 A. D., until the end of Emperor Haile Selassie in 1974 used Biblical references to emphasize state and king legitimacy (Ullendorff 1988).They referred to themselves as the Conquering Lions from the Household of Judea. They recount biblical references such as "Ethiopia shall stretch her hands unto God" and Old Testament historical incidents that refer to Ethiopia/Kush in favorable lights as divine testimonials vouching of Ethiopia's sacredness. Abyssinian political culture before the onset of the secular regimes in the form of communism or the current agnostic liberalism was deeply rooted in biblical references which were then integrated into the system and practice of government.

The Arab Paradigm in Africa. Africa's interaction with the Middle East throughout the ages has not been one in which Arab contributions can be pointed out as a visible and enduring legacy, except in religious matters. Africans cannot reflect on the relationship without contemplating the effects of Arab slavery and Islamic proselytization as a mix of hurtful legacies that had not been redressed. Today, Islam is energized due to the influx of Wuhabits revivalists supported by the extravagance of limitless petro-Dollars.

Islam instructs the believer to obey Allah's orders. Allah's orders are narrowly defined to accommodate a modicum of tolerance, but broadly defined to take advantage of the vicissitudes of time and place in order to escape the damning effects of unrighteous actions (Lewis 1994). They were communicated through the Prophet Muhammad, a person who repeatedly acknowledged that he was less than perfect in his judgments, while attributing them as Allah's words. In the Quran, the dictates of an authoritarian doctrine and a totalitarian system preclude any defense for those who refuse to accept Islam as the only faith and Mohammad as the only messenger of Allah. Mohammad carries a scepter of truth with absolute authority to bring wrathful judgment on those who refuse to believe in his teachings. Embracing the teachings of Islam brought safety to conquered lands; rejecting Islam brought persecution, exile, and summary killings. These acts were demonstrated during the founding of Islam when Mohammed forced the Jews of Medina to convert and those who refused to accept his teachings, he exiled or massacred (Kennedy 1986:40)

Islam in its fresh vibrancy was full of self-confidence. "There is not God but Allah and Mohammad is the messenger of Allah" meant all other faiths had expired; all past prophets and their teachings are obsolete, and the teachings of Mohammad displace all other principles of faith.

European interaction on the basis of reciprocal religious edification and sharing of theological and doctrinal values was reduced when the Vandals ransacked North Africa in 426 A. D. and weakened Africa's religious link with Europe. The Vandal invasion was superficial and African Churches and synods quickly recovered with the aid of Emperor Justinian in 533. As the fortunes of the Byzantine Empire and its religious traditions faced precipitous decline, its ability to ascertain its presence in Africa disappeared (Murata &Chittick1996: 32-34). The final mortal blow to African Christianity came between 670-700 A. D. when the Arabs invaded North Africa (Isichei, 1995:41-44). The African Christian churches in Morocco, Algeria, Tunisia, and Mauritania faced a momentous decline and decay. St. Augustine's monastic orders, the prodigiously productive theological centers, the hermits, and the Desert Saints declined with their source of recruitment and as membership renewal dried out. The celebrated voices of theological innovations and inspirational treaties from the world's greatest theologians of the time was silenced as Islam, in its most inhospitable attitudinal manifestations, restricted and eventually extinguished them. The Fatimid Dynasty started the process and the Mamluks completely obliterated African Christianity from Algeria, Tunisia, Libya, Morocco, Mauritania, and severely restricted it in Egypt. J. Spencer Trimingham observed:

> Christian Africa was abandoned to its fate. Egypt remained a Christian country for a long time with the Muslim as the dominant ruling minority, but through the machinery of the State the Church was slowly strangled and more and more of her peoples were absorbed into the new religion until in the course of time Egypt became a Muslim state with the Christians the subject minority they remain to this day (Trimingham1965: 42).

The Islamic conquest brought to light the plight of Christianity in places where Christianity had been institutionalized. With exception of the Abyssinian Church that had fought valiantly endless battles against Islamic jihad, the rest of African Churches atrophied in the intolerant climate that Islam brought to the lands it conquered. The vibrant intellectual centers and warship centers of Africa were ruined, their clergy persecuted and murdered or forced into exile.

The European Paradigm in Africa. With the Arab conquest of North Africa to the era of exploration in the fifteenth century, the evolution of religious advances was characterized by European evangelization and Islamic resistance. The African traditional religions were cast in paternalistic assumptions stridently defining Africa as having nothing to offer by way of cultural and civilizational enlightenment. Africa became the "Dark Continent," and African faith was declared as "pagan" and a base form of occultism and witchcraft. The traditional religions whose spiritual and textual foundations did not differ from Christianity or Islam in the deification of God mattered little to Europeans or Arabs. This created a crisis of faith and culture where Christianity, Islam, and African traditional faiths competed to find internal rationale for dominance.

Each of these faiths has a specific paradigm that was dogmatically cast as a superior to the other religionsand able to bring the Dark Continent to light. Christian missionaries from Portugal, Spain, France, and Belgium emphasized Catholicism mostly in Western and Southeastern Africa. They mixed their missions with zeal for spreading the Gospel and, at times, participating in the slave trade rationalized as an antidote to backwardness (Hastings 1994 :173 -221).

> The great weakness of the Christian enterprise in black Africa in the Middle Years was its close association with the slave trade. There was a basic contradiction between converting Africans and purchasing them as slaves. . . . Some priests traded in slaves. The Church in Angola derived much of its income by instructing and baptizing the enslaved, and the end of the slave trade caused financial crisis for the Luanda. (Isichei1995: 71).

Catholicism displayed an inconsistent pattern of teaching and preaching in its devotional and evangelistic endeavors in Africa. Its clergy were full of kindness and generosity. They navigated deserts, crossed rivers, penetrated jungle forests, and captured the attention of native Africans in the deepest interiors of Equatorial Africa, such as Angola and the Congo. Yet, in all of their spiritual toils, they could not elevate their aim beyond the paternalistic superficial kindness.

Their teaching was limited to the rudiments of catechisms. They deliberately withheld education at the elementary level. In all of the three to four centuries that they had been in Africa, there never was a college or a university in any of the Portuguese, French, or Spanish colonies of Africa. Hospitals and medical facilities were part of the colonial apparatus utilized to facilitate and support colonial personnel with little access available to the natives. Catholicism's vision of winning souls was blinded by their unwillingness to impart educational opportunities and the pecuniary interests they aided in preserving for the colonial rulers. Centuries of colonial and evangelistic endeavors left African colonies at a level of development that was no better than they were in pre-colonial years. The African Church under their watch stagnated at the inspirational level of a shallow spiritual initiation. Crawford Young describes the Belgian educational policy in the Congo as follows:

> In the cultural domain, the Catholic missions were indispensable auxiliaries. Their task was to displace customary African religion with Christianity, an alteration which, according to a leading Catholic prelate, was commanded by the conviction that "only the Christian-Catholic religion, based on authority, is capable of changing native mentality,

of giving to our Africans a clear and intimate consciousness of their duties, of inspiring in the respect for authority and a spirit of loyalty towards Belgium" (Young 1994: 255)

The subservient status that the Church expected of the native African Christian did not materialize, because, as Young observed, "In manifold ways, African society displayed a capacity for evasion and inner autonomy."

After the Second World War when decolonization began, the missionary churches were transferred to African natives. A new way of interpreting Christianity by integrating traditional beliefs with biblical principles flourished. In the meantime, the worldly habit of substandard faith that was the cause of the schizophrenic attitudes affected even the native church.

Conclusion

There is tendency in the scholarly world to judge Africa wrongly; and the scholarly verdict and intellectual judgments often seem to be dismissive, ambivalent, selective and tainted with heavy doses of begrudged and qualified acknowledgement (Davidson, B. 1987). According to Davidson, the selective amnesia on African civilizational and traditional values became common after the fifteenth century when imperialism and colonialism began to expand in coastal Africa. Before that, Africa was regarded by Europe and Asia with equal regard, and given the wealth in bullion and precious commodities that were abundant for African potentates to display; there was genuine admiration of Africa's rich and exotic image. By the sixteenth century, Africa's image was soiled and historians like Gibbons cast Africans as "savage" and as barbarians (Gibbons 1913).

The unifying features of IT are plausible in their theoretical elegance. They chart a path of optimistic feature where global crisis can be quantifiably identified and tackled with wisdom and cosmopolitan civility. The realist school will disagree by referencing to man's penchant for warmongering. They cite eventualities that often explode on the African religious and political landscape to corroborate their theories.

Looking at Africa, and from the perspectives of the twenty-first century and going back for the last millennium, the pessimism of the realists Africa's image is one of destitution and human misery. The parameters of respectability and civilizational dignity seemed to have been set too high for Africa to measure up to the levels the Westerners desired. Africa has been subjected to the outside influences of Christianity and Islam and each non-African religion continues to contend for the Africa's soul. The friction generated by the clash of Christianity and Islam in the African landscape does not inspire optimism.

References

Braudel, F. (1991). *Civilization & capitalism: 15-18th century: The structure of everyday life.* Berkeley, CA: UC. Press.

Budge, S. W. (1928). A History of Ethiopia Nubia and Abyssinia. London: Methuen and Co. Ltd.

Davidson, B. (1970). *The Lost cities of Africa*. Boston, MA: Little, Brown and Company.

Gibbons, E. (1952). *The decline and fall of the Roman Empire*. Chicago, IL: William Benton Publisher.

Isichei, E. (1995). *A History of Christianity in Africa: From antiquity to present*. Lawrenceville, NJ.: World Press, Inc.

Hastings, A. (1994). *The Church in Africa*: 1450-1950. New York, NY. Clarendon Press.

Kennedy, H. (1986). *The Prophet and the age of the caliphates: The Islamic Near East from the sixth to the eleventh century*. London, UK. Longman.

Kuhn, T. (1970). The *Structure of Scientific Revolution*. Chicago, IL. University of Chicago Press.

Lewis, B. (2009). *What Went Wrong: Western Impact and Middle Eastern Response*. New York: Oxford University Press.

Merrills, A. H. &Miles, R. (2010). *The Vandals*. West Sussex, UK. Wiley-Blackwell.

Murata S. & Chittick, W. C. (1996). *The Vision of Islam*. London, UK.I. B. Taurus Publishers.

Smkaange, S. (1971). *African saga: a brief introduction to African history*. Nashville, TN.:Abington Press.

Stigler, J. W. (2003). *Globalization and its Dscontents*. New York: W. W. Norton & Co. Inc.

Targowski, A. (2009). *Information technology and societal development*. Hershey & New York: IGI Global.

Targowski, A. (2011). *Cognitive informatics and wisdom development: Interdisciplinary approach Hershey & New York*: IGI Global.

Trimingham, J. S. (1965). *Islam in Ethiopia*. London, UK. Frank Cass & Co. LTD.

Ullendorff, E. (1973). *The Ethiopians: an Introduction to Country and People*. London, UK. Oxford University Press.

In: Spirituality and Civilization Sustainability ...
Editors: Andrew Targowski and Marek J. Celinski
ISBN: 978-1-53610-729-6

Chapter 15

RELIGION VERSUS THEOLOGY: ITS IMPACT ON CIVILIZATIONS

Walter Benesch*
Department of Philosophy & Humanities
University of Alaska Fairbanks, Alaska, US

ABSTRACT

In order to generate more light than heat in any discussion of religion, a critical distinction between *religion* and *theology* needs to be made. The Latin root of 'religion' is *ligare* which means 'to tie' or 'bind' and *re* which means 'back'. Thus *religare* means in some sense to 'tie back', 'to restrain', 'to support,' or 'to commit'. Examples of this meaning are found in terms like *ligament, ligature (something that binds or connects).* I would suggest that just as *ligament* refers to physical and structural aspects of human beings in general, there are corresponding mental and emotional structural aspects that apply to human beings, e.g. interpreting, affirming, denying, believing, doubting reasoning, wondering, asking, answering, etc.. Humans rely upon their physical ligaments to move, upon their mental structural processes to think, and upon their innate emotional processes, feelings, attitudes, desires, likes and dislikes, etc. to relate to one another as social beings. *Religion* I would equate with the relating processes of *living, moving, thinking, feeling human being.* For example, hopefully, we *religiously* stop at stop signs, love and feed our families, respect and empathize with one another, and tend to dichotomize our values and political choices, etc.

THE THEOLOGY - ORIENTED MINDSET

Unfortunately, in the minds of theologians, it is 'theology' that is often intended when they think of 'religion'. *The* or *theo* means 'god or gods' and *logy* as in 'biology, geology, psychology' means theories of, study of the laws/logic of 'bio, geo, psyche', etc. These '*ogies'* are the 'study of" they are not whatever it is that is being studied. Biology is not

* E-mail: wbenesch@alaska.edu

'living' though we may consider it the study of process we call 'life'. So it is with theology which is not 'god or gods', though we may consider it the study of what we call the 'supernatural or gods. However, if one equates religion with theology, one may then and especially then religiously practice violent, racist, dogmatic brands of theology, particularly against those who would suggest one's religiously practiced brand of violent theology is not 'religion'. Xenophanes in the 6th Century BCE seemed to have had theology in mind when he suggested that "*If oxen or lions had hands which enabled them to draw and paint pictures as men do, they would portray their gods as having bodies like their own: horses would portray them as horse, and oxen as oxen*" (Wheelwright 1985). As a capable observer who religiously watched others, Xenophanes also noted that "Aethiopians have gods with snub noses and black hair, Thracians have gods with gray eyes and red hair.".(*Ibid*) Xenophanes insights are echoed 600 years later in the *Nag Hammadi* texts in the Gnostic *Gospel of Phillip II, 3* :"*God created man. [But now men] create God. That is the way it is in the world---men make gods and worship their creation. It would be fitting for the gods to worship men!*"(Robinson 1977).

THE EMPATHY FACTOR

I would offer two suggestions to those who study and write about 'religions' and 'theology'. *First*: I would suggest that theological systems should be clearly defined and distinguished from the uses of the word 'religion. This would simplify identification of meaning and purpose of terms used in any discussion of religion and theology. *Second:* I would suggest that in view of the biological and anthropological researches over the last hundred years, there is a common emotional and social reference point for both theology and religion, and a common source of both which in part explains why we confuse them. This common source is *empathy.*

En or em means to put into or onto, e.g. 'enact' (put into action). *Path* or *pathos, pathy* means feelings and emotions When *em* is combined as a prefix with *path* or *pathy,* one has *empathy* which means the unconscious projection of one's feelings into or onto the 'other. This 'other' can be an animal, another human being, a flower, or the environment. The important point here is that the feeling is unconscious – though it can be developed and consciously acted upon. A good example would be unconsciously 'yawning' or 'smiling when someone else smiles or yawns. The Dutch Primatologist, Frans Waal suggests that

> "We can't feel anything that happens outside ourselves, but by unconsciously merging self and other, the other's experiences echo within us. We feel them as if they're our own. Such identification...cannot be reduced to any other capacities, such as learning, association, or reasoning. Empathy offers a direct access to the 'foreign self'(Waal 2009).

The German Neurobiologist, Gerald Hüther, like Frans Waal ,would extend a basic capacity for empathy to all creatures who possess a brain. Hüther sees empathy as an innate neuronal phenomenon which is understood by other members of a species or group. He suggests it is the most important form of intra-species communication and is most highly evolved in species where such communication is essential to species survival. He also suggest that it is "*...still laid by us in the cradle at the time of birth in the form of a certain genetically programmed neuronal circuits in our brains*" (Huther 2006).

Of course, as Huther suggests, what happens to innate empathy as the individual develops will vary from individual to individual and in humans from group to group.

Once one has experienced and understands empathy, whether it is with an animal, another human, or the old oak tree in the park that is to be razed to make way for a new shopping mall, one is ready to return to the distinction between religion and theology. Empathy, and religion as the experiencing of empathy, has both positive and negative aspects. It is positive in enabling the group, whether rats or humans, to survive, but for that very reason it can set the members of a group against 'outsiders'. For example, in any war it is necessary to stress empathy toward 'our side' as opposed to discouraging empathy for the enemy or 'their side' in order to facilitate killing them. Even killing, as the Hebrew Book of *Numbers* proposed, in addition to enemy combatants, the other's women and children.(*Numbers 31:17*) We substitute negative images and invent special names for the foe in order to negate any empathy which might block the 'sacred slaughter'. In this respect, one need go no further in the modern world than to examine any major political or military conflicts, the US public health insurance debate, the issues of abortion, gay marriage, euthanasia, spousal abuse, etc. Thus where *religion* can mean innate and even unconscious 'empathy' *theology* and theological systems can be called upon to argue views that emphasize empathy within the group while de-emphasizing-empathy with the outsiders.

Perhaps one of the most interesting examples of what happens when theology is confused with religion as empathy is found in the first two creation stories in Genesis – where in the first an androgynous and empathetic deity creates humans, male and female, in his/her image and tells them to multiply their kind. However, the theologians in Judaism, Christianity, and Islam and sub-sets tend to ignore Genesis 1 for Genesis 2, where the deity uses a male rib to make a female companion for the first male. As the witch-hunters of the 16th Century, Kramer and Sprenger pointed out, a rib is a 'bent bone' and so the woman was defective from the beginning (Kramer, & Srenger 1971, 2009). No wonder that St. Paul doesn't want 'females teaching' and Islam wraps them up in personal tents. A similar situation prevails in civilizations around the world when the theologians get to work on negating empathy. In India it occurs in the *Laws of Manu* and in the *Hymn to Visvakarman,* which outline the divine origins of the castes. The Buddhists suggest in the *Jataka* that *"The nature of the woman is hard to know. Tis like the ways in water of the fish. Lies are to them as truth, and truth as lie...She bandits are they, cruel and malign, and hard and fickle*"(Davids 1989).

THE SECULAR STATE VERSUS THEOLOGY AND RELIGION

Is there another approach to equating religion with theology? I think so. Just as theology needs constantly to be re-examined, so too does empathy/religion, which can use theology to attack the 'other' and needs to be re-examined. In short, as in a 'secular state', the 'people' need to be educated, understanding, and alert – so must this education, understanding and critical alertness carry over to the connection of theology with religion! The US Constitutional Fathers made an attempt at this possibility when they tried to separate 'religion' and 'government'. However, the cure is, I think, even more radical---I suggest that civilizations and nations must remove theology and the theologians from the *justification business.* Civilizationists, in turn, need to clearly distinguish the one from the other and their inter-relationships. The secular state, imperfect as it is, must work out its laws without theological justifications which enable suicide bombers, territorial rapists, religious haters of races, ethnic groups, genders and gender orientations to proclaim that whatever happens, good or bad, it is a reward or punishment of the gods. Of course, in theological systems which rely heavily upon proceeds from real estate sales on the other side, this may hurt financially.

Another approach to melding religion and theology is found in civilizations East and West. This is *pantheism*, that is the view that humans and the rest of nature as well as the god or gods are all aspects of a harmonious whole. *Pantheism* arises in response to human experiencing of the world as a *Nature/Mind Continuum* which manifests itself in 'imitating processes' in nature, e.g. evolution and reproduction, and in mental imaging and imaging processes in human thinking, e.g. products of the imagination in languages, concepts, interpretations, etc. This combination of 'world' and 'image of world' in the human imagination generates the paradoxes that humans seek to resolve with their imaginations in theological systems. The nature and significance of these paradoxes was clearly recognized in classical philosophical traditions East/West. For example, the *Kena Upanisad* in a series of questions wonders about the possibility knowing and not knowing consciousness:

> By whom impelled soars forth the mind projected?
> By whom enjoined goes forth the earliest breathing?
> By whom impelled this speech do people utter?

The answer provided by the Risis is less an answer than a lesson on answering:

> There the eyes go not;
> Speech goes not; nor the mind.
> We know not, we understand not.
> …
> It is conceived of by him by whom It is not conceived of.
> He by whom It is conceived of, knows It not.
> It is not understood by those who [say they] understand It.
> It is understood by those who [say they] understand It not…](Radhakrishnan 1957).

The practical yet mystic Chinese Taoist, Chuang Tzu choose to speak of the unspeakable, however…:

> Heaven and earth were born at the same time I was, and the ten thousand things are one with me.We have already become one, so how can I say anything? But I have just said that we are one, so how can I not be saying something? The one and what I said about it make two, and two and the original one makes three. If we go on this way, then even the cleverest mathematician can't tell where we'll end, much less an ordinary man….Better not to move, but to let things be!(Watson 1968).

And Sextus Empiricus in his discussion of the Greek Socratic philosopher, Gorgias of Leontini claimed that Gorgias was the father of three fundamental propositions:

> "...firstly that nothing exists, secondly that even if anything existed it could not be known by men, and thirdly that even if anything could be known by anyone it could not be communicated to anyone else"(Wheelwright 1966).

This perspective was affirmed by Gorgias' contemporary, Socrates who 'knew that he did not know.' Socrates possessed, what the modern Chinese philosopher, Feng Yu-lan would call *no-knowledge*, as opposed to the ignorant individuals who *have-no* knowledge (Yu-lan).

In these passages, and they are but a fraction of similar texts by other philosophers and other schools, there would seem to be a clear insight that the possibility *of consciousness* or *reflexive self awareness* cannot be reduced to one or more possibilities *for consciousness* as products of nature and/or mind.

Some of the most significant illustrations of the application of this insight are found in the logical systems that many classical traditions and schools developed, e.g., the Jaina 'nayavada', 'syadvada' and 'saptabhangi' which emphasize subjects and points of view; the Nyaya and Buddhist five part experiential 'syllogism' and the 'catuskoti' which emphasize situational encounters of subjects and objects; and Taoist-Neo-Confucian process logics which emphasize a synthesis of aspects of and perspective upon subjects, objects, and situations. These are logics in which there is a critical step or rule or level which will preclude the possibility of mistaking the products of the logic for either the world, or the possibility of the consciousness of the thinking logician who employs it. One might speak here of a synthesis of *neti neti* and *tat twam asi.* These logics and their traditions represent what I would call the *dimensions* of wisdom or *philosophical space*.(Benesch, 1997)

A progression from Polytheism or dualistic monotheism is illustrated in the Hindu *Brihadaranyaka Upanisad* in India in the 7th Century BCE . Here a student asks the philosopher, Yajnavalkya:

> "How many gods are there, Yajnavalkya?"
>
> He (the philosopher) answered..."As many as are mentioned in the Hymn to All the Gods, namely, three hundred and three, and three thousand and three [3306]"
>
> "Yes", said the student, but really just how many gods are there, Yajnavalkya?"
>
> "Thirty-three."
>
> "Yes", said the student," But really, really now just how many gods are there, Yajnavalkya?"
>
> "Six."
>
> "Yes", said the student, "But really, really, really now just how many gods are there, Yajnavalkya?"
>
> " Three."
>
> "Yes", said the student, "But really, really, really, really now, just how many gods are there Yajunavalkya?"
>
> "Two."
>
> "Yes." Said the student, "But really, really, really, really, really now, just how many gods are there, Yajnavalkya?"
>
> "One and a half."
>
> "Yes," said the student, "But really, really, really, really, really, really now, just how many gods are there, Yajnavalkya?"
>
> "One..."
>
> "....Which is the one god Yajnavalkya?" asked the student.

> "Breath" said Yajnavalkya, "They call him Brahman, the Yon" (Radhakrishnan 1957).

In this dialogue, which occurs in India in the *Axial Age*, the philosopher, Yajnavalkya is reducing a *pluralistic polytheism* of many gods to a *pantheistic monism* which holds that all that exists is a manifestation of *Brahman* or *Cosmic Consciousness/Breath.* Confucius, when asked about 'serving spiritual beings and about death replied "If we are not yet able to serve man, how can we serve spiritual beings?... If we do not yet know life, how can we know about death" (Chan 1973). According to the *Analects* there were three things Confucius would not discuss: 'strange phenomena', 'physical exploits', and 'spiritual beings'. (*Analects 7:20)*

Conclusion

An interesting aspect of modern physical science around the world is its acceptance of a pantheistic view of the world which entails the ultimate open-ended challenge to universal certainties. The scientists' attention is focused increasingly upon the nature of human awareness as it relates to 'actual experience' and all of the puzzles and problems involved in inter-relating actual experiences. This is a relating which is achieved in the human intellect and as a result a relativistic world view emerges in the 19th and 20th Centuries. Physicist John Wheeler described the role of the scientific observer within this view as both 'spectator' and 'participant'.

> "...in the quantum principle we're instructed that the actual act of making an observation changes what it is that one looks at. To me, this is a perfectly marvelous feature of nature... So the old word observer simple has to be crossed off the books, and we must put in the new word participant. In this way we've come to realize that the universe is a participatory universe" (Buckley 1979).

Physicist Erwin Schrödinger remarked "...it may perhaps be possible for logical thinking to disclose at least this much: that to grasp the basis of phenomena through logical thought may in all probability be impossible, since logical thought is itself a part of phenomena, and wholly involved in them."(Schroedinger, 1983) The consequence of 'thinking about the unthinkable' is that the logician, like all thinkers, lives in what the physicist John Wheeler calls a 'participatory universe' where the very act of observation changes the observed (Buckley 1979).

It is amazing how close in understanding, and that across six centuries, modern physics and biology are to the Neo-Confucian Philosopher, Wang Yang-ming's continuum view of 'innate knowledge': "The innate knowledge of man is the same as that of plants and trees, tiles and stones....Heaven, Earth, the myriad things, and man form one body. The point at which this unity is manifested in its most refined and excellent form is the clear intelligence of the human mind"(Chan 1963). The French mathematician and physicist, Henri Poincare maintained that the very process of generalizing implies a belief in the unity of the world: "if the different parts of the universe were not like the members of one body, they would not act on one another…know nothing of one another, and we…would know only one of these parts. We do not ask if nature is one, but how it is one"(Poincare 1946).

The position on mind and nature of Amit Goswami, professor of physics at the Institute of Theoretical Sciences at the University of Oregon, would also seem consistent with that of Wang Yang-ming. Prof. Goswami suggests that the heliocentric universe is again becoming geo- or human centered in that it is "*… formless potentia … and becomes manifest only when observed by conscious beings….Of course, we are not the geographical center, but that is not the issue. We are the center of the universe because we are its meaning"*(Goswami 1993).

Finally, as Michael Faraday (1791-1867) wrote of his own experience: "In our conceptions and reasoning regarding the forces of nature, we perceptually make use of symbols which, when they possess a high representative value, we dignify with the name of theories….Such conceptions have their advantages and their disadvantages; they afford peaceful lodging to the intellect for a time, but they also circumscribe it, and by and by, when the mind has grown too large for its lodging, it often finds difficulty in breaking down the walls of what has become a prison instead of its home"(Blin-Stoyle 1960).

References

Benesch, W. (1997). *An introduction to comparative philosophy, a travel guide to philosophical space.* New York: Macmillan/St. Martins.

Blin-Stoyle, R.J. (1960). *Turning points in physics, a series of lectures given at oxford university in trinity term 1958.* (2 ed., p. 1). Amsterdam: North- Holland Publishing Co.

Buckley, P. & Peat, F.D. (1979). *Conversations in physics and biology.* Toronto: University of Toronto Press. p. 53-53.

Chan, W. (1973). *A source book in Chinese philosophy.* Princeton: Princeton University Press. Analects 11:11, p. 36.

Chan, W. (1963). *Instructions for practical living and other neo-Confucian writing by Wang Yang--Ming,* New York: Columbia University. p. 221.

Davids, R. Transl. (1989). *Stories of the Buddha, being selections from the Jataka.* Dover, NY: Carolline AF.p.67.

de Waal, F. (2009). *The age of empathy.* London: Harmony Books.p.65.

Goswami, A. (1993). *The self-aware universe.* New York: G. P. Putnam Sons.p.141.

Huther, G. (2006). *The compassionate brain.* Michael Kohn trans. London: Harmony Books.p.112-113.

Kramer, H. & Srenger, J.(1971, 2009). *The malleujs maleficarum.* Dover, NY: Digireads.com Publishing.

Poincare, H. (1946). *The foundations of science.* Halsted, G.B. Trans. Lancaster, PA: The Science Press.p.130.

Radhakrishnan S. & Charles, M. (1957). *A source book in Indian philosophy.* Princeton, NJ: Princeton University Press.p.42-86.

Robinson, J.M. Ed. (1977). *The Nag Hammadi library.* New York: Harper & Row. P.143.

Schroedinger, E. (1983). *My view of the world.* Hastings, C.Tran. Woodbridge, CT: Ox Bow Press.p.19.

Watson, B. Trans. (1968). *The complete works of Chuang Tzu.* New York: Columbia University. P.43.

Wheelwright, P. (1966). *The presocraics, "sextus empiricus 'against the logicians*". New York: Macmillan.p.256.

Wheelwright, P. (1985). *The presocratics*. New York, NY: Collier Macmillan.p.69.

Yu-lan, F. *A short history of Chinese philosophy*. New York: Macmillan/ Free Press.p.117.

In: Spirituality and Civilization Sustainability ...
Editors: Andrew Targowski and Marek J. Celinski
ISBN: 978-1-53610-729-6

Chapter 16

Religion for a Sustainable Civilization

Michael Andregg*
University of St. Thomas, St. Paul, MN, US

Abstract

This chapter looks at a paradox of large religions in the modern world, some driving us toward endless war even though all the founding prophets spoke about peace, citing Golden Rules of very similar meaning. It identifies "authoritarian law and militant religion" as interacting evils wrapped in soft words of scriptural origin. It applauds the emergence of "sustainable stewardship" as a counterpoint to more primitive "multiply and dominate" theologies. It shows how "people of faith" and "people of reason" coexist in many churches, but differ in how they evaluate the world. The author discusses why we need a civilizational religion that could manage the planet and the people on it more humanely, instead of subjugating and exploiting them for anyone's short term benefit. And he ends with a concrete list of characteristics that global religion should have.

Introduction

Religion presents a critical paradox to those who work on civilizational and human survival. On one hand, some religions point the way toward a sustainable, humane and ethical civilization. On the other hand, others drive us toward a fast Armageddon of war with weapons of mass destruction, or a slower death by environmental collapse and civilizational decay. Understanding both sides of this paradox is one key to the happier outcome.[1]

Because the stakes are so high, I begin this essay with some axioms that may be controversial for some who read them. First, whatever God is (or Allah, Yahweh, Atman, The

---

* E-mail: mmandregg@stthomas.edu

[1] For 23 years I studied why wars begin to write a book that won a National Peace Writing Award in 1999 (On the Causes of War, 1997, 1999). Two chapters in that book address the main challenges that animate this edited work, #13 on Authoritarian Law and Militant Religion, and #31 on Spirituality Without Churches. Concepts developed there in more detail are summarized here and supplemented with context appropriate to civilizations.

Force, Wakan Tanka or whatever name you prefer) it cares about life, truth, and love. Second, "religion" is not the same thing as "spirituality". "Religion" is more organized than mystic spirituality, and often far more aggressive. The churches, mosques, synagogues and temples that are most convinced they are God's elect doing God's will on earth are powerful forces driving us toward global war over which is "the best". I believe that is the opposite of God's desire. Why?

Well the answer to that question is the essence of this essay. One reason is because churches[2] are often bound to words in books written thousands of years ago by tribal peoples (and often edited by many hands thereafter). Inspired by God these words may be, but they had to pass through the minds of people from very primitive cultures, and were necessarily expressed in human languages which are always profoundly limited. Besides, God appears to have spoken with a great many people through time in every language there is. It is hubris to think that spirituality cannot progress beyond that comprehended thousands of years ago,[3] or that God needs permission from certified clergy to speak to other human beings.

Another reason why organized churches and the religious extremists attracted to some of them are driving us toward global war is because the churches themselves are living systems. They compete in a Darwinian universe that is ruthless, extremely self-centered and sometimes cruel. Churches compete for limited resources just like bacteria, hyenas and trees. But the feedstock for churches (synagogues, mosques and etc.) are human beings willing to give treasure and sometimes their lives in service to the church, which alleges that doing so is the same as serving God. Sometimes they offer special rewards for risky service, like 72 virgins alleged for martyrs.

Yet another reason why some churches drive us toward death instead of life, and toward hate instead of love, is because some churches and people are quite hostile to "science" as a discipline and to "reason" as a way to discern truth. They prefer "revelation" from designated prophets or church leaders, although sometimes they allow that God may talk to anyone it desires.

It is also important for this essay not to become a mere diatribe against the sins of churches. Churches provide some very essential services to society and to billions of human beings. In fact, good churches are a critical part of the solution to our crises. Unenlightened churches are a cause of the same crises. Churches are complicated, and one often finds authentically spiritual people, inspired by God and doing good works every day, side by side in churches with individuals of more limited vision who really believe that God loves them exclusively.

Finally, we must acknowledge here that the living system of our Earth is experiencing an existential crisis on a scale seen only five times before in the geological history of the planet.[4]

---

[2]For most of the rest of this essay I will use the Christian term "churches" for all houses of worship of any faith rather than repeating "churches, mosques, synagogues and temples" over and over. The belief that God loves one form but not the others is one of the core illusions that blinds many organized religions. This is closely bound to the equally false belief that God loves only one religion or one group of people and not all or any others.

[3]Another errant conclusion of the fundamentalist views I describe alleges that God says exactly the same thing to everyone all the time. Another is that God never uses metaphor or symbolic language forms. Such beliefs contribute to the ignorance of fundamentalist literalism. This matters due to resulting wars over whose truth is THE TRUTH.

[4] These were the great extinctions known as the Cretaceous-Tertiary, End Triassic, Permian Triassic, Late Devonian and Ordovician-Silurian extinctions, the most famous of which was about 65 million years ago when dinosaurs and about 20% of all other species disappeared in the blink of a geological eye. The prime theory today is

This crisis began long before the term "sustainability" gained traction, or "climate change" or other current expressions of the global environmental crisis. It began with exponential increases of human populations and the wave of extinctions of other species that inevitably followed. That decay accelerates each day. Any religion for a sustainable civilization must therefore have some core elements that respond to the biological aspects of the crisis before us.

Churches rooted in the words of tribal peoples thousands of years ago find it difficult to change their dogmas as fast as the living system is decaying today. One obvious example is bans on birth control and other pronatalist policies. Tribal people thousands of years ago suffered very high mortality rates, had life expectancies of 40 years if lucky; half their babies died very young and they competed with aggressive others for land and every other critical resource. Aggressive breeding was essential to group survival then. Today it is a formula for global disaster. Some churches have come to understand that, but the fundamental wing of many organized churches is still caught up in trying to outbreed the others with disastrous consequences for all. This is a "tragedy of the commons" phenomenon of the first order.

At the same time, many churches include an ecumenical element that recognizes some validity to other religious perspectives and organizations. Most include authentically spiritual people as well as those who just memorize words, and all claim to worship a God that loves people, life and the Earth. So the seeds of enlightenment are there, and nourishing those seeds is a task implied by the title of this book.

The remainder of this essay will address the following subtopics. "Authoritarian Law and Militant Religion" focuses on why some churches are so violent, and why that drives us toward global war. "Sustainable Stewardship" focuses on how undue emphasis on one sentence from Genesis (1-28) in the Bible / Torah leads some people and institutions to support destruction of the living system by trying to outbreed each other, and to oppose many social actions that might solve that problem. Enlightenment here means simply attending to other phrases in the sacred texts that promote stewardship of life on earth. "People of Faith versus People of Reason" aims to defuse that tragic war between worldviews, because it appears that both are legitimate ways of learning, each with different virtues and flaws. Listening carefully to the best of both reveals many important perspectives on how to deal with the great challenges that civilizations must if they want to survive and prosper in the Third Millennium after the birth of Jesus Christ. Finally a conclusion will come where I try to show in simplest form the path from here to there.

Authoritarian Law and Militant Religion

Militant religions tend toward authoritarian or even totalitarian politics and law because they think they know *exactly* how God wants people to live, and are distinguished from peaceful churches by their willingness to force those views on others. Since they are also aggressively pronatalistic they inevitably come into contact with other aggressively expansive social groups, often after driving off or killing less aggressive native peoples. Compromise is

collision by comet or asteroid, but maybe one of the dinosaurs caught "religion" and tried to dominate all of the others with weapons of mass destruction such as we have developed today. Anyone who thinks science knows for sure what happened 65 million years ago has elevated science to a quasi-religious status that it neither deserves nor desires.

difficult between true believers, and there are a thousand varieties competing for the crown of God's "favorites".

An Israeli counterterrorism expert with 20 years experience in the Israeli Defense Forces thought as hard as he could about why some people become violent when exposed to "religion" (Guiora, 2009)[5]. He also teaches Constitutional Law at an American law school so he is very reluctant to recommend restraints on either free speech or religion, but in the end he does. Having looked very closely at religious extremism as a phenomenon and at actual terrorists as people he interrogated, he then consulted scholars and counterterrorism practitioners in four other countries with relevant cases to study; Turkey, Britain, the Netherlands and the U.S.A.

The case he examines in Israel is not of suicide bombers, but rather the ultra-right wing Jewish forces that assassinated Israeli Prime Minister Yitzhak Rabin on November 4, 1995. The shooter was a man named Yigal Amir, but the shot was preceded by extremely vigorous and public appeals for the death of the Prime Minister by extremist rabbis associated with the settler movement that occupied parts of Gaza and much of the West Bank in a quest for Eretz Yisrael[6].

These are the same rabbis who promote the most orthodox, or fundamentalist interpretations of the Torah, and who oppose any steps toward peace with the Palestinian people whose land they are slowly digesting. Sharing is not an option to them (nor to religious extremists on the Palestinian side). The rabbi's counterparts in the Muslim Ummah are those radical imams who urge imposition of Sharia law in countries they take over. The most extreme of all urge global war against the West in general, and that call is echoed by extremists of the Christian variety who truly believe that a global war that kills most people on earth is actually God's will. They have been confused by a foolish interpretation of "Revelations" and other Biblical passages.

Sincere confusion is not a valid excuse for genocide, in my opinion; a topic to which we will return. Thus we observe today a "global war on terrorism" (the GWOT in military jargon) which can change names and targets, but has no definable end. The sustainable civilization we desire will have to deal with a great many of these disturbed individuals and groups for as far as my eye can see, because many have weapons and lethal intent. In fact the most violent are eager to acquire the weapons of mass destruction (WMDs) invented by civilizations before them, so we do not have eternity to contemplate this problem and to end the GWOT because it becomes a fuse heading toward a real Armageddon that no one in their right mind wants.

The phenomenon of terrorists seeking weapons of mass destruction has spawned libraries of literature, much relevant to this topic. Here I will focus on a neglected dimension. These groups and churches and individuals are not actually religious, in my trying-to-be-humble opinion. Rather, they express mere linguistic and cultural variations on a much more ancient theme, the simple but ruthless Darwinian competition for resources. That process is described

[5] Guiora's term "religious extremism" is a virtual equivalent to my term "militant religion." We both focus on those forms of "religion" that urge holy wars or personal violence against people who are not members of the sacred club.

[6] EretzYisrael or "Greater Israel" is a term for all land from the Nile to the Euphrates Rivers which many orthodox settlers believe is the actual land God gave their ancestors which must be occupied only by Jews to fulfill His Will.

by Richard Dawkins (1976) among many others. The law of the jungle works in jungles, but it cannot work for a sustainable, global, high tech civilization capable of building WMDs.

That kind of "religion" is *not* a spiritual phenomenon at all. Rather it is simple selfishness wrapped in pious cloth. That some pretend these thoughts are derived from God is hubris.

Prohibition of birth control, repression of women's freedoms in general, indifference to the devastation that follows population pressure and destruction of biological habitats, and predatory attitudes toward neighbors not of the same "church" are also all associated with these tribal belief systems justified by allegedly sacred words of men long dead.

This is not "spiritual" at all – it is all about power and resources, veiled by a mask of piety. The color and details of the masks vary from fundamental Christian, orthodox Jew or Wahhabi Muslim on some lesser jihad. And remember, there are almost always some excellent people in all of those groups, doing God's actual work in much quieter ways while the extremists fight and kill. These forms of pseudo-religion lead to endless wars because each truly believes that they are the one and only God's favorite. And all of that, in my opinion, is just the selfish Darwinian drive to dominate and ultimately to outbreed others expressed in religious and political language. That drive to dominate the entire earth also leads to destruction of ecosystems that sustain us all, religious and secular alike, by reckless growth and greedy consumption of scarce resources not all of which are renewable. But secular governments have been very reluctant to address this threat, and very weak even in recognizing how fundamental this threat is to the very existence of the secular state and to civilization itself.

SUSTAINABLE STEWARDSHIP VERSUS "MULTIPLYAND DOMINATE" THE EARTH

In the Christian and Jewish scriptures there is a particular passage of special relevance here. Genesis 1:28 of the American King James version of the Bible claims that God spoke to a first couple, Adam and Eve thus: "And God blessed them, and God said to them, Be fruitful, and multiply, and replenish the earth, and subdue it: and have dominion over the fish of the sea, and over the fowl of the air, and over every living thing that moves on the earth." This passage has been used to justify occupying every spot on Earth that can sustain human life and quite a few that cannot without sending in provisions. Extinction of species increases quickly.

This passage has also been used to justify genocide and near equivalents against competitors, especially native or indigenous peoples who happened to occupy territories the eager breeders wanted to exploit. So long as the indigenous did not belong to the organized church with the best weapons and most aggressive military cultures of their time and place, this was also often blessed by ecclesial authorities of their time and place as "God's will".

But after several generations of growing evidence of the gradual destruction of the ecosystems that sustain us all, Evangelical Christians in America discerned that stewardship (conservation and maintenance for the long term) of natural resources and of the Earth could also be inferred from this same passage. The point here is that even fundamentalist churches can change their interpretations of scripture and grow spiritually; they just do so very slowly.

After centuries of hostility to science in general and to reason as a path to knowledge rather than faith in what was delivered in churches by certified clergy of the Roman Catholic Church, even a Pope allowed in 1996 that evolution was probably a correct description of how life emerges and changes on our planet. He also wrote that belief in evolution was "compatible with Christian faith" (Pope John Paul II, 1996). This was a shock to those who still believed that God created humans *de novo*, along with every other species on earth, approximately 6,000 years ago as proclaimed by theologians who counted genealogies written in the Bible. Those passages, as noted often here, were written by tribal peoples thousands of years ago who had never heard of DNA or ecosystems, much less of evolution.

Despite that Pope's enlightenment, it bears emphasis that far more people in America today remain skeptical of evolution than are literate in it, and contests between creationists and biologists recur each year in some school board in America. People change slowly, cultures change slowly, and there is something much more comforting about "faith" for large numbers of people than "objective" and often sterile science can provide.

It also merits emphasis that every step of this glacial process of enlightenment has been accompanied by and sometimes catalyzed by "people of faith" working within institutions that were generally hostile to change. The father of classical genetics was a Catholic priest named Gregor Mendel who noticed patterns of inheritance among his garden peas. He studied, recorded and ultimately published his results according to the scientific method that developed during the general Enlightenment in Europe. My main university is named for another Catholic priest and theologian (St. Thomas Aquinas) who opined in *Summa Theologiae* and *Summa Contra Gentiles* that reason might be, or even must be, a legitimate way for human beings to learn about the universe.

This was very controversial in his time, and remains disputed to this day by those who believe that there is some intrinsic conflict between people who use evidence and reason as their guides, versus "people of faith" who never challenge knowledge as delivered by their certified clergy.

This conflict between "people of faith" and "people of reason" is so fundamental to the task at hand that I treat it separately in the next section. Here my goal is integrating the good in both.

People of Faith versus People of Reason

First and most importantly, this alleged conflict between different ways of knowing and understanding the world is itself half illusion. Most people obviously use both styles to inform their conclusions about the world. But it is also an illusion that is vigorously promoted by some who feel threatened by modern science and especially by evolution and ecology. On the other side of this chasm are extremists of the "rational" type, who reject any insights of the intuitive, mystic or charismatic kind, including actual evidence of phenomena that they cannot understand by their paradigm (e.g. paranormal phenomena like remote viewing which the US Army and CIA used for over 20 years because it sometimes worked). Things that only work sometimes or only for some people are anathema to the hyper-rationalists, just as evidence that the Earth was formed much more than 6,000 years ago is annoying to extremists on the other side.

My Ph.D. professor happened to be the son of a Russian Orthodox priest and one of the most famous evolutionary biologists of his time (Theodosius Dobzhansky). He reconciled this paradox very concisely by saying that "Evolution is God's way of creating life on Earth." (Dobzhansky, 1962). Because he was one of the founders of the modern, synthetic theory of evolution he was asked hundreds of times to debate with the creationists of his day, but found most to be impervious to the mountains of evidence that biologists, geologists and others had found to support the theory of evolution over other theories of the genesis of life on earth.

He also observed to me privately that the extremists on the 'rational' side were probably equally confused. By those he meant "fundamentalist" scientists who dismiss anything they can't understand as unreal, but especially notions of spirits or souls or ghosts or heaven or hells or any alternative dimensions of reality accessible by means other than repeatable, physical experiments. In my own, un-humble opinion, those pseudo-scientists have made a religion of their "science" and are just as dogmatic as the faith-based folks that they reject, because there are undoubtedly phenomena on Earth that contemporary science cannot explain at all.

So the second most important thing to stress here is the extremely important role that churches and faith have played in the evolution of civilizations and still do serve in the daily lives of billions of people on this earth today.

Churches and temples and priests of a vast array of nameable religions have been repositories of culture since the beginning of recorded history. Beyond storing, duplicating, and passing on treasures and skills (like writing), churches provided resources for specialized classes of people who could then learn more about astronomy, bureaucracy, and biology, for example. Without the Muslim Arabs of the late-first millennium where would math and science be today? Without Jewish artists, writers and jurists laboring away in their harsh Diaspora of two millennia, where would culture, art and law be today? Very impoverished I would say. So those who would build a better religion for a new millennium should be very careful to retain what is good of the ancient religions, which you can be certain are not going to vanish under any circumstances less than the catastrophic wars that some think are God's plan for Earth. Besides, as a practical matter, churches are built by true believers, not by mystic intellectuals (Hoffer, 1954).

A comprehensive treatment of these topics would require a *magnum opus* to bring in the great religions of Asia and the nature based (but often unwritten) religions of Africa and the Western Hemisphere. But for this simplistic, synthetic essay it is better to focus on the many very good and sometimes essential things that organized churches do today for their peoples and the world.

The average person on Earth struggles with many difficult daily challenges of survival, and worries about the welfare of his or her children now and when the parents are gone. One of the few things every church acknowledges is that every human dies, and one of the greatest things that churches provide for people is some comfort that even then something greater will care about their children and the Earth that sustains them. A related service of churches for ordinary people is some story about the meaning of life, and of death, that makes sense to them and helps us with those daily struggles and with the occasional terrifying moments of birth and death.

That is not a trivial service to provide. Far beyond charity, the churches provide comfort, meaning, and dignity for the half of humanity that scholars often forget, the half with IQs under 100, whose fear of death and of the unknown is as great as any others'. Churches also provide a matrix of community which, when functional, helps to solve a great variety of community problems as well as to assure worried parents that someone will be there if disaster strikes.

Any plan to promote a "religion" for a "sustainable civilization" that can survive the third millennium must provide equivalent services to the people. This function, often dismissed by atheists and by all too many scholars, is quite essential. But there is more.

Churches, traditionally, have taken ethics seriously. Despite their many errors in that domain, this is quite essential too. Without someone thinking seriously about ethics we are doomed, so it helps when churches encourage people in business, for example, to think hard about business ethics. It helps when military professionals engage in creating rules of war, lest barbarians with weapons of mass destruction ruin everything. Who did western warriors look to when their moment came? To Just War Theory, developed by ancient Catholic scholars like St. Thomas of Aquinas and even more by St. Augustine of Hippo who pondered similar problems long ago. Even ethics for spies is developing, although that is a difficult birth (Andregg, 2010).

Spiritual or mystical warriors know that there is more to their profession than winning battles of bullets, and they have been around since at least the time of Sun Tzu 2,500 years ago. His *Art of War* is reprinted today because it is so profound. In fact, it is scripture for warriors although many soldiers do not realize that. For example in the 3rd lesson of his first chapter he alleges that the first of the fundamental factors in war is the moral (Sun Tzu, as translated by Samuel Griffith, 1963).

Science, business, and the military are not notorious for spending excessive time on "ethics" so it is important to note how critical the people are who create and promote professional ethics in each of these domains. The most relevant discipline, law, spends much more time on such concepts, but the dreadful reputation of lawyers shows some limits of progress there too. Most of all, law illustrates the phenomenal difference between deeds, and words on paper or uttered by mouths. Law also illustrates the corrosive roles of hubris and the love of money and power.

Who wrote "The root of all evil is love of money"? A man named Timothy inspired by God (or Jesus) thousands of years ago, it is alleged. Those words have been copied more than the vast majority of words written by anyone, so I should not be rash when criticizing ancient people or the churches that labored very hard to bring those words to my attention. Who wrote the Golden Rule? Well, Jesus is alleged to have said it, but before him were the authors of Leviticus who said it also, and Confucius wrote a version and, in fact, this appears to be an even more universal concept than the dangers of loving money too much. All those pearls of wisdom were brought to the third millennium by scribes of various kinds, often employed and equipped by churches who took ethics seriously. We should not forget them at the same time that we warn about the zealots who burn books and kill scholars in their wars over whose god is the real God and similar issues.

Scientists who work hard on the frontiers of knowledge know that there is so much more to understand about the universe than the minuscule amount we understand now, that what we know is like a grain of sand in the Sahara desert or a drop of water in the ocean. So religion for a sustainable civilization should call off the stupid war[7] between people of faith and

[7]While praising the good works of churches, secular states can never forget that people who truly think they are serving God may come at any time with heavy weapons to mow down the intellectuals, enslave non-believers,

people of reason. It should recognize instead that both faith and reason are legitimate ways of knowing that can be tested against the evidence of an external world and the universe around us.

Getting from Here to There

The complex crises confronting civilizations today are so daunting that they challenge the greatest minds of our time. Compounding the obvious problems of war, poverty, injustice and destruction of the living system is the fact that the powers that actually rule the earth today are heavily invested in the *status quo* and resist change vigorously (military, financial and energy interests, along with those dinosaur churches I have been criticizing here).

But change agents should recall that these are all human beings in the end, confused though they may be. All institutions are staffed by humans, who have children usually. So the vast majority of the powers that be on Earth still care about the future of the Earth, and especially about the welfare of their children who must inherit whatever we leave behind, so there is hope even for dedicated non-believers in anything beyond their personal power and wealth.

Plus, we all die in our due time, so even the most fanatic suicide bomber, or dedicated Air Force bomber, worries at some level about whether God will agree in the end that they lived their lives well or poorly according to the desires of Allah (or whatever you choose to call the Creator of us all). Comforting this almost universal fear of death is one of the classical functions of churches, along with giving guidance on how to lead the moral life, and promoting community.

A religion for sustainable civilization cannot abandon these basic functions. In fact, it must do better than most religions do today to cultivate the enlightened morality of world citizens that all the Buddhas, sages and prophets wrote about in ancient times.

Since churches and governments have fought so often and so fiercely about which truth is *the* truth, and which power structure "owns" which pieces of land on earth, some of our deeper thinkers spend considerable time searching for a universal ethic of some kind. One example was Hans Kung and Helmut Schmidt's Global Ethics (1998). Kung was a famous theologian and Schmidt a retired chancellor of Germany. Kung brought together religious people from a vast array and Schmidt brought together parliamentarians to consider the same basic questions.

On another front, engineers, physicists and others have been slaving away on energy issues for at least two generations (since nuclear bombs were dropped on children in Japan anyway) and biologists have been slaving away seeking solutions to the biological problems that the global environmental crisis presents. So there are solutions out there, many, once the will to seek them exists. Lots of solutions exist that have not been adopted by the powers that rule our Earth today, and some have been actively suppressed when they threatened lucrative franchises.

---

and impose their rigid codes of "sacred law" on all. This is the paradox of "religion." If civilization is to endure it must defeat those dark forces physically and on the fields of philosophic battle, without destroying collateral goods.

Reform of the UN is another of those institutional challenges that seems impossible on the surface. Most everyone who knows the UN knows that its voting system is archaic, based on the distribution of major powers in 1945, that its budget is ridiculous, that its bureaucracy is a model of inefficiency, and that all the permanent seats in the security council are reserved for the biggest nuclear powers who are paradoxically the only ones who could blow the whole place up. Any of them can veto any substantive decision, a formula for glacial change. As such the UN is constrained by its charter to tiny problems and is almost powerless to deal with big ones.

But answers are out there, solutions exist, ready for the day when humankind actually wants answers and solutions that work instead of just rationalizing the way things are today. Joseph E. Schwartzberg has written extensively about those issues (2009) along with Kofi Annan, Boutros Boutros-Ghali and a host of other internationalists who would much prefer a system that works to fulfill the UN mandates rather than an institution paralyzed by squabbling among its members.

So the religion for a sustainable civilization can only be an ecumenical system that, a) rejects war as a legitimate instrument of statecraft for anything less than unambiguous self-defense, b) promotes global citizenship, c) recognizes the biological crisis and promotes environmental and economic sustainability on Earth, d) preserves the ancient virtues (like charity) and the essential functions of traditional churches while waging a war of words, hearts and minds (and as seldom as possible bullets) against the fundamentalists, fascists and militant extremist terrorists who are willing to destroy everything in their misguided fights over who knows God's will best.

TURKEY AND IRAN AS CURRENT EXAMPLES

Two Islamic countries illustrate well the cross currents of old religions struggling with the challenges of modernity. They are Turkey and Iran, and like every other subject considered here, there is only space for the highlights.

When Mustafa Kemal took over the reins of Turkish power in 1922 after defeat of the Ottoman Empire in World War I, he recognized that this 98% Islamic nation could not compete with Europe and America without a radical reorganization to bring it into the modern world. Very few leaders have accomplished such radical change without destroying their countries.

First, he declared that Turkey would henceforth be a secular state, anathema to Islamic fundamentalists who believe that the church should *be* the state and that governments should be subservient to Islamic clerics and Sharia law. That law imposes punishments derived from 7th century Arab culture that many find draconian, like stoning adulterers to death (if they are female, males get much more lenient treatment) or cutting off the hands of thieves.

Then he empowered the Army to guard this secular state, which was accomplished at great pain to many other constituencies. As part of this package he also transformed the Turkish language (adopting the western European alphabet instead of cursive Arabic calligraphy), liberated women from bondage to men (another vestige of Arab culture not actually commanded by the Holy Qur'an) required training and certification of imams and other religious teachers in schools funded and controlled by the secular state, and other drastic transformations.

Despite vast problems that remain, Turkey today is the only Islamic country with a real chance to join the European Union, and is far more modernized than most Islamic countries which cannot even form a modern bank (because interest is forbidden by Sharia law).

Iran was propelled into forced modernization when British oil companies objected to nationalization of Iranian oil. With operational help from the young American CIA, they deposed democratically elected Prime Minister Mohammed Mosaddeq in 1953 in Operation Ajax. The PM was replaced by an ancestral heir to power named Mohamad Reza Pahlavi who became a dictatorial monarch called the Shah. Iran modernized quickly after that, but at a great price.

Ruthless repression of dissent was organized by the Shah's secret police, created by the CIA and called SAVAK. Depletion of the only Iranian resource (oil) able to generate large amounts of foreign cash accelerated, some invested in development while most of the money went overseas or into the Shah's accounts. This eventually resulted in a chaotic people's revolution in 1979, organized by some of the most radical clerics who had relocated to Paris and London. When they returned to power, they established a new dictatorial rule by the most Islamic of Islamic scholars as determined exclusively by a group of senior imams and ayatollahs.

So today one of the cradles of civilization, with 5,000 years of recorded history, is in thrall to two great problems with implications for us all. One is enormous tension between the very old and exclusively male mullahs who want to retain 7th century Arabic cultural norms (not Persian, the Persians have fought many wars with Arabs) and a population half of which is under 25 years old, and half of which is female. Most of them would rather be free than slaves to a bunch of bearded old guys. The other great problem is an urgent quest to achieve nuclear weapons capability, which frightens everyone in the neighborhood but especially Israel and NATO.

There are many ironies in this if you can step back from details to take a God-like, detached view of the region. Iran is surrounded by nuclear weapons powers (Russia to the north, China, Pakistan, and India to the north and east, France, Britain, and America to the west-NW, and Israel to the southwest) which has very graphically offered to destroy Iran if it becomes too frightened. So the mullahs press on with their program to build weapons that should be totally forbidden by strict interpreters of the Holy Qur'an, which strictly forbids murdering children, other Muslims, and the many other innocents who would certainly die if nuclear weapons are ever used again.

Turkey, Iran and Israel are therefore crucibles today where we shall learn whether secular states and the people who create them can control the religious extremists who threaten to destroy today's civilization if they cannot rule it all. A modern, civilizational religion could help.

God informs the mystic ecumenicals, but not, I think, the violent terrorists of any persuasion. God is love, life and truth, not necessarily in that order. I urge readers to use those guides as you reform the institutions. For the strictly atheistic I can offer Bertrand Russell and Albert Einstein's advice: "Remember your humanity, and forget the rest" (1954).

CONCLUSION

Religion for a sustainable civilization able to meet the challenges of the Third Millennium after the birth of Jesus of Nazareth should express the following qualities.

- It should be more spiritual than hierarchically organized, and more ecumenical than exclusive.
- It should express the Golden Rules and therefore it must reject war as a legitimate instrument of statecraft except in unambiguous cases of literal self defense.
- It should vigorously promote environmental and economic sustainability on earth, because it is aware of the crisis in the living system here and now, and because
- It should recognize Stewardship of the living system as a primary spiritual responsibility of human beings.
- It should preserve and cherish the ancient virtues like charity in particular, and the duties to help, heal and educate those less fortunate or enlightened.
- And it must defeat the false religions of fascists and militant extremist terrorists who use "religion" as a cover for their quests for absolute power, without destroying innocents in the area or the ecumenical spirit of the Creator who loves us all.

These are my opinions on the topic of human survival and enlightened religion.

REFERENCES

Andregg, M. (1997, 1999, 2001). *On the causes of war*. St. Paul, MN: Ground Zero Minnesota.

Andregg, M. (2010). Ethics for intelligence professionals. In Johnson, L. (Ed.) *The Oxford Handbook of National Security Intelligence* (pp.735-753). London, UK, Oxford University Press.

Aquinas, St. Thomas. (~ 1273 CE). *Summa theologiae*, and *Summa contra gentiles*. Italy.

Dawkins, R. (First edition 1976, 30th anniversary edition, 2006) *The Selfish gene*. London: UK, Oxford University Press.

Dobzhansky, Th. (1962, reprinted in 2009). *Mankind evolving: the evolution of the human species*. New Haven, CT: Yale University Press.

Guiora, A. X. (2009). *Freedom from religion: rights and national security*, London, UK: Oxford University Press.

Hoffer, E. (1951, 23rd edition 2002). *The true believer: thoughts on the nature of mass movements*. New York, NY: Perennial Classic Books.

John Paul II, Pope of the Catholic Church. (1996). *Letter to the Pontifical Academy of Sciences*, delivered in plenary session.

Kung, H. & Schmidt, H. (1998). *Global ethics and global responsibilities: two declarations*. Norwich, UK: SCM Press.

Russell, B. & Einstein, A. (1954). "The Russell-Einstein manifesto," senior author Russell, but signed by Einstein on his death bed; delivered by Russell on BBC radio Dec. 23, 1954 and very widely quoted due to the prominence of both men in their relevant ways.

Schwartzberg, J. E. (2007). *Universal regional representation as a basis for security council reform*. Presented on June 6-8, at the Twentieth Anniversary Meeting of the Academic Council on the United Nations System, CUNY Graduate Center, New York, NY, USA.

Sun Tzu. (1963). *The Art of war*, as translated by Griffith, S.B. London, UK: Oxford University Press. Original written about 400-500 BCE in China.

PART C

THE ROLE OF SECULAR THINKING IN CIVILIZATIONAL DEVELOPMENT

In: Spirituality and Civilization Sustainability … ISBN: 978-1-53610-729-6
Editors: Andrew Targowski and Marek J. Celinski

Chapter 17

GLOBAL RELIGION AND ITS CIVILIZATIONAL REPERCUSSIONS

Andrew Targowski * ***and Edward Jayne*** ‡
Western Michigan University, Kalamazoo, MI, US

ABSTRACT

The purpose of this chapter is to define the centrality of the Global Financial Crisis in 2008-09 and its following stage - the Great Recession, which are controlled by business "religion" of the emerging global civilization. When democracy defeated totalitarianism in 1991 with the removal of the Berlin Wall, we achieved a New World Order. For a long time nobody could explain its meaning and practicality, since nobody was able and willing to decompose the emerging Global Civilization into its pieces -- religion, culture and infrastructure. Global culture and global infrastructure could be recognized and somehow defined and practiced, but "global religion" was unrecognized. No sacred religions could be accepted as the world universal religion! However, business apologists have assumed that our new global religion is no longer sacred, but secular under the guise of *business*.

This premise will be investigated in this paper. The global civilization is characterized and its behavior upon well-being of people is assessed. The framework of business "religion" as the new "religion" of the Global Civilization is modeled and characterized.

The future of business "religion" is evaluated and the means to develop the sustainable and wise civilization are offered. The issues of "ecoism" and Oriental versus Western Civilizations are excluded from this investigation.

* Andrew.taregowski@wmich.edu; President of the International Society for the Comparative Study of Civilizations
‡ Edward.jayne@wmich.edu

INTRODUCTION

The purpose of this investigation is to define what might be the roots of the Global Financial Crisis in 2008-09 and the Great Recession that has followed[1]. The most salient outcome of this collective economic meltdown has been the prolonged, if not permanent, leading to high unemployment among nations belonging to Western Civilization, most notably the United States, the primary source of the world's present crisis. The most troublesome aspect of this crisis has not been the "recession" itself, but its ongoing misunderstanding among our nation's financial community as well as the media and the political and intellectual elite. This has resulted in reduced effectiveness in taking appropriate steps toward repairing the economy and improving the well-being of our population as a whole. Perhaps the best explanation of this misguided economic ideology is what might best be described as a decline of Christian morality and values which have supposedly characterized Western Civilization in the past.

The Great Recession since 2008 can be blamed on a variety of problems. However, the most basic cause of its prolongation beyond normal economic expectations is a drastic decline of purchasing power resulting from the large-scale outsourcing of industrial jobs to off-shore producers in non-western nations. The ownership of outsourced factories remains the same, and both productivity and bottom-line profits have skyrocketed resulting from drastic reductions in labor and environmental costs. The formula sounds great, but its more basic consequences are not worth the economic benefits obtained, as any half-educated economist could have predicted. Only a new and more extravagant spirituality provides a cogent explanation of how and why such a catastrophe has been promoted by our economic leadership.

For example:

- At least forty thousand or more factories have been exported abroad over the past decade, resulting in a net zero growth in job creation under President Bush during his entire presidency. This outsourcing of labor has apparently been subsidized by the Overseas Private Investment Corporation (OPIC), which has linked U.S. corporations with as many as 150 countries through large structural business loans, small business loans, political risk insurance, and investment funds.
- Nearly 30 percent of American manufacturing jobs disappeared during the eight years of the Bush administration. There are now less than 12 million manufacturing jobs in the United States – fewer factory jobs than at any time since the beginning of World War II. (Bernie Sanders website, Jan. 18, 2011).
- Since 1986, as many as 15 million high-paying manufacturing jobs have left the US and American workers. The foreign workers who have replaced them earn a small fraction in wages and without any fringe benefits. In many cases any sum above a dollar per day is the beginning of middle-class status and a vast change of lifestyle (Shery 2011).

[1] The issue of sustainable civilization is beyond the scope of this consideration, as is "ecoism" versus capitalism and socialism (Esty 2009, Hawken and Lovins 2010, Targowski 2011). Also excluded from consideration is the rapid development of Oriental Civilization in Far East, resulting from the decline of Western Civilization (which is very apparent in 2008-2011). An entirely separate investigation seems appropriate in addressing these issues.

- Since the Great Recession began in late 2007, the U.S. has lost more than 8.4 million jobs. Over 2 million of these were in manufacturing, the kind of jobs that have traditionally supported American families in the middle class. In 2009 alone, America lost 1.2 million jobs. (Huffington 2010:20).
- An estimated 0.1 percent of the richest families (about 150,000 households with income above $400,000) received 23 percent of the total income in 2007. This resembles the same pattern in 1928 that led to the Great Depression in 1929! Meanwhile, the wages of the typical American has hardly increased in the last 30 years relative to inflation, leading to the crash of 2008. (Reich 2010:20).
- Last years' (2010) corporate profits were at $1 2/3 trillion dollars (in the US measure), a record high at the same time as our official unemployment statistics were at 9.8 percent of the total work force. Why? To a large extent because of increased productivity at least partly resulting from cheap labor and environmental costs in outsourced factories abroad. (Catherine Rampell, NYT Nov. 23, 2010).
- In 2009 the top twenty-five hedge-fund managers were paid on average more than $1 billion apiece. (Freeland, 2011:48).

All these decisions have been undertaken by ambitious top executives essentially stateless corporations. These executives do not seem to care anymore about their own countries, and their exclusive goal is to increase their shared wealth at any cost. They minimize their reliance on American and other such advanced industrial workers, since these have become "too expensive," but of course they continue to depend on American consumers as well as sympathetic American politicians. As a result, our nation's developed economy has become a service economy too weak to support the American standard of living for the population as a whole, as was the case in the years of 1947-75.

Today the most available jobs include: 1. Waiters and waitresses, 2. Janitors and cleaners, 3. Food preparation, 4. Nursing aides, orderlies and attendants, 5. Cashiers, 6. Customer-service representatives, 7. Retail salespersons, 8. Registered nurses, 9. General and operational managers, 10. Teachers. Only three of these positions require a college degree; the rest rely on basic job training. (Dobbs 2006:112-113).

Do we therefore need 4,000 colleges and universities in the U.S.? More specifically, how long can we teach MBA and engineering programs without students having any prospect of employment? But the problem is more pervasive than that. Today there are between 25 and 30 million unemployed, including those who have given up job hunting and are therefore not included in official statistics. All of these are victims of this globalization strategy. How many more can we expect to be victimized in the coming years? The stimulus packages of President Bush and President Obama temporarily slowed down the Great Recession in last four years. However, it was insufficient to eliminate the more basic economic and social crisis. The question is why more has not been done to reverse this trend? What is the impediment?

As with the successful effort to deny the impact of global warming in order to protect smokestack industries from being forced to install more expensive filtration equipment, our nation's political, intellectual, and media-oriented elite have imposed tacit censorship regarding the impact of globalization in having reduced the United States from an industrial economy to a service economy.

Neither politicians nor journalists dare to mention this trend, much less betray any willingness to identify the corporations and banks implicated in making it happen. For these profit-driven enterprises have become sacred cows too unimpeachable to be tarnished by such considerations.

No longer is the well-being of America or even the world as a whole the primary consideration, but the well-being of mostly global corporate investors who comprise an entirely new priesthood, their Bible consisting of the Dow Jones big board and all the data needed to play its game. In other words, bottom-line business profits have taken precedence over our nation's economy as a whole. The two are not exactly the same despite vigorous protestations otherwise, and obviously one of them has been sacrificed to maximize the other. Any basic and truly objective investigation would prove that business's role nowadays has become excessive, far less healthy than in earlier years. But no such investigation is forthcoming.

From Empire to Nation and Civilization

Since the Roman Empire, the world was ruled by consecutive societies, such as the Frank Mongolian, Ottoman, Portuguese, British, and Soviet (in the East). In the 19thcentury the rise of a nation concept took over the political map of the world. In the 21st century however, largely due to the Internet's ability, globalization has accelerated the growth of the World's Economy. The main component of this economy is not a nation but a global corporation. This kind of corporation penetrates all civilizations, taking advantage of each one based on the exploitation of its available resources – raw materials and/or cheap labor.

To analyze the new world organization one must reexamine the concept of civilization as a large society economically independent with an advanced culture and infrastructure (Targowski, 2009:14-16). According to Toynbee (1995), there have been as about twenty-six different civilization in the last 6,000 years and each of those civilizations is oriented by a specific religion. Nowadays, there are eight heirs: the Chinese (Buddhism and Confucianism), Japanese (Buddhism and Shinto), Western (Christian; Protestant and Catholic), Eastern (Christian-Orthodox), Islamic (Islam), Buddhist alone, Hindu alone, and African (eclectic) (Targowski 2009:8). In the twenty first century, all of these have more or less converged in an inclusive Global Civilization as shown in Figure 1. The Internet and global transportation systems support operations of this new world-wide civilization as do the banks and financial markets. Needless to say this Global Civilization, just about 10 years old, has already replaced much of Western Civilization, which is about twenty-six hundred years old if ancient Greece is included in the tally. This transformation which is taking place during our lifetime for some ones is difficult to notice. But their impact is tremendous, particularly in the area of culture and its morality, values, symbols, and patterns of behavior.

The Decline of Western Civilization

Western Civilization has been the most successful civilization in the world history. It is most accomplished in intellectual and material contributions.

Since Western Civilization has such the impressive developmental history and is full of the greatest minds in science, engineering, medicine, art and literature and politics. It had not surprisingly created a lot of conflicts, wars, and revolutions of all kinds. On one hand it has made possible very successful people and organizations, but on the other hand it has created a lot of poverty and social and personal tragedies. Some perceived in the Western path the ultimate destiny of decline and fall, as in fact too many other civilizations have undergone a comparable outcome.

One of the first to notice this pattern was Nikolay Yakovlevich Danilevsky (1822 –1885), a Russian naturalist, economist, ethnologist, philosopher, historian, who in his book *Russia and Europe* previewed the insights of Western Civilization. Aspects of Danilevsky's book prefigured some of the theories in Oswald Spengler's *The Decline of the West* (1917). Whose argument was based on the structure of civilization. According to both, the process is always similar and takes 1000–1200 years to run its course. In their final 200–300 years, Spengler said, all civilizations stiffen into rigidity and formalism; creativity dies out and cynicism surges, the countryside empties and cities grow gigantic, and continuous warfare ends in coalescence of a political-economic world state. Writing that book in 1910-1915, he evaluated Western Civilization as already embarked well into this phase. Later events, especially the collapse of Germany after two World Wars, confirmed his prediction to certain extent and led his popularity among his country compatriots, and beyond.

But, Germany is just one of many nations belonging to Western Civilization and it quickly recovered after the Second World War and became the strongest state in Europe. Western Civilization was in good shape as long as Soviet Civilization persisted, justifying enormous defense expenditures on both sides of the Cold War. When the Soviet Empire dissolved in 1991, supposedly a great victory against communism, Western Civilization paradoxically began to decline in real terms.

In 1990 by President George H.W. Bush envisioned both a New World Order and “eternal peace,” but Francis Fukuyama, an experienced specialist in foreign relations published a best-selling book *The End of History and the Last Man* (1992) suggesting a far more pessimistic outcome. Since everything has been experienced by humans and it is the time to return to the ideals of the French Revolution, which waited too long for implementation, Fukuyama argued that the advent of Western liberal democracy may signal the end point of humanity's socio-cultural evolution and the final form of human government:

> "What we may be witnessing is not just the end of the Cold War, or the passing of a particular period of post-war history, but the end of history as such: that is, the end point of mankind's ideological evolution and the universalization of Western liberal democracy as the final form of human government."

It turns out he was wrong. The New World Order imposed a new kind of molting pot, and we encountered not Western, liberal happiness but what amounts to an Eastern challenge in economy and values. Most of this challenge is triggered by our steadily declining economy. Without any notice we have entered Global Civilization and its new morality and values in the 21st century, no longer limited by Western Civilization’s earlier rules of behavior.

The Emergence of Global Civilization

In the twenty-first century, the eight sacred religion-oriented civilizations, mentioned at the beginning, have more or less converged in an inclusive Global Civilization(in the 21st century, Figure 17.1). But what is the identifiable religion of this Global Civilization? Certainly it is not to be confused with any of those sacred religions of those eight civilizations.

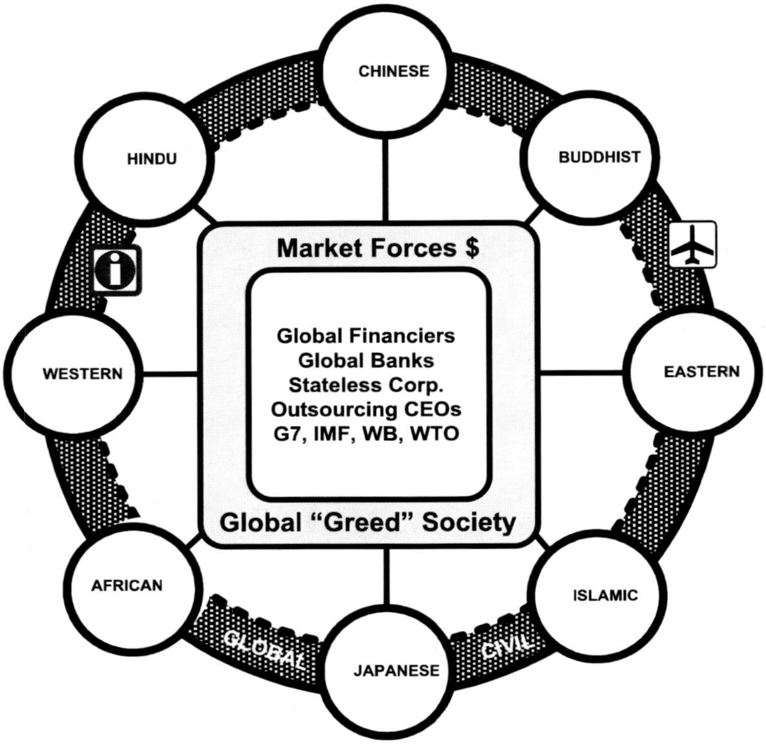

Figure 17.1. The Emergence of Global Civilization in the 21st Century[2].

Its spiritual mission is in the pursuit of business as a strictly secular belief system, the first of its kind in the 6000-year history of civilization. The Athenian, Roman, and comparable ancient civilizations certainly thrived on trade across the Mediterranean region, but not on a comparable scale, and not with anything approaching the amazing convergence of standards and attitudes now in effect at least among the wealthier classes. Today, Global Civilization is both supported and controlled by the Global Economy, which integrates the world's trade relations with a relatively free and unrestricted movement of goods, services, and labor, in the latter instance by bringing work to the inexpensive workers rather than the other way around. Tariffs still take effect as well as the subsidization of products to enhance their competitive possibilities abroad, but as a whole trade barriers are far lower than before.

[2] In this model of the current civilizations the Islam Civilization is not categorized into its sub-civilizations such as Sunni, Shia, or Sufism, and so forth.

THE SIGN OF GLOBAL CIVILIZATION'S BEHAVIOR AND MISBEHAVIOR

The "Silicon Valleys" of the "Third World" in places such as Bangalore are often displayed as the beneficial product of globalism, when just a few blocks away from the internet cafes and computer shops rural India continues to be aggravated by its population explosion. According to United Nations statistics, this stark economic contrast in India is beginning to manifest itself in non-western societies. The rise of large, cross-border regions in Europe, in North America, and in Asia has borne similar consequences. These regions do attract business enterprises that undoubtedly contribute to a higher standard of living, but they operate according to the rule of the market and at this point without a political framework that makes possible costly regulations (Moller, 1991).

Most of the world's population does not have running water, most are illiterate, most have less than a high school education, and many are malnourished. With the exception of the Group of Eight industrialized countries (G8) -- all of which but one are western -- the majority of people on this globe do not truly benefit from this globalization, nor do they play a crucial role except as a source of almost astonishingly cheap labor. In other words, globalism as a "religion" benefits a dispersed elite that is relatively small. At this time its primary beneficiary is G8 economic and cultural hegemonism that ultimately depends on financial institutions linked with Wall Street. (Aung-Thwin2001). So what exactly are the assets and liabilities of globalism right now? For the purposes of clarification, the following table might be useful in helping to sort out the various categories involved as shown in Table 17.1.

Table 17.1 Advantages and Disadvantages of Global Civilization

ENABLING FACTORS	GLOBALIZATION BENEFITS	PROBLEM CAUSING FACTORS
Advances in transportation and communication	Higher economic growth of global corporations, China, and India	Digital divide
Manufacturing and information technology outsourcing	Poverty reduction in China and India	Inequality, declining middle class in developed nations, Financial Crisis in 2008-09
Lowering tax barriers	Basic life quality improvement in non-western societies	Volatility in advanced corporate societies
Media support	Widely heard advocacy	Anti-globalization movement
Creation of WTO	Corporate entities thrive	Traditional institutions in decline
Wealth allocation	Quick investment based on comparative advantage	Cultural decline, from welfare of disadvantaged to welfare of rich

Of course the categories can be expected to change over time, but the current profile seems sufficiently stabilized to suggest the advantages and disadvantages as listed will continue into the indefinite future.

Right now the world's elite are leading the march toward globalism, but millions of laborers, either employed or unemployed, see themselves as losers resulting from the elimination of national trade barriers. Those supranational enterprises foster extreme economic disparity among workers and an elimination of transparency as much as possible in order to obscure this disparity. A sustained public relations campaign unavoidably tells on one page of a newspaper that a corporation has eliminated 8,000 workers, while on another page perhaps a few weeks later tells of this corporation's CEO earning a $25 million bonus.

It seems almost impossible to exaggerate what is happening. As earlier indicated, the top 25 hedge-fund managers were paid on average more than $1 billion apiece in 2009, when Wall Street was supposedly in a free fall and our nation's economy was on the brink of a major depression. On the other hand even slave labor is tolerated in non-western nations. For example, most of the cell phones, DVD players, video games, and many of the computers used across our nation and abroad are produced by underpaid workers in Chinese factories, but the coltan (or tantalum or columbite-tantalite) crucial to the operation of these luxuries is actually mined by slave laborers in the Congo. Granted, major electronics corporations have not directly employed this slave labor themselves, but they have had no compunctions about dealing with the Congo war lords who have used profits from this labor to buy weapons from abroad.

The managerial class is of course confident that it can take care of itself and is surprisingly indifferent what happens to the rest of the people. The media owned by billionaires and mega-millionaires has effectively diverted public resentment to other issues (welfare, socialism, the free use of guns, abortions, etc.), but increasing number of population is becoming aware of the charade. And this resentment can only intensify if the trend persists. Globalism has accordingly produced three dangerous sources of reaction: nationalism, populism and the authoritarian pursuit of oppressive solutions (Annan, 1998). The public can go either liberal or conservative in any number of ways, and the task of our nation's corporate leadership is to take whatever steps seem necessary--for example through contributions to libertarian causes--in order to guide the public in the most harmless direction relevant to corporate needs.

A New Secular "Religion" of New Global Civilization

According to the Oxford dictionary a religion is "the belief in and worship of a superhuman controlling power, especially God or gods." As an intentional oxymoron, the word combination secular religion can be used to describe ideas, theories or philosophies which involve no spiritual component yet possess qualities similar to those of a religion. Such qualities include a system of indoctrination, the prescription of an absolute code of conduct, designated enemies, unquestioning devotion to a higher authority and an ideologically tailored creation story and millenarian narrative.

The secular religion operates in a secular society by filling a role which would be satisfied by a church or another religious authority. Social philosopher Raymond Aaron (1957) notably uses the term to refer to Communism. Philosopher of science Michael Ruse (2003) made use of the term in discussing evolution theory and Darwinism. And the last but not the least, Thomas Frank (2000) suggests that the free market has become a secular religion in the United States.

Ideologies such as atheism, agnosticism, skepticism, Marxism, secular humanism, and existentialism have also been recognized as secular religions since the Enlightenment (McDowell and Stewart 1991).

If westerners dominate Global Civilization, the question is justified exactly what is its religion? Christianity? Not at all. Granted, religion influences nearly everything in our daily lives, from buildings, the food we eat, and the books we read to the rituals of marriage and death, and the customs of court room and government. It shapes our beliefs, moral codes, and sense of national identities. Both individuals and nations describe themselves in religious terms -- Christian or Jew, Hindu or Muslim, Buddhist or Shinto, and so forth.

On the other hand, secularization has mounted since the seventeenth century, and today one's status as a businessperson does not require further *religious* identification, since business itself has become a "religion." Not only is greed good, as Gordon Gekko so persuasively insists in Oliver Stone's famous "Wall Street" episode, but, beyond that, it is virtuous, and in fact it is a religion of its own that is free and clear of its earlier involvement with Protestantism as described by Max Weber. It now throws a wider net than the northern European Protestant sect could ever have imagined.

The belief in gods and goddesses was once important, but nowadays the most successful mortals--inclusive of our nation's 400 mega-billionaires--take on this role to a certain extent. Morgan and/or Rockefeller now sit on heaven's throne, if such exists, or perhaps Ford hand-in-hand with his friend Edison, or perhaps Hayek and Friedman despite the September 2008 embarrassment.

It means that business emerges on a global basis as a secular "religion" of Global Civilization. Because it is based upon a *business doctrine* composed of the following elements in the 21st century:

- *Business Faith* emphasizes markets know best, "the sky is the limit," permanent growth, expanding market share, bottom-line avarice, individual bonuses, super-consumerism, downsizing as the source of bigger profit and bonus, walmartization (toward the largest scale through automated simplification), globalization as a platform for growth and bigger market share, and the shared assumption that wealth is "virtue."
- *Business Knowledge* is taught at business colleges that serve as for-profit seminaries at which the business faith is taught by business faculty who act as business priests and monks/nuns. Research conducted by business faculty and subsidized by business itself presumably augments and refines the application of business faith.
- *Business Liturgy* -- involves endless business meetings/conferences and by the media, all of which feature information convenient for the Business Doctrine in order to keep citizens as consumers and faithful believers in super-consumerism and Fun Society's simplistic lifestyle rooted in insatiable consumerism.

Business "religion" Doctrine is what keeps business as "religion". It is demanded by CEOs of Big Business who act as *Business Bishops and Cardinals*. They as the business' top elite define vision, goals, strategies, principles and rules of current global capitalism, which form the Business "religion" Doctrine. As such it later becomes the *creed* for most of executives and managers of global capitalism.

For example, in the 2010s this doctrine is based on the following rules:

- Rule 1: The elimination of governmental regulations is necessarily beneficial, since it encourages growth.
- Rule 2: Lowered the taxation of wealthy taxpayers creates new jobs[3].
- Rule 3: The removal of safety nets for displaced workers is justified because it minimizes business costs so as to be more competitive globally.
- Rule 4: The offshore outsourcing of manufacturing is good for consumers since prices of imported goods are cheaper.
- Rule 5: Unemployed workers do not have the right skills so it is their obligation to seek appropriate job training to find employment elsewhere.
- Rule 6: As much as possible loyal employees need to avoid taking these and other such issues into consideration. They should concentrate on their jobs without concerning themselves with supposedly irrelevant matters.

At least the first five of these rules are highly debatable. Contrary to the first rule, for example, the 2008 collapse of Wall Street resulted as much as anything from a lack of regulation; and contrary to the second rule, President Bush's generous 2001 and 2002 tax cuts had no appreciable impact on unemployment level at the time. The next three rules bear obvious consequences that need to be weighed against the needs and expectations of the public as a whole as well as the sustained health of the nation's economy in its entirety – indeed the world economy in its entirety. And finally the sixth and largely unspoken rule bears upon the alienation of Americans in general as was featured by C. Wright Mills and numerous other sociologists almost three generations ago. Unfortunately, the media discourages the discussion of these issues, since such inquiry might chase away advertisers and commercial support. In practice media accept these rules as "divine" ones, which as "religious dogma" cannot be debated. As the result of this shared perspective, one in six Americans lives in poverty, totaling 46.2 million citizens.[4] (Poverty is defined as a family of four living with an income of $22,113 or less).

Business "religion" Doctrine is what codifies business as "religion". The CEOs of Big Business have acted as *Business Bishops* by having codified business as a "religion". The most influential of these convene at *conclave*s to decide about the current curse of world business affairs. In turn *Business Cardinals* are selected from Wall Street's biggest banks, and government's most prestigious officials who come to annual January meetings at Davos, the posh ski resort nestled in the Swiss Alps. They form the so-called Party of Davos. Some 2,000 business leaders will show up to discuss the world's problems as defined by *Business Cardinals* who own or manage the great global concentration of wealth (Microsoft, Citigroup,

[3] A March 2011 NBC News/Wall Street Journal poll found 81 percent of those surveyed would support a tax on millionaires that would be used to for deficit reduction. An April, 2011 CBS/New York Times poll revealed 72 percent of people favored raising taxes on the wealthy to reduce the deficit. However, politicians refuse to listen to the people who put them into in office and continue to spout misinformation about what citizens really want?

[4] Lisa Erikson. "What Will Take to Get Republicans to Listen?" *Kalamazoo Gazette*, OPINION, September 25, 2011, p. A9.

Siemens, Nestle, Nomura Holdings, Saudi Basic Industries, etc.). The Party of Davos is the virtual network that governs the global market in absence of an official world government with these powers. The UN's claims to this status notwithstanding. Discussions at Davos are doctrine and strategy-wide, prepared by the *Commission for Business Faith Standards*, whose members come from other think tanks such as:

- Bilderberg Group – the informal network which creates connections between Europe and America. It meets at on invitation-only annual conferences of about 100 leading figures in business, politics, the media, and academia. The agenda is public, but the discussions are off the record, inviting speculations as what is discussed, agreed, and decided when people of such power congregate.
- Bohemian Grove - This is a site of an annual "summer camp" (at the Grove Hotel, a former provincial estate in the English countryside) to which a secret list of leading figures from within the USA and beyond are invited. Members have included every U.S. president since John Kennedy, cabinet officials, and heads of large corporations including banks, military contractors, oil companies, and the media. It is an elaborated bonding ritual that has attracted much suspicion.
- Caryle Group – the largest investment group in Washington D.C., managing billions of dollars of equity capital, it specializes in politically sensitive areas as aerospace, and has interest in several military contractors, and in contracts with Saudi Arabia.
- Trilateral Commission – foster closer co-operation between Japan, Europe and North America, its membership has broadened to include China. It includes about 350 leaders in media, academia, public service, labor unions, and other non-governmental organizations, but excludes those currently holding government positions. It is an influential grooming ground for emerging political leaders.
- Kissinger Associates – founded by Henry Kissinger in 1982, the firm assists a selected group of multinational companies to identify strategic partners and investment opportunities, using the foreign-policy experience of its associates to facilities relations with overseas governments. The company does not disclose the names of its corporate clients but they are thought to include Coca-Cola and American Express.
- G8 – The group started meetings in 1970s as a world economic summit, but now provides an opportunity for heads of governments to discuss a wide range of issues without a formality normally associated with top-level inter-government relations. It includes such nations as; the U.S., Canada, Japan, Germany, United Kingdom, France, Italy, and Russia.
- Many other smaller groups are emerging in the last years of the 21st century, such as; the Bao Forum on China's Hainan Island, Clinton Global Initiative, Google's Zeitgeist, Aspen Institute's Ideas Festival, Marie-Josee Kravis Manhattan Dinner, where typical conversation is about thinking "outside the box" and "killer apps" (computer applications) (Freeland 2011:49), (Burman 2007:94).

There is nothing wrong if influential people meet and talk about world issues. This is particularly true if they take into account world peace, the well being of people, climate control, and the economic sustenance of civilization (Targowski 2011). However, this is almost entirely not the case. They prefer consulting about *Business Doctrine* and its applications in global economic practice that undoubtedly features current benefits, but just as surely, one suspects, without adequately taking into account the long-term destabilization of civilization. Heavenly optimism entails the immediate pursuit of profit maximization, but without sufficient effort to avoid incurring massive negative consequences suggestive of punitive hellfire as depicted in the New Testament's Book of Revelation. Not that such an outcome is seriously taken into account.

Today's successes predominate as the most important issue, while their increasing negative impact is disregarded as an irrelevant issue in the unforeseeable future, much as CEO's too often seek immediate corporate profits at the expense of long-term corporate growth. What primarily concerns these individuals is quick benefits during their half dozen years in command, and later consequences simply don't matter. But not true.

The most visible supreme authority in the application of *Business "religion" Doctrine* is of course the president of the United States, who serves as the Business World's *Holy Father* in executing this doctrine, whatever the ultimate cost to the health and well-being of the world's population. His Secular Holiness collaborates with others across the world who enjoy comparable if subservient high status, and their representatives run the World Bank, the International Monetary Fund (IMF) and World Trade Organization (WTO) to implement their doctrine as a world mini business government. The *de facto* global system supported by these banks is necessarily elaborate and without definitive rules and boundaries, but it can be charted any number of ways, as illustrated on the architecture of business "religion" depicted here (Figure 1). What is interesting to notice that the president of the U.S. does not control business "religion"? He just implements it according to the invisible hand of business "religion's" bottom-line agenda.

At the lower echelons, medium and small businesses are managed by *business priests* and *deacons* under the authority of the above-mentioned business "religion's" leaders. Also notable are the many *Business Saints*: Adam Smith, Henry Ford, Andrew, Mellon, John Rockefeller, Sam Walton, Bill Gates, Warren Buffet, and others. They are supported by *Business Apostles* such as Frederic Taylor (scientific management), Peter Drucker ("business is everywhere"), Bill Clinton ("New Economy"), Lawrence Summers ("too big to fail"), Timothy Geithner ("less regulations the better"), Thomas Friedman ("almost every American should outsource"), Jagdish Bhagwati ("globalization is good"), C.K. Prahald ("core competency is good, everything else outsource"), Gregory Mankiv ("making hamburgers at MacDonald is manufacturing"), Steve Forbes ("sky is the limit"),and too many others to count.

The interaction among these and other players in the global system may be diagrammed as follows in Figure 17.2.

Whatever its baroque extravagance, the model serves its purpose well precisely because of its excesses. It is significantly different from the structure of our nation's government mandated by the Constitution, as much as anything because it represents a new and different power-elite resulting from the exponential growth of our nation's economic institutions since the inception of the Federal Reserve Board preceding World War I began.

The 1929 financial crisis was followed by a Rooseveltian interlude that gave the middle class respite from this plutocratic trend, but profit maximization resumed in full force starting with President Reagan in the 1980s, and here we are now. Everybody who is anybody has a finger in the pie, and complicated strategies occur to launch any potentially lucrative game plan once its rhetoric is effectively couched for public consumption.

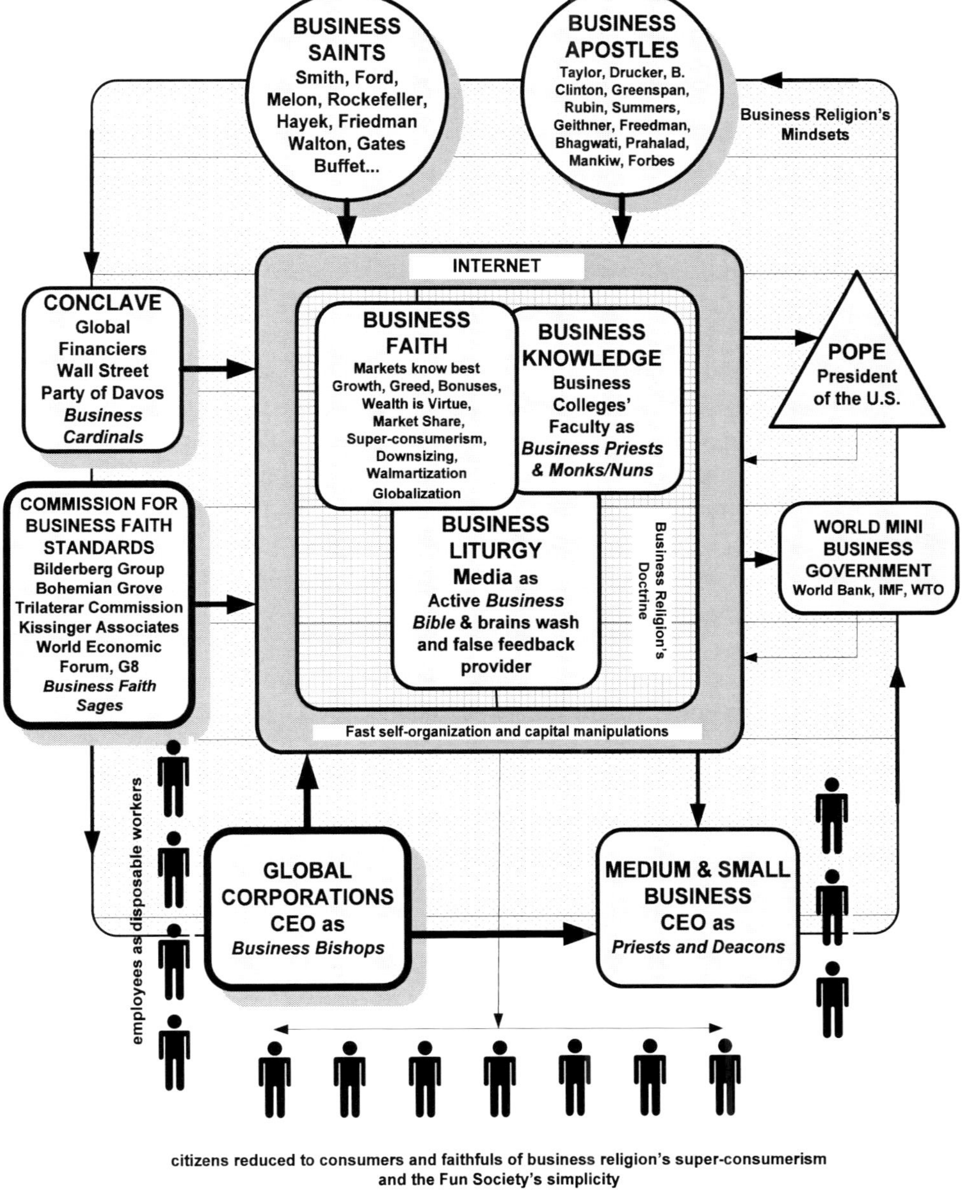

Figure 17.2. The Architecture of business as the religion of Global Civilization and main relations among the entities.

This thoughtless effort to maximize corporate success in the global context, whatever its cost, too often bears less than satisfactory collateral damage despite the high profits obtained. This is the case, for example, if and when the work ethic declines, loyalty goes dead, corporate trust declines, and/or strategic effort specifically relevant to social need simply dissolves. (Sennett 2006:63). The pithy but dangerous slogan "grow or die" takes precedence minus the recognition that misguided growth as exemplified by cancer, shoddy products, and shoddily constructed housing projects almost inevitably accelerates catabolic trends.

In the short run these issues don't matter, but in the long-term the "religion" of business strictly meeting the needs of the elite cannot survive the anger and disappointment lower down on if the business ladder. *Business "religion"* cannot ignore the basic needs of the masses, but this is exactly what it is doing. If, big business has a "religion", it is a "religion" that needs further refinement in serving the needs of the people. Just as Christ's version of faith benefited from Paul's modifications, somebody somewhere in the business world must find a way to ameliorate the near-sighted ideological extravagance of the bottom liners today. The *Business Cardinals and Bishops* justify themselves by insisting that their strategy is to continue business growth till the level of the American Way of Life can be enjoyed in every corner of the world, particularly in China and India. However, two to three planets would be needed additional to the Earth to provide the needed volume of strategic resources for such an outcome, even assuming that the rest of the world would be satisfied with the high but gradually declining standard of life that Americans experience today. (Targowski 2009a:17).

The fact is that two entirely distinct economies (Figure 17.3) have emerged over the past couple of decades: the global economy run by the Global Elite (our latest Ruling Class) and the scattered local economies that is run by small businesses and their workers, many of whom live from paycheck to paycheck, even from hand to mouth. Typically, righteous pundits aligned with the elite blame world poverty on laziness and inferior work skills supposedly typical of these local economies, but western and non-western workers are fully aware that this transparent excuse is used to rationalize their exploitation -- some of them as underpaid workers without fringe benefits, and others as a surplus population neglected by both western and non-western governments mostly dedicated to the benefit of the global elite.

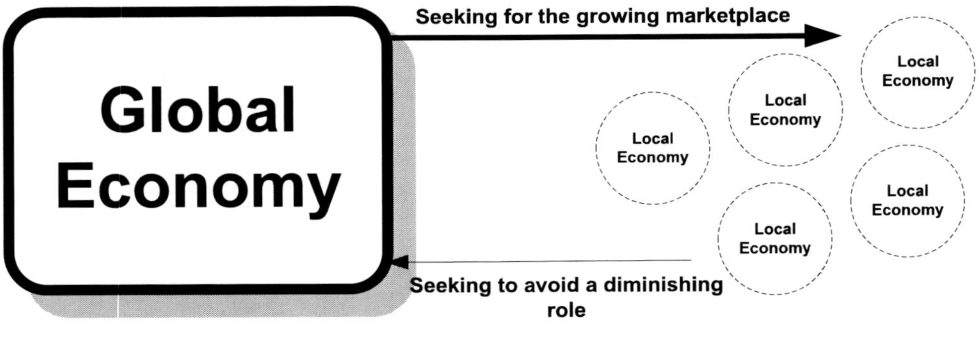

Figure 17.3. Global and local economies in confrontation in the 21st century.

Chrystia Freeland from the *Atlantic* (2011:55) is ambivalent about what can be done. In one context she argues that "America does need many of its plutocrats . . . who produce goods and create jobs," ignoring the fact that these plutocrats primarily invest abroad, for example by having created 1.4 million jobs abroad in 2010 as opposed to zero job growth in the United States (Gogoi 2010). Local economies abroad are driven into poverty by trade favors to foreign competitors, just as the labor force at home is forced to accept lower wages and increased layoffs.

On the other hand, she argues that super-elites have two ways to survive: by suppressing dissent (which is being done today) or by sharing their wealth, as Bill Gates and Warren Buffet have argued in proposing that 50 percent be given away. Freeland hopes that "the plutocrats aren't already too isolated to recognize the benefits of this second alternative." The authors think that she is too optimistic.

THE FUTURE OF BUSINESS "RELIGION" AND LENIN'S ROPE

In the twenty-first century, the business "religion" eagerly transforms America from an industrial to a service economy that cannot sustain the American Dream. Honestly speaking, the service economy does not provide a healthy future for Americans (and Westerners). Big Business advocates the idea of a service economy as a replacement for the industrial economy, but this is simply wrong. It might be difficult for some to understand, but what is good for bank and corporate profits can sometimes be harmful to the economy as a whole, just as what is good for General Motors, as Charles Wilson once proposed, is not what's good for our nation.

If our nation's entire economy (for example inclusive of federal entitlements and the services provided by state and local governments) is trimmed to maximize the profits of banks and large corporations, the arrangement can bear negative consequences for all involved, inclusive of the banks and large corporations themselves. By killing their particular goose to retrieve another golden egg or two, these venerable institutions will have brought to an end sustained benefits for all concerned. The steady-state momentum of our nation's economy can only suffer, and with negative consequences for everybody involved. Corporate strategy today reminds one of what has been described as Lenin's rope. In Russia a hundred years ago, any banker who lent money to somebody who wanted to buy a rope to hang him with was the victim of his own greed. In other words, the banker brought from his own destruction in the near future by lending to an anarchist dedicated to such an outcome. In similar fashion, Big Business can only be described as having been insane in having de-industrialized our own country by exporting factories to other countries in order to augment profits through diminished labor and environmental costs. As a result, predictably, the American people have become more useful to our nation's corporations as consumers than as workers in a situation that cannot last for more than a generation or two. The financial benefit of this arrangement for corporations is only temporary, and when losses continue to mount elsewhere in our nation's economy, the negative consequences will be shared by all. To restore the health of our economy, if such be possible at this point, it would be essential to bring back manufacturing and the services linked with its operation. We might not be able to restore the ratio whereby 25 percent of our work force is involved in manufacturing, as was the case in the 1970s, but at least 15 percent of the labor force should be employed to produce goods for our society as well as export abroad. Another 60 percent should work in services linked with manufacturing. Since every job in manufacturing generates 3-5 jobs in services, one can assume that these alone should play a major role in mitigating our nation's current unemployment statistics. Altogether, it can be estimated that 75 percent would gain employment by reindustrializing our economy, and the remaining 25 percent could work elsewhere, including banks, other financial institutions, and federal, state, and local government.

Of course one can argue about the scope of these targeted ratios, but the question seems academic at this point, since there is no chance that the current state of affairs has any prospect of even beginning to restore these earlier ratios. The problem is that any major overhaul as proposed here would be almost impossible to bring about. For the barn door is open and all the horses are gone.

Needless to say, this situation has not gone unnoticed. In TIME, one of the two most popular American weeklies, Zachary Karabell writes:

> "The decline in domestic jobs is the result of technology and globalization, both of which have enhanced prosperity. There is no going back, and the manufacturing jobs that have been lost are gone forever."
> (TIME January 17, 2011:32)

What Karabell doesn't realize is that the Crash of 2008-10 was not a sign of prosperity, but vice-versa it signified globalization's failure. In the same issue of TIME, (pp. 32 and 25), another writer, Bill Saporito writes:

> "It's more evidence that America is facing a bifurcated employment future. At the top end is highly educated, technically competent workforce attuned to the demands of the global marketplace. At the other end is a willing but under-skilled group that is seeing its prospects undermined by workers like in China in low-end manufacturing and by a mismatch of emerging markets."

Neither writer seems to recognize that about 30 million American workers today and potentially 50 million in the near future simply do not fit into the global marketplace of labor. Right now (2011) the official unemployment figures are in the range of 9 percent, not including those who have given up the effort to seek employment. How soon can this figure drop to 6 percent, or 4 percent? Can any incumbent elected official hope to win reelection if this doesn't happen? And what of their replacements? To what extent will economic crisis generate political crisis, and that in turn to crises in foreign relations?

If the United States could be a small country, this problem might eventually be compensated by new job specializations. However, in a nation the size of the United States, it will always be the largest portion of the public who do not have the advanced education that would help them to find employment beyond the services jobs already mentioned. Should the national government provide welfare benefits to these unwashed masses and otherwise forget about them?

Will wealthier Americans need to enclose themselves more effectively in gated communities in order to avoid unpleasant encounters with their less fortunate compatriots? Do we truly want a simplistic economic Darwinism to engulf civilized society according to the new business "religion"? Is the globalization of business at the expense of almost everybody involved a determined future for American society into the indefinite future?

Conclusion

1. What is good for General Motors, CITI Group, Wal-Mart, Exxon, or Microsoft is no longer good for the U.S. and its citizens. These Big Businesses have become outdated because they paid insufficient attention to the American middle class and its need for a secure and comfortable standard of living. In effect, the U.S. is in danger of becoming a Third World nation (Huffington 2010) because of them.
2. NAFTA, the WTO, and similar "free-trade" international agreements are in fact socially corrupt arrangements among the global elite (*Conclave, Business Bishops and Apostles*) and undermine the social contract to minimize the benefits of democratic capitalism which used to be shared broadly among majority of citizens (Faux 2006).
3. Globalization's business "religion" that emphasizes a continuing pursuit of free trade and futuristic technology (Grey 2007)], in order to make the rich even richer, can only push Western Civilization into severe decline that provokes social unrest at dangerous levels. This is when the Great Recession 2008-11 will lead to an even greater depression followed by *a necessarily conservative populist reaction*, in the desperate effort to sustain law & order (Targowski 1982).
4. As Toynbee argues, civilizations have arisen when "creative minorities" devised solutions to the great crisis of the age. On the other hand, they have perished when they failed to resolve that crisis – just as happened to the Roman Empire. According to Patrick Buchanan, "We are entered upon the final act of our civilization" (2006:60). Obviously, the last scene will be the destruction of our nation, but what is the next to last scene? Paradoxically, this is now under way through the unimpeded invasion of the non-western world by major corporations assisted by Wall Street banks.

If Americans want to rescue the American Dream, then something must be done to harness the outsourcing of the U.S. economy. Other changes seem potentially useful along following lines:

1. American nation's military emphasis should be significantly reduced. We do not need between 700 and 1000 military bases abroad and the futuristic weapons systems developed by major corporations primarily intended to augment aggregate demand. Nor do we need to be involved in more foreign invasions than the rest of the world combined since World War II as supported by a military budget comparable to that of all the rest of the world combined. If the financial health of the military-industrial complex is considered a major Keynesian need, as seems to be the case, domestic projects such as free higher education and the development of bullet trains should be sufficiently enlarged to supplant the aggressive pursuit of warfare abroad. This has happened elsewhere. It can happen here.
2. A better and more effective mixed economy is needed along lines already pursued in Western Europe. Neither socialism alone nor free enterprise alone is sufficient. Social services and entrepreneurial capitalism should coexist, and with sufficient regulations to curtail potential excesses by both.

3. Ecoism as the development of alternative energy sources should be pursued as a sustainable "deep" economy (environmentally and socially accountable) to replace turbo-capitalism.
4. Lobbying should be curtailed, and improved feedback should be emphasized between elected officials and the electorate.
5. The now prohibitive cost of campaign advertising should be reduced, as is done for example in European nations where candidates are given free access to prime time TV in the early evening for a few weeks before elections. If this alternative is taken for granted in Europe, there is no reason why it can't be done here. Otherwise, wealth buys up TV advertisement slots and almost totally dominates elections, guaranteeing the plutocratic excesses our nation endures today.
6. Citizens should learn to accept higher levels of taxation, particularly on a graduated scale with progressive taxes emphasized instead of regressive taxes. As a rule of tomb, billionaires and mega-millionaires should pay proportionally higher taxes than the rest of us[5].

In a broad sense, business as "religion" in its present formulation should be either revised or eliminated from the minds of national and local politicians, businessmen, intellectuals, and business faculty. Whatever the benefits of our nation's major corporations, their impact become toxic, their only defense is a "religion" that doesn't quite work except for themselves—and ultimately not even for themselves.

REFERENCES

Annan, K. A. (1998). A secretary-general of the United Nations, New York, These remarks are taken from a speech at Harvard University, September 17. New York: U.N.

Aaron, Raymond (1957). *The Opium of the intellectuals*. London: Secker & Warburg, pp. 265-294.

Aung-Thwin, M. (2001). *Myth & history in historiography of early Burma: pardigms, primary sources, & prejudices*. Athens, OH: Ohio University Press.

Brown, Ch. (2009). Commentary: solidarity and universalism as premises of overcoming the perils of liberal globalization. *Dialogue and Universalism*. (XIX), pp.11-12.

Bhadwati, J. (2007). *In defense of globalization*. Oxford & New York: Oxford University Press.

Buchannan, P. (2006). *State of emergency*. New York: THOMAS DUNNE BOOKS.

Burman, St. (2007). The State of the American empire. Los Angeles: University of California Press.

Dobbs, L. (2006). *War on the middle class*. New York: Penguin Books.

[5]A group of two dozen millionaires stormed Capitol Hill on November 16, 2011, demanding lawmakers raise their taxes. "We want to pay more taxes," said California millionaire Doug Edwards, a former marketing director for Google. "If you're fortunate, and you make more than a million dollars a year, you ought to pay more taxes." The millionaires want Congress to allow the tax cuts passed during the George W. Bush administration to expire. Some want higher taxes generally (retrieved on 11.18.2011 from http://www.kesq.com/politics/-29787390/detail.html).

Esty, D. C.& A. S. Wiston. (2009). *Green to gold: how smart companies us environmental strategy to innovate, create value, and build competitive advantage*. New York: Wiley.

Faux, J. (2006).*The global class war*. Hoboken, NJ: John Wiley and Sons.

Faux, J. 2006). The party of Davos. *Nation*, February 13, pp. 18-19.

Freeland, Ch. (2011). The rise of the new ruling elite, how the global elite is leaving you behind. *The Atlantic*, vol.307, nº1.

Fukuyama, F. (1992). *The end of history and the last man*. New York: Penguin Group.

Gogoi, P. (2010). "Job market booming overseas for many American companies." *Huff Post Business* (published 12-28).

Grey. J. (2007). *Black mass, apocalyptic religion and the death of utopia*. New York: Farrat, Straus, Giroux.

Hamel, G. and C.K. Prahald. (1996). *Competing for the future*. Boston: Harvard Business Scholl Press.

Hawken, P. and A. and L. Hunter Lovins. (2010). *Natural capitalism: creating the next industrial revolution*. Boston: Back Bay Books.

Huffington, A. (2010). *The third world America*. New York: Crown Publishers.

McDowell, J. and D. Stewart. (1991). *Understanding secular religion*. Manitou Spring, CO.: Summit Ministries.

Moller, J.O. (1991). *Technology and culture in a European context*. Copenhagen: Nyt Nordisk Forlag.

Prahald, C.R. (2009). *The fortune at the bottom of the pyramid*. Upper Saddle River, NJ: Pearson Education.

Reisch, R. (2010). *After-shock*. New York: Alfred A, Knopf.

Ruse, M. (2003).Is evolution a secular religion? *Science*, vol. 7, nº 3.

Sennett, R. (2006). *The culture of new capitalism*. New Haven and London: Yale University Press.

Shery, N. Out sourcing America: job loss and unemployment. retrieved on 1-7-2011 from http://www.the7thfire.com/Politics%20and%20History/Norma_Sherry/out_sourcing_america-job%20loss%20and%20unemployment.htm

Targowski, A. (2004). From global to universal civilization. *Dialogue and Universalism, vol.* XIV, n. 3-4, pp.121-142.

Targowski, A. (2009). *Information technology and societal development*. Hershey & New York: IGI.

Targowski, A. (2009a). Will business end or revive Western Civilization? *Proceedings of the 39th International Conference of the International Society for the Comparative Study of Civilizations*. Kalamazoo, MI: The ISCSC.

Targowski, A. (1982). *Red fascism*. Lawrenceville, Virginia: Brunswick.

Thomas. R. (2000)."The Rise of market populism: America's new secular religion", *The Nation*, October 30.

Toynbee, A. (1995). *A study of history*. New York: Barnes & Noble.

Wilkinson, P. (1999). *Illustrated dictionary of religions*. New York: A DK Publishing Book.

In: Spirituality and Civilization Sustainability …
Editors: Andrew Targowski and Marek J. Celinski
ISBN: 978-1-53610-729-6

Chapter 18

CORRUPTION OF INSTITUTIONS AND THE DECAY OF CIVILIZATIONS

Michael Andregg*
University of St. Thomas, St. Paul, MN, US

ABSTRACT

This chapter discusses the dangers of corruption of institutions, especially governments, and how such corruption can be exposed and partially cleansed. Theories about the decay phase of civilizations are briefly cited, and examples of corrupted forms of six professions illustrated (military, law, medicine, journalism, business and the clergy). Parallels between large organizations and the human body are shown to illustrate system consequences of dysfunction. An enduring theme is the need for constant, built in mechanisms to reduce corruption in living systems, including the largest scale of civilizations. Some solutions to these problems are mentioned, but readers are also challenged to do better since the problems of corruption of governance have been eternal and have successfully resisted many reform efforts.

INTRODUCTION

Civilizations are living systems, so like any living system they need at least 19 subsystems to acquire and process food, water, energy and information, to safely dispose of toxic byproducts or wastes, to avoid being eaten themselves, and otherwise to stay alive and to reproduce themselves. In one sense all these life functions are equally "essential" (Miller, Living Systems, 1978). Still I will maintain here that cleansing a civilization regularly of corruption (or empire or nation state) is especially important. Why?

First, because corruption is corrosive and feeds on itself. Very high corruption cripples economies, nations and other social groups, so mechanisms must be built into any social organization with a desire for a long life to keep corruption below toxic concentrations, which

* E-mail: mmandregg@stthomas.edu

includes civilizations. Many examples show, however, that high levels of corruption can also be sustained for long periods. They tend to be examples of very poor, dysfunctional countries though.

Second, because corruption is inevitable. Corruption is a form of sloth, and sloth is actually favored in living systems to save energy. As Lord Acton noted, "power corrupts and absolute power corrupts absolutely." Many thoughtful observers have agreed, and nothing we have seen in 150 years since gives us reason to question this conclusion or Acton's wiser corollaries.[1] Corruptions shielded by official secrecy are especially pernicious. Some amount of corruption may be necessary to avoid death by bureaucracy or boredom. But in general corruption leads to bad decision-making, inefficiencies, gross injustices, and crime, and ultimately corruption of governance is deeply related to the decay phase of historic civilizations.

Spirituality may once have served as a partial check on the tidal force of corruption, but when it was weakened by organized religions other institutions were also compromised. A chapter on that factor is elsewhere in this book so I won't write much more here. Both have value, but one is more advanced and enlightened than the other. The distinction between authentic spirituality and organized religion is important to any project on "Spirituality and Civilizational Sustainability."

After a brief introduction to that "Decay Phase" of civilizations alluded to above, I will illustrate more clearly what I mean by corruption of institutions by six examples that are especially relevant to the health of modern societies.

Corrupt Forms of Important Institutions and the "Decay Phase" of Civilizations

One of the great pioneers of civilizational theory, Carroll Quigley of Georgetown University, wrote the following words about decay in his classic "Evolution of Civilizations" (1961).

> "The Stage of Decay is a period of acute economic depression, declining standards of living, civil wars between the various vested interests, and growing illiteracy. The society grows weaker and weaker. Vain efforts are made to stop the wastage by legislation. But the decline continues. The religious, intellectual, social and political levels of the society begin to lose the allegiance of the masses of the people on a large scale. New religious movements begin to sweep over the society. There is a growing reluctance to fight for the society, or even to support it by paying taxes."

Quigley also wrote that a turning point occurs when the masses of a population's citizens stop following the moral examples of elites, because those elites have become contemptible rather than inspirational. Quigley's synthesis is unique, but overlaps well with his British

[1] My favorite among those is "Everything secret degenerates, even the administration of justice; nothing is safe that does not show how it can bear discussion and publicity." Found in a letter of January 23, 1861, published in *Lord Acton and his Circle,* Letter 74, edited by Abbot Gasquet, 1906. This wisdom was preceded by Irish statesman Edmund Burke, 1729-1797, who wrote in a letter to the Sheriffs of Bristol on April 3, 1773: "...among a people generally corrupt liberty cannot long exist."

predecessor Arnold J. Toynbee, another world historian who helped start the systematic study of civilizations.

Corruption brings down empires, but it is not unique to governments; every profession has a corrupt form. Here are six examples.

Military: Ideal warriors are guardians of the people, of innocence in particular, and of the state that supports and empowers them. Mercenaries kill whomever their employers desire, but they both wear uniforms, carry weapons and master essentially identical skills. Their cardinal differences are all in the mind, and in the missions they choose to execute. A close corollary is police, who may protect and serve their society, or be just thugs in uniform. In police states, they spend most of their time repressing domestic critics and very little on protecting the innocent.

Law: Ideal attorneys are defenders of justice, the innocent and the weak. They provide essential order without which large scale business is impractical, prosecution of criminals and defense of innocents from overzealous prosecutors, and relief for people besieged by bureaucracies. Some lawyers just sue people for a living, badger the weak or poor, and tie their societies in knots, creating thickets of regulations that stifle everything unless some lawyer or official is paid off. Some attorneys rationalize any crime for their rich or powerful employers, like those who made torture official U.S. policy.[2] Both types are lawyers, but one is hated while the other is loved.

Medicine: Ideal doctors, nurses and other health professionals are our hope when we are sick, and devote their lives to healing whether they know the Hippocratic Code or simply follow the spirit of compassion that guides this profession. Quacks, cranks and predatory nursing home owners or pharmaceutical companies exploit the sickness of their patients or the weakness of their minds to use and abuse the elderly, ill, innocent or otherwise vulnerable for commercial or other exploitative purposes. Both wear white clothing, but one is a gift from God while the other is a predator in deceptive garb. As in every other area, the common key is what lies in the hearts and minds of the professionals in question. The systems they work in matter greatly as well, because very good people working in very bad systems end up serving evil despite their best intentions.

Journalism: Ideal journalists bring the real news of social concern to citizens and elites alike, "without fear or favor" (a phrase we encounter among intelligence professionals[3] as well). Without good and sometimes brave journalists, the noble experiment called democracy would be impossible because one of the earliest forms of corruption of governance is habitual, casual lying by the political class. Bad journalists simply put their names on press releases of the powerful, read trash that other people write, or bully marginal people of their society to please their rich employers. The internet is providing a great challenge to all

---

[2] Examples of these would be John Yoo and his former colleagues at the Office of Legal Council to U.S. President George W. Bush. When asked, they wrote opinions that he could violate *any* law when at war.

[3] "Intelligence professional" is an insider term for spies, intelligence analysts, covert operators, technical collectors and dozens of other varieties of people employed by governments in their clandestine services. They have important roles in modern societies, but are called the world's "second oldest profession" for a reason. Spies have been here forever and are far more common than most people know. Having spent several decades studying spies extremely closely I am always tempted to bring them into stories about social dynamics. The analysts are very much like journalists and professors except for the obsession with secrets that so dominates spooky-luky land. Hubris is also especially common there, which is corrosive to all the good values that corruption of governance also destroys.

journalists in these times, but it is also an opportunity to rise above the bonded servitude to power that so many endure today.

Business: Ideal businessmen and women generate wealth, employ people, solve vast practical problems, and make money for investors who include many of our elderly in modern societies. Bad businessmen in *laissez-faire* economies victimize the vulnerable, exploit workers, despoil the environment, corrupt governments, and often run off with their loot just before peasants with pitchforks put them in jail or to the torch. Very bad businessmen, like very bad politicians or dictators, are functional psychopaths, indifferent to the suffering of the multitudes they injure. Like all the other professions, the core of business corruption lies in the mind. This matters greatly because businessmen can do so much good or evil depending on their souls and goals.

Clergy: Ideal clergy of any faith, church, temple or non-scriptured naturalist spirit clan comfort the sick, console the bereaved, bless babies and marriages, counsel those concerned about moral dilemmas or afterlife, and otherwise serve as agents for the Creator of us All. Corrupted clergy form cults, confusing themselves or their organizations with "God." A chapter on this factor comes elsewhere since it is so central to spirituality for a sustainable civilization.

So I will repeat the main theme only here: although related, spirituality and religion are not the same domains. Churches are like the elementary schools of education about afterlife, spirit world, and ultimate meanings of life. Good churches promote communities (instead of wars) and provide many really valuable services to troubled souls searching for truth and love on this earth.

I bug them to rise above these good but elementary things because so many vocal churches and alleged "religions" have become stuck in idolatry of words of men long dead, especially literalist interpretations of words written by tribal peoples thousands of years ago. We have learned a few things since then. When inevitable differences of scriptural detail lead to wars in the modern era, too many churches, mosques and synagogues become microphones for those who bray for war, believing strangely that "God" is on "their side" and wants us to kill each others' children.

Specifically, when "religions" call for killing groups of other human beings they violate the most basic guidelines and desire of the Creator of us All. When they oppose healing the earth because they want to grow and dominate more, they threaten All under Heaven. So I say, bless the good works of the elementary schools of spirituality, churches, but do not confuse them with universities.

Gandhi the Mahatma was more concise when he tried to convey similar concepts in his rendition of the seven deadliest sins that worked against authentic spirituality.

They were:

- Wealth without work
- Pleasure without conscience
- Science without humanity
- Knowledge without character
- Politics without principle
- Commerce without morality
- Worship without sacrifice

As Quigley noted elsewhere in his *magnum opus*, civilizations do not start in the "decay phase." Something much more inspirational guides them during their growth and climax periods when leadership is less predatory (at least internally – many slaughtered multitudes outside the empire) and more authentically spiritual. It may be written somewhere that decay is inevitable, but all of the great historians pondered this because they did not want their own children or the children of their nations to suffer the terrible consequences of civilizational collapse. Neither do we; so we shall see whether our "modern" civilization responds to its challenges in time or not.

Quigley was preceded by another great world historian, Arnold J. Toynbee, who finished a 12 volume "Study of History" in 1961 that he started in the early 1930's. This was partly inspired by the global war he saw coming, and it was a standard reference for a generation of British historians to follow. Toynbee distilled the common follies of failing civilizations into three factors. 1 – Resting on their Oars (in Quigley this correlates to declining real investment); 2 – The Suicidalness of Militarism (imperial overreach in Quigley); and 3 – the Ideology of the Ephemeral, or making absolutes of trivial things. In each of these instances corruption plays a role, the first in business, the second in the military, and the third among the political and intellectual elite.

I am a warrior and write here because the children are in danger and the nations are in peril. Do not take this issue lightly, because it is everyone's responsibility to act when such conditions occur. You are not a moron or you would not be reading this book. Look around, use the brains God gave you, and then do whatever you can to correct the corruption that is currently ruining "All under Heaven", as the Chinese say. The corrupt form of professors is dilettante intellectuals.

THE NEED FOR CONSTANT ANTI-CORRUPTION PROCESSES TO PRESERVE "CIVILIZATION"

Since corruption is inevitable, corrosive and destroys civilizations, mechanisms to combat it must be permanent, built-in, and operate almost constantly like pumps at the bottom of a mine that floods with groundwater. As James Stewart put it, "This is one of the reasons you cannot abolish the Department of Justice." Mr. Stewart won a Pulitzer Prize in 1988 for reporting on the stock market crash of 1987, and later became a page 1 editor of the Wall Street Journal. Then he wrote "Tangled Webs: How the Epidemic of Lying is Undermining America Today" when a plethora of other crimes and systemic lies produced the Great Recession of 2007 on.

There are individual instances of greed and lies that harm people on a retail level, like Bernie Madoff's[4] Ponzi scheme or a thousand other examples, and there is systemic lying that harms millions or even billions of human beings. The crash of the U.S. housing market from 2007 on for several years was fueled by thousands of mortgage brokers generating mortgages they knew would fail, then Wall Street firms packaging them into complex securities that

[4] Bernie Madoff was a particularly famous fund manager who bankrupted hundreds of thousands of investors when his 20-50 billion dollar Ponzi scheme collapsed in 2008. In terms of corruption his crime is less significant than the failures of empowered regulators to stop him even though they were warned repeatedly over many years that he was running an illegal scam that would certainly collapse some day.

were rated investment grade by rating firms that knew they were bad. Junk bonds were then sold by brokers who knew they stunk (like Goldman Sachs which famously bet its own money against securities it was selling to investors who trusted them). No one from Goldman Sachs went to jail, while millions of poor thieves do. This was all driven by professionals seeking easy money from people less intelligent or ruthless than they. When the bubble burst, trillions of dollars of middle class assets were lost in the debacle, and tens of millions of people were thrown into poverty. The already poor suffered even more, but even that tragedy was small compared to some international examples.

Many scholars have observed that one of the larger causes of poverty in Africa is corruption of governance (along with other causes). Fewer have noticed the role that international banking played in this tragic affair, especially when large volumes of "petrodollars" needed to be parked somewhere. One ploy was to talk dictators of small, impoverished Third World nations into taking huge loans, at interest, from the northern banks in the names of their nations.

Many would take large sums, put them back into Swiss (or other western) banks, and then leave the debts on the books of their impoverished peoples. One of the executives who promoted this for a lucrative living suffered crises of conscience over about 20 years, finally writing a book in 2005 called "Confessions of an Economic Hit Man." In addition to promoting loans that could never be repaid by the leader who signed for them, they used many other methods from the dark arts. Perkins wrote that "Economic hit men (EMHs) are highly paid professionals who cheat countries around the globe out of trillions of dollars …" by cajoling and blackmailing foreign leaders into serving U.S. foreign policy and awarding lucrative contracts to American business.

Many businessmen and professors of business have told me that a certain amount of kickback, "baksheesh" and other terms for the same bribery process are simply the norm in international business and essential for success. That may be, but it impoverishes many to enrich a few. Saddam Hussein took 10% off the top of oil contracts when he ruled Iraq to finance his palaces and secret police, and Libya's Muammar Gadhafi took 20% until he too was deposed. Some professors claim that the lack of regulation in international business is at fault, implying that regulatory agencies are the solution. Partly true, but the record of regulatory agencies being captured by the industries they are intended to regulate is legendary[5], and that is just for "regular" businesses.

There are at least two other areas where corruption of governance has been raised to an art form. One is international crime and the other espionage. I first encountered the phrase "the fine art of human corruption" while studying spies. Spies need people who will commit treason in their countries by revealing secrets, and big time criminals need corrupt officials to not enforce laws forbidding their daily work. Cultivating government officials who will look the other way when smuggling drugs or weapons or human beings or any other valuable good across international borders, for one example, has been a method of criminals since the beginning of organized borders.

So there are special groups that use corruption of governance as a toolkit, e.g. spies and crime. Did I forget politics? Life is too short to describe the many ways that politicians

[5]An academic presentation to the U.S. Congress about this process was provided in 2010 by Sidney Shapiro, a professor at Wake Forest University School of Law at a hearing on: "Protecting the Public Interest: Understanding the Threat of Agency Capture." It is accessible at http://www.progressivereform.org/articles/Shapiro_AgencyCapture_080310.pdf

manage to be corrupt, much less the artful ways they rationalize that to their constituents, spouses, and even to themselves. In fact, the deepest and most painful corruptions often begin with lying to one's self.

I struggled with this problem as best I could in a chapter on "Corruption of Governance" in a book ***On the Causes of War*** that won a national award long ago. The biggest challenge there was finding meaningful solutions, since corruption tends to feed on itself and is so strongly defended by the politicians who benefit so much from it. One paragraph conveys that essence:

> "In America today, corruption of governance is so embedded that many of its basic features are accepted as common practice, so routine they are no longer noticed, like the buying of Congressmen by moneyed special interests. Every year, someone decries this legal bribery, and every year it is ignored. Bills are presented to Congress for reform, and rebuffed with the most amazing rhetoric. The opponents are outraged, OUTRAGED, that anyone would suggest they could be influenced by money. Then they refuse to pass the simplest reforms. So general welfare is sacrificed annually to enrich those who are already powerful." [From page 87 in chapter 14 of "On the Cause of War," 1997, 2001]

Things have gone downhill in America in the 16 years since those words were written. No matter how artful any regulatory scheme, we are dealing with human beings with all our weaknesses, temptations, pressures and personal crises. People can get around any fence they build, so regulation is at best a partial answer. Corruption is something that begins in the mind and tarnishes the soul. Religion claims to have some solutions for that, and authentic spirituality certainly does, but if those were easy to master we would have many less problems on Earth than we observe today. So I will conclude this chapter with a section on solutions after one more metaphor that attempts to make simple something that is actually quite complex.

The Human Body Metaphor

Systems theory is too abstract for many people, but there is at least one complex system we are all intimately familiar with; our bodies. Deep thinkers through history have often used body metaphors to try to convey how systems work, or should work. Consider a civilization like some kind of super-organism. How would "corruption" manifest in a body, and how do actual human bodies deal with these kinds of problems?

One clue is provided by that seminal thinker, Carroll Quigley, again. He observed elsewhere in his book that a distinguishing feature of the decay stage is when agencies of government begin serving their own bureaucratic interests instead of the functional purposes for which they were created. Sound familiar? Thus when police stop protecting the population and start repressing critics of the government which provides their budgets, or when a military system becomes merely parasitic instead of truly defensive, these would be examples of corruption at the level of civilizations. How does this compare to bodies?

The parallel is autoimmune diseases, where white blood cells and a larger immune system that properly exists to detect and destroy disease organisms turns to attack healthy tissues instead. It is not that white blood cells are intrinsically bad, or that their power to destroy is immoral, rather, they have lost sight of their proper targets and proper function serving the larger body.

In fact, growth of ANY tissue beyond its proper bounds can kill a human body – we often call this cancer. Those breast or lung or skin or bone cells are supposed to be doing useful things, and to occupy a defined space consuming proportionate resources, but when they grow beyond limits and consume ever more resources they can consume the whole body of the organism of which they should be only one part. That proper function is supposed to be well coordinated with the many other functions of many other tissues that make up a whole human body.

How cells of a healthy body "know" what their proper boundaries are, what their proper functions are, and how these should be and usually are well coordinated with the rest of the kaleidoscope of human biochemistry is one of the great mysteries and miracles of nature called physiology. And what we don't know about physiology greatly exceeds what we do know despite the best efforts of physicians and scientists for centuries. Homeostatic mechanisms for control and integration are especially complex and mysterious. Perhaps they have tiny cell 'brains' and chat with each other like we do. Maybe they even have souls of some itty, bitty kind, that commune with the Creator of us all for guidance.

That may seem too romantic and New Age for a scientist. We could wave the wand called "chemical communication" and pretend we understand it, but the problems of corruption and how to fix them have defied solution by the greatest minds of our time, so I say **be bold** and reach out for anything that might solve this perennial problem. Feel free to do much better than I can in this last section on solutions.

SOLUTIONS

At this point, good government types may cite a number of excellent ideas that have helped prior campaigns to combat corruption in governments and societies like: transparency of institutions and decision making processes, strict campaign finance laws (in democracies) and strict enforcement of those, free press with protections, a vigorous NGO sector (like Freedom House, Transparency International, or the Committee to Protect Journalists, all NGOs devoted to missions that include protecting those who expose corruption), protections for government or corporate whistleblowers, independent judiciary with enforcement of ethics codes, strong oversight institutions like IG offices (Inspectors General) that work at their ideal mission (e.g. rooting out corruption or unprofessional behaviors, not mere flak control units) and so forth and so on. These are all good ideas, excellent ideas, truly, but since they also always fail to root out the heart of corruptive processes, and since new corruptions are invented every day, I am going to focus on something at once ancient and extremely novel in academic prose today.

Most, if not all people appear to have souls, and what we do in this life has large consequences thereafter. If people with power and wealth actually believed this, our problems with corruption could be dramatically smaller. If ordinary people actually believed this, ordinary life would be gentler, kinder and a good deal less materialistic than we observe today. And if kings and presidents believed it there would be far fewer wars.

But of course, a great many professors and public intellectuals long ago dismissed the stories of churches as quaint, tribal tales backed by scant or no evidence as recognized by modern science. So as a scientist, I offer a scrap of data you may not have noticed from the evidence based world.

For 20 years the U.S. Army, then the Defense Intelligence Agency and finally the CIA sponsored teams of "remote viewers" as part of their more esoteric intelligence collection arsenal. They did not get involved without millions of dollars in testing by prestigious academic research units like the Stanford Research Institute. Brutally summarized, certain adept or highly trained individuals would sit in bland rooms at Fort Meade, Maryland (which also houses the super-secret National Security Agency) and receive 'targets' assigned by their commanders. Then they would go into something we will call a trance-like state, extend their minds far across the globe to watch and otherwise sense something forbidden by another state or clandestine group. I confirmed the existence of the program from none less than a former director of Central Intelligence, Admiral Stansfield Turner, who told me the evidence that most convinced him that this esoteric technique could actually work and was worth funding for so long.

But don't believe me, try reporter Jim Schnabel's 1997 book for an objective review. After that you might try reading any of several memoirs by some of the best remote viewers. For this discussion, I will cite in particular the 6 page chapter on "Afterlife" by Lyn Buchanan. Like any informant or commentator, you can believe, disbelieve, dissect or criticize any of his claims.

Focusing on the prime claim for this topic, Mr. Buchanan writes that he was tasked to follow at least 67 persons through the death transition for various reasons, and he was sobered by observing that there were 4 distinct outcomes. Some went to a place remarkably like stories of heaven (he could never stay, but he could watch for a short time before being ushered off by something like spirit guardians). Some went to a place remarkably like stories of hell (he never stayed there more than moments because the fear and dread he felt were horrific). A smaller fraction appeared to reincarnate, and the details of that are interesting. Another small fraction simply disappeared, or ended at the moment of death, with no sign of any afterlife at all.

Remembering that these were all "intelligence targets" of one kind or another, Buchanan does not speculate on what relationship people's lives had with these different outcomes, and he is quite frank about his religious upbringing and the limits on accuracy among remote viewers and on the whole process which was constantly monitored and measured, not least because some remote viewers were far more accurate than others. He had access to that data because he was one of the best, but still, this is just another human report about things that are very hard for other humans to experience directly (like the top of Mount Everest, or the bottom of the deep ocean).

So take this whole section as a simple encouragement to consider the possibility that afterlife might actually be a real phenomenon, that something like souls might actually exist, and that conduct on Earth might actually have consequences beyond the obvious. If the people driven to acquire large amounts of money or power truly believed this, corruption would be much less.

Some may note that many people have rejected stories of afterlife often, and that crime is eternal. True–that's why the good government rules and enforcement systems are also required.

Money and power seek each other out like teenagers in the night, and they seldom care much about rules imposed by elders. Corruption in government and business is as natural as nature and midnight liaisons, so combating corruption must necessarily be an endless process. I encourage considering and implementing all the good government methods, tools and laws that appear appropriate to particular national circumstances, but since the captains of industry and politics are also masters of circumventing mere rules, and rationalizing catastrophes thereafter, I also encourage a little rethinking about where you are actually going.

Mr. Buchanan was extremely impressed by "hell" and would do anything to avoid that.

One final note on hubris: very, very bright people (like you!) are regrettably prone to hubris, an originally Greek word that translates roughly into "overweening pride." Very powerful people are notorious for this, and very rich people have been known to indulge. In every sector hubris is extremely corrosive of wisdom and other good things. Corruption and hubris love each other. The very bright may come to think they know everything (even though what they don't know is billions of times greater than what they do) which effectively stops their learning processes. Hubris makes smart people dumb. The very powerful may come to believe they are invulnerable, which led to bromides like "pride goes before the fall." Hubris makes the powerful weak, and the very rich may come to believe that they can buy their way into heaven, a thought encouraged by certain churches that confuse themselves with the Creator of us All.

No matter the person or details, we all die in the end, and what happens next is not entirely up to us, no matter how smart, powerful or rich we may be. So be wary of hubris, and open to the possibilities of forms of spirituality appropriate to a global civilization of the Third Millennium after the birth of Jesus of Nazareth.

Feel 100% free to improve on my attempts in this direction, because we who have children or love children would like them to endure. You have probably noticed that our civilization is in trouble, so it is time for a transformation of our civilizational habits appropriate to a new age. Like butterflies emerging from caterpillars, we must transform, lest we decay and die from endlessly repeating errors of our past.

CONCLUSION

Civilizations are always at a "crossroads of history" of one kind or another, but the transition to the Third Millennium is especially rocky due to the convergence of explosive new technologies (the internet as much as weapons of mass destruction, although WMDs are special since only they could end our civilizations entirely) with the population growth that is already damaging our life support systems severely. Desperate people are prone to fighting over resources, people oppressed by corruption and systemic injustice are prone to fighting for freedom, and both have much to fight over today. The information revolution also makes the poor and dispossessed more aware of injustices today and sometimes more able to do something about that.

Finding and cultivating forms of spirituality that can promote global harmony instead of global war thus becomes a paramount task of our time. Feel free to do better than me, but I warn all to avoid the original sin of churches, which is to think that their way is the only way to "God" or to enlightenment. Thus begin the religious wars that torment prophets in their graves who devoted everything to teaching about peace, life, love and right relationships with the universe.

Other crises beckon that I have barely mentioned here. "Global warming" (or whatever term you prefer) is a symptom of the much larger assault on the living system that we are witnessing today, but doing almost nothing about. Loss of biodiversity is occurring on scales seen very rarely in the entire geologic history of the earth, and "peak oil" promises to make these problems more expensive much faster than we would prefer.

As noted so often, desperate people sometimes resort to desperate measures. Those don't help with problems like this, so I encourage all to heed the wisdom of sages from civilizations past to help create the better forms of both civilization and spirituality that can endure and even prosper in the world to come.

REFERENCES

Andregg, M. M. (1997, 1999, 2001). Corruption of governance. In *On the Causes of war* (Chapter 14). St. Paul, MN: Ground Zero Minnesota. Accessible at: www.gzmn.org

Buchanan, L. (2003). *The Seventh sense: the secrets of remote viewing as told by a "psychic spy" for the U.S. Military*. New York, NY: Paraview Pocket Books.

Gandhi, M. His seven deadly sins, or more accurately Seven Blunders of the World, is a list that he gave to his grandson Arun Gandhi on their final day together, shortly before his assassination on January 30, 1948. Arun added an eighth sin, "Rights without Responsibilities."

Miller, J. G. (1978). *Living systems*. New York, NY: McGraw-Hill.

Perkins, J. (2005). *Confessions of an economic hit man*. New York, NY: Plume Publishing.

Quigley, C. (1961). *The Evolution of civilizations: an introduction to historical analysis*, New York, NY: Macmillan.

Schnabel, J. (1997). *Remote viewers: the secret history of America's psychic spies*. New York, NY: Dell Publishing.

Shapiro, S. A. (2010). Testimony of August 3, before the Subcommittee on Administrative Oversight and the Courts of the U.S. Senate Committee on the Judiciary on "Protecting the Public Trust: Understanding the Threat of Agency Capture." Accessed on Feb. 28, 2012 at: http://www.progressivereform.org/articles/Shapiro_AgencyCapture_080310.pdf

Stewart, J. (2011). *Tangled webs: how the epidemic of lying is undermining America today*. New York, NY: Penguin Press.

Toynbee, A. J. (1947). *A Study of history*. Abridgement of Volumes 1-VI, by D.C. Somervell. London UK and New York, NY: Oxford University Press.

Toynbee, A. J. (1950). *War and civilizations*. Passages from Toynbee's "Study of history" selected by Albert V. Fowler. London UK and New York: Oxford University Press.

In: Spirituality and Civilization Sustainability … ISBN: 978-1-53610-729-6
Editors: Andrew Targowski and Marek J. Celinski

Chapter 19

TOYNBEE'S PERCEPTION OF DECLINING WESTERN VALUES

W. Reed Smith*
Jefferson Parish, Louisiana, US

ABSTRACT

This chapter presents a brief examination of Arnold Joseph Toynbee and his perception of declining Western values and the processes thereof. Toynbee's life is briefly discussed. The reader is then introduced to some of Toynbee's ideas on civilizations and the state of the Western Civilization in particular, including Toynbee's very well-developed concepts regarding the breakdown and disintegration of civilizations. Toynbee's later move toward contemplation of a world-wide Westernized civilization is discussed. It is simply too early to tell whether Toynbee's ideas on religion will pan out. The idea of syncretistic world spirituality does not seem to have any support aside from Western intellectuals. The reality continues to be that of religious or religion-inspired conflict, best exemplified by the 9/11 attacks and the Arab-Israeli conflict. In that vein, Samuel Huntington has challenged Toynbee's "Westernizing world" with his concept of the clash of civilizations, in which the still extant non-Western civilizations are modernizing but not Westernizing, and re-asserting themselves against the West.

INTRODUCTION

This chapter will present a discussion of Arnold Joseph Toynbee and his perception of declining Western values and the processes thereof. First, Toynbee's life will be discussed briefly. Then, the reader will be introduced to some of Toynbee's ideas on civilizations and the state of the Western Civilization in particular. Toynbee's later move toward contemplation of a world-wide Westernized civilization will be discussed. Finally, perhaps the most important, existential question facing the Western Civilization at present will be posed.

---

* E-mail: wrsmithjd@yahoo.com

A discussion in just a few pages of Arnold Toynbee's perception and understanding of declining Western values will by definition need to be severely truncated. Toynbee was extremely prolific: in addition to his twelve volume *A Study of History*[1] (the "*Study*"), he wrote dozens of other books and articles. Therefore, by necessity this chapter will barely scratch the surface of Toynbeean thought.

TOYNBEE'S LIFE

Arnold Joseph Toynbee was born April 14, 1889, in London, at the height of the British Empire. He came from an upper or upper middle class family, and his uncle and namesake was the economic historian Arnold Toynbee. Thus, presumably Toynbee was exposed to the academy from infancy on.

Toynbee was educated at Oxford, where he began teaching in 1912. He held various teaching positions throughout his life, including Director of Studies at the Royal Institute for International Affairs from approximately 1925 to 1955, during which period he edited the Institute's annual *Survey of International Affairs*.

Toynbee was also active in diplomacy. He attended both the 1919 Versailles Peace Conference and the Potsdam Conference after World War II.

In the 1940's and 50's Toynbee and his ideas enjoyed considerable popularity (and endured sometimes savage criticism). He was the subject of numerous articles in the press, and he appeared on the cover of *Time* magazine on March 17, 1947.

Toynbee died on October 22, 1975. Thus, his life spanned both World Wars, the decline and disintegration of the British Empire, and the unofficial transfer of power from London to Washington. In other terms, in one lifetime he saw the transition from horses to space flight and the moon landings, from gunpowder to thermonuclear bombs. Tellingly, the last thirty years of his life were the first thirty years of the Cold War, and the conflict between the West and the Soviet Union was a major pre-occupation of the later volumes of the *Study*.

TOYNBEE THE CIVILIZATIONIST

Toynbee championed the concept of *civilizations* as opposed to *civilization*: Toynbee believed that civilizations are regional, self-contained "intelligible fields of study".[2] The Western Civilization is the one exception. Toynbee believed that the Western Civilization has become world-wide. As a necessary condition of a world-wide West, he further believed that the non-Western world was not just modernizing; rather, the whole world was also Westernizing.

[1] Toynbee, A. J. (vols. 1-6 1939; vols. 7-10 1954; Vol. 11 1959; Vol. 12 1961). A study of history. London: Oxford University Press. Many of the footnotes to this chapter refer to the abridgement of Toynbee's Study (Abridgement) in two volumes by D. C. Somervell, for ease of reference. In the Preface to both volumes of the Somervell Abridgement, Toynbee acknowledged that he had read and approved the Abridgement and that the work should be considered his as well as Somervell's.

[2] Somervell, Study (Abridgement), Vol. 1, p. 35.

Toynbee identified twenty-one civilizations, although in his later years he admitted that there may have been more.[3] However, of the twenty-one civilizations identified by Toynbee, all are either dead or in a state of serious breakdown, except one: the West[4], which Toynbee also admitted was in distress if not breakdown. Toynbee was concerned exclusively with the study of high cultures or civilizations, and not primitive cultures, which are not included in his conception of civilizations.

According to Toynbee civilizations or societies come into existence as a result of "challenge and response"; in other words, when a "creative minority" offers a successful response to a problem confronting a region, a society emerges. For example, the challenge which gave rise to Western Civilization around 1000 A.D. was how to civilize and reach a *modus vivendi* with the Germanic barbarians who had invaded the Roman Empire. The problem was solved by the Roman Catholic Church, which civilized the barbarians by converting them to Christianity, which then became the basis of Western Civilization. (The term Western Civilization refers, originally, to Western or Latin Christianity as opposed to Byzantine Civilization and Eastern Orthodox Christianity, and not to any particular geographic region. Thus, Poland and the Baltic States are undeniably part of the West.)

Toynbee theorized that societies are driven by "mimesis", or imitation.[5] According to Toynbee, a society is led by a creative minority which produces the original successful response to the initial problem confronting the society. For a time the society exists on its success, but eventually another challenge arises. At that point in a healthy society either the same or a new creative minority arises and produces successive successful challenges to responses confronting the society. During these successful challenge-response cycles, the rest of the society follows the creative minority through the process of mimesis. In other words, as long as the creative minority is successful, everyone else is only too happy to follow: everyone else wants to *be in* the creative minority, and thus tries to imitate its manners, religion, clothing, etc.

When the creative minority's responses are no longer successful, societal breakdown occurs. The minority uses force rather than creativity to get the rest of the culture to follow it and thus becomes the dominant minority. The rest of the society becomes the oppressed "internal proletariat", and the barbarians outside the now fixed borders of the society become the excluded "external proletariat".

According to Toynbee the dominant minority can keep the genie in the bottle for only so long, normally in the guise of a "universal state" which rules the entire civilization (e.g. the Hellenic Civilization's universal state was the Roman Empire). Toynbee referred to the "coma of a universal state" which blinds the population with the "mirage of immortality".[6] The dominant minority may produce several responses which may appear to work and which may even lead to rallies in the society, such as occurred in the long history of the Roman

[3] Somervell, *Study* (Abridgement), Vol. 1, p. 34. Later Toynbee added two more civilizations for a total of twenty-three, but he admitted there may be more. See Huntington, Samuel, *The Clash of Civilizations*, p. 44; Toynbee, *A Study of History, The First Abridged One-Volume Edition* (Oxford University Press, U.S. American Heritage Press, New York 1973), pp.70-72.

[4] Mason, *Toynbee's Approach to World Politics*, pp. 81-82.

[5] See discussion Somervell, *Study* (Abridgement), Vol. 1 pp. 279-83.

[6] Somervell, *Study* (Abridgement), Vol. 1 p.532; Toynbee's reference to "the mirage of immortality" is mentioned by Huntington in *The Clash of Civilizations*, p. 301. In comparing the universal state to a coma, Toynbee echoed Oswald Spengler's concept of a Culture past its prime hardening into Civilization. See Spengler, *Decline of the West*, pp. 24-26.

Empire. However, unless the underlying challenge is successfully faced, each rally wears off, and as the challenge re-surfaces, a relapse occurs.

Eventually, oppression, the *taedium vitae*, and the inability of the society to solve the problem cause the internal proletariat to become despondent. Toynbee referred to the internal proletariat as being in, but not of, the society. The internal proletariat is too weak to overthrow the dominant minority, so the internal proletariat secedes from the society, often spiritually, which may produce a higher religion (e.g., the Hellenic Civilization's internal proletariat produced Christianity).

When the civilization and its power structure are unsupported by the masses, the dominant minority seeks allies from without. Normally the universal state fixes and defends its borders, which Toynbee called the *limes* after the Roman borders. Outside the *limes* are the barbarians, the external proletariat. The barbarians enter the stage first as hostages, then as mercenaries, and finally as raiders. Once the barbarians are allowed entry in any large numbers as mercenaries, they perceive the utter weakness of the society, leave to inform their fellows on the outside of the *limes*, and return as raiders. Eventually the raiders become powerful enough to overthrow the universal state and thus the civilization. Before that happens, however, something ominous occurs. The dominant minority begins more and more to adopt the manners (clothing, weapons, hairstyles, etc.) of the barbarians. As discussed below, Toynbee called this process "barbarization".

The barbarian successor states that then take over simply do not have the capacity to govern the universal state: Toynbee likened them to "the vultures feeding on the carrion or the maggots crawling on the carcass".[7] They are ephemeral and short-lived. However, the barbarians may well claim that they are the heirs of the universal state and may pretend to be continuing it in order to gain some semblance of legitimacy. Thus, consider, e.g., (1) the frescoes in North Africa of toga-clad Vandals eating grapes and drinking wine in the manner of Romans, the former owners of their villas, and (2) the German pre-occupation with the Holy *Roman* Empire. The result is an interregnum, usually a dark age, until a new society emerges.

It will be seen that the secession of the internal proletariat and the invasion of the barbarian external proletariat are two sides of the same coin, which is the internal disease of the society, which Toynbee called "some kind of spiritual breakdown".[8] The barbarians are essentially latecomers, that is, just an afterthought. The fact that they are allowed into the civilization at all is impossible without the underlying internal disease of the society.

It is also worth noting, in this age of nuclear proliferation, whereby non-Western developing countries are acquiring nuclear and other weapons of mass destruction such as biological and chemical weapons, along with the technologies that produce them, that Toynbee anticipated these phenomena in his discussions of the relations of barbarians with the civilization to which they are appended. He was particularly concerned with the transfer of military technology to the barbarians:

> [W]e may now... watch the barbarian make his first appearance on the stage as the dominant minority's apprentice; see the dominant minority begin to "go native"; ...and

[7] Somervell, *Study* (Abridgement), Vol. 1, p. 14.
[8] Somervell, *Study* (Abridgement), Vol. 1, p.259.

> finally watch the ci-devant dominant minority lose the last traces of its original form by sinking to meet the triumphant barbarian at a common level of unmitigated barbarism.[9]

In reading that passage one cannot help but remember that the technology that enabled the Japanese to defeat the Russians in 1905 and attack Pearl Harbor in 1941 had been taught to them by well-meaning Westerners, as was the nuclear technology that allowed Pakistan to produce the nuclear weapons it holds. Similarly, the West has either directly or indirectly educated the Iranian nuclear scientists who are on the verge of producing nuclear weapons, and the 9/11 terrorists were Arab students in the United States. Furthermore, the West has been only too eager to supply the developing world's almost insatiable hunger for modern weaponry. The spectacularly successful economies of China, India, and several other such countries are the direct result of transfers of Western know-how and the education of exchange students in the West.

The West has been incredibly short-sighted in this regard. Western leaders and intellectuals have utterly forgotten the maxim that "The road to Hell is paved with good intentions." In short, the West transfers its technology at its own peril.

PROCESSES OF DISINTEGRATION

> [O]f the three factions into which a disintegrating society is apt to split, it is the dominant minority that succumbs most readily to the sense of promiscuity, and the ultimate result of this proletarianization of the dominant minority is a disappearance of that schism in the body social which is the index and penalty of social breakdown. The dominant minority in the end atones for its sins by closing a breach that has been its own handiwork and merging itself in its own proletariats...
>
> [T]he course of this process of proletarianization [proceeds] along its two parallel lines—vulgarization by contact with the internal proletariat and barbarization by contact with the external proletariat....
>
> A. J. Toynbee: Somervell, Study (Abridgement) Vol. 1, p.456 (See explanation in endnote 1).

Perhaps the most interesting aspect of Toynbee was his application of his theories to Western Society. Toynbee was rather closed-lipped about exactly where he believed the West was in its development (or devolution). However, he did every now and again in his writing apply his principles to the West. I believe Toynbee was well aware of how far the disintegration of the West had progressed.

At present, some forty years after Toynbee stopped writing, the application his theories to the West is unsettling, to say the least.

---

[9] Somervell, *Study* (Abridgement), Vol. 1, p. 461.

Proletarianization

> In all cases of symbiosis between the dominant minority and the internal proletariat both parties are affected, and the effect on each of them is to set them in motion on a course which leads to an assimilation of the other class. On the superficial plane of 'manners' the internal proletariat moves towards enfranchisement and the dominant minority towards vulgarization. The two are complementary and both are taking place all the time; but, while it is the enfranchisement of the proletariat that is the more conspicuous in the earlier phases, in the later chapters it is the vulgarization of the dominant minority that forces itself on our attention.
>
> A. J. Toynbee: Somervell, *Study* (Abridgement) Vol. 1, p.458.

To use the United States (the core state [according to S. Huntington] of the Western Civilization at present and arguably its universal state [according to Toynbee]) as an example of the process described in foregoing quote, it will be seen that the lower classes have been steadily enfranchised over the course of the history of the Republic. At its inception only white, male landowners could vote. First non-landowners, then blacks, then women could vote. Suffrage is now so universal that some object to the requirement that a picture identification be shown before a person is allowed to cast his vote.

Also, in the larger sense, the lower classes have been enfranchised by compulsory public education, labor laws, the welfare state, anti-discrimination laws in housing and public accommodations, etc.

However, what of Toynbee's rather ominous thought that in the later stages (of disintegration) it is the vulgarization of the dominant minority—the upper classes—that becomes obvious? If the vulgarization or proletarianization of the dominant minority is in full swing, then according to Toynbee we should be in the later stages of the disintegration of Western Civilization.

Rampant pornography, illegitimacy, foul language in public discourse, etc., are all examples of what Toynbee would call increasing vulgarization or proletarianization[10] in society, which he opined would increase in the disintegration stage of civilization. Such proletarianization is the effect of the increased influence of the lowest classes (Toynbee's internal proletariat[11]) on the culture.

This trend in the West is depressingly obvious; if the reader has any doubts, simply look at a movie from the 1940's or 1950's and compare the number of curse words and nude sex scenes in it with a similar movie today. Or make a similar comparison of advertisements. Or compare the sheer volume of pornographic materials available in 1950 and at present.

Proletarianization now reaches the highest levels of Western Society. In March 2010, U.S. Vice President Joe Biden introduced President Obama at the White House signing of Obama's Healthcare legislation. Unaware that the microphone was on, Biden told Obama "This is a big f__king deal!"[12] Former Vice President Dick Cheney[13] and convicted former

---

[10] Somervell, *Study* (Abridgement), Vol. 1, p. 455 et seq. Toynbee treated vulgarization/proletarianization and barbarism as subparts of promiscuity; I have separated them to a certain extent for purposes of this chapter.

[11] Somervell, *Study* (Abridgement), Vol. 1, p. 375 et seq.

[12] abcnews.go.com, March 24, 2010, "Was Joe Biden's Swear a Big Deal?"

[13] www.washingtonpost.com, June 25, 2004,Helen Dewar and Dana Milbank, "Cheney Dismisses Critic with Obscenity".

Governor of Illinois Ron Blagojevich[14] are guilty of similar obscene remarks. A few decades ago, such speech was confined to only the lowest levels of society.

About a year ago on my commute home from work I heard a local radio talk show host[15] opine that porn star Jenna Jameson's father must be very proud of her because of the millions of dollars that she has amassed. The radio host would not be persuaded otherwise. Such are the effects of proletarianization.

Of course, in the context of proletarianization Toynbee was referring to vulgarity and vulgarization in the original Latin sense, which simply means "common" and does not necessarily entail obscenity. Thus, vulgarization/ proletarianization also applies to fashion (and art, language, religion, etc.). Perhaps the most obvious "gift" of the United States to the world has been the American teenagers' uniform—blue jeans and t-shirt—which also happens to be nothing more than common laborers' clothing (i.e. dungarees and an undershirt). Compare the popular garb sixty years ago: when in public, ladies wore white gloves and skirts and gentlemen wore suits and ties.

Perhaps the best way to understand proletarianization is on the macro level. The overthrow or suppression of the power of first the monarchy, then the hereditary aristocracy, and concurrent rise of commercial interests is most clearly visible in the history of England. It is also the history of Rome, in both Toynbee's view and that of his predecessor, Oswald Spengler.

Toynbee believed that the Roman Empire's inception was the triumph of the commercial interests or middle class over the traditional aristocracy (the Senatorial class). For the next four or five hundred years, the emperors tried to maintain the supremacy over the lower classes, or internal proletariat, by means of bread and circuses (*panem et circenses*), for example. However, eventually the lower classes prevailed by means of their spiritual secession, i.e. the adoption of the passive Christian faith. In 313 A.D. the Emperor Constantine famously adopted Christianity as the Roman state religion, and the handwriting was on the wall as to the fate of the Hellenic Civilization.

Today in the West, a similar process is taking place. The monarchs and nobility of Europe (and even the plantation owners of the American South) have been overthrown or at least have had any real power suppressed by the commercial interests. Those commercial interests, now in the guise of conservative political parties, are having an increasingly difficult time keeping the socialists and labor unions in check, despite massive welfare states in which even the poorest people have access to practically limitless food, the latest consumer goods, health care, and housing. The masses receiving government assistance of one sort or another continue to grow, and the democratically elected governments of the West are powerless to do anything about it.

Remember, in broken down and disintegrating societies, the problem is a "some kind of spiritual breakdown". That breakdown is perhaps best described by the phenomenon of the upper classes (both the financial interests and what is left of the aristocracy) taking on the manners of the proletariat.

---

[14] www.huffingtonpost.com, Janan Hanna, June 24, 2010, "Blagojevich Tapes Played in Court: Ex Gov Irked by 'Thankful' Message from Obama Aide".

[15] The said comments were made by John Osterlind, WRNO, 99.5 FM, approximately April 20, 2011.

Barbarization

> The fatuousness of the 'chocolate box' style is so desolating that it has provoked our own generation into attempting desperate remedies. Our archaistic flight from vulgarity into pre-Raphaelite Byzantinism is discussed in a later chapter, but in this place we have to take note of the contemporary and alternative flight into barbarism. Self-respecting Western sculptors of to-day who have not found a congenial asylum in Byzantium have turned their eyes toward Benin; and it is not only in the glyptic branch of art that a Western World whose resources of creativeness have apparently run dry has been seeking fresh inspiration from the barbarians of West Africa. West African music and dancing, as well as West African sculpture, have been imported, via America, into the heart of Europe.
>
> A. J. Toynbee: Somervell, Study (Abridgement) Vol. 1, p. 466.

To Toynbee, closely related to proletarianization is increasing barbarization[16] in the disintegration stage. Barbarization (or barbarism) can be defined as the dominant minority's (and internal proletariat's) acceptance of the primitive and often violent habits and customs of foreign barbarians (Toynbee's external proletariat[17]) who clamor for entrance into a civilization during its disintegration stage. The archetypical barbarians were the principally Germanic tribes that toppled the West Roman Empire in the Fourth and Fifth Century A.D. The modern analogy is the huge migration of non-Western masses who have been allowed to come into Western Civilization in the last fifty to sixty years. Increasing barbarization is the acceptance of the manners and customs of barbarians by the population of a civilization, which presupposes that large numbers of barbarians have been allowed into the civilization.

Writing some seventy years ago, Toynbee pointed to West African art and jazz music as an example of a barbarian influence on the West.[18] Other examples today are just as obvious: tattoos, nose rings and body piercing are all barbarian or foreign practices now popular among the general public in the West, particularly the youth. In particular, in Western Culture tattoos were once confined to common seamen; an officer would never dream of getting a tattoo. Visit a university now and you will soon lose count of the visible tattoos on display on students of both sexes.

Also interesting in this regard are the rather contradictory comments made by Bundeskanzler Angela Merkel on or about October 17, 2010, that in Germany "the approach [to build] a multicultural [society]... has failed, utterly failed", but that immigrants are nevertheless welcome in Germany.[19] Ms. Merkel also cited recent comments by German President Christian Wulff that Islam is "part of Germany", which in terms of historical accuracy is a clearly false assertion brought on by a perceived political need to accept the millions of Islamic foreigners in Germany as a *fait accompli.*

Similarly, the present rise of nationalist, "anti-immigrant" parties in Europe is nothing more than a reaction to the massive influx of non-Western, mostly non-Christian foreigners and is certainly not due to some mysterious, base evil inherent in the anti-immigrant parties and the millions of people who support them. In other words, elements of the European

16 Somervell, *Study* (Abridgement), Vol. 1, p. 455 et seq.
17 Somervell, *Study* (Abridgement), Vol. 1, p. 403 et seq.
18 Somervell, *Study* (Abridgement), Vol. 1, p. 460, 466.
19 www.bbc.co.uk October 17, 2010, "Merkel says German multiculturalism has failed".

population are resisting the tendency toward increasing barbarism. This trend of resistance, although unpleasant and even disturbing in certain respects, is an indication of not of weakness but of some level of vitality of Western Culture.

In fact, Toynbee specifically discussed the fact that at about the middle of the Fourth Century A.D., the Germans in the service of Rome began to retain their German names and not take Roman ones, as they had previously done. In much the same way, many foreign immigrants to the West today keep their own names, religions, and customs in the name of multiculturalism and diversity (and as another example, many American blacks simply make up African- sounding names, invent fashions, speak their own dialect, and/or even become Muslim, all in an effort to define themselves as distinctively black). As Toynbee put it:

> This new insistence on their cultural individuality did not evoke on the Romans' part any counter-demonstration of anti-barbarian exclusiveness. So far from that, the barbarians in the Roman service began, at this very time, to be appointed to the consulship, which was the highest honor that the Emperor had to bestow.[20]

In other words, the Romans were too far gone to preserve themselves or the Hellenic Civilization. Obviously, judging from the reaction the multiculturalists would have if someone were to call for, say, all immigrants to take Western names, wear Western clothes, and adopt Christianity, the West is in at least the same stage of disintegration as the Fourth Century Romans. About a century later the inverse trend began: the Romans began taking barbarian names. By the time of Charlemagne everyone of note in Gaul, for example, had a German name.

Promiscuity

> A sense of promiscuity is a passive substitute for that sense of style which develops pari passu with the growth of a civilization. This state of mind takes practical effect in an act of self-surrender to the melting-pot; and in the process of social disintegration an identical mood manifests itself in every province of social life: in religion and literature and language and art, as well as in the wider and vaguer field of 'manners and customs'.
>
> A. J. Toynbee: Somervell, Study (Abridgement) Vol. 1, p. 455.

According to Toynbee, the disintegration stage of a civilization is also characterized by an increasing sense of "promiscuity"[21], which is related to both proletarianization and barbarism. Promiscuity can be defined as the willingness of the upper class (Toynbee's "dominant minority") to accept the manners and customs of and mix with other classes within and without the civilization.

The wedding of William, Prince of Wales, and Kate Middleton, a commoner, was held on April 29, 2011. William's choice of a mate is a classic example of promiscuity of manners in the literal sense. Promiscuity has been a problem for modern royal families since Edward VII married Wallis Simpson and the deposed Crown Prince of Germany became a supporter of an Austrian corporal, Adolf Hitler.

---

[20] Somervell, *Study* (Abridgement), Vol. 1, p. 463.

[21] Somervell, *Study* (Abridgement), Vol. 1, p. 455 et seq.

Promiscuity also applies to religion. For example, post-Vatican II Catholicism celebrates the Mass in vulgar languages and in unadorned, Protestant-style churches, and the Popes have had numerous meetings with the leaders of other faiths, in the name of ecumenism. Furthermore, in America the Lutheran and Episcopal Churches have essentially merged.[22]

But promiscuity operates on every level. The miscegenation rate has skyrocketed since the 1960's. Far from being shunned, mixed race individuals are celebrated, particularly in advertisements. Immigration--legal and illegal--shows no sign of abating. One can even eat a "Southwestern egg roll" while listening to "Afro-Celtic" music.

I would be remiss if I did not mention the best example of proletarianization, barbarism and promiscuity all rolled into one human being: President Obama. The product of literal promiscuity, Obama's mother was a white American leftist and his father was a non-Western, Kenyan communist.

From a young age he has allied himself with the Left and with the poorest elements of American society. Internet theorists question whether he is really a Western Christian or a Moslem, and the "birther" movement believes he was not born in the U.S., thus rendering him constitutionally unqualified to be president. Even members of Obama's own party (Sen. Harry Reid and the man who would become Obama's Vice-President, Joe Biden), not to mention then-President Bush, quipped that Obama was electable because is articulate or he can speak without a black accent[23], which--along with the fact that he is half-Caucasian--made him acceptable to white voters.

Thus, Obama is a figure who can only exist in the disintegration stage of a civilization. Obama's counterparts in Rome were Germanic barbarian or semi-barbarian generals like Stilicho, Martius Aetius, and Odoacer, the man who deposed the last West Roman emperor and set himself up as ruler of Italy, in violation of the Roman constitution.

Furthermore, consider also the juxtaposition of Obama and his Republican rivals. In 2008 Obama faced and defeated Sen. John McCain, a white, aging Vietnam War veteran, partially crippled, who was portrayed in the press as old, tired, and having no new ideas. Obama's rival in 2012 was Mitt Romney, a spectacularly successful businessman, white, who was portrayed in the media as stiff, out of touch with "the common man", and, once again, devoid of new ideas. Whether any of these characterizations are true or not is irrelevant. The point is that Obama is portrayed as "cool", young, vigorous, well-spoken, and intelligent; his motto is "Hope and Change".

I do not wish to argue for or against President Obama or any of his rivals. The intention here is to highlight the radically changing sentiments of the people of the Western Civilization with regard to a black man, half-foreign, and probably nominally Christian at best. There is no question that the rise and popularity of Obama is a demonstration of Toynbee's proletarianization, barbarization, and promiscuity at work.

---

[22] Stammer, L. B. (July 19, 1997). Episcopal, Lutheran accord heralds new era of worship. Retrieved April 14, 2009, from http://articles.latimes.com/p/1997/jul/19/news/mn 14267.

[23] Sen. Harry Reid's comments that Obama is "light-skinned" and has "no Negro dialect" are discussed in voices.washingtonpost.com, "The Fix", by Chris Cillizza, January 9, 2010; then-Senator Joe Biden called Obama "articulate" and "clean", while President Bush deemed him "articulate": www.usatoday.com, January 31, 2007, Fredereka Schrouten, "Biden burned by 'clean' language".

Toynbee's Shift

Volumes I –VI of Toynbee's Study were published in the 1930's, prior to World War II but during the period of the Nazis. Toynbee wrote from the highest echelons of British Society, from the Royal Institute for International Affairs, at the very center of the British Empire, which was then still perceived as the most powerful state on earth.

World War II changed all that. Although the U.K. was nominally a victor, in real terms the War was a catastrophe for her. At the end of the War the real power as the leader of the West undeniably shifted to Washington, Britain's former colony, and within a very few years the British Empire disintegrated almost entirely. When in the late 1940's the West became locked in the life and death struggle with the Soviet Union, Britain was a second rate power that relied on the U.S. for protection.

Furthermore, World War II had produced a technological revolution. When the War started, the combatants still used horses on the battlefield. It progressed with radar and strategic bombings, including fire bombings, of cities. The War ended with the use of long distance rockets, jet engines, and of course, atomic bombs. Furthermore, the intentional, workmanlike extermination of millions of civilians brought into intense focus the terrible possibilities of industrial society.

All these influences had a profound effect on Western intellectuals. In Toynbee's case, there was a marked shift in his thought in Volumes VI-XII of the *Study*: his outlook became less Western and more cosmopolitan or world-wide. Toynbee was famously optimistic, but in a sense, his writing became more forlorn. He abandoned the idea that civilizations produce higher religions; Toynbee eventually came to believe that the higher religions created civilizations around them instead of the other way around.

Toynbee said that he wrote Volumes VI-X of the *Study* from "the Indian standpoint"[24]. He concentrated on the Cold War "world situation" and proposed a solution through the development of a new world spirituality built on mutual tolerance and respect among the higher religions: Christianity, Islam, Hinduism, and Buddhism. Thus, he emphasized a unified world, which he assumed would be "Westernized".[25]

This emphasis was a real departure from Toynbee's earlier writing, but one might argue that the shift to the world-wide viewpoint was the inevitable, inescapable result of the fact of the (Anglo-American) West's dominance of the entire planet other than the Soviet Union after World War II. Toynbee believed that even Soviet communism was a Western political movement which was paradoxically being used by the Russian offshoot of the Orthodox Christian Society to oppose the West. Thus, the West had become the only civilization ever to dominate the entire planet. One could now travel by jet plane around the whole world in a day. There were hundreds of millions of non-Westerners being ruled by the West, many of whom had religions and civilizations far older than those of the West. How could the West (and the world) survive in any manner, without becoming the totalitarian Nazis who had just been defeated in the most destructive war in history? Toynbee answered that question with his call for a world-wide spirituality and mutual respect among the higher religions.

---

[24] Mason, H. *Toynbee's Approach to World Politics*, p. 92, New Orleans: Tulane (1958); citing A. Montagu, ed., *Toynbee and History: Critical Essays and Reviews* (Boston 1956), p. 7.

[25] See for example Somervell, *Study* (Abridgement), Vol. 1, p. 414, 418, 516.

Keep in mind that Toynbee considered ideological conflict to be a problem akin to religious conflicts, which could be overcome only by tolerance and compromise, and not by force of arms.[26] Furthermore, he considered nationalism and the worship of nation-states to be a form of idolatry which would require an unprecedented moral response if Western Civilization is to survive.[27] The imposition of a traditional universal state would be *a priori* insufficient to solve the problem, as by definition the universal state is imposed by force by the dominant minority only after the breakdown of the civilization.[28] Toynbee theorized that another solution was possible: that of an (admittedly vague) "fresh and unprecedented spiritual advance"[29]. Such a spiritual advance would lead to a syncretistic understanding between the higher religions, which would produce a sort of voluntary ecumenical state[30] based on "multiplicity in unity".[31] Toynbee never defines this term, but he uses some examples to indicate what he means: The medieval Respublica Christiana, the Ottoman Millet System, and to a certain extent, some aspects of the Roman Empire.

Obviously, Toynbee's religious aspirations are far beyond the realm of possibility for the four higher religions at this time. Furthermore, Toynbee is really grasping at straws when he proposes his religious solution: he is internally inconsistent. For example, of his three at least partial models for "multiplicity in unity", two (the Ottoman Empire and Rome) were universal states, and the third (medieval Christianity) aspired to be. Also, as noted above, Toynbee himself discussed at length that in the disintegration stage of civilization, through promiscuity there is increasing syncretism in religion[32]; yet now Toynbee proposes that very syncretism as a solution to the problems facing the West and the world.

Furthermore, for all his supposed optimism, one might argue that Toynbee only emphasized the "Indian standpoint" after World War II, i.e., after it was obvious that the West was in such dire straits. Of course, an even more cynical view is that Toynbee's shift was an attempt to lay a groundwork for appeasement and co-operation with non-Western peoples, such as the Indians, Chinese, and Africans, in the Cold War struggle against the Soviet Union. Still, his call for a global spirituality was far ahead of its time when he wrote in the 1950's.

CONCLUSION

It is simply too early to tell whether Toynbee's ideas on religion will pan out. The idea of a syncretistic world spirituality does not seem to have any support aside from Western intellectuals. The reality continues to be that of religious or religion-inspired conflict, best exemplified by the 9/11 attacks and the Arab-Israeli conflict. In that vein, Samuel Huntington has challenged Toynbee's "Westernizing world" with his concept of the clash of civilizations, in which the still extant non-Western civilizations are modernizing but not Westernizing, and are re-asserting themselves against the West.[33]. Thus, the question arises: What is the Western Civilization today? Or to be more exact, what are its boundaries? Is the West the white

[26] Mason, *Toynbee's Approach to World Politics*, p.108.
[27] Ibid., pp.56-57
[28] Ibid., pp. 81-82.
[29] Toynbee, Study, Vol. IX, p. 344.
[30] Mason, *Toynbee's Approach to World Politics,* p. 83.
[31] See discussion in Mason, *Toynbee's Approach to World Politics,* pp. 86-92.
[32] Somervell, Study (Abridgement), Vol. 1, P. 473-482.
[33] Huntington, *The Clash of Civilizations*, pp. 56-78.

continents of Europe east to Belarus and part of the Ukraine, Australia, North America, perhaps South America, and a few outposts here and there? Or is the West now truly the entire world, as Toynbee posited? In other words, is the West truly a global civilization, as Westerners sometimes seem to act as though it is, or are Western intellectuals just pretending, with too much hubris? The way the reader answers those questions depends in large part on whether the reader favors the early Toynbee who analyzed the decline of Western values, or the later Toynbee, who called for the global spirituality. Toynbee was truly an optimist, and stubbornly so, in at least one sense. He adamantly stated that he was not a prophet, that no one can foretell the future, and, *contra* Spengler, that there is no guarantee that the West or any living civilization would come to an end.

According to Toynbee, however unlikely it might be, a civilization can regenerate itself through a successful response to the challenges facing it at any point. Only time will tell if the West will survive. However, one thing is certainly working in the West's favor: Thanks to Toynbee, the modern West has the capacity for self-awareness; we can reflect on our present predicament and contemplate our own survival. Whether the politicians and the general public choose to do so is another question.

Toynbee is relevant for one final reason: himself. Toynbee was a classical scholar of the Victorian type. A professor and career diplomat, he was comfortable in Latin and Greek; and while he was accused of being pedantic, his writing is somehow scholarly but still readable.[34] He was also a member of a dying breed: he was an English gentleman in the sense that he was very genteel, even with his critics, a bulwark of courtesy and refinement against the very vulgarity and barbarism that he prophesied.

REFERENCES

Huntington, S. P. (1996). The clash of civilizations and the remaking of world order. New York: Simon and Schuster.

Mason, H. (1958). Toynbee's approach to world politics. New Orleans: Tulane (1958)

Somervell, D.C. (1946 & 1957). A study of history (Abridgement). New York and London: Oxford University Press, (Vol. I-VI: 1946; Vol. VII-X: 1957).

Spengler, O. (1926). The decline of the west. Vol.1. English trans. Atkinson, C. F. (1926). New York: Alfred A. Knopf. Originally published (1918) as Der Untergang des Abendlandes, Gestalt und Wirklichkeit. Munich: C. H. Beck'sche Verlagsbuchhandlung. Vol. 2. English Trans. Atkinson, C. F. (1928). New York: Knopf. Originally published (1922) as Der Untergang des Abendlandes, Welthistorische Perspektiven. Munich: C. H. Beck. One-Volume ed. published (1932) New York: Knopf.

Toynbee, A. J. (1972). A study of history, the first abridged one-volume edition. Oxford University Press; New York: U.S. American Heritage Press (1972).

Toynbee, A. J. (vols. 1-6 1939; vols. 7-10 1954; Vol. 11 1959; Vol. 12 1961). A study of history. London: Oxford University Press.

[34] Despite his penchant for the unnecessary use of the past perfect tense.

In: Spirituality and Civilization Sustainability … ISBN: 978-1-53610-729-6
Editors: Andrew Targowski and Marek J. Celinski

Chapter 20

REVIVING BUSINESS ETHICS FOR SUSTAINABLE CIVILIZATION IN THE 21ST CENTURY

Elaine E. Englehardt*
Utah Valley University, Orem, UT, US

ABSTRACT

This chapter examines the view that businesses have an ethical responsibility to promote sustainability, not just economic profit. It discusses the possibility of businesses being committed seriously to values that support sustainability for future generations, while at the same time carefully pursuing profitable ends. Some businesses merely give "lip service, or web service" in pledging their commitment to such values, but true commitment is not reflected in their daily practices. Finally, the paper addresses questions about the relationship between sustainability and spiritual and religious values. When sustainability is approached from a spiritual perspective, it can be embedded both within a personal or an organizational ethic. The earth and her resources can be seen as family members to be protected and sustained for posterity. Religions can give support to such spiritual views by explaining to members the importance of caring for and loving one another. Insofar as businesses operates with a mission that respects sustainable development should review its action plans often and carefully and implement them daily.

INTRODUCTION

Defining Sustainability

The words *sustainable* and *development* are both necessary in order to define our need to address serious ethical challenges for business regarding the present and future. This is not merely a local concern, but a national and global matter. The United Nations has been addressing sustainable development for more than 25 years. It states: "Sustainable

* E-mail: elainee@uvu.edu

development is the development that meets the needs of the present without compromising the ability of future generations to meet their own needs" (United Nations World Commission on Environment and Development, 1987, p. 43). On a national level, the Environmental Protection Agency (EPA) bases its principle of sustainability as:

> "Everything that we need for our survival and well-being depends, either directly or indirectly, on our natural environment. Sustainability creates and maintains the conditions under which humans and nature can exist in productive harmony, that permit fulfilling the social, economic and other requirements of present and future generations. Sustainability is important to making sure that we have and will continue to have, the water, materials, and resources to protect human health and our environment." (United States Environmental Protection Agency)

Questionable Commitment to Sustainability

Numerous scholars and organizations agree with the basic definitions provided by the UN and the EPA. This paper examines the view that businesses have an ethical responsibility to promote sustainability, not just economic profit. It discusses the possibility of businesses being committed seriously to values that support sustainability for future generations, while at the same time carefully pursuing profitable ends. Some businesses merely give "lip service, or web service" in pledging their commitment to such values, but true commitment is not reflected in their daily practices. Finally, the paper addresses questions about the relationship between sustainability and spiritual and religious values.

Some businesses take these challenges seriously, but with mixed results. For example CVS prides itself in being a socially and environmentally responsible corporate citizen. It has a corporate website devoted to proper disposal of chemicals and other hazardous material (CVC Environmental, 2010).

Additionally, in its 2010 Corporate Social Responsibility Report, "Innovation, Leadership, Commitment," CVS details significant investments in programs in sustainability. Sustainability includes corporate social responsibility for CVS, so their mission statement not only discusses environmental features, it also includes providing free flu shots to people in need, investing in disaster relief and supporting people with disabilities (CVC Environmental, 2010). In addition to the environmental web site, CVS adopted a long-term target to reduce carbon emissions to show a commitment to environmental stewardship. However, on November 24, 2010, CVS paid nearly $270,000 in penalties for improperly dumping photo-processing chemicals and drugs into wastewater at many of its nearly 140 stores in Connecticut. According to Department of Environmental Protection Commissioner Amey Marrella:

> "This case shows the importance of monitoring compliance with laws designed to protect natural resources and the public health. CVS simply failed to ensure the proper handling of wastewater from processing photos and failed to ensure the proper and safe disposal of pharmaceutical products. The company is now taking steps to change its business practices and come into compliance with the law." (qtd. in Dumped, 2010)

The Connecticut Department of Environmental Protection announced that the Woonsocket, Rhode Island-based CVS and its subsidiary, Connecticut CVS Pharmacy LLC, agreed to a settlement that includes paying $223,900 to the state's General Fund and $45,000 to a project to study ways to reduce storm water in sewer systems in Bridgeport and New Haven. The company also agreed to make improvements in its environmental practices (Dumped, 2010). It appears that the problems didn't stop in 2010. On April 19, 2012, CVS was ordered to pay $14 million to different government entities in California for mishandling the disposal of photo chemicals and drugs (Settlement, 2012).

It took very little to taint the work and reputation of this organization, and very little effort was shown on the part of individuals hired to care for and properly dispose of chemicals and drugs for the giant firm. Strangely, CVS has not updated its on-line corporate responsibility statement online since 2010, even with a mention of an impending 2011 update. However, in 2010 it implemented a "CVS Caremark Environmental and Climate Change Policy" available to define priorities in this area for the corporation:

> "The link between human health and the health of our planet is becoming increasingly apparent. As a company dedicated to improving people's lives through innovative and high-quality health and pharmacy services, we are committed to operating in a manner that meets or exceeds applicable environmental regulations; reduces our environmental and climate- related impacts; and contributes to the long-term sustainability of our business. CVS Caremark's enterprise-wide environmental strategy, goals and quantifiable targets are established and overseen by senior leaders who comprise our Environmental Leadership Council, and, as appropriate, are reviewed by the company's CEO for approval. The process for developing our strategy, goals and targets involves engagement with colleagues from across the enterprise and third-party environmental experts." (CVS Caremark, 2012).

Did priorities change for this firm between the posting of environmental and social responsibility policies and the chemical mishandling problems? Did proper care for disposal of toxins into the environment become less important? Many businesses and individuals like CVS have the goal of adopting and implementing a full plan for a sustainable civilization within the next twenty years. However, the focus of this paper extends beyond this to include the entire 21st century. Will a sustainable civilization be possible in this century?

Milton Friedman's Warning on Socialism with Sustainability

Support for sustainability in its many forms is practiced by students in K–12 and is a movement at many colleges and universities. States, cities, towns and counties have programs for sustainability. Many businesses proclaim their sensitivity to various concerns about sustainability. However, in some circles, practices supporting sustainability are seemingly regarded as unnecessary, reactionary, and even "socialistic." The words of Nobel Prize winning economist Milton Friedman often haunt the discussions of business, sustainability and ethics. Friedman, a main force behind the Chicago School of economics sternly proclaimed:

> "The businessmen believe that they are defending free enterprise when they declaim that business is not concerned 'merely' with profit but also with promoting desirable 'social' ends; that business has a 'social conscience' and takes seriously its responsibilities for providing employment, eliminating discrimination, avoiding pollution and whatever else may be the catchwords of the contemporary crop of reformers. In fact they are - or would be if they or anyone else took them seriously - preaching pure and unadulterated socialism. Businessmen who talk this way are unwitting puppets of the intellectual forces that have been undermining the basis of a free society these past decades." (Friedman, 1970, pp. 122-26)

In this '70s statement, Friedman particularly denies that "avoiding pollution" is a special responsibility of corporations. Friedman and his supporters will not move from the position that a corporate manager is an agent of the stockholders and any diversion of resources from the task of maximizing stockholder wealth amounts to spending the stockholder's money without their consent. He further argues that government, and perhaps religions, are the institutions best suited for solving social problems. Business, according to Friedman, is not well suited to solve social problems. In practice, however, many businesses find extreme difficulty in drawing a line between spending the stockholder's money for charity and spending it in the "enlightened self-interest" of the firm.

Friedman does not consider the possibility that business activity may at times injure others and that it may be necessary to regulate the social consequences of one's business activities to consider the needs of the community, particularly in the area of sustainability. These needs will include economic gain, but there are also needs for sustainability, safety, spirituality, and cooperation.

Government, community, education, and religion cannot effectively tackle problems of pollution and sustainability without the assistance of socially responsible businesses. Businesses need to acknowledge that they have an obligation to help solve some of the problems of the society. First, to at least some extent, they bear some responsibility for causing these problems. Second, their very existence depends on support from the communities in which they reside. Third, especially given the first two factors, it seems reasonable expect them to reciprocate as good citizens. Awareness of the need for sustainability should exist in an organization's interactions with its employees, customers, suppliers, owners, creditors, government associations, religions, and cultural and societal institutions that support and inform the organization. Business as an institution exists primarily because it is sanctioned by these many forms of society.

Friedman's views aside, much progress in sustainability has been made in various businesses, government sectors, communities and religions. However, advocates understand the need to habitually practice and remind others of the principles of sustainability. In the political climate of 2012, Friedman's views seem to be as popular in some circles as they were in 1970 when he wrote his essay. Some politicians believe government has no business telling business to be involved in sustainable practices; seemingly, for them, business profits come before the ethics of sustainability.

REQUIRING AN ETHICS OF NO HARM IN PROFIT-MAKING

Should business profits come before the ethics of sustainability? Organizations can fulfill their profit-making function; however, in doing so they should always minimize social injury. We should be able to devise laws or even social programs that minimize the injury that citizens will suffer at the expense of those who question the importance of ideas of sustainability. Decency may be expected, but justice, in the minimal sense of not injuring others, can be required of all. Certainly, it is difficult to devise laws that legislate showing continual love and kindness to one another. Reasons why certain corporations or organizations will not, or should not, be required to pursue sustainability or even moral good in all situations may exist. However, it is difficult to find reasons why these same institutions should be excused from injuring others, particularly in creating a sustainable present and future. H. L. A. Hart and A. M. Honoré (1959) find that we are equally obligated to avoid or correct any social injury.

In the moral judgments of ordinary life, we have occasion to blame people because they have caused harm to others, and also, if less frequently, to insist that morally they are bound to compensate those to whom they have caused harm (Hart & Honoré,1959).

Within comparative ethics, there are no societies exempt from the imperative against harming others. The specific form or harm or social injury may differ, as well as the method of rectification; nevertheless, the requirement is in place. Philosopher Holmes Rolston III notes:

Ethics in the modern West has been almost entirely interhuman ethics, persons finding a way to relate morally to other persons—loving our neighbors. Ethics seeks to find a satisfactory fit for humans in their communities; and this has meant that ethics has often dwelt on justice, fairness, love, rights, or peace, settling the disputes of right and wrong that arise among us. But ethics now is anxious about the troubled planet, its fauna, flora, species and ecosystems. (2012, p.14)

Rolston's case for love and fairness is laudatory. However, the case for sustainability could be made merely within the imperative to avoid harm. Certainly notions of the public good and the values that we actively seek to implement are subject to great disagreement. This may result in moral pluralism, which most of us would regard as healthy debate. However, we may be able to establish grounds for a social injury caused by years of harm to an environment that belongs to all of us. Corporations may bristle at this imperative, but the global demand to refrain from harming the environment has been in the making for many years.

UN SOCIAL CONTRACT FOR SUSTAINABLE DEVELOPMENT

In 1992 the United Nations Conference on Environment and Development (UNCED) assembled more than 40,000 individuals to form a social contract for sustainable development. This group included delegations from 178 nations—virtually every nation in the world. There were 118 heads of state and government ready to sign an agreement. The request was to foster sustainable development (Rolston, 2012, p. 7). The agreement promised continued growth or development, but in a way that sustains opportunities for the future. Over 150 nations endorsed sustainable development.

In 2005, the United Nations World Summit Outcome Document asked for the "three components of sustainable development—economic development, social development and environmental protection—as interdependent and mutually reinforcing pillars" ("World Economic Situation," 2005, p. 12). These interdependent pillars bring different meaning to developing nations than they do to developed nations. Businesses in developing nations may term sustainability as survivability, while developed nations understand well what sustains their economic practices and how these can conflict with sustaining environmental protections.

This sustainable development debate asks governments and societies to consider how they can best manage their resources. The difficulty of determining levels of sustainability center on effective pricing of our important natural resources: the air we breathe the climate that sustains us, the water we drink, the rivers and oceans that provide food for us. The World Business Council for Sustainable Development (WBCSD) utilizes the term eco-efficiency in asking members to think clearly about sustainable development in terms of economic development, social development and environmental protection. They believe that "eco-efficiency is reached by the delivery of competitively priced goods and services that satisfy human needs and bring quality of life, while progressively reducing environmental impacts and resource intensity through the life cycle to a level at least in line with the earth's carrying capacity" (Rolston, 2012, p. 8; DeSimone & Popoff, 1997, p. 47).

SHARED VALUE PROMOTES ETHICS AND PROFITS

In an ethical move that brilliantly circumvents Friedman, Michael Porter and Mark Kramer (2011) outline a theory that fully benefits both the business and community in which the business is operating. It encourages an ethical, social and financial benefit for a business and the community. The ethic states that companies must do more than think about profits: "Companies must take the lead in bringing business and society back together" (Porter & Kramer, 2011, p. 63). "The solution lies in the principle of shared value, which involves creating economic value in a way that also creates value for society by addressing its needs and challenges" (p. 64). They believe that society and business have been pitted against each other for many years, and that the two can develop shared values designed to show appreciation for sustainability with a thorough examination of the societal needs, bases of productivity, and collaboration across profit and non- profit boundaries (p. 64). For example in farming, Porter and Kramer do not recommended donations or inflated prices to the farmer:

> "A shared value perspective, instead, focuses on improving growing techniques and strengthening the local cluster of supporting suppliers and other institutions in order to increase the farmer's efficiency, yields, product quality, and sustainability. This leads to a bigger pie of revenue and profits that benefits both farmers and the companies that buy from them." (p. 65)

Porter and Kramer believe that many companies have lost sight of the most basic question: "Is our product good for our customers?" As an example they point out food companies that have traditionally based profits on high levels of consumption. They challenge these companies to focus products on health and nutrition improvement (2011, p. 67). They credit Wells Fargo with developing products and tools to assist customers with budgeting, managing credit and paying down debt. They also focus on General Electric's Ecomagination products, which are financially successful, yet also have an impact in stabilizing the environment (p. 68).

The Porter and Kramer approach is highly critical of the theory of Milton Friedman, explaining that it is a dated notion that focuses on short-term performance pressures from shareholders by enticing consumers to purchase more and more inferior products. To continue making profits when following the Friedman model, companies may restructure and move off shore to produce at lower costs. This move harms the community that loses the business, and places the business in a location where societal needs are even more pressing. This brings little true innovation, slow organic growth, commoditization and no clear competitive advantage (Porter & Kramer, 2011, p. 65). The Porter and Kramer view is to reconceive products and markets; redefine productivity in a value chain; and build supportive industry clusters at company locations. They believe the net effect will reset the boundaries of capitalism by better connecting a company's successes with societal improvement (p. 67). They find there are many ways to serve new needs, gain efficiency, create differentiation, and expand markets.

Within this theory, companies that do move to developing countries should build shared value with these new communities. They note that in Kenya, Vodafone's M-PESA mobile banking service provided low-priced cell phones with capabilities of mobile banking services. This shared value helped the poor save money, and also gave small farmers the ability to market their crops. Within three years Vodafone signed up 10 million customers, representing 11% of the country's GDP (Porter & Kramer, 2011, p. 66). This interconnectedness is referred to as "clusters" to develop business and endorse sustainability. As another example, in India, Thomson Reuters developed a monthly service that provides weather and crop-pricing information and agricultural advice. An estimated 2 million farmers use the service and research indicates that 60% have increased their incomes (p. 66).

Porter and Kramer present a formula for creating shared value by first identifying all the societal needs, benefits and harms that are, or could be, within the reach of the firm's product. Next, they affirm that opportunities are constantly changing as technology evolves, economies develop, and societal priorities shift (2011, p. 69). The redesign of products and distribution methods can assist in sharing values between the company and community. The rewards can be big for businesses, as ongoing exploration of societal needs should lead companies to discover new opportunities for differentiation and repositioning in traditional markets. The companies could also discover potential in markets previously overlooked (p. 70).

Does Shared Value Avoid Sustainable Development?

With its creative sustainable development structure, the shared value model also has its problems. The shared value argument switches between categorizing capitalism's present issues as an "image problem" and as a "substantive problem" (Denning, 2011). It is argued that these issues are essentially being used to keep capitalism as it is now intact; it is being used as a cover to make people believe that sustainability really matters and that business values are changing. Denning says that the true problem is that the marketplace has changed and management has failed to follow. Shared value, even if it is well meaning, is just another tool to allow management to avoid the changes that will bring about sustainable development. Denning explains:

> "The principal reason why the private sector is experiencing declining returns is that the marketplace has changed and management hasn't. In the marketplace, there has been an epochal shift in the power from seller to buyer. As a result, the "inside-out" perspective of value chains (we make it and you take it) is failing fast and needs to be replaced by an outside-in perspective." (Denning, 2011)

Denning claims that Porter and Kramer aren't doing enough with the simplicity of a theory based on "we want to understand the customers and their problems and find ways to solve those problems." Sustainable development is not helped when new products are essentially "plugged in" to the current method of business. There is an appearance that companies are making changes in the ways they do business, but in actuality they are preserving the status quo (Denning, 2011).

While the case against shared value has some valid points, it doesn't necessarily rule out shared value as viable new tool in sustainability. Those practicing shared value theories must constantly focus on the theories of sustainable development, and understand that capitalism as it is being practiced today must not harm the many tomorrows to come, particularly in developing countries.

SUSTAINABLE PRACTICES AND SPIRITUALITY

Chief Seattle

> "Man did not weave the web of life-he is merely a strand in it. Whatever he does to the web, he does to himself." —Chief Seattle, 1854

These remarks were made in 1851 when Chief Seattle of the Suquamish was offered $150,000 for 2 million acres of land located in part in the Puget Sound area. The Chief delivered a profound, spiritual address when he sold the land. What follows are few of his words:

> "Yonder sky that has wept tears of compassion upon my people for centuries untold, and which to us appears changeless and eternal, may change. Today is fair. Tomorrow it may be overcast with clouds. My words are like the stars that never change. Whatever Seattle says, the great chief at Washington can rely upon with as much certainty as he can upon the return of the sun or the seasons. The white chief says that Big Chief at Washington sends us greetings of friendship and goodwill. This is kind of him for we know he has little need of our friendship in return. His people are many. They are like the grass that covers vast prairies. My people are few. They resemble the scattering trees of a storm-swept plain. The great, and I presume—good, White Chief sends us word that he

wishes to buy our land but is willing to allow us enough to live comfortably. This indeed appears just, even generous, for the Red Man no longer has rights that he need respect, and the offer may be wise, also, as we are no longer in need of an extensive country. . . . Our dead never forget this beautiful world that gave them being. They still love its verdant valleys, its murmuring rivers, its magnificent mountains, sequestered vales and verdant lined lakes and bays, and ever yearn in tender fond affection over the lonely hearted living, and often return from the happy hunting ground to visit, guide, console, and comfort them. . . . Day and night cannot dwell together. The Red Man has ever fled the approach of the White Man, as the morning mist flees before the morning sun. However, your proposition seems fair and I think that my people will accept it and will retire to the reservation you offer them. Then we will dwell apart in peace, for the words of the Great White Chief seem to be the words of nature speaking to my people out of dense darkness. . . . We will ponder your proposition and when we decide we will let you know. But should we accept it, I here and now make this condition that we will not be denied the privilege without molestation of visiting at any time the tombs of our ancestors, friends, and children. Every part of this soil is sacred in the estimation of my people. Every hillside, every valley, every plain and grove, has been hallowed by some sad or happy event in days long vanished. Even the rocks, which seem to be dumb and dead as the swelter in the sun along the silent shore, thrill with memories of stirring events connected with the lives of my people, and the very dust upon which you now stand responds more lovingly to their footsteps than yours, because it is rich with the blood of our ancestors, and our bare feet are conscious of the sympathetic touch." (Chief)

Many spiritual leaders have felt compelled to explain their views on the earth, sustainability, and the harm that others can do to the earth through destructive practices. Leaders such as Chief Seattle, the Dalai Lama, and Mahatma Gandhi offer spiritual advice on our need to care for the earth. Chief Seattle's statement affirms that his people's commitment to sustainability is like the return of the day and night. He isn't sure that the US government will share this same commitment to the environment. He emphasizes the ability to revisit sacred environmental sites, and that these sites should not be harmed. In reflection, we see how some of the land has been preserved while other acres have been developed in ways that would be defined as harmful by Chief Seattle.

HIS HOLINESS THE 14TH DALAI LAMA OF TIBET

Other Spiritual leaders offer similar advice on sustainability and the environment. *His Holiness the 14th Dalai Lama of Tibet explains the simplicity of sustainability and spirituality as:*

"You see, taking care of the planet is nothing special, nothing sacred, and nothing holy. It is something like taking care of our own house. We have no other planet or house except this one. Although there are a lot of disturbances and problems, this is our only alternative. We can't go to other planets. For example, take the moon; it looks or appears beautiful from a distance but if you go there and settle there it is horrible. This is what I think. So you see, our blue planet is much better and happier. So, therefore, we have to care of our- own place or house or planet." (Tenzin, 1990)

The *Dalai Lama* questions the intelligence of human beings when compared to simple creatures such as ants or bees, who require no police force or constitution. He challenges humans to develop a greater respect for this simplicity because they live in harmony, "through the natural law of existence or nature's law or system" (Tenzin, 1990).

MAHATMA GANDHI

In furthering the spiritual elements of sustainability, Mahatma Gandhi said, "You have to be the change you want to see in the world" (Kumar, 2012). With this in mind, some of his followers claim it is essential that globally we adhere to new concepts of spirituality when working within concepts of sustainable development, capitalism, social entrepreneurship, and corporate social responsibility (Kumar, 2005).

RELIGIOUS ETHICS IN SUSTAINABLE PRACTICE

Catholic Bishops

Some formal religions have expressed views on the morality of businesses practices that harm the environment and the poor. For example in the Pastoral letter *Economic Justice for All* (1986), the Catholic Bishops remind global business leaders that the human being is a strong part of business decisions. The letter first asks businesses to cooperate with their communities in caring for the poor. "In our teaching, the human person is not only sacred but also social. How we organize our society—in economics and politics, in law and policy—directly affects human dignity and the capacity of individuals to grow in community" (qtd. in Englehardt & Schmeltekopf, 2010, p. 415). The letter asserts that global financial support is worthy, but more important is a commitment to the poor in one's community. "The obligation to 'love our neighbor' has an individual dimension, but it also requires a broader social commitment to the common good" (2010, p. 415).

The Catholic Bishops further focus on sustainability by pointing out that everyone on the planet shares the same ecological environment. They explain that today's depletion of natural resources, such soil and water, endangers future generations. "Pollution of air and water threatens the delicate balance of the biosphere on which future generations will depend" (qtd. in Englehardt & Schmeltekopf, 2010, p. 417). The Bishops hold that, though nations are separated by geography, ideology and culture, they are joined by a complex environmental framework. The resources of the earth "have been created by God for the benefit of all and we who are alive today hold them in trust" (p. 417).

Community well-being and environmental sustainability are at the center of the Bishops' case. An impoverished and ravaged area of a city can be restored and revitalized and made sustainable again. People in this area can also assist in and benefit from the restorations. The aesthetic, environmental and community rewards can be rich if planned in advance, and worked on a daily basis as part of the sustainable business efforts. Citing studies that describe chemical and other pollution dumping in poor rather than the affluent communities, the Bishops focus their attention on themes of corporate sustainability and justice in society.

The Bishops regard the economic system of a country as tied to an essential spirituality. This system should strive to maintain the dignity of human life by supplying "food, clothing, shelter, rest, medical care, education and employment" for all citizens (qtd. in Englehardt & Schmeltekopf, 2010, p. 416). The Bishops maintain that governments should make more prudent expenditures, particularly in regard to weapons of war. They point out that US Defense Department expenditures are more than $300 billion per year and urge that the funds be spent in bettering human life, particularly through building better spiritual societies rather than tearing them down. "Some of the poorest countries of the world use scarce resources to buy planes, guns and other weapons when they lack the food, education and health care their people need" (p. 418). The Bishops insist that a first step in sustainable development is removing this emphasis on war and weapons of war.

Jewish Perspective

Jewish scholar Ronald Green holds that Jewish and Catholic thinking share a spiritual perception, "that all good fortune, whether personal or material, proceeds from God's hands" (2010, p. 443; see also Gannon, 1987). Green asserts that those who have been blessed by wealth, health, or ability have a "corresponding duty to use their resources to aid those less fortunate, and they subvert this understanding when they turn their blessings into merited possessions they can use to the neglect or detriment of others" (Green, 2010, p. 444). Green adds that the Jewish tradition insists it is important for the sake of dignity that people "work for and have stewardship of" their lives and possessions. Sustainability is increased through the stewardship process. However, Green realizes that poverty-stricken people in some societies do not have belongings and, therefore, need aid.

The focus in Jewish thinking is not economic efficiency, but concern with the dignity of individual human beings, especially the needy and disadvantaged. Green points out commitment to human dignity has always been a commitment in Jewish thinking. "The paramount moral theme has not been the right to the ownership and use of one's own property, but one's responsibility for the just stewardship of that property" (2010, p. 443). This position emphasizes the importance of the 24th Psalm which states, "The earth is the Lord's, and the fullness thereof; the world, and they that dwell therein. For he hath founded it upon the seas, and established it upon the floods" (Psalms 24:1–2). This means that for a business person, sustainability of the earth is an imperative, first because everything belongs to the Lord, and as individuals we are to be caring stewards of these resources. Second, the resources are to be shared with others, particularly the poor and vulnerable.

Conclusion

This chapter has emphasized the importance of the business world, seriously embracing the idea of sustainable development. The EPA reminds us, "Everything that we need for our survival and well-being depends, either directly or indirectly, on our natural environment. Sustainability creates and maintains the conditions under which humans and nature can exist in productive harmony, that permit fulfilling the social, economic and other requirements of present and future generations" (United States Environmental Protection Agency).

Some businesses do embrace the serious challenge of sustaining the planet for future generations while still carefully developing business. Other businesses give "lip service, or web service" to commitment to sustainability, but true commitment is not reflected in their daily practices. When sustainability is approached from a spiritual perspective, it can be embedded both within a personal or an organizational ethic. The earth and her resources can be seen as family members to be protected and sustained for posterity. Religions can give support to such spiritual views by explaining to members the importance of caring for and loving one another. Insofar as businesses operates with a mission that respects sustainable development should review its action plans often and carefully and implement them daily.

References

Chief Seattle's 1854 Oration. (n.d.) Retrieved from http://www.halcyon.com/-arborhts/chiefsea.html CVC Environmental. (2010). Home page. Retrieved from http://www.cvcenvironmental.com/ CVS Caremark. (2012). Environmental Policy. Retrieved from http://info.cvscaremark.com/our-company/corporate-responsibility/environment/our-carbon-footprint

Denning, S. (2011, December 20). Why 'shared value' can't fix capitalism. *Forbes*. Retrieved from http://www.forbes.com/sites/stevedenning/2011/12/20/why-shared-value-cant-fix-capitalism/

Desimone, L. D., & Popoff, F. (1997). *Eco-efficiency: The business link to sustainable development*. Cambridge, MA: MIT Press. Dumped CT chemicals costs CVS $269K. (2010, November 23). *Hartford Business Journal Online*. Retrieved from http://www.hartfordbusiness.com/news15731.html

Friedman, M. (1970, September 13). The social responsibility of business is to increase its profits. *New York Times Magazine*, 122–26.

Green, R. (2010). The Catholic challenge to the American economy. In E. Englehardt & D. Schmeltekopf (Eds.). *Ethics and life: An interdisciplinary approach to moral problems*. (pp. 428–35). New York: McGraw-Hill.

Hart, H. L. A., & Honoré, A. M. (1959). *Causation in the law*. Oxford: Oxford UP.

Kumar, S. (2012, April 30). Transformation: The spiritual imperative. *Life Positive*. Retrieved from http://www.lifepositive.com/Spirit/Enlightenment/The_Spiritual_Imperative 102005.asp

National Conference of Catholic Bishops. (2010). Economic justice for all: Catholic social teaching and the U.S. economy. In E. Englehardt & D. Schmeltekopf (Eds.), *Ethics and life: An interdisciplinary approach to moral problems* (pp. 414–26). New York: McGraw-Hill.

Porter, M. E., & Kramer, M. R. (2011). Creating shared value: How to reinvent capitalism—and unleash a wave of innovation and growth. *Harvard Business Review*, January/February, 63–70.

Report of the World Commission on environment and development, United Nations, 42nd Session. (1987). Development and International Economic Cooperation: Environment.

Retrieved from *http://daccess-dds-ny.un.org/doc/UNDOC/GEN/N87/184/67/IMG/N87-18467.pdf?*OpenElement United States Environmental Protection Agency. (n.d.). Sustainability. Retrieved from http://www.epa.gov/sustainability/basicinfo.htm

Rolston, H. (2012). *A new environmental ethics: The next millennium for life on earth.* New York: Routledge.

Settlement in Chemical Disposal Case Against CVS. (2012, April 19). *KQUED Radio.* Retrieved from http://www.kqed.org/a/kqednews/RN201204190904/b

Tenzin G. (1990). Spirituality and nature. *His Holiness the 14th Dalai Lama of Tibet.* Retrieved from http://www.dalailama.com/messages/environment/spirituality-and-nature World economic situation and prospects 2005. (2005). United Nations World Summit. Retrieved from http://www.un.org/en/development/desa/policy/wesp/wesp_archive/2005-wesp.pdf

In: Spirituality and Civilization Sustainability ...
Editors: Andrew Targowski and Marek J. Celinski
ISBN: 978-1-53610-729-6

Chapter 21

AUTOMATION WITH HUMAN FACE

Andrew Targowski[1*] and Vladimir Modrák[2‡]
[1]Western Michigan University, Kalamazoo, MI, US,
[2]Department of Manufacturing Management,
Technical University of Košice, Prešov, Slovakia

ABSTRACT

This chapter views the impact of automation and new globalization phenomenon, outsourcing on sustainable economic growth. Its main scope is to analyze the impacts of advanced automation and offshore outsourcing in manufacturing on a human capital and an acceleration of structural unemployment. Simultaneously, in this chapter are compared two concepts by which a company can tend to attain a position of manufacturing excellence. Further is given a special emphasis to the automation driven shrinking of the middle class in countries that are passing to the phase of deindustrialization. Finally some laws of automation in manufacturing are formulated and few ideas and recommendations for the future are outlined.

INTRODUCTION

The purpose of this investigation is to assess the question: is automation the right strategy for the developed nations which practice relentless economic grow, regardless of social consequences? In order to answer this question some review of current automation trends is provided, their advantages and disadvantages are assessed, the automation and outsourcing's impact on industrial decline is addressed, which can lead to the judgment that automation is at the cross-roads. In order to apply wise automation, three laws of automation are formulated

* E-mail: Andrew.targowski@wmich.edu; [1]Professor of Computer Information Systems; President of the International Society for the Comparative Study of Civilizations
‡ E-mail: Vladimir.modrak@tuke.sk; Professor of Manufacturing Technology, Technical University of Košice, Head of Department of Manufacturing Management, Prešov, Slovakia

and conclusions are drawn, among one of them is the proposal for the development of Technosophy, which should be observed by all stakeholders of the wise automation technology and strategy.

Automation in manufacturing is rapidly unfolding, automated factories become a growing reality whether one likes it or not. This trend is logically associated with the substance of the global economic system that *is set* up in a manner to gain profit and in which automatic factories are inevitable. But the global economic system is also affected by complex social, political and strategic factors that are to a lesser extent predictable than technological changes.

For example, cost of computer and telecommunication technologies are decreasing dramatically while their speed is increasing exponentially and it is reasonably expected that these tendencies will continue in the future. Similarly, it is possible to presage inter-sectoral shifts of the labor force in response to technological changes. The employment shift from agriculture sector to manufacturing that was initiated with the industrial revolution culminated in the 1950s and consequently began declining while the percentage of the labor force employed in services grew rapidly (Miles, 1993).

Analogically, when automated factories will be in developed countries widespread, then manufacturing employment will be dramatically reduced to the indispensable minimum and presently dominating sector of services will expand further. However, the inertial need for higher productivity in the service sector will further decrease traditional employment and would require new sources of generating work for those becoming unemployed through the widespread use of super-automation (Makridakis, 1995). Moreover, employment in developed countries is endangered by subsequent phenomena that are connected with new forms of organizations such as telework, subcontracting, outsourcing, offshoring and others.

The problem is diversified in nature that requires not only specialized researches but also use of multidisciplinary approaches. In this paper we intend to explore selected aspect of automation in manufacturing as well mentioned phenomena in the organization of firms related to structural unemployment issues.

LITERATURE REVIEW

During the last decades, advanced automation technologies have become more and more omnipresent in manufacturing industries. Automation devices that are sourced from reputed manufacturers are noteworthy from a cost and performance standpoint.

But, their increasing development influences so much the organization of socio-technical systems, that the traditional relationship between humans and machines, in the broad sense of the term, has been strongly altered (Mayer, 2008). In order to make visible this interaction between Humans and advanced automation technologies, a new concept so called “challenging automation engineering” is formed (Nof et al., 2006; Jämsä-Jounela & Zühlke, 2006).

One of the necessities of this concept is that many younger people have kept away from jobs in manufacturing industries because of their "3K" reputation (*kitsui, kitanai, kiken* - hard, dirty and dangerous) and found jobs in service industries. Consequently, manufacturing industries have employed fully automated and unmanned systems and excluded workers from the workshops.

According to Nakazawa (2011) this way of change may have, for example, the following problems in the future:

- Since fully automatic unmanned manufacturing system is highly synchronized and adjusted, when a problem occurs in the system, the system falls down into a logical conflict and therefore fully automatic unmanned manufacturing systems will have very restricted and low level functions.
- Techniques and skills are created and advanced by humans, and they are transferred from human to human. If fully automatic unmanned systems are realized, actual manufacturing processes are isolated from human; and humans cannot see, touch and listen to actual processes directly. This may mean that further progress of technique and manufacturing technology stops, and better systems than before may not be realized again.
- Even fully automatic unmanned manufacturing systems may still require some workers, for instance, for loading and unloading operations and supervisory and maintenance operations which are very difficult to implement in technical terms. This means that the human is also treated as a component of the manufacturing systems.

The last mentioned problem can be one of great importance but also can build the causal foundations for the 'challenging automation engineering' concept, as it is apparent that advanced manufacturing systems tend to sacrifice human dignity.

According to some manufacturers, advanced automation does not necessarily increase the productivity, but vice versa in some cases. Especially in cases when implementation of advanced technology is not accompanied by a coherent labor strategy and operated by skilled technicians (Daude et al. 1998; Jensen 2001). The integration of people and technology in the factory is considered as essential to improving productivity (Filip et al. 2002; Suksawat et al., 2006).

In this context it seems appropriate to see 'challenging automation engineering' as integration of automation engineering and social sciences to a systems engineering approach with the aim to achieve holistic vision of automation technologies (Mayer & Stahre, 2006). In order to establish basic framework for such systems, Halpin (1995) proposed a conceptual scheme of a socio-technical automation technology.

Keeping in tune with the article scope, we will further focus on offshoring and offshore outsourcing related especially to unemployment problems.

According to Varadajaran (2009), outsourcing refers to the practice of a firm entrusting to an external entity the performance of an activity that was performed erstwhile in-house. Offshore outsourcing can be defined as the practice of hiring an external firm to perform to perform non-core business processes in a country other than the one where the products or services are actually developed or manufactured. It can be contrasted with offshoring, in which the manufacturing or service functions are performed in a foreign country through a foreign subdivision. Sometimes offshoring is performed through offshore outsourcing, that is, when a company hires an external company to perform a service in another country (Messner, 2008).

Offshoring and offshore outsourcing are considered to be controversial subjects because there are different views on these matters. But, it has to be also said that offshore outsourcing along with foreign direct investment present the main features of process globalization during the recent decades (Feenstra, 1998; Krugman, 1995). Doh (2005) in his essay discusses the implications of the debate over offshoring and concludes that "offshoring is likely to present challenges to societies, corporations, and stakeholders for many decades". Bryce & Useem (1998) were stated that determination of the precise amount of outsourcing impact on firm's value is nearly as elusive as measuring the mass of a neutrino. Findings of Cranfield study by Kakabadse & Kakabadse (2002) show that activities and functions that are outsourced are seen as critical to the future survival of the enterprise, particularly for European companies.

Results obtained from Japanese manufacturing industries indicate that core business-related outsourcing, offshore outsourcing, and shorter-term outsourcing positively effected on outsourcing firms' market value. Conversely, non-core business-related outsourcing, domestic outsourcing, and longer-term outsourcing were not found to enhance firm value (Jiang et al. 2007).

The Pros and Cons of Using Advanced Automation

The effects of a new technology and its importance to leverage economic growth have been a matter of dispute since the Industrial Revolution. In spite of that, at the beginning of the twenty-first century, it is not possible unambiguously to contain the effects of a new technology and automation, because impacts of technological changes are very complex including such factors as pollution, unemployment, and threats to privacy. Moreover, it has to be considered that technological changes often had different effects on various groups in the society and something is more important for some than for others.

Obviously, automation brings many advantages for manufacturers, especially in increasing production efficiencies and maximizing profits. Moreover, firms can achieve through automation many further effects such as error reduction, higher quality performance, reduction the need for work in harsh physical environments and others. In this connection, our intention in this section is to share some thoughts on this issue.

There is quite known fact presented for instance by Travers & Decker [23] that "jobless growth has been one consequence of new technologies the introduction of which has been accompanied by the globalization of capital, the internationalization of work, and the downsizing of government" However, this view is not fully shared among advocates of automation. For example, Brennan et al. (2008) claim that "the high degree of automation in modern manufacturing systems, factory automation and control systems have become central to companies' responsiveness, and arguably the key to competitiveness". According to Groover [12] and Dorf & Kusiak, (1994) "some workers who qualify for jobs in today's conventional factories will not qualify for indirect labor positions in highly automated factories and will not be employable". But they add that "if companies do not automate their factories for the future, there is likely to be no future for these companies".

We think, that the right question which should be contested is "What is probability that for companies that will prefer the conventional factory model will have no future?". To find a satisfactory answer to this question in a direct way is rather impracticable. But we could indirectly investigate relevant potential differences between the conventional factory model and the automated factory. The automated factory can be viewed for this purpose as an integration of new advanced manufacturing technologies (AMT), not all of which are computerized, through computer hardware, software, and databases with computer-controlled machine tools, automated material handling and robotics to form a highly automated and flexible manufacturing system (Attaran, 1989). We can certainly assume, that automated factory at least from competition point of view ranks to a position of World Class Manufacturing (WCM) or World Class Factory. Generally, a status of WCM can be achieved by two concepts: Advanced Manufacturing Technology and Manufacturing Excellence (ME), as it is depicted in Figure 21.1. This persuasion is shared, for example, by Hammond (1998) who pointed out, apart from other incentives, that "By not ruling out any means to attain competitive advantage, U.S. industry will again attain its position as a World Class Manufacturer.

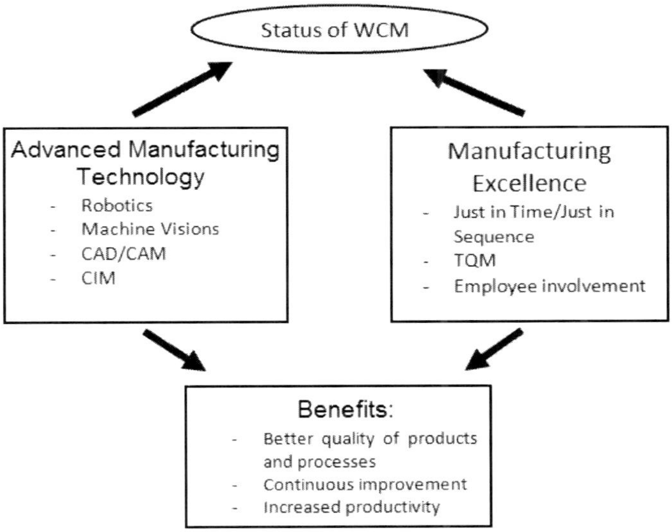

Figure 21.1. Two routes to achieving WCM status.

In generally, separate ways to WCM are characterized as follows. First of them is based on implementation of AMT that includes such tools as robotics, machine vision, computer integrated manufacturing and other automated technology and presents the technical route to achieve the WCM status. For the second way that is also called soft technology, it is necessary to adopt such tools as Just in Time/Just in Sequence, TQM and Employee Involvement methodology. These concepts provide soft enhancements of hard technological solutions.

One of the things that differentiate these two concepts is the necessary level of investment. Naturally, an adoption of AMT involves a high level of investment in contrast with an introduction of Manufacturing Excellence, for which only a considerable managerial effort has to be provided. The major effectiveness indicators of the AMT project are costs and benefits. The problem is that while the costs are ordinarily easily quantifiable, the benefits are often very difficult to quantify. Chen & Small (1994) in this sense emphasize importance of strategic benefits such as; early entry to market, perceived market leadership, or improved flexibility, but simultaneously they note that they are not readily convertible into cash values.

Ingersoll engineers came up with a set of surprising results from a survey of British manufacturing regarding the risk of introducing new technology in manufacturing firms (Mortimer, 1985). They recognized only an 18% rate of success in firms that went for the high technology option; 34% rate of success in firms that invested to the medium level of technology; 60% rate of success in cases when companies underwent only partial equipment change with reorganization; and with an 84% success rate in firms that staked mainly on organization changes, introducing only a minimal changes in equipment. The results obtained may be graphically presented as it is shown in Figure 21.2.

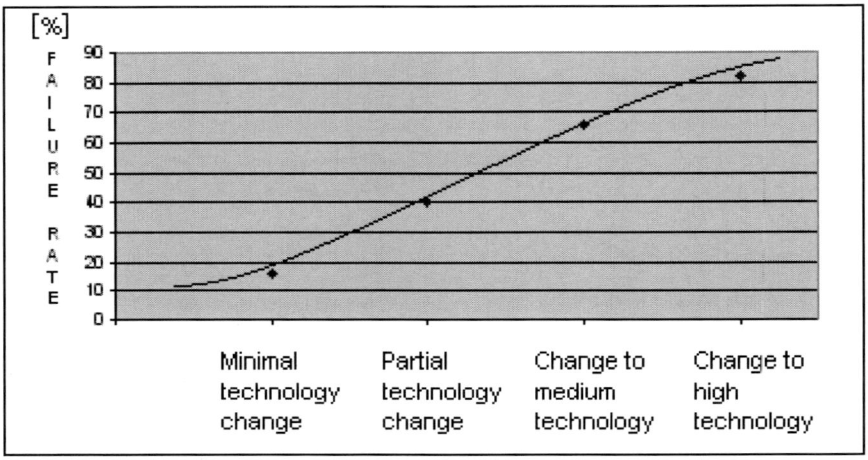

Figure 21.2. Assessing the failure rate of introducing new technology in manufacturing industry.

To prevent a potential risk related to low rate of return of AMT-oriented investment for firms, Schonberger (1990) recommends investing in the simplest equipment possible and improving present equipment before considering new equipment and automation. Summarily, a highly anticipated comparison of these two concepts based on decisive criteria is shown in Table 21.1.

Table 21.1. Comparison between the AMT route and ME route

CRITERIA	AMT-oriented approach	ME-oriented approach
Managerial effort	Lower	higher
Level of investment	Higher	lower
Negative environmental impacts	Higher	lower
Rate of employment	Higher	Lover
Benefits	Comparable	

Thus, a dependence of the competition ability on the extent of investment to the AMT and extend of managerial effort to ME, respectively, can be modeled as depicted in Figure 21.3.

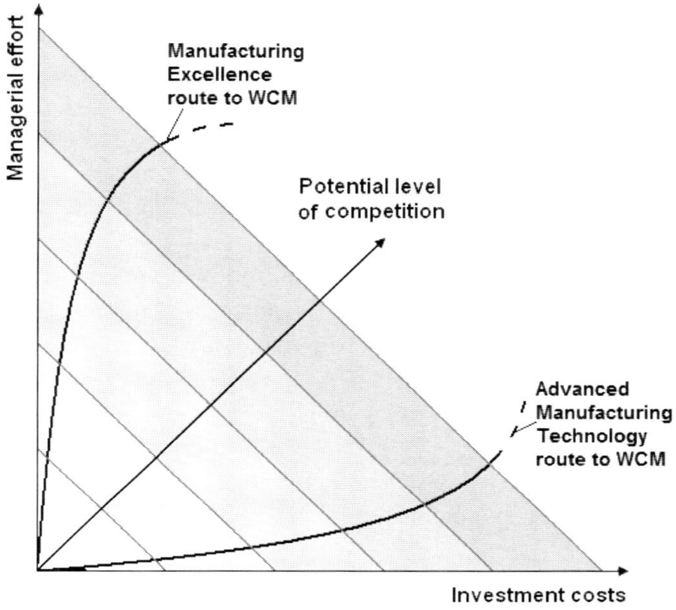

Figure 21.3. Model of a dependency of the potential level of competition on the optional routes.

Assuming results of comparison of values from Table 21.1, it is quite evident that debatable quoted above opinion: "if companies do not automate their factories for the future, there is likely to be no future for these companies" has a low probability of being true. But, even though, investing into advanced manufacturing technologies (ATM) and in general in automation is potentially risky, the technically-oriented approach remains only a promising one. Needless to say that these two approaches are frequently mixed what can be optimal solution to attain expected positive results.

Automation and Outsourcing's Impact on Industrial Decline

In the last 50 years one can recognized the following approaches towards automation: (a) developing separate components of automated systems, which can fit in most of integrated configurations; (b) developing flexible integrated systems which can optimize overall performance; (c) developing data mining systems, which generate knowledge rules about their functionality and can control adaptively according to new emerging situations. However, in the 2000s, along with the advanced applications of the Internet in manufacturing (d) a new trend of outsourcing takes place, particularly in countries such the U.S., United Kingdom, and to certain degree in Germany, where the expensive labor is being replaced by less costly labor in developing countries such as China and India.

In effect, a concept of automation in so far advanced countries (mentioned above) is marginalized, since these countries are passing to the phase of deindustrialization. Consequently, a reform of the manufacturing industry is now a core strategy for government and private sector. In this context a new term "the automation of custom manufacturer" is introduced and new CIM concepts and technology-intensive industrial structures are anticipated. What factors will motivate decisions for automation in the near future? Three decenniums ago, there were a number of economic and social factors that provided motivation for automation in manufacturing such as, increased productivity, lowering high cost of labor, avoiding labor shortages, improving the use of expensive raw material by better engineering and automation, reducing manufacturing lead time, reducing of in-process inventory (Groover, 1980).

Will they be the same as before? In our opinion, following reviews of automation in the last 100 years will look not at the technical advantage of automation but at its social implication. Mostly it will be looked into following factors:

a) How automation results in the subjugation of the human beings by machines in times of population growth?
b) How reduced labor force by automation impacts unemployment rates?
c) How automation reduces purchasing power of eliminated labor force employed in manufacturing?

Thomas Friedman (2006) in his best-selling book "The World is Flat" noticed that the transfer of services and manufacturing from the developed to developing nations also transfers wealth. As a result of it, the world becomes economically "flat." It is interesting to notice that the main tool of this flattening process is the Internet, which was not developed because it was financed by wise capital, as it is true in many other technologies. In fact, the Internet was developed by the military and scientific community.

With offshore outsourcing strategy and free trade policy of the Global Economy, more and more western businesses are closing up shops in the United States (about 40,000) in Germany and the United Kingdom as well, and moving elsewhere (mostly to Asia), taking millions of jobs with them. The result is a sharp drop in American middle class' standard of living. This was a proud fruit of successful 200+ years of the American Way of handling economic development. Suddenly, these two hundred years of steady climbing to the highest standard of living (by a large country) in the world are put in a reverse gear and leading to the Big Crash 2008-2011 of the American middle class. It leads to a national divide between the global elites (a New Ruling Class) and those have been left behind.

Needless to say that exporting jobs to Asia and Mexico, the corporate elite is destroying the American dream and profiting from the exploitation of sweatshops. Abandoned by their government, American workers (and English ones too) are being forced to compete with cheap Third World labor and are inevitably losing out (Buchanan, 1998).

Global and stateless corporations are profitable, but the competitiveness of the people, business, and communities rooted in the U.S. economy is relentlessly deteriorating. American (and to certain degree English and German as well) workers, from the unskilled to highly educated engineers and research scientists, have been set adrift in a sea of dog eat-dog competition that guarantees a substantial drop in their living standards (Faux, 2006).

Outsourcing and offshoring can be compared with traditional market competition expanded in a global economy, and enabled by an increasingly robust information infrastructure. Market economies are relentless in their drive for efficiency and productivity. Historic barriers of transportation logistics, off-site management, and knowledge transfer have been greatly reduced by information and transportation technologies. There are obvious short-term financial benefits available to companies by moving well defined systems and processes to lower cost areas of the world. Short-term effects on developed societies are less attractive than they are to companies, with less available jobs and fewer opportunities. Long-term consequences for everyone are open to debate, and potentially foreboding.

Forrester Research estimated in 2004 that American companies will move 3.4 million jobs offshore by 2015. About a third of those jobs pay $46,000 per year or higher (Atkinson, 2004). Labor union AFLCIO in 2007 estimates that the United States lost about 2.7 million manufacturing jobs between January 2001 and August 2004 (AFLCIO, 2007). The U. S. Government Accounting Office indicates that services associated with offshoring grew from $21.2 billion in 1997 to about $37.5 billion in 2002, an increase of more than 76 percent. But exports from the U. S. of those same types of services also increased by over 48 percent (Hughes, 2002).

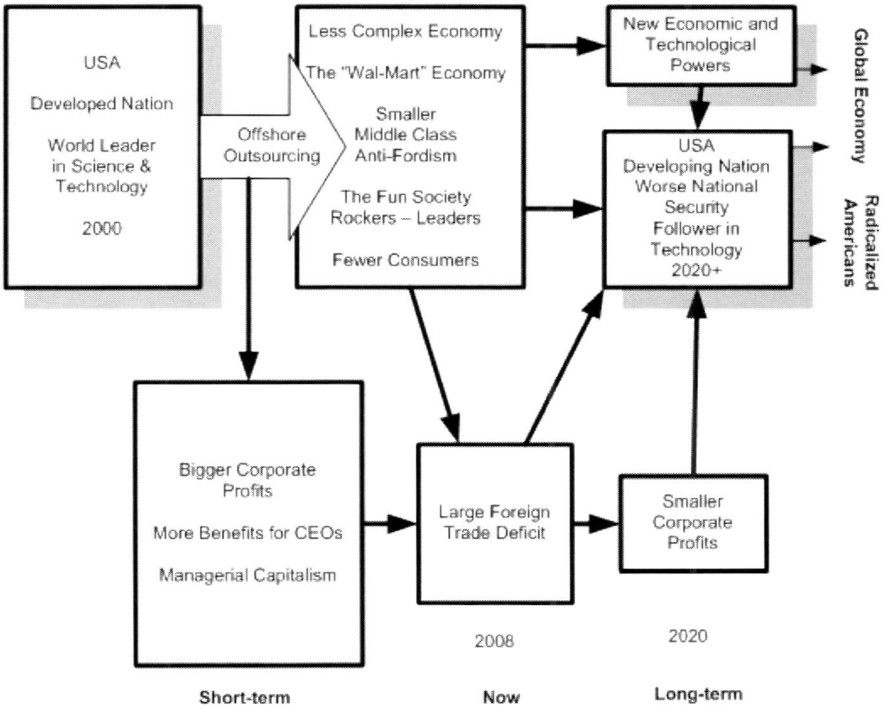

Figure 21. 4. A model of the consequences of offshore outsourcing for the U.S.

Figure 21.4 describes the long-term effects of continued job losses from offshoring. Short term profits for U.S. companies improve from lower costs but long term effects of a less complex economy resulting from the loss of the country's manufacturing base, the proliferation of low paying service jobs, a shrinking middle class, and large trade deficits produces a new world economic order in which the United States will play a much less prominent role. In this scenario, the country experiences lower national security becomes a follower rather than a leader in technology and education, experiences a decline in standard of living for its citizenry, and has to contend with a much more radicalized political structure.

The following conclusions on offshore outsourcing can be offered:

1. Outsourcing needs sophisticated management that balances short-term profit with long-term investment in competitive position.
2. Manufacturing and information technology offshore outsourcing is a potential strategic threat for the American economy and society.

Impacts of the Rapid Changes in Manufacturing

The offshoring manufacturing to China, India, Eastern Europe and other countries have cut the wages in Western Civilization and put workers out of jobs. Manufacturing now accounts for only 12 percent of that civilization's jobs. If manufacturing is declining in the West, then automation loses its broad application. As the result of it, all precautions taken into considerations during the development and operations of automation are missing the point.

The MIT economist David Autor (2011) published a report that looked at the shifting employment landscape in America. In his report, Autor says that a leading explanation for the disappearance of the middle class is "ongoing automation and offshoring of middle-skilled 'routine' tasks that were formerly performed primarily by workers with moderate education (a high school diploma but less than a four-year college degree)." Routine tasks, he explains, are ones that "can be carried out successfully by either a computer executing a program or, alternatively, by a comparatively less-educated worker in a developing country." The culprit, in other words, is technology. The hard truth—and you don't see it addressed in news reports—is that the middle class is disappearing in large part because technology is rendering middle-class skills obsolete.

"People say America doesn't make anything anymore, but that's not true. With the exception of a few short lapses, manufacturing output has been on the rise since the 1980s. What is true is that industrial robots have been carrying ever more of the manufacturing burden on their steely shoulders since they appeared in the 1950s. Today, a Japanese company called Fanuc, Ltd., has industrial robots making other industrial robots in a "lights out" factory. (That's the somewhat unsettling term for a fully automated production facility where you don't need lights because you don't need humans.) That's where we're headed. It's not just manufacturing, either. Automated call centers are replacing customer-service agents. Automated checkout stations are replacing grocery-store clerks. When the science of computer vision advances sufficiently, we'll have algorithms, not humans, evaluating X-rays at airport security checkpoints and screening user-generated content for sites like Facebook." (Price, 2011).

Western Civilization is losing an economic battle, a battle that the majority of Westerners think was mismanaged for years. For example, since 1975 the United States has traded at a deficit, importing far more goods than has been exporting. Its levels of production have dropped, to the detriment of its ability to innovate and train workers. Western Civilization's economic system is in shatters and it is going to continue to face repercussions if something drastic is not done to put the control of its future back in their own hands.

AUTOMATION LAWS FOR THE 21 CENTURY

A number of important questions one can asked and reply about the effect of automation on society in developed countries:

a) *Will automation raise standard of living*? Perhaps *moderate* automation could. But today in developed economies we deal with the declining automation due to the trend of outsourcing manufacturing and service to less developed nations where labor cheaper than automation. As the result of it, the middle class is declining in these nations and its standard of living.
b) *Does automation create unemployment*? Yes, it creates unemployment in developed nations. But because automation's processes being outsourced can be instantly online controlled by the Internet from the developed countries.
c) *Will more skill be demanded or less*? In developing nations, the deindustrialization reduces complexity of economy which as service-oriented does not need high science and engineering-oriented skills. In developing nations automation-oriented priority is not the issue, since cheap labor competes with westernized automation.
d) *Will workers get more satisfaction from their jobs*? No. Since they move to service jobs which do not require intellectualization of their work.

However, certain automation of global information systems provides manufacturing and service jobs in developing countries. Because distance is "dead" and electronic management of global, dispersed enterprises is possible. This is considered by the developing nations as the historic justice accomplished and the problem of the North-South colonial issues is being resolved.

The real danger is not that automation and robots will make us mad with power, or that human-like humanoids will themselves become super intelligent and take over the world. The consequences of their introduction will be subtler. Inexorably, we will interact more with machines and less with each other. Already, the average American worker spends astonishingly large percentages of his/her life interfacing with machines. Many return home only to log in a new.

Human relationships are a lot of trouble, forged from dirty diapers, lost tempers and late nights. Machines, on the other hand, can be turned on and off. Already, many of us prefer to forge and maintain relationships via e-mail, chat rooms and instant messenger rather than in person. Despite promises that the Internet will take us anywhere, we find ourselves - hour after hour - glued to our chairs. We are supposedly living in a world with no borders. Yet, at the very time we should be coming closer together, it seems we are growing further apart. Humanoids may accelerate this trend (Ethical Considerations, 2010).

In 1942 – Isaac Asimov wrote "Runaround," a story about humanoid robots which contained the "Three Laws of Robotics":

I. A robot may not injure a human, or, through inaction, allow a human being to come to harm.
II. A robot must obey the orders it by human beings except where such orders would conflict with the First Law.
III. A robot must protect its own existence as long as such protection does not conflict with the First or Second Law.

In 2009-Andrew Targowski (2009) defined Laws of Service:

I. Do not develop service systems without human presence.
II. Do not develop service systems which harm society.
III. Do not develop service systems which endanger human race.

Law I protects people against passivity. Law II protects society against structured unemployment. Law III protects the human race against the bifurcation into two kinds of species.

Targowski & Modrák (2011) offer the following Laws of Automation in Manufacturing:

I. Do not implement high automation technology before you are not sure that same goal can be achieved by another means.
II. Do not implement automation technology with aim to totally eliminate human presence in manufacturing process.
III. Do not develop automation which harms society or endanger human race.

It would be necessary to organize a forum for suggestions which could improving the laws and promote their applications. Thereafter it would be useful to open even wider forum for discussion, making preconditions and recommendations how future manufacturing systems should be developed and managed in a responsible manner for the good sake of Society.

Conclusion

According to known facts, factory automation caused during the last decade worldwide decline in manufacturing jobs, not only in developed countries but in developing countries as well in a uniform manner. Hence, the laws of Robots, Service and Automation Systems should be implemented into society undertaking as follows:

1. The automation systems are one of the most complex systems in civilization which triggered tremendous developmental trends in science and technology in the 20th century. They looked very promising at their early stages, but later provide many doubts about their positive role in Society.
2. The automation systems designed for better effectiveness and reliability & quality are as long positive as long they do not harm and endanger human beings and society.

3. The presented Laws of Robotics, Service Systems, and Automation should be included in codes of ethics of appropriate professional associations.
4. The governments should established national policies for applying these Laws of Robotics, Service and Automation.
5. The professional education should include in its research and teaching these Laws of Robotics, Services, and Automation as securing ones of societal well-being and civilization sustainability.

In order to integrate all these laws into one coherent discipline, a new one should be pursued. Perhaps it should be covered by Technosophy, which should investigate wise engineering for wise civilization. Technosophy is relatively a new term which is needed to identify a purely techno-scientific approach to technology. According to Levy & Junkar (2001), Technosophy suggests the need to develop wisdom to accompany the science of technical artifacts. This kind of engineering should be only developed today and aimed at the sustainability of our civilization in times of shrinking strategic resources of the planet. It is widely known that population becomes too big to sustain our western styles of life, even in short-term future. Therefore, many leading corporations comprehended these challenges and adopted sustainability planning over the past few years as a tool to achieve strategic dominance (Modrak & Dima, 2010; Zajac, 2006). Hence, the future is now and Technosophy is, in our opinion, needed today as never before.

REFERENCES

AFLCIO (2007). Retrieved November 20, 2007 from http://www.aflcio.org/issues/ Jobseconomy/exportingamerica/

Asimov, I. (1942). Runaround. New York: Street and Smith Publications, Inc.

Atkinson, R. D. (2004). Understanding the offshoring challenge. Retrieved January 22, 2005, from http://www.accra.org/newsletter/PPIoffshoring.pdf

Attaran, M. (1989). Strategic issues in the automated factory. *Industrial Management & Data Systems*, 89 (4), 14-19.

Autor, D. (2011). The Polarization of job opportunities in the U.S. labor market. Boston: MIT Department of Economics and National Bureau of Economic Research.

Brennan, R.W. et al. (2008). Developments in dynamic and intelligent reconfiguration of industrial automation. *Computers in Industry*, 59 (6):533-547.

Bryce, D. J. & Useem, M. (1998). The impact of corporate outsourcing on company value, European Management Journal 16 (6): 635–643.

Chen, I. J. & Small, M.H. (1994). Implementing advanced manufacturing technology: an integrated planning model. *OMEGA, Int. J. of Management Science*, 22 (1): 91–103.

Daude, R., Wenk, C., Westerwick, A., Henning, K., and Weck, M. (1998) Supporting skilled workers at shop floor machine tools, *AI & Society*. (12): 29-37.

Doh, J.P. (2005) Offshore outsourcing: implications for international business and strategic management theory and practice. *Journal of Management Studies* (2005), 42(3): 695-704. Hoboken, NJ: Wiley-Blackwell.

Dorf, R., & Kusiak, A. (1994). Handbook of design, manufacturing and automation. New York: John Wiley. Ethical Consideration (2010). Retrieved on December 25 from https://inlportal.inl.gov/portal/server.pt/community/ethical_considerations/543).

Faux, J. (2006). The global class war. New York: John Wiley & Sons, Inc.

Feenstra R. C. (1998), 'Integration of trade and disintegration of production in the Global Economy'. *Journal of Economic Perspectives*, 12(4):31–50.

Filip, F.G., Donciulescu, D.A. and Fillip, Cr.I. (2002) Towards intelligent real time decision support systems for industrial milieu. *Studies in Information and Control*, 11:303-311.

Friedman, T. L. (2006). The world is flat: a brief history of the 21st century. New York: Farrar, Straus and Giroux.

Groover, P. M. (1980). Automation, production systems, computer-aided manufacturing. Englewood Cliffs: Prentice-Hall.

Groover, M. P. (1987). Automation, production systems, and computer integrated manufacturing. Englewood Cliffs: Prentice-Hall.

Halpin, T.A. (1995). Conceptual schema and relational database design. In: 2nd edition. Sydney, Australia: Prentice Hall.

Hammond, R. W. (1988). Manufacturing excellence in support of the technological Solution. *SME Technical Paper*, MM88-267.

Hughes, N. C. (2002). China's economic challenge: smashing the iron rice bowl. Armonk, NY: M. E. Sharpe.

Jämsä-Jounela S.L., Zühlke D. (2006). 50th Anniversary of IFAC: present and future of automatic control. *Journal of Automation Technology in Practice*. 2:4-5.

Jensen, P.L. (2001). Human factors and ergonomics in the planning of production. *International Journal of Industrial Ergonomics*. 29:121-131.

Jiang, B,. Belohlav, J. and Scott, T. (2007). Outsourcing impact on manufacturing firm's value: Evidence from Japan. *Journal of Operations Management*, 25(4):885-900.

Kakabadse, A., & Kakabadse, N. (2005). Outsourcing: current and future trends. *Thunderbird International Business Review*, 47(2):183-204.

Krugman, Paul (1995). Growing world trade: causes and consequences. *Brooking Paper on Economic Activity*, 1:327-362.

Levy, P. & Junkar, M., 2001 Technosophy: strategic approaches to the assessment and management of manufacturing technology innovation. *NATO ASI Series 4. Science and Technology Policy* - Vol. 21, Dordrecht The Nederland: , Kluver Academic Publisher.

Makridakis, S. (1995). The forthcoming information revolution - it's impacts on society and firms. *Futures*, 27(8):799-821.

Mayer, F. & Stahre J., (2006). Special section on human-centred systems engineering. *Annual Reviews in Control* (Elsevier). 30/2:193-195.

Mayer, F. (2008) Social impact of automation trends and issues: an human centered systems engineering perspective. In *Proceedings of the 17th World Congress* of *The International Federation of Automatic Contro*l, Seoul, Korea, July 6-11, pp. 5251-5256.

Messner J.I. (2008) Offshoring of engineering services in the construction industry. In: The offshoring of engineering: facts, unknowns, and potential implications, National Academies Press, pp 137-148.

Miles, I. (1993). Services in the new industrial economy. *Futures*, 25(6):653-672.

Modrak, V. & Dima I.C., 2010. Conceptual framework for corporate sustainability planning, *International Business Management*, 4 (3):139-144.

Mortimer, J. (1985). Ingersoll engineers: integrated manufacture. Bedford: IFS Publications.

Suksawat, B, He, W., Hiraoka, H and Ihara, T. (2006) Optimization of scheduling method for anthropocentric manufacturing system, In: *Proceedings of the 7th Asia Pacific Industrial Engineering and Management Systems Conference 2006 17-20 December 2006*, Bangkok, Thailand, pp. 1634-1644.

Nakazawa, H. (1993) Alternative human role in manufacturing, *AI & Society*, 7:151-156.

Nof, S.Y., Morel G., Monostori L., Molina A., Filip F. (2006) From plant and logistics control to multi-enterprise collaboration. *Journal of Annual Reviews in Control*, 30:55-68.

Price, A. (2011). Automation insurance: robots replacing middle class jobs (retrieved on Nov. 22.2011 from http://www.good.is/post/automation-insurance-robots-are-replacing-middle-class-jobs).

Schonberger, R. J. (1990). World class manufacturing: the next decade. New York: Free Press.

Targowski, A. (2009a). Information technology and societal development. Hershey and New York: IGI Global.

Targowski, A. (2009b). Cognitive informatics and wisdom development. Hershey and New York: IGI Global.

Travers, A. & Decker, E. (1999). New technology and critical pedagogy. Radical Pedagogy, 1(2).

Varadajaran ,V. (2009) Outsourcing: think more expansively. Journal of Business Research, 62(11):1165-1172

Zajac, J. (2006) Chemical management in mass industry. In: *International scientific conference on flexible technologies - MMA2006*. - Novi Sad,15-16 June, pp. 177-178.

In: Spirituality and Civilization Sustainability ...
Editors: Andrew Targowski and Marek J. Celinski
ISBN: 978-1-53610-729-6

Chapter 22

COULD COMPOSITE ALTRUISM BECOME A UNIVERSAL COMPREHENSIVE SPIRITUALITY MODEL FOR THE PLANET?

Richard Zinser*
Western Michigan University, Kalamazoo, MI, US

ABSTRACT

Throughout the centuries and around the globe nearly all moral systems have included the virtue of altruism, the unselfish interest in the welfare of others. The opportunities and challenges created by globalization have given rise to the need for a spirituality that serves all of humanity, so by extension altruism includes what is best for the planet and the future as well. Altruistic attitudes and behaviour can and should be taught to both children and adults. Education for altruism often takes the form of the comparative examination of religions and cultures through stories and international case studies, through ecology and future consciousness, and by spiritual reflection and meditation. There is a current sense of urgency to practice altruism throughout the world because civilization is nearing the point where decisions need to be made that will have enormous consequences.

INTRODUCTION

> All the joy the world contains has come through wishing happiness for others.
> (Shantideva, 8th century, India)

Altruism may be one of the few universal concepts among cultures. The majority of religious, spiritual, and philosophical traditions throughout civilization include a form or version of altruism. Similarly, there are 21 religions that have a type of Golden Rule (Religious Tolerance, 2010). Although there have been, and continue to be, conflicts between

* E-mail: Richard.zinser@wmich.edu

different systems of ethics and morality, most people would agree that—at minimum—others should be treated well. Even secular institutions such as business schools are re-examining their curricula to consider adding a more humanistic component. Because of this, altruism has the potential to become the basis for a world spirituality.

The term *altruism* is usually understood as interest in and action for the welfare of other people. It is similar to, but not the same as, *agape* or unconditional love from the Christian tradition, and *loving-kindness* practiced in Buddhism. Altruism also has elements of compassion and empathy in that it recognizes the feelings of others and seeks to be emotionally with others. It is sometimes thought of in connection with holistic views or big-picture thinking in which the individual is part of, and has a relationship with, a larger community, organization, or environment. Altruism is also related to philanthropy and charity, but in altruism the beneficiaries are often indirect or unknown; for example many people plant trees and use recycling services simply because they feel it is the right thing to do for the environment and the future. What's more, there is a purely logical argument for altruism: the needs of the group are more important than the needs of the individual.

A key feature of altruistic behaviour is that the person doing the good deed has no expectation for reward. Some writers are sceptical that behaviour can be purely altruistic because there is always some self-interest such as the psychic benefits of feeling good about oneself or the unconscious hope of compensation in the future. However, there are many examples of heroic efforts by people spontaneously helping complete strangers, without regard to their own safety in some cases, and certainly with no thought of being paid back somehow (Oliner, 2004). Nonetheless, when discussing altruistic situations, it may be difficult to disentangle the benefits for other and self, although the argument may be largely irrelevant.

Over the centuries, religions and spiritual traditions have encouraged the love for others, and have developed methods or models to help people become more altruistic such as sacred writings, formal precepts, rituals, and service to the community. Ideally a person would internalize and grow in love for others and have a transformative experience; the person then may feel less isolated and less ego-centered, resulting in a shift to an expanded worldview. Altruism and compassion for people naturally arise as a result (Vieten, Amorok, & Schlitz, 2006). Secondly, there is a growing sense of love and conscientiousness for the *planet* which means having positive regard for all societies, species, and ecosystems. Third, humans should feel a sense of responsibility and selflessness to the society of the *future* which will certainly be affected by the decisions made in the present.

There is no current theory that satisfactorily explains why people are altruistic. A recent literature review found articles on altruism related to anthropology, religion, philanthropy, blood donors, organ donors, recycling, ecology, evolutionary biology, psychology, organizational behaviour, economics, and management. The theories can be grouped into two broad categories: In the theory of *evolutionary* altruism, people exhibit helping behaviour which benefits others in the community--even at significant cost to the individual—because it is a survival strategy. In *psychological* altruism people are intrinsically motivated to increase the welfare of others which may or may not be reciprocal. Or maybe altruism is just a human mystery that will remain unknowable.

Due to the complexity of modern life and the potential for worldwide crises, generalized altruism is all the more important for the advancement of the human race. Therefore altruism should be taught and encouraged especially for young people. Education for altruism has the unique feature of being culture-neutral and therefore may transcend the arguments over what to teach or whose values to teach. It will likely take a universal form such as *global citizenship* and might utilize widely accepted pedagogical methods such as service learning and international case studies. Of course there are many barriers to overcome, but since civilization seems to be at a tipping point where significant change is needed, widespread altruism will certainly contribute to the solution.

WHY NOW?

On a global scale, all people breathe the same air and drink the same water. However, through electronic communication—and more recently with digitalization and the Internet—the peoples of the world have become connected in a much more tangible way. The instantaneous transfer of data, ideas, and dollars among diverse points on the planet has facilitated connections and collaborations without precedent. Satellite photographs demonstrate the movement of weather across the globe ignoring international "boundaries". The powerful image of the Earth viewed from space suggests a perspective that all peoples of the world are one people—a global society. Although that ideal is far from being realized, the pace and scope of transformation has reached a time where decisions will be made over which direction the world will take.

In the global economy states are more connected and dependent on others. The increased physical and psychological proximity removes barriers between states which results in sharing both opportunities and challenges; because of this complexity every success or crisis in one country quickly spreads to others. At the social level, if people feel separated from the world then problems seem to be caused by external agents, but if people perceive that they are connected to the world then they possibly will see that they are part of the problem and part of the solution. This relationship has lead to thinking about humanity as one community.

For example, in 1993 the Council for a Parliament of the World's Religions issued a *Declaration of the religions for a global ethic* (Kung, 1993) which stated that: "...we all have a responsibility for a better global order; that involvement for the sake of human rights, freedom, justice, peace and the preservation of the earth is reasonable and necessary". It describes how every human being is precious and as an inalienable dignity which all peoples and states are obliged to honor. The declaration is eclectic because it created a theme taken from all religions, a composite, and is therefore not associated with any one religion. The declaration spells out four "directives" based on the opening statement with the hope that these principles can rise above the current differences among ethical systems. Although freedom and justice may have different meanings around the world, perhaps most people can at least agree with the concept of altruism, that reciprocal cooperation is required to sustain society.

A second example comes from a UNESCO conference which advocated for the comparative study of cultures (Schafer & Amenta, 1992). Learning about other cultures will help increase the understanding and tolerance needed for global citizenship. It will help people to see the needs and values of others, to take on their perspective; people will be more disposed to work together and compromise, with the ultimate result to "create a moral responsibility to humanity" (p. 16). Therefore it is crucial to recognize that all people are connected and have the same basic needs. Like the strings in a fishing net, when one string is pulled it affects all the others which are connected in all directions; the individual strings may appear different, but from the perspective of the fisherman the differences are miniscule and do not affect the functioning of the net.

Civilization is quickly reaching the stage where conflict among societies, or acting in disregard of other societies, will no longer be an option. Economies based on natural resources are not sustainable and lead to environmental degradation while enriching a very few people. As resources dwindle, and those that are left are contaminated, conflict is inevitable. But because of instantaneous communication and the proliferation of weapons technology every war will be a world war. Yet just as people in communities have learned to work together for their mutual benefit, so must the community of nations see that universal altruism may help prevent such conflicts. The alternative is to wait for compliance with the threat of mutual destruction.

THE DIMENSIONS OF ALTRUISM

Among the many ways to think about altruism, it may be useful to divide the topic into three dimensions: altruism for people, for the planet, and for the future. The definitions of each should be made clear, as much as possible, and the strategies to teach them can be delineated.

Altruism for People

Altruism for people can be defined as selfless behaviour and the concern for others without expectation for reward. Young people probably begin feeling altruistic toward those in closest proximity--family and neighbors—and then progress in increasing circles toward friends and schoolmates, and eventually include co-workers, community and the region, nation and the world. Ideally, they learn that all people have fundamental needs such as health and prosperity. Students may realize that people can fulfill their own hopes as humanity as a whole achieves theirs; in other words, self-interest can be combined with interest in others, or helping oneself can result in helping others. This is an extension of the Golden Rule, suggesting that people should treat others as they would like to be treated, a version of which appears in many religions and philosophies. It does not mean that if a person wants to be treated well then they should treat others well (which is conditional); rather it means that the way they want to be treated is the standard for how they should treat others, which is altruistic. “Pure” altruism is helping others simply because they need help.

There have always been altruistic people. A good example would be many of the Christian saints who worked for the poor and the dying. It may be tempting to suggest that there are less altruistic people today but that may be more of a perceptual issue due to the negative network news. Every day there must be countless acts of selflessness by people all over the world that never gets reported. There are millions of people in the traditional helping professions such as medicine, law, and education that have dedicated their careers to improving the lives of others. Religious institutions of every kind have numerous initiatives both local and around the world for the sole purpose of relieving others' suffering. There are scores of average people who volunteer in many worthwhile organizations like homeless shelters and hospices. Finally there are limitless instances of everyday helpfulness from anonymous people who lend a hand, offer their seat, or provide an encouraging word.

In Buddhism there is the concept of *unconditional compassion* which recognizes that all people suffer and therefore deserve compassion. It should not be reserved just for those deemed "worthy" (Shantideva, 2006). If one person harms another they should not be resented because their behaviour is likely a result of their own suffering. In fact when people provoke negative reactions it should be seen as an opportunity to practice compassion. Just ask: How do other people feel when I do those things? Meditation on this concept involves the sympathetic imagination of projecting oneself into the position of others.

People can even practice *intentional altruism* which involves "exchanging oneself and others" (Rinpoche, 1998). The meditator observes or imagines a person suffering; they imagine giving them all health and happiness, then imagine taking on all their suffering and that they become free. In the course of daily life when something bad happens, imagine all the other people that have had similar experiences and have compassion for them; when something good happens, wish that all beings may benefit from it. This is called "boundless impartiality" which means giving up attachment to some and aversion for others and having an even-minded attitude toward all. It is similar to the love of parents for their children—ignoring their difficulties and ingratitude, doing everything possible for their well-being. The process increases awareness of one's responses that are conditioned and leads to disengaging from the usual reaction which helps break habits, increases well-being, and decreases focus on self. In the long-term it reduces ego needs and, by definition, increases concern for others. Meditation is "a powerful means of engaging a universal psychological process—that of shifting one's preoccupation with self to a sense of connectedness with others" (Kristeller & Johnson, 2005, p. 404). There are factors from across traditions that help people maintain altruism such as having a community of shared beliefs and experiences, a common language, continuing to learn, and daily practice and reminders.

Although there may not be agreement on the teaching of values and morality (e.g. "character education" or "pro-social behavior") in public schools, altruism has the potential to transcend the debate over what to teach. Children need to be socialized into the helping process by teachers and adult role models, while older students can develop the cognitive ability to take the perspective of others. Classrooms should provide opportunities for students to connect and help each other, to discuss and write about the behavior and moral dilemmas of characters in the media, to identify their feelings and those of others. Young adults often research community service organizations and participate in service learning projects. The idea is to develop personal values by showing how positive behavior contributes to the good of the group (Robinson & Curry, 2006).

Altruism for the Planet

This is a concept that will become increasingly important as the realization grows that the planet is the origin and sustainer of life, the principal resource shared by all. It can no longer be exploited by local individuals for short-term gains (for which everyone pays the long-term cost). Therefore young people will need to be *ecologically literate* which is "to understand the principles of organization, common to all living things, that ecosystems have evolved to sustain the web of life" (Capra, 2002, p.230). Based on the principles of ecology and interdependence, human responsibilities expand if seen from the biological community rather than a solely economic development viewpoint. Interdependence means that the wellbeing of one species is connected with the wellbeing of all species; the needs of the group are more important than the needs of the individual, yet the individual thrives as the group thrives (MacPherson, 2005). From this perspective, all living things are equal residents of the Earth with the right, and necessity, to survive. Economic values are often the default basis for international negotiations, but altruism for the planet could become a universal ethic, a common ground for communicating, the standard for decision making. The "world" may refer to the total human population, while the "planet" refers to all life on the globe.

Ecological literacy can be taught through interdisciplinary studies with ecology as the central theme. Science and technology education for example should include environmental ethics and study the impacts of human activities on other systems. There are also many practical ways that teachers can instill a sense of compassion for all living things. In the younger grades for instance children can be made aware of the interdependence of life through demonstration and participation by planting trees for the benefit of the next generation. In high school students could track the waste stream to understand that trash does not get "thrown out", it gets thrown *in* (… in a landfill, in the ocean).

College level learners may apply ecological principles through projects related to their specific course of study. For example, a study of the fishing industry may show that the quantity of fish in certain species has been reduced to unsustainable levels. Further, systems theory demonstrates that if all the fishermen cut back on their catch, by say 30 percent, then the species will thrive and the fishing can continue indefinitely. However, if even one selfish fisherman exploited the "extra" fish for himself then the conservation strategy would collapse and all would lose. Such a case study might provide the means to utilize problem-solving skills and realize the benefits (and dilemma) of altruism.

Altruism for the Future

Altruism for the future is having concern and positive regard for the people and the planet of the next generations. It begins with an awareness of time and the process of change: understanding past efforts, appreciating the present, and preparing for the future. The paradox is that the present moment is all that exists, yet remembering the past and imagining the future can improve the present. His Holiness the 14th Dalai Lama recently stated that "World history is a record of the effects of the negative and positive thoughts of human beings … By reflecting on these past occurrences, we can see that if we want to have a better and happier future, now is the time to examine the mindset of our present generation and to reflect on the way of life that it may bring about in the future" (Gyatso, 2010, p. 1). Therefore, keeping the future in mind influences present behavior which influences the future. This *future consciousness* (Lombardo, 2009) requires a critical evaluation of current events to consider where they are leading; it helps individuals prepare for the future and hence be open to change.

People can be taught to be more responsible for their actions by considering possible futures. "Humans by their behavior constantly shape their natural and social environments and, in so doing, shape their own future, although not always in ways that they intend or understand" (Bell, 1998, p. 323). People have an image of the future based on their intentions and beliefs about what may and should happen, and can expand their choices through objective analysis. They make choices based on *their* values, but *universal* values are based on whether they contribute to the health, happiness, freedom, and survival of society. In other words, individual choices in the present affect not only the individual's future but may have an impact on the future of all, so thinking altruistically about the future could result in wiser choices.

Young people can readily see that having a budget deficit, decimated ecosystems, and nuclear waste for example have tremendous implications for the imminent society of the world. Future consciousness can serve as another organizing principle for integrating studies across disciplines. Using a variety of contexts, it has the potential to teach foresight, critical thinking, planning, problem solving, and decision making. Similar to other process skills, students can use case studies and potential scenarios to increase their awareness, such as how the introduction of certain drugs or products had unintended consequences. Ideally, altruism for the future would be the catalyst for implementing sustainable systems which not only prevents negative consequences, but creates tangible benefits for people and the planet yet to come.

Thinking about the future can influence how it unfolds; therefore it may be wise to focus on positive and universal attitudes, rather than with expectations for specific results, or fear of certain events, which only limit the possibilities.

THE ROLE OF EDUCATION

Children typically learn, for better or worse, a code of ethics from their parents and extended family, and later perhaps at church or school. These principles may range from an elementary sense of right and wrong to highly-articulated moral values. However the beliefs remain largely unconscious for children until they reach the age where they can use judgement and discrimination. For this reason the role of teachers is critical in the development of altruism for adolescents and adults. Ironically the practice of teaching is itself altruistic because teachers are doing what they believe to be the right thing for their students with no immediate or direct reward. Teachers, and all adults working with young people, are in a position of potential influence over their learners and therefore need to be conscious, unbiased, and moral. Students, especially adult students, are taught to distinguish between good and bad, whatever the subject is, using the process of "reflective discernment" (Brookfield, 1998, p. 284) which is facilitated by the teacher. As people mature they develop an awareness of others, they are able to delay personal gratification, and therefore learn to be helpful and live in community. They transcend the needs of one's self through a range of behaviours from accepting simple inconveniences while assisting others to taking serious risks for the good of the group.

One of the purposes of education is to develop citizenship, and within the context of globalization effective citizenship requires the ability to engage peacefully with other cultures around the world (Reimers, 2006) or *global citizenship*. Because of its broad scope, educational institutions may be in a better position than families, religions, workplaces, and governments to promote "global civility". Within education different people and societies have diverse views on what should be taught; the concept of citizenship is in fact value-laden. For example some countries may think of citizenship as promoting nationalism, state religion, or democracy, but perhaps most agree on altruism which could serve as the common language and framework for education. Ideally, this would lead to a commitment to the universal values of human rights and tolerance. They are universal because they are not defined locally but are gleaned from many different philosophies, religions, and cultures around the world.

Schools could do more to emphasize universal values or altruism; their focus is still mainly regional so they may not be keeping up with changes in the world. However the opportunities associated with globalization create pressure to expand education. As a starting point, Merriman and Nicoletti (2008) recommend the study of core topics, the big issues that affect everyone: Technology and its many uses; human rights and tolerance; personal and planetary security; environmental and ecological concerns; population growth and available resources; economics; health and wellness. "We should all want to help all members of the communities in which we live to be educated because we will all benefit from everyone being educated, perhaps beyond the benefits that particular individuals can capture. As the communities in which we live are increasingly also global, we extend the same reasoning to a commitment to the education of our global neighbors" (Reimers, 2006, p. 284).

Certainly there are pockets of this level of education happening already in many countries. Perhaps there could be developed a set of international best practices, not necessarily a curriculum where the subject of altruism is taught directly, but rather by infusing strategies that inculcate altruism. This would provide the scaffolding so that altruism is learned through a variety of contexts as the "moral of the story". History and literature are rich in examples of plausible dilemmas and conflict-resolution scenarios, although teachers must be careful to present them in an unbiased manner, not ethnocentrically. Students learn from good role models how people are interdependent through examples of common good or win-win situations. The study of stories and cases can help them identify their own ideas about altruism; it can help them understand multiple perspectives, that in many cases there is no "right" or "true" way to do things. They will learn to judge characters and circumstances from their context--not by current or individual criteria; they would see the wisdom of balancing short- and long-term goals, of balancing individual and other's interests. Such strategies will also require teachers to use a more interactive approach for which they may need professional development and even a curriculum handbook. Of course educators may be resistant to change: this will be more work, it's inconvenient, it will not increase test scores. There is no simple answer, but the hope is that students who are more altruistic would also be more motivated and better behaved.

Higher education is increasingly focused on extrinsic values such as career advancement. The scientific model emphasizes analysis and quantification rather than human qualities such as judgment and reflection; and economics is based on a pessimistic view of human nature instead of building students' character. In many cases not much from the humanities or liberal arts is included, in fact some students resent having to take general education courses that are not directly relevant to their major. Yet even in business schools curricula can create a synthesis of the technical and the human dimensions (Birnik & Billsberry, 2008). Subjects do not have to highlight either one or the other; faculty can create a fusion of the two, called "righteous management", again through case studies and such. Business students would learn the ethic of reciprocity, the paradox of egoism versus altruism, that group interest is not incompatible with self-interest.

In management education courses students are learning that employees increasingly want to bring their "whole selves" to work including the spiritual dimension (Pielstick, 2005), so leaders and managers need to be prepared to work in a more humanistic system. Although spirituality has never been a core subject in business, faculty can use the topics of ethics and values as the context emphasizing that spirituality is related to employee health, motivation, and effectiveness. In this way educators can introduce spirituality while maintaining separation from religious dogma. Another popular strategy is the use of ultimatum games such as the prisoners' dilemma to initiate discussion on the complexity of human interaction (Morris, Urbanski, & Hunt, 2011). Results of these games typically show that students generally take a conservative approach even though the potential benefit is much higher, and that they will punish unfair behavior even if it means loss to themselves, an interesting variation of altruism. There is some evidence that humans have evolved a universal moral instinct that enhances cooperation and restrains selfishness. By extension, analysis of organizational behavior sometimes fails to consider that workers are also social who know that sometimes what serves them best is to serve others' interests.

Conclusion

The pace and scale of change in the twenty-first century, and the pressure to take advantage of the benefits while minimizing the crises it has caused, makes predicting the future more complex and uncertain. The education of global citizens through universal values such as altruism, therefore, will certainly contribute to whatever scenario may unfold (Zinser, 2012). In this schema altruism includes positive regard and action not only for people but also for the planet and the future. Because meeting these challenges is no doubt a long-term process it puts teachers in a unique position to influence the next generation which will assume much of the responsibility.

There has been progress during the last few decades in the growing awareness of problems that affect all people, and prominent voices from many sectors calling for action, particularly in Europe and America. However, at the same time developing countries seem to be making the same social and environmental mistakes, only now the stakes are higher because the point-of-no-return may be just around the next corner. Technology has narrowed the dimensions of time and distance between countries thereby dramatically increasing the interaction effects, intended or otherwise. As the world becomes more uncomfortably crowded a new etiquette seems to be necessary to sustain society, perhaps a collective belief system based on altruism—doing what's best for the most. People can increase altruism through religious experiences and meditation, and through ecological literacy, global citizenship, future consciousness, and many others means.

How can people be convinced to sometimes sacrifice their own interests for the benefit of others? Is altruism a rational decision, or do people have an inherent sense of justice, or is it provoked by certain circumstances? Perhaps the mind can be trained like the Buddhists of a thousand years ago to disengage from habitual reactions and make conscientious choices; or perhaps today's teenagers can be taught to appreciate the perspectives of others rather than acting from fundamentalist beliefs. In a political election, for example, with several candidates and many important issues, certain individuals and groups may vote for the candidate that is most likely to support *their* interests rather than voting for the candidate that is most likely to address the big issues that affect *everyone* such as energy and health. If people take the altruistic position that all of humanity has the same basic needs and desires then they may not feel that some should win and some should lose. Even though people have about 99.9 percent of the same genes they focus so much on the minor differences in size, shape, and color which appear only on the surface.

The situation is similar to waves on the ocean: if one looks closely at individual waves there will be differences in the size and shape of the waves, even though it's all the same water. In fact when the wave hits the beach it dissipates back into the body of water and becomes other waves. But from the perspective of the ocean or a sailing ship the differences in waves are irrelevant.

Do the best for the most.

REFERENCES

Bell, W. (1998). Making people responsible: The possible, the probable, and the preferable. *American Behavioral Scientist, 42*(3), pp.323-339.

Birnik, A. & Billsberry, J. (2008). Reorienting the business school agenda: The case for relevance, rigor, and righteousness. *Journal of Business Ethics,* 82(4), 985-999.

Brookfield, S. (1998). Understanding and facilitating moral learning in adults. *Journal of Moral Education, 27*(3), 283-300.

Capra, F. (2002). *The hidden connections: Integrating the biological, cognitive, and social dimensions of life into a science of sustainability.* Doubleday: NY.

Gyatso, T. (2010). Loving the enemy. *Tricycle: The Buddhist Review,* quoted from the online magazine [www.tricycle.com/-practice/loving-enemy].

Kristeller, J. & Johnson, T. (2005). Cultivating loving kindness: A two-stage model of the effects of meditation on empathy, compassion, and altruism. *Zygon: Journal of Religion and Science, 40*(2), 391-407.

Küng, Hans (1993). *The Parliament of the World's Religions Declaration toward a Global Ethic.* Paper presented at the Parliament of the World's Religions conference, Chicago, September 4, 1993. available at http://groups.yahoo.com/group/kerygma/message/1265

Lombardo, T. (2009). Understanding and teaching future consciousness. *On the Horizon,* 17(2), pp. 85-97.

MacPherson, S. (2005). Educating ecological citizens of The Blue Planet. *Canadian Journal of Environmental Education, 10,* 141-156.

Merriman, W. & Nicoletti, A. (2008). Globalization and American education. *The Educational Forum, 72*(1), 8-22.

Morris, J, Urbanski, J. & Hunt, J. (2011). Unto others: Illustrating the human capacity for cooperation. *Journal of Management Education, 35*(2), pp. 260-281.

Oliner, S. (2004). Extraordinary acts of ordinary people: Faces of heroism and altruism. In Post, S., Underwood, L., Schloss, J. & Hurlbut, W., eds. (2004). *Altruism and altruistic love: Science, philosophy, and religion in dialogue.* Oxford University Press: New York.

Pielstick, C. (2005). Teaching spiritual synchronicity in a business leadership class. *Journal of Management Education, 29*(1), pp. 153-168.

Reimers, F. (2006). Citizenship, identity, and education: Examining the public purposes of schools in an age of globalization. *Prospects, 36*(3), 275-294.

Religious Tolerance (2010). *Versions of the golden rule in 21 world religions.* Available at Religioustolerance.org/reciproc.htm

Rinpoche, P. (1998). *Words of my perfect teacher.* Translated by the Padmakara Group, Boston: Shambhala.

Schafer, P. & Amenta, S. (1992). *An image of the educated person of the future.* UNESCO conference: Geneva, Switzerland. ED 366 541.

Shantideva (2006). *The way of the bodhisattva.* Translated by the Padmakara Group, Boston: Shambhala.

Vieten, C., Amorok, T. & Schlitz, M. (2006). I to we: The role of consciousness transformation in compassion and altruism. *Zygon: Journal of Religion and Science, 41*(4), 915-931.

Zinser, R. (2012). A curriculum model of a foundation for educating the global citizens of the future. *On the Horizon, 20*(2).

In: Spirituality and Civilization Sustainability … ISBN: 978-1-53610-729-6
Editors: Andrew Targowski and Marek J. Celinski

Chapter 23

UNIVERSAL SPIRITUALITY AS A CONDITION FOR A SUSTAINABLE CIVILIZATION

Andrew Targowski*

Western Michigan University, Kalamazoo, MI, US

ABSTRACT

This chapter offers a diagnosis of contemporary civilization, characterized by a lack of wisdom and numerous conflicts of various natures, which its decline causes. Saving this civilization in decline consists in promulgating the development of a wise universal-complementary civilization. Its control component is *Spirituality 2.0*, which is a Decalogue of complementary values, drawn from the contemporary 9 civilizations. The development of civilization so far has been controlled by religions, which are in a structural, permanent and ever-growing conflict at the dawn of the 21st century. Lessening of inter-civilizational conflicts (as illustrated by the present war on terror) is only possible when religions come to consensus, which is not very likely at present. The only practical solution is the introduction of Spirituality 2.0, which introduces a shared supra-platform for shared values and secures tolerance and the application of Religions 1.0. The likelihood of the introduction of the enforcement of Spirituality 2.0 is currently very small but given the good will of those involved, and particularly if they prove wise, might be possible, providing people demonstrate wisdom in the solution of the problems of the contemporary civilization.

THE DIAGNOSIS OF THE CONTEMPORARY, UNSUSTAINABLE CIVILIZATION

The progression of civilization is in its sixth millennium. By the time of the Industrial Revolution it had been slow. In the second millennium of the contemporary era, the world's population grew twenty two times, income *per capita* went up by 855% and the income of the

* E-mail: andrew.targowski@wmich.edu; , President of the International Society for the Comparative Study of Civilizations

whole world grew 300-fold. It was only as of the Industrial Revolution that civilization started growing tremendously fast. Within 800 years, i.e. from 1000 to 1820, income *per capita* had grown a mere 53%, while from 1820 to 1998 it grew eight times, with the population growing five times (500%) (Maddison 2001). The average life expectancy increased in this millennium from 24 to 78 years in the developed countries. One could say that an average man was just a little better off in 1800 than someone living 6,000 years ago. Owing to the growing population most average people fared even worse than their forefathers. People in the UK and the Netherlands were better off but normal people living in the immobile societies of Japan and China lived close to the level of cavemen. They were subject to Malthusian selection where births were leveled off by deaths. Any growth in the number of births diminished the level of per capita income. The paradox of the then civilization was about wars, epidemics, diseases, chaos and lack of hygiene boosted living standards as it reduced population.

The Industrial Revolution, which introduced machines in place of the muscular effort of men, produced a surplus of goods, which was a rationale for the growth in population, and even forced it, as the industrial business needed more and more clients – this developed scientific and technical knowledge, and in consequence developed the techniques of production and distribution. In effect, per capita income and the living standard grew at an accelerated pace. At the beginning of the 21st century, about 2 million people are living in very good conditions, while 5 million are still living in poverty. This means a formation of a systematically expanding rift between the rich and the poor. It can be statistically estimated that the rich live 7 times better that the poor, if we take the whole world as a system of reference (Targowski 2009). If civilization maintains the current pace of the economic growth, using the calculations analogous to the ones of the 2nd millennium, at the end of the third millennium, the population may grow to the absurd level of 180 million people, whereas our ecosystem can maintain 8 million people only. If we want to keep living on Earth, the economic growth in the 3rd millennium, over the next 1,000 years, should grow 3% only for the end of the period. This is a growth rate planned for one year rather than the whole millennium. The nonsense of upholding the present economic strategy, which is about securing an economic growth of 3% annually to secure employment in the economy for a population thus expanding, is that a bigger supply of goods not only fosters employment but stimulates the number of births in families that have an adequate income. It is a repetition of the Industrial Revolution strategy, investigated in the relationship between the economic growth and population growth. Table 23.1 represents the situation of the planet if China and India keep growing as fast as the USA.

Table 23.1. If China and India keep developing like the USA

Country	Population (million, 2005)	% of global resources used (2005)	American Way of Life— % of resources used (2005)
USA	298	27	27
CHINA	1,300	5	117
INDIA	1,100	2	99
R.O.W.	3,700	66	66
TOTAL	6,465	100	**309**

Sources: Pocket World in Figures, The Economist, 2008 plus the author's estimates.

The data shown in Table 23.1 imply that at present it takes three planets like Earth to secure the American Way lifestyle to China and India, assuming that the rest of the world, i.e. 50% of the population live the way they live today, in poverty. If those remaining poor people want to live like the Americans, then it takes 6 planets like Earth to secure this lifestyle or 5 billion people need to be transferred to other planets, which for now seems impossible. In conclusion of the hopeless situation of the civilization, the following opinion by Lester Brown (2001) could be quoted:

- If the Chinese wanted to eat as much beef as the Americans, they would have to have 343 million tons of cereals annually, which is as much as an annual volume of production in the USA.
- If the Chinese wanted to eat as many fish as the Japanese, they would need to consume 100 million tons of seafood, i.e. as much as is being hauled from waters around the globe nowadays.
- If the Chinese wanted to have 2 cars in each family, they would have to use 80 million barrels of oil daily, which is as much as is being mined globally. Incidentally, they would need to expand the parking area by 31 million hectares, where they currently produce 132 million tons of rice, which is their staple food.
- If the Chinese want to be better educated, they would need to increase the use of paper from the present 35 to 342 kilograms per person (this is how much Americans are using), and this is more paper than its annual production volume around the globe.

The above example of estimates that lead to absurdities is just about China. India's needs might be similar. The conclusions simple: if the Terrestrial Civilization is to last, it needs a new political-economic system. The present one is characterized by solutions which are adequate for the 19th century but not for the 21st century;

- The policies of steady economic growth for the sake of securing new jobs for the growing population, which supports these policies, is growing in a positive spiral, leading the problem of overpopulation to self-entanglement and self-destruction of the population.
- The policy of improving the organization and efficiency of agriculture and industry is a fundamental paradigm of contemporary business and business schools. In consequence, it leads to a vast nonsensical concentration of businesses, automation, robotization, informatization and virtualization, which curtail employment where the labor market is on the rise.

In the USA 4 companies have come to dominate most of the farming business, causing the local farmers to go bankrupt. Big companies supply food which is unhealthy and tasteless whereas local farmers produce food which is both healthy and tasty. In the USA, 81 per cent of beef is supplied to the market by 4 companies only [(Scharplatz 2003)]. Cargill, Inc. controls 45% of global cereal farming; Archer Daniels Midland controls 30% of these farms in the world (Lowrence 2004). Four international companies control over 70% of liquid milk production in the USA, with an Ohio-based company producing 3 billion eggs annually (Schmid 2003). A company in Utah breeds 1.5 m swine and has a problem with excrements, comparable to the problem of a major city of Los Angeles (Halwei 2004). A huge pig farm in North Carolina generates more feaces than the states of California, New York and Washington on aggregate (Imhoff 2003). A typical morsel of food that an American eats travels the average 2,000 km from where it came from until it lands on the table. Transporting a box of Kellogg's flakes to a shop takes 7 times more energy than what the contents of the box contain (McKibben 2007).

In the name of enhancing productivity and efficiency, 200,000-acre farms are set up, run by one manager and several people supervising automated machine systems. This concentration of agricultural production in the name of its bigger efficiency makes 6 million Americans yearly suffer from diseases resulting bad food, 300,000 end up in hospital, with 5,000 dying (Pretty 2002).

In Western Civilization, almost each country witnesses this type of concentration of agricultural production, which results in the low prices of food, but also bankruptcies of the small local farms. The environment too undergoes increasing erosions a result of this large scale of production and feaces that are hard to process. Some provincial regions of the USA are called *food desert,* with churches and main streets of towns virtually deserted. Concentration of farming may be good for global corporations, but small farms are still more effective in output by hectare, whether calculated in tons, calories or dollars, not to mention its better quality. The success of the strategy of sustainable development is about supporting small and medium-sized farms rather than the huge ones. Small and medium-sized farms do well with water and energy provision, as well as waste disposal. Super-farms face tremendous problems in this respect and these destroy the environment, degrading the civilization

The Agricultural Wave (Toffler 1980) started the civilization of man and sustained man for 5,800 years until the Industrial Wave took over the leading role in the development of civilization 200 years ago. The West developed the super-consumption strategy alongside a perfectly organized production so as to supply more and more goods in the subsequent generations. The point is for the customer to keep buying something new, even if it is unnecessary. In 1970-2000 the industry of the West introduced advanced systems of automated and robotized production saturated with information technology, having superbly educated and specialized engineers and managers. During the Information Wave (Internet) of the end 20th century, the intensified industrial production was moved to Asia. For the second time in the history of the world, the West used the "slave" labor of Asian workers to reap exorbitant profits – what better term can you think of to denote work done in Asia for a dollar per hour?

In consequence, the West (North America and Europe) was flooded with cheap products, which were also sold in the Asian market. In 2011, 16 million cars were sold in China. And here begins the possible end of civilization. One cannot stop the ambitious Asians use the benefits of hi-tech production by saying that Earth's strategic resources will not suffice for all if they keep buying so many cars and other goods. This would be immoral on our part. Thanks to the industrialization of Asia by means of the Western global business, the world 'is flattening'(Friednman 2005). The capital gains from the West move East and the gap in standards of living tend to narrow down, particularly in Asian cities.

In the eyes of a number of humanists, this trend is positive for the world, and never mind that it is taking place at the expense of Western Civilization. They think it might even be advantageous that the things are that way as this is how the wrongs of the West (the USA) can be redeemed and its mistakes corrected as regards the colonization and slavery.

The contemporary plight of civilization is filled with contradictory economic and political trends and strategies, which in effect accelerate the decline of civilization. The confusion is exacerbated by the virtualization of the society, caused by social networks. These networks lead to the replacement of representational democracy (MP's) by direct democracy.

The latter democracy is a step backwards in social progress since it introduces populist and radical politics. Obviously this new Virtual Civilization cannot be regulated as shown in the failure to pass the ACTA treaty on copyright and prosecuting online dissemination of contents that lead to real-life crime. The community of Internet users blocked the treaty in the name of freedom of information circulation in the Internet. For fear of failure to be reelected, politicians in a number of countries succumbed to the direct democracy in 2011-2012. This is not a wise strategy, but apparently it is not what is wise but, rather, what is convenient for the masses that have become a sort of oracle, dictating how to judge and select solutions.

In conclusion of the crisis of Contemporary Civilization, a following picture emerges:

1. Mass production of food poses a threat to consumer health and destroys the natural environment.
2. Cheap industrial production boosts ultra-consumerist attitudes and leads to the exhaustion of strategic resources within a few dozen years.
3. Automation, robotization and informatization generate unemployment at a time when there is uncontrollable population growth and available manpower soars.
4. Virtualization leads to people being brainwashed by representative democracy having been replaced by direct democracy, i.e. radicalism, extremism and chaos.
5. Market economy has turned into the market society, where almost anything is for sale, and the common good has been replaced by individual advantage.
6. Instead of serving the society, business demands that it be served by the society.
7. Politicians oriented to being elected in short 2-4-6-year cycles demonstrate no commitment to correcting disadvantageous long-term trends within civilization. Politics is not founded upon spirituality (either religious or civic) and the ethics/morality it generates.
8. Societies have very little confidence in politicians who do not promote the common good and issues that are vital for the people at large.
9. The political crisis handed over the development of societies to managers and technocrats, who negate the value of the common good and replace it with a business approach, oriented towards profit for the private operator, who has been entrusted with the lease of a prison, hospital, school, park, theatre, museum, rail or even military operations (in Iraq and Afghanistan, the number of people hired to provide services for the military exceeds the number of soldiers; these operators treat this as great business, generating the more profit the longer it lasts).
10. Universities support passé status quo with their know-how in order to preserve the benefits from the cooperation in research and consultations.

Thoughtless continuation of the processes mentioned, based on the wisdom of the market only, will inexorably lead to the decline and fall of the civilization as we know it and one we dream of. This is why we need to move on to develop a civilization based on wisdom, or at least try to approach it mentally (conceptually), which is a duty of intellectuals, if not politicians. Perhaps the readers of this concept might take it up.

The development of civilization so far, over the 6,000 years is characterized by a continuum of conflicts and wars, stimulating the progress of technology, science and politics. Wars regulate population levels in some ways, but the means is too radical. Therefore this option needs to be rejected and a situation ought to be reached where world peace will create a bigger stability of societies and a lesser pressure for the development of lethal technology and science as well as domineering policies of aggression.

Striving for world peace is a domain of international organizations such as the UN Security Council. Countries that have good reasons to go to war pay little attention to this body. In the 21st century we are facing a conflict between the Civilization of Islam and the Civilization of the West and the East. It is a clash of the moralities of these civilizations. Such conflicts are on the rise and often assume a local character, such as between ethnic groups. Since organized religion deals with moral issues, they ought to try and handle the conflicts. Alas, this is practically impossible.

Even within Christianity, Pope John Paul II endeavored to befriend Protestantism in the so-called ecumenical process, but he failed. Attempts to enter into co-operation with the Orthodoxy failed, too. It is hard to imagine Islamic authorities striking a consensus with the leaders of Christianity. We cannot count on churches, mosques and synagogues to bring peace on Earth, even though in all those places the clergy and the believers pray for this kind of peace every day. Notably, they chiefly pray for peace for their own fold. They do not say that, of course, even if they do think this way. And this is what they communicate to their god.

TENETS OF A SUSTAINABLE UNIVERSAL-COMPLEMENTARY CIVILIZATION

From Religion 1.0 to Spirituality 2.0

The first condition of the design of the architecture of a Sustainable Civilization is civilians undertaking to introduce the second level of complementary religion, which can be called Spirituality 2.0. It does not replace any of the existing Religions 1.0, which would not only be a heresy, but an outrageous revolution, impossible to win, but also an unnecessary and harmful one. The point is not to fight religion but that it should grow at the global level rather than in some areas of the world. Spirituality 2.0 would teach complementary morality, founded upon the most essential values of the particular Religions 1.0. These were listed in Table 23.2.

A semantic-logical aggregate of the above values constitutes the morality of the Spirituality 2.0, which will control the need to develop the Universal-Complementary Civilization (UCC), as common for the whole world. UCC is not a loose cluster of the remaining civilizations – it is simply the highest level of world civilizations, beneath which there are levels of the civilizations known to date. In this way, an American or Pole, or any other terrestrial will practice the moral values of at least 2 civilizations. One can imagine following the norms of three or more civilizations simultaneously.

Table 23.2. Complementary values of Spirituality 2.0

CYWILIZATION	VALUES OF RELIGION 1.0 AS CONTRIBUTION TO UNIWERSAL-COMPLEMENTARY SPIRITUALITY 2.0
AFRICAN	Spiritual contact with ancestors
BUDDHIST	Morality
CHINESE	Worship of elders and a sacred character of family
HINDU	Moderation
ISLAMIC	Crime and punishment
JAPANESE	Co-operation and worship of nature
EASTERN	Devotion and sacrifice
WESTERN	Free election, tolerance, technology
GLOBAL	Human and citizen's rights, international law; free flow of ideas, people, goods and services
UNIVERSAL-COMPLEMENTARY	The above plus wisdom, integrity, conditional forgiveness, equal access and sustainable development

Shall we say a couple live in the Western Civilization and each of them come from a separate civilization? This civilizational mix forms a complicated "cloudy" model of civilization that might have to be observed so that tolerance to others might become a morality practiced locally and globally.

How do we successfully phase in the morality of Spirituality 2.0? This may take several generations or more. It took Christianity 300 years until it was recognized. Today, thanks to excellent communication systems, this should take faster. Spirituality 2.0 needs to be launched at schools and universities and 2-5 generations need to pass (50-100 years) for the first positive effects of the process to come to light. Spirituality 2.0 cannot surely be enforced immediately at the level of adults; neither can it be imposed by legislation. This religion needs to be implanted in all world civilizations, which may prove impossible. The religions of these civilizations will consider this process an assault on them and will seek to undermine the credibility of Spirituality 2.0 in the eyes of their adherents. The paradox of the potential conflict is about these religions not being mutually preclusive with their ideas – they are meant to complement each other and continue their mission for the sake of humanism.

Failure to enforce Spirituality 2.0 into the observance of the Universal-Complementary Civilization will make it impossible to eliminate or even limit wars waged on premises of morality clashes both now and in the future. The author knows of no better solutions for the time being.

From Capitalism and Socialism to Ecologism (Eco-Supremacy)

Over the last 200 years, civilization utilized three socio-political systems: Capitalism, Socialism and Communism, as well as their various combinations. None of these systems can control the Universal-Complementary Civilization.

Capitalism in its present form of turbo-Capitalism is subservient to global business and its bosses and is controlled by lobbyists, thus losing its democratic and liberal character. Its main objective is generating exorbitant profits for a narrow elite (1%). Apple had $100 billion cash in 2012 and decided to pay a dividend to its shareholders -- $2 per $600 worth of share, which for small capitalists is a ridiculously negligible capital gain, amounting to 0.003%. The bosses of the corporation, though, regularly pay themselves dozens of millions of dollars in bonuses.

The strategy of global business is a pursuit of a steady increase in the productivity of resources by an ever growing concentration of companies in a given branch, monopolizing the market and expanding target markets.

Socialism, even democratic, is too costly to be applied to the population at large, whether it is 7 or 9 billion. Communism proved to be a doctrinaire, murderous system, even for its own people, and one destructive to the environment.

In this situation, a new socio-political system needs to be developed, which will be called Ecologism, from the word ecosystem, a synonym of biosphere. The following objectives will be set before it:

- Mission: implementing the policies of sustainable development of civilization.
- Aim: controlling population growth and the consumption of resources in such a manner that the next generation will have the same living conditions as the previous one.
- Strategy: sufficiency versus efficiency, with the society evolving towards a wise society.
- Main policies:
    1. Nature is the most important.
    2. People are more important than markets.
    3. People's health is more important than money.
    4. Sufficiency is more important than efficiency.
    5. Business is subservient to and controlled by society.

Ecologism includes the following subsystems:

A. Eco-education – based on eco-knowledge and wisdom.
B. Wise society – trained and educated in the knowledge of eco-education and having qualifications to wise decision-making.
C. Eco-democracy — all equal to each other but not to the environment, which is supreme to man.
D. Eco-justice – any violation of the law must also be assessed against and possibly punished for possible harm done to the environment.
E. Eco-infrastructure – operates in harmony with Nature and protects it against destruction.
F. Deep economics – includes environmental and social costs alongside those of business and administration into cost-effectiveness calculations.
G. Deep media – comprehensively and impartially inform the society of the plight and development of the sustainable civilization.

The architecture of Sustainable Civilization is presented in Figure 23.1. Three elements play a vital part in the architecture of Sustainable Civilization: Eco-education, Spirituality 2.0 and Wise Society, which decide the success of the remaining five. The three decide people's consciousness and their wise attitude to each other and Nature. These also decide a successful transformation from the present *paranoia* to the expected *metanoia* (Kolakowski 2010).

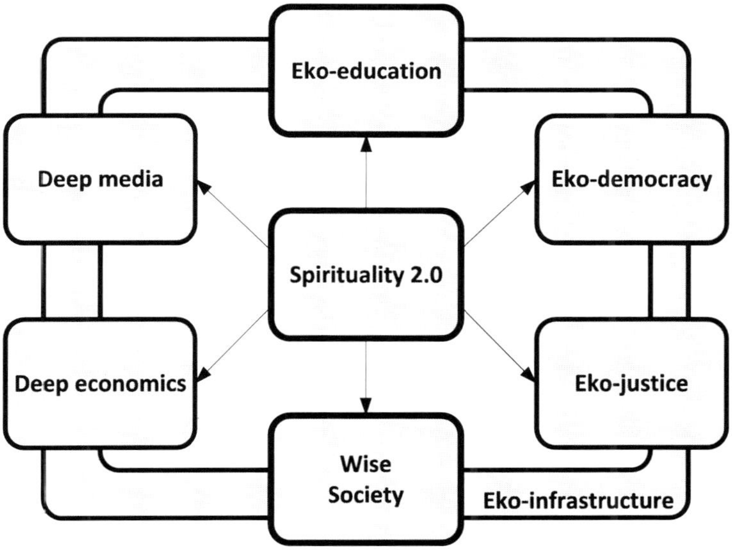

Figure 23.1. The Architecture of a Sustainable Civilization.

Sustainable Civilization can function provided that it is supported by Wise Society. This kind of society is constituted by Wise People, who can use four minds: *basic, reasoning, global and universal* and have mastered a wise *art of life*.

The development of Sustainable Civilization will not begin if it is left to the popular *laissez-faire* of today. The danger of civilization collapse indicates that a certain dosage of social engineering is necessary. It would be about a mix of *a bottom-up* and *top-down approaches*. The role of organizations such as the UN is as indispensable as the involvement of NGOs. Even today every school and university ought to apply itself to developing eco-knowledge and wisdom, as well as training wise graduates. Those will be candidates for wise citizens, workers, leaders, who will apply wise solutions in their positions, ones which would develop Wise Society and Sustainable Civilization.

CONCLUSION

1. The development of civilization so far has been controlled by religions, which are in a structural, permanent and ever-growing conflict at the dawn of the 21st century.
2. Lessening of inter-civilizational conflicts (as illustrated by the present war on terror) is only possible when religions come to consensus, which is not very likely at present.
3. The only practical solution is the introduction of Spirituality 2.0, which introduces a shared supra-platform for shared values and secures tolerance and the application of Religions 1.0.
4. The likelihood of the introduction of the enforcement of Spirituality 2.0 is currently very small but given the good will of those involved, and particularly if they prove wise, might be possible.

REFERENCES

Brown, L. (2001). *Eco-economy.* New York: W. W. Norton & Co., p.17.

Friedman, T. (2005). *The World is flat. The brief history of the twenty-first century.* New York: Farrar, Straus and Giroux.

Halweil, B. (2004). *Eat here: reclaiming homegrown pleasures in a global supermarket.* New York: W. W. Norton & Company.

Imhoff, D. (2003). *Farming with the wild.* Healdsburg, CA: Sierra Club Books.

Kołakowski, L. (2010): The New stage of *dialogue and universalism. individuality and infinity. metanoia* – solidarity. *Dialogue and Universalism*, No. 7–8.

Lowrence, F. (2004). *Not on the label.* New York: Penguin Books.

Maddison, A. (2001). *The World economy, a millennial perspective.* Paris: OECD, pp. 17-31.

McKibben, B.(2007). *Deep economy, the wealth of communities and the durable future.* New York: Times Books, Henry Holt and Company.

Pretty, J. (2002). *Agri-culture.* London: Earthscan Publishing, Ltd.

Scharplatz, J. (2003).Weeding out the skilled farmer. *Prairie Writers Circle*, November 26.

Schmid, R. (2003). *The Untold story of milk.* Washington, DC: New Trends Publishing.

Targowski, A. (2009). Will business end or revive western civilization? *The Proceedings of the 39th International Conference of the Society for the Comparative Study of Civilizations.* June 3-7, Kalamazoo, Michigan, pp. 7-37.

Tofller, A. (1980). *The Third wave.* New York: Bantam Books.

PART D

THE CONCLUSION

In: Spirituality and Civilization Sustainability ...
Editors: Andrew Targowski and Marek J. Celinski

ISBN: 978-1-62618-587-6

Chapter 24

CAN SPIRITUALITY SAVE CIVILIZATION?

***Andrew Targowski*[1] ** and Marek Celinski*[2‡]**
[1]Western Michigan University, Kalamazoo, MI, US
[2]Private practice in psychology, Toronto, Canada

ABSTRACT

This chapter is about the synthesis of the II Great Crisis of Civilization and evaluation whether religious and secular spirituality can save the civilization as we know it. A new model of spirituality for the Third millennium is supported under the form of Spirituality 2.0. This model should allow for the development of Wise Civilization. A new model of the sustainability strategy is defined, too. Can the current generation implement a Wise Civilization? This is the question. This new Spirituality 2.0 positions itself inside and outside of religions; the latter means "spiritual but not religious" and believe in the existence of different "spiritual paths," emphasizing the importance of finding one's own individual path to spirituality. However, as an example of mutual tolerance of different believes, this new spirituality argues that in order to save our further existence and farther progress of humanity, both kinds of spirituality (1.0 and 2.0) should be applied in agreement. The main ideas of that agreement have been defined in this chapter.

INTRODUCTION

The purpose of this concluding chapter is a synthesis of the II Great Crisis of Civilization that is taking place in the 21st century and suggesting the strategies of overcoming it. Possibilities in that respect will be analyzed as regards religious and secular spirituality. In consequence, a new form of spirituality will be defined as theoretically capable of overcoming this crisis, but its enforcement into human practice nowadays is hardly probable. However, given concerted efforts are made, a new spirituality is enforceable. The question is

* E-mail: Andrew.targowski@wmich.edu
‡ E-mail: marekcelinskil@rogers.com

whether there is enough time to prevent man and human civilization from being overcome by the crisis.

People have become confused about the origin of their spirituality and about its content. Many currently believe that their cultural tradition and their own sense of what is important provide sufficient background for creating one's own meaning and purpose of human life.

It is evident from a historical perspective that spirituality was initially externally imposed on masses of people (as exemplified in the story of Israelites' Exodus from Egypt). Originally spiritual values were regarded as objective, sacred and absolute. In the course of centuries, during which these values were internalized, people started to regard their spirituality as their own creation, and therefore as subjective, relative and potentially dispensable if causing conflicts and inconvenience. While doing this they lost connection with the most powerful meaning of spirituality as the representation of "natural laws" of human development and history, which has the potential of changing the psychosocial reality. In antiquity, a sense of justice or of human dignity perhaps inspired in some people considerations for more humane treatment of slaves and was most strongly manifested in Spartacus' rebellion; the same eternal inspiration eventually caused a universal condemnation and abolition of slavery .

The current meaning of human rights also represents today's understanding of who we are as humanity. Probably it will be further changed to express a meaning of equality and justice more suitable for the future living conditions.

However, for spirituality to be a powerful instrument of social change, it must be regarded as an internal representation of objective principles and values that are not changeable in themselves but subject to various interpretations that reflect our forever incomplete ability to appreciate their full meaning. We have to be patient and tolerant as the awareness of what the adequate interpretation for our times is may only develop through a a confrontation of contrasting views that can be painful.

The term "spiritual" is often used in contexts in which the term "religious" was formerly employed (Sheldrake 2007). This understanding of spirituality, can be of secular character too; secular spirituality emphasizes humanistic ideas and values such as love, compassion, patience, tolerance, forgiveness, contentment, responsibility, harmony, and a concern for others.

Spirituality is understood as follows:

> "Spirituality exists wherever we struggle with the issues of how our lives fit into the greater scheme of things. This is true when our questions never give way to specific answers or give rise to specific practices such as prayer or meditation. We encounter spiritual issues every time we wonder where the universe comes from, why we are here, or what happens when we die. We also become spiritual when we become moved by values such as beauty, love, or creativity that seem to reveal a meaning or power beyond our visible world. An idea or practice is "spiritual" when it reveals our personal desire to establish a felt-relationship with the deepest meanings or powers governing life (Fuller 2011)[1]."

[1] Fuller, R. C. *Spiritual, But Not Religious*. beliefnet.com. Retrieved on: 2011-12-03.

It is important to notice that secular spirituality includes aspects of life and human experience which go beyond a purely materialist view of the world, without necessarily accepting belief in a supernatural reality or divine being. Through the history of Western Civilization humans gradually were developing new spiritual values in the addictive process as it is exemplified in the Table 24.1. (Targowski & Ajnenkiel 2000).

Table 24.1. The Additive Development of Values within the Western Civilization

Period	Stages of Western Civilization	Human Values In The Additive Process
XXI	Globalization	Business is always right, low ethics, vulgarization of culture, the stronger takes all
XX-XXI	Postmodernism	Love, relative truth, hope, autonomy, responsibility, creativity, self-accomplishment
XX	Democracy	Equality, human and civil rights, self-determination of nations, private property, free market, free press, free elections
XIX	Capitalism	Free market, competition, and social-democracy
XVIII-XIX	Romanticism	Patriotism and cult of feelings
1789	French Revolution	Liberty, equality, and fraternity
1776	American Revolution	Individualism and liberalism
1688	English Revolution	Parliamentarism and political pluralism
XVIII	Enlightenment	Knowledge, rationalism, freedom of ideas, tolerance, and pluralism
XV-XVI	Renaissance	Fullness of human development
I CE	Christianity	Faith, hope, and love
I BCE	Ancient Rome	Law
V-III BCE	Ancient Greece	Truth, goodness and beauty
XX-I BCE	Judaism	Servicing to God and people, justice and dialogue

II Great Crisis of Civilization vis-a-vis Spirituality

I Great Crisis of Civilization occurred after the fall of the Roman Empire and lasted for about a millennium until the Italian Renaissance. The causes included the fall of moral integrity of the Roman elite and invasions of barbarians (such as Vandals) from Northern Europe. The so-called dark ages lasted for about a millennium; during that period the Classical (Greco-Roman) Civilization was in decline.

Among the powerful drivers of the Renaissance was the 1453 development of print by Guttenberg, which began the dissemination of knowledge, development of science, technology, education and industrialization. Another factor that made a powerful impact on the Renaissance was a positive spiritual evolution of the societies of the nascent Europe, whose moral signpost was Christianity with its 'love your neighbor as you love yourself.'

As of the Enlightenment Era and the French Revolution and along the Industrial, Bolshevik and Mexican Revolutions as well as the Polish Solidarity (1980-89), civilization has made spectacular progress, interrupted only by two world wars (1914-1918 and 1939-1945) but continued with a rising momentum after World War II on both sides of the Iron Curtain. The Arms and Technology Race during the Cold War (1945-1989/91) led Civilization – the Western variety in particular – to the climax of its development and a feeling that "sky is the limit for the human potential."

The feeling of man's dominion over the world, that is, our arrogant behavior on the small planet Earth had led to the II Great Crisis of Civilization, the beginnings of which are clearly seen in this early 21st century. As Targowski[2] puts it, this Great Crisis is characterized by 16 major specialist crises in politics, global business, administration, religion, technology, science, education, nutrition, ecology, population, resources, war, super-capacity, over-communication and media. Therefore the 21st century Great Crisis of Civilization is a fact (Figure 24.1.) as it stems from a cross-influence of as many as 16 crises. However, its main cause is a crisis in ideas and morality (based on the satisfaction of one's own interest Goldman 2011:249), which leads to the crisis in the ecosystem and the fall of the civilization as we know it.

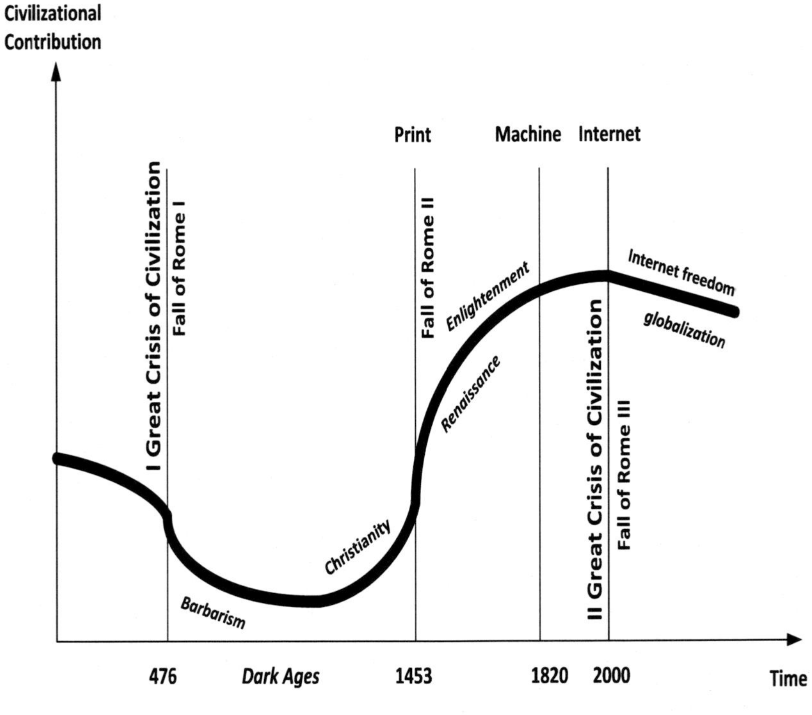

Figure 24.1. The Timeline of Great Civilization Crises.

Evidently, both great crises of civilization result from a spirituality crisis. The great civilizational progress, compounded by the arrival in the late 20th century of the Information Wave, made Lech Zacher[3] wonder whether man is possibly seeking an 'over-civilized'

[2] Chapter 2.
[3] Chapter 3.

presence on Earth. The same author is optimistic[4] in seeing man as likely to return to reasonable civilizational framework thanks to the potential of the mind, but he perceives this as conditioned by man forgoing a change in the nature of societies by means of technology; conversely, man must free themselves from it and change their ways upon the importance of observing values and attitudes leading to the necessary positive changes in the processes of their civilization.

In the 20th and 21st centuries, so rich in conflicts and the achievements of science, technology and economy, man managed to make ends meet in poverty, ways out of which were sought at all costs, but once attaining welfare and prosperity, such as in the Western Civilization, man got confused and put material goods first, placing those above spirituality and morality. Man forgot – so it seems – that they are different from animals in having a culture that controls their bestial instincts with values and symbols which promote behaviors that follow some patterns. In this process of materializing their being, man has neglected models of moral conduct, and in effect man has led to the II Great Crisis of Civilization.

The progress of science and industrialization loomed large to man, who thus neglected the need to be spiritual. Psychologist Marek Celiński[5] argues that civilized man is governed by three processes: biological evolution, manifesting itself by instincts as well as spirituality, resulting from internal conditions that are dependent on faith, but in the event of these two processes clashing, man has at their disposal a decisive, culture-inspired, decision-making process oriented towards a wise judgment and choice (Targowski 2011).

This thought is further developed by Stephen Borthwick[6], who reminds us that civilized man is man organized into the communities of village, town, city, state or empire, where they pledge allegiance to an overlord: on the one hand this is God, but on the other, it is natural or externally imposed law. In democracy, the sovereign is the people made up of individuals who think that they can arbitrarily make laws, disregarding objective values and consequences. Where there is no sovereign from outside the system, the civilization collapses. Evolution of spirituality over millennia locates the origin of spirituality from the external, sacred and absolute to the internal, secular and individual. Figure 24.2. illustrates the evolution of spirituality over millennia.

What, then, is the role of a sovereign in the 21st century Western civilization or the Global variety that has taken it in? Which sovereign is losing significance?

History of Civilization teaches us that, according to II Great Law of Civilization:

> People seek freedom, whose extent and intensity depend on the level of knowledge in the society, its ability to communicate and its familiarity with the international community. (Targowski 2009:35).

In the 6,000 years of the history of civilization, people have made great progress in liberation, though at the expense of great sacrifices made during major social revolutions and hundreds of wars. The biggest freedom was attained thanks to the Internet, which in the 21st century has given man unlimited access to information, knowledge, communication, organization and even staging revolutions (Arab Spring of 2011).

---

[4]Chapter 5.
[5]Chapter 1.
[6]Chapter 4.

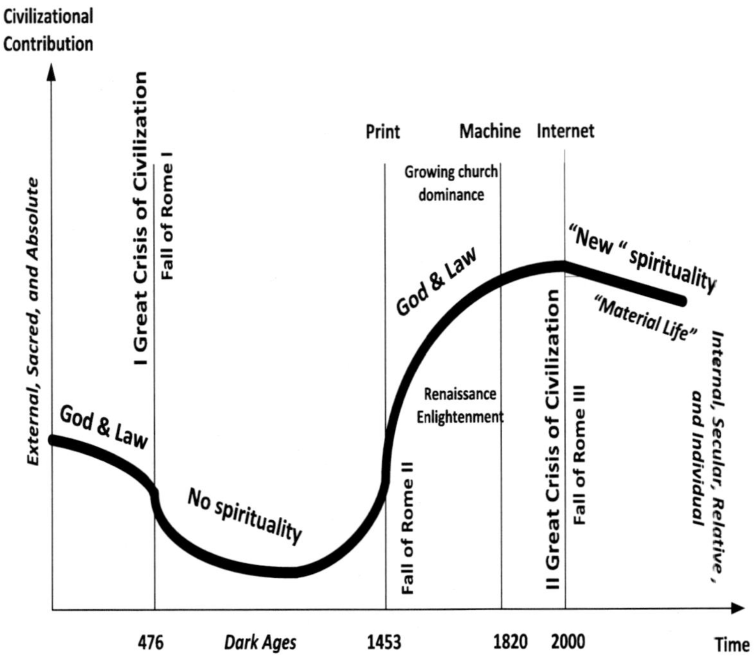

Figure 24.2. The Role of Sovereign (God & Law) and Spirituality in the Rise and Fall of Civilizations.

Thanks to the Internet, man has been freed from the limitations of family, neighborhood, as well as the local and national communities. Now one hardly knows their neighbor but has hundreds of acquaintances scattered all over the world, and in this way become a virtual citizen of the world, psychologically and informationally free as one who understands their world and can speak out on global issues as well as get organized in a community of like-minded individuals. Thanks to that the citizen of the world opposes any regulations limiting information circulation in the Internet, such as the ACTA treaty, which defends authors and is supposed to counteract plagiarism; they also support WikiLeaks even if these reveal secret information that exposes the way their real government operates.

This psycho-informational human freedom of 21st century man resembles George Santayana's interpretation of total freedom, which is about writing checks to be cashed from an account that is non-existent in the bank. Although the famous philosopher lived over half a century ago, his concept of total freedom was, as it were, adopted by Wall Street, who put clients' money at risk and take over their money by cashing huge bonuses without being held accountable either financially or legally when their 'horses' lose. In this way they contribute to the moral decline of the Western Civilization and the world entering the II Great Crisis of Civilizations in the 21st century.

The paradox of the II Great Crisis of Civilization is about civilization failing to become wiser thanks to the Internet, as opposed to the days in which books and print did enhance wisdom. Man did become more free thanks to the Internet but did not become wiser if they are causing the II Great Crisis of Civilization. Having found it a rule that spirituality is the greatest cultural factor deciding man's and human civilization's success or failure, it will now be investigated what kind of spirituality might take man and their civilization away from this major crisis.

ORGANIZED RELIGION CANNOT SUPPORT SUSTAINABLE DEVELOPMENT

Religions characterize civilizations, which was stated in plain terms by the founder of the scientific concept of civilizations, Arnold Toynbee (1934). This was upheld by Ashok Kumar Malhotra[7], who said that religions delimit reasoning and spirituality within the civilization. Therefore, in his opinion, the role of religion in the development of civilization is fundamental.

Religions have ruled civilized people for several thousand years. For two thousand years the monotheistic religion of Christianity has been ruling 33.32% of the global population, followed by Islam, controlling 21.01% of the people, with Hinduism holding sway over 13.26% and Buddhism – 5.84; the remaining religions are authorities for 12.48% and 14.08% of people profess no religion (Wikipedia). This calculation implies that 8,6 out of 10 people are controlled by religion; it is a very high percentage, but are these people being properly spiritually inspired?

The biggest religions – Christianity and Islam – are in a crisis. In the Western (Atlantic) Civilization, only up to 10 per cent of people go to church, which means that only one person in ten is subjected to spiritual influence of a religious nature (Anderson *et al.* 2008), which is one of the main reasons for the downfall of the Western Civilization. The countries of Islam are under transformation, as evidenced by the Arab Spring, which has been going on since 2011 in North Africa (Libya and Tunisia) and the Middle East (Egypt, Bahrain, Syria). David Goldman says Islam is in a crisis in the 21st century (2011:4).

It can be posited that the more educated the society the lesser the religious influence in it. The Internet contributes to it by informing the people on the developing countries of the lifestyle in the developed ones, where people have been 'freed' from organized religion and spirituality has been replaced with a pursuit of the greatest possible wealth here and now.

Obviously, each religion preaches the only and best possible spirituality; there can be no surprise about that. Religions are fighting for their markets as organized religion is good business for the people in permanent employment there. Therefore, the many religions are conflicted within and without. Each of those has in its dogmas some solutions that can be worth using, and if those were selflessly applied, there would be none of these conflicts. Yet, in practice, the dogmas are sound and wise only on paper.

None of the major religions preach inter-religious reconciliation, except the Japanese Buddhism (functioning alongside Shintoism – the cult of Nature), which is emphasized by Hisanori Kato[8]; other religions do not worship Nature, which establishes the environment in which people live, but which people systematically destroy. If all religions but one have no respect for the natural environment of man, there can be no wonder man destroys it and in doing so contributes to the II Great Crisis of Civilizations.

However, were it not for religions, they would need to be invented, as no other institution teaches morality from cradle to deathbed. On the other hand, it is a fact that organized religions are preached by people who either cannot demonstrate a connection between spirituality and the quality of life or, being chiefly interested in controlling their own fold as well as securing their institution sufficient means and resources, they nurture the same

[7]Chapter 6.

[8]Chapter 9.

illusion of the superiority of matter over mind as is embraced by secular people and, as a result, their actions alienate the faithful from another kind of "administration" of the type that regulates the lives of men.

For the above reasons, it cannot be hoped that great religions with their forms of spirituality will lead civilization out of the crisis in the 21st century. This is not to say that they should not pursue the development of the values that are basic for and shared by humanity, which are supposed to enable the survival of mankind and a higher quality of life.

The Secular Spirituality Practised Cannot Save Civilization

Supplying man with spirituality based on secular ideas has dominated religious spirituality in the 21st century. It is taking place on a long timeline of civilization at a time when the Western Civilization has come to know prosperity and considered it the supreme objective of life. Generally speaking this prosperity is enjoyed by 1 per cent of the people with the other 99 per cent only aspiring to it. None the less, it is this minority that sets the trends in the life of societies and promotes policies oriented at boosting material well-being.

In the opinion of 1 per cent of the people, business is the most important in society, as it determines income, which should be as high as possible, no matter at what expense it comes. Particularly great profit is generated by the global business that has caused the transformation of the Western Civilization into the Global Civilization of the 21st century. So, what is the religion of the new civilization? The answer comes from Targowski and Edward Jayne[9] - it is "business" that preaches maximum profit within the so-called 'shallow economics,' which ignores social costs and the environment being devastated. The result is the destruction of the middle class (felt by the 99%) in the USA and Western Europe, the destruction of social cohesion (which at some point used to be an advantage of the Western-Atlantic Civilization) and replacing it with class struggle, so criticized and unimaginable in the West. (Stiglitz 2012:xvi, Faux 2006).

It is true that the globalized economy accounts for the annual growth of 3-5%, which means a global rise in employment and the $1 trillion growth in goods and services. However, this causes an accelerated growth in population, exhaustion of strategic resources and the destruction of the natural environment, whose annual cost is estimated at $4.5 trillion. This kind of negative effects of globalization are called by Graeme Maxton (2011:I) the "end of freedom."

Grand economic projects in the world, particularly in the developing countries are launched thanks to the growing corruption. Michael Andregg[10] holds that corruption has a similar impact on the society as cancer has on the body: it slowly consumes it and in the end – kills. Corruption has become art of the secular spirituality of societies, which want to be rich at any cost forgetting that securing a high quality of life is even more important. Alas, it leads to no prosperity, but what it does is contributing to the moral decline of civilization.

---

[9] Chapter 17.

[10] Chapter 18.

Reed Smith[11] notes that the process of a moral decay of civilization was already marked in the 1930s by Arnold Toynbee (1934), when he listed such factors as proletarianization, barbarization, (particularly in primitive art), sexual promiscuity and others. In the 21st century these processes became exacerbated in pop culture, characterized by chaos in pop music, untidiness in clothing and hairstyle, violence in films, conversations using vulgar catchwords (eg. f....excited, fun, etc.) and even several symbols used in e-communication as well as the online freedom of expressing whatever comes to ones mind in the interactive blog communication.

Along the negative symptoms of this secular spirituality, suggestions surface of how to make these more noble. Elain Englehart[12] things that the application of ethics in business ought to be enlivened, which not only should be oriented at making a profit, but should secure a sustained development of the economy. Alas, in that respect, business only does it "lip service" and "web service", which in practice frees business from the policy of sustainable development.

In the days when the hi-tech business has made the society accustomed to producing and applying ever new electronic gadgets to the policy of an ever more widespread automation, robitization and informatization, Andrew Targowski and Vladimir Modrak[13] propose the idea of "automation with a human face." These tools of advanced technology should only replace human labor when an environment is involved that is dangerous for man, the work is too hard, etc. The authors introduce three laws of automation which, in order to be applied, must be adopted by professional associations so they will be included in the codes of good practice of respective professions.

Spirituality in a very important and manifold manner contributes to the quality of human life. Unlike instincts which through various biological pressures and demands focusses our attention on survival, which sometimes leads to ruthless exploitations of others, spirituality offers a perspective that human life is more than survival. This higher level of understanding of ourselves is achieved by an awareness of cultural (collective), historic and biological factors along with a recognition of what is temporary and specific to certain psychosocial conditions, and what is eternal and ubiquitous. In the end people create on an individual and collective basis some meaning of life which gives them a sense of value for their own life and for life in general, and orientation for their efforts thus enabling developments of specific goals both for humanity and for individuals.

Another important point is with respect to social relations and connectedness among people. In order that the relations be mutually satisfactory there is a need that the intentions express certain goodness commonly recognizable as such by people of different cultures. Considering that cultures are different, we have to refer to the core set of values and ideas that are appreciated by people living in various cultural and religious environments, and at different times in history. Approaching others without malicious intentions to manipulate, control or exploit is the basic principle of good relations.

Spirituality inspires us to extend further our understanding of humanity by referring to the sense of solidarity; from such a perspective all human beings share the burden of responsibility for the quality of our life and our future growth. Human solidarity sometimes

[11]Chapter 19.
[12]Chapter 20.
[13]Chapter 21.

demands from us to act not only with compassion and altruism but also with an acceptance of painful sacrifices in the name of truth, justice, equality or other values. While this may sometimes be difficult to bear, we have to remember that this is the best warranty of sustained and peaceful continuity of civilizations.

Should man only do what pays? Richard Zinser[14] claims that man also needs to be altruistic, interested in involvement in issues that affect people and the environment in a global scale. So that one will become such an altruistic 'citizen of the world,' one must be taught that as early as in childhood, but then in youth and adulthood, too.

Can the 'new man' – ethical and selfless as well as wise in the application of science – overcome the 'spirituality' as promoted by business – particularly the global business in the era of internet freedom? The answer appears to be negative. An entirely new model of making man spiritual needs to be proposed that would on the one hand continue the best that the 6,000-year-old civilization has to offer but, on the other, could meet the challenges of the III millennium.

CAN A NEW MODEL OF ENSPIRITING POSSIBLY SAVE CIVILIZATION?

A new model of spirituality of the III millennium was proposed by Andrew Targowski[15] as Spirituality 2.0., which is universal and complementary and should be accepted by the great religions. It is a pseudo-religion, whose aim is not abrogating the hitherto religions 1.0 but, rather, provide a superstructure of spirituality, whose Decalogue is made up of the most important values adopted from the functioning civilizations, as illustrated by the Table 24.2.

Table 24.2. Complementary values of Spirituality 2.0

CYWILIZATION	VALUES OF RELIGION 1.0 AS CONTRIBUTION TO UNIWERSAL-COMPLEMENTARY SPIRITUALITY 2.0
AFRICAN	Spiritual contact with **ancestors**
BUDDHIST	**Morality**, based on the unity with the Universe and its creatures
CHINESE	Worship of **elders** and a sacred character of family
HINDU	**Moderation** in satisfying desires and appetites
ISLAMIC	Awareness that **crime** will be met with **punishment**
JAPANESE	Co-operation and **worship of nature**
EASTERN	Devotion and **sacrifice** inspired by a sense of being a part of the collective
WESTERN	**Free election, tolerance, technology** based on the discovery of nature laws and their applications
GLOBAL	Human and citizen's rights, international law; free flow of ideas, people, goods and services, tolerance for other views
UNIVERSAL-COMPLEMENTARY	The above plus wisdom, integrity, conditional forgiveness, equal access and sustainable development

[14] Chapter 22.
[15]Chapter 23.

This type of spirituality, founded upon tolerance, ought to be taught along the principle "love your own alien" whereas the present turbo-capitalism (21st century), deprived of its once democratic character, ought to be replaced with the system of Ecologism, having this meaning that in the event of a conflict between man and nature, the interests of the latter will have a priority. The model of the system of Ecologism as one supporting Wise Civilization, is presented in Figure 24.3.

Wise Civilization can function provided that it is supported by Wise Society. This kind of society is constituted by Wise People. Is it possible?

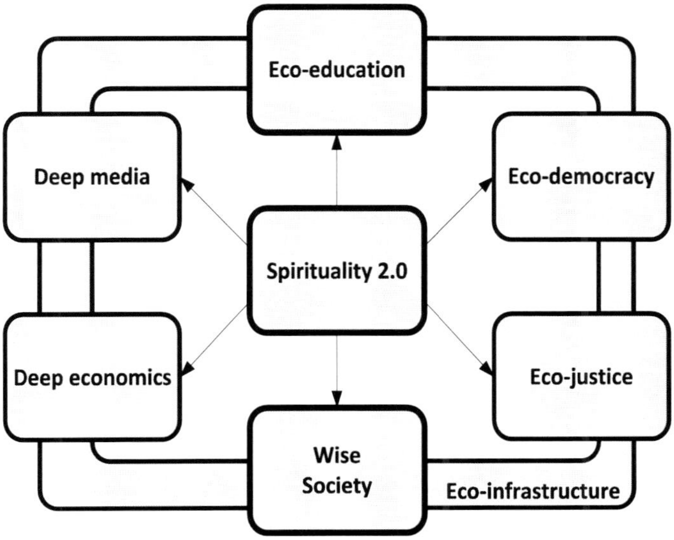

Figure 24.3. The Architecture of a Wise Civilization.

The process of reaching the Wise Civilization is *currently* characterized by the triple bottom line, as illustrated by the following:

- Economic vitality
- Environmental accountability
- Social responsibility

Furthermore, the concept of "good life" and life success currently defined in material and economic terms, should be replaced by a broader concept of "quality of life" which includes spirituality, primarily manifested as care for human beings and their environment.

Alas, the model of contemporary sustainability strategy does not feature the requirement of spirituality and therefore it will be proposed that this process be included in the general model of sustainable development as illustrated by the model in Figure 24.4.

A new set of sustainable criteria, will be called the *quadruple bottom line*, since it is composed of the following ones:

- Spirituality
- Economic vitality

- Environmental accountability
- Social responsibility

However, spirituality is embedded in every other criterion, as its illustrated in Figure 24.4.

Figure 24.4. Model of Sustainability Strategy.

The development of Wise Civilization will not begin if it is left to the popular *laissez-faire* of today. The danger of civilization collapse indicates that a certain dosage of social engineering is necessary.

It would be about a mix of *a* bottom-up and top-down approaches. The role of organizations such as the UN is as indispensable as the involvement of NGOs. Even today every school and university ought to apply itself to developing eco-knowledge and wisdom, as well as training wise graduates. Those will be candidates for wise citizens, workers, leaders, who will apply wise solutions in their positions, ones which would develop Wise Society and Wise Civilization.

SPIRITUALITY AND THE PROSPECT FOR SUSTAINABLE CIVILIZATION

The most important points regarding the relations between spirituality and prospects for sustainable civilization are as follows:

1. Crisis was the product of the mentality developed in the 19 the century oriented towards maximizing profit through economic expansion and unlimited access to resources.
2. Competition that aimed at "outsmarting" and "outdoing " was the primary motive behind industrial relations, and relations between various nations.

3. The current economic crises that affected the most advanced parts of the industrialized world showed that there are limits for improvements in the quality of life with respect to its material aspects. The price that we pay for such a standard of life is reflected in national debt. In a long run, this strategy is unsustainable.
4. We propose a strategy for "sustainable civilization" that would maximize prospects for the majority of people to enjoy life consistent with the present understanding of the "quality of life".
5. We postulate that the objective and necessary changes may be achieved by a reference to universal spirituality which as its primary tenet refers to human solidarity in facing common life adversity. From this should follow understanding that profit, competition and economic expansion cannot be the foundations of socioeconomic life in the future.
6. The new socioeconomic activity should be therefore primarily oriented at sustainability rather than expansion (or expansion may be limited to some domains such as medical science, more effective use of energy, agriculture, etc.).
7. This will increase the roles of governments and international institutions that will establish quotas for resource utilization and production.
8. People would be initially opposing such proposals and for this reason efforts are needed to develop and propagate ideas of "universal spirituality" which will present a set of values and guidelines about how to cope with life adversities and problems not only from the perspective of individual interests or one's own nation's survival but from the perspective of the whole humanity. To this end people have to believe that life is worth living and that reaching out to other opportunities for living decent life is the best foundation for the continuity of our civilization.

In summary, one can recognize that the main targets of human race are: sustainable civilization and a high quality of life.

To accomplish these targets, one must emphasize the importance of the societal processes, such ones as:

- Spirituality 2.0-driven process
- Solidarity-driven process
- Knowledge-driven process
- Sustainability-driven process

which have to be practiced together with supporting them: education, politics, culture (broadly treated) and infrastructure. The model of these components and their relations is shown in Figure 24.5.

Conclusion

1. The development of civilization so far has been controlled by organized religious spirituality, which is losing its power in the 21st century.

2. The II Great Crisis of Civilization in the 21st century is triggered by the secular morality, which promotes mostly materialism and moral relativism, similarly to the cause of the I Great Crisis of Civilization (GCC) which began after the Fall of Rome in the 5th century and lasted almost 1000 years till the Italian Renaissance.
3. Lessening of inter-civilizational conflicts (as illustrated by the present war on terror) is only possible when religions come to a consensus, which is not very likely at present.
4. In order to get out of the II GCC a new spirituality is necessary that can propose a universal Spirituality 2.0 – a complementary set of values adopted from contemporary civilizations.
5. This new Spirituality 2.0 positions itself inside and outside of religions; the latter means "spiritual but not religious" and believes in the existence of different "spiritual paths," emphasizing the importance of finding one's own individual path to spirituality. However, as an example of mutual tolerance of different believes, this new spirituality argues that to save our further existence and further progress of humanity, both kinds of spirituality (1.0 and 2.0) should be applied in agreement. The main ideas of that agreement have been defined in this chapter.
6. Today's objective of man should be a strategy of sustainable development, which can secure to as many people as possible a life quality which is consistent with our aspirations and an understanding of human nature. In order to develop Wise Civilization, this strategy ought to be implemented in: *economic vitality*, *environmental accountability* and *social responsibility* and each of these ought to be supported by Spirituality 2.0 (compassion for Wise Civilization).
7. The likelihood of the enforcement of Spirituality 2.0 is currently low but given the good will of those involved, and particularly if they prove wise, it might be possible.

REFERENCES

Anderson, J., G. John Ikenberry, and Thomas Risse. (2008). *The end of the west? Crisis and change in the Atlantic Order*. Ithaca and London: Cornell University Press. p.256.

Buchanan, P. J. (2006). *State of emergency*. New York: Thomas Dunn Books.

Faux, J. (2006). *The Global class war*. Hoboken, NJ: Wiley.

Fuller, R. C. (2011). *Spiritual, but not religious*. beliefnet.com. Retrieved on: 2011-12-03.

Goldman, D.P. (2011). *How civilizations die*. Washington, DC: Regnery Publishing, Inc., p.249.

Homer-Dixon, Th. (2006). *The upside of down*. Washington, DC: ISLAND PRESS.

Huffington, A. (2010). *Third world America*. New York: Crown Publishers.

Maxton, G. (2011). *The end of progress*. Hoboken, NJ: Wiley.

Sheldrake, P. (2007). *A brief history of spirituality*. Hoboken, NJ: Wiley-Blackwell. p. 1-2.

Stiglitz, J. E. (2012). *The price of inequality*. New York: W. W. Norton & Co.

Targowski, A. & A. Ajnenkiel, Edts. (2000). *Losy Polski i Swiata (Faiths of Poland and the World)*. Warsaw: Bellona, p. 385.

Targowski, A. (2009). *Information technology and societal development*. Hershey, PA & New York: IGI Publishing.

Targowski, A. (2011). *Information technology and wisdom development.* Hershey, PA & New York: IGI Publishing.

Tischner, J. (1984). *The spirit of solidarity.* San Francisco: Harper & Row, Publishers.

Toynbee, A. (1934). *A study of history.* Oxford: Oxford University Press

Wikipedia-- http://en.wikipedia.org/wiki/Major_religious_groups. Retrieved on: 2012-8-4.

INDEX

A

B

C

Q

R

S

T

U

V

W

Y